Ralph [illegible]

August 2001

Attack Bombers We Need You

Ralph Conte

ISBN 0-9712387-0-7

Ralph Conte
2300 NW 5th Avenue
Mineral Wells, TX 76067
(940) 325-1076

Cover design by Ron Watson.

Book design by JM Press, Nashville, Tennessee
www.publishyourbook.com • jmp@nashville.com

PRINTED IN THE UNITED STATES OF AMERICA

Contents

INTRODUCTION

"AMERICA WON'T FORGET YOU BREED OF MEN"

A memorable remark by the Executive Officer of the 668th Squadron of the 416th Bomb Group. Lieutenant Colonel Chester Wysocki (Retired) wrote in his compilation of information on the activities of his squadron, which by extension, said the same thing of all members of the group. It could not have related only to the flying crews, because without the ever present energy, ability, and enthusiasm of the ground personnel, nothing could have been accomplished. He did, however, highlight the missions the group flew, mentioning members of the 668th who participated in them

His warm, respectful description of events of his squadron were recorded on a daily basis, as he put it, "written at the time it occured." Chet included input from fellow squadron members and official documents. The 225 page typewritten documentary was presented as the Operational History of the 668th squadron to the Commanding Officer of the post- war 416th BombWing, (H) (SAC) established in 1948 at Griffiss Air Base, in Rome , New York . That SAC Wing includes B-52 Bombers.

That Wing hosted a re-union for the 416th Bomb Group in 1966. The new Wing Introductory Booklet distributed to the 416th Group re-union includes the statement:

THE WING'S TITLE WAS CHANGED TO THE 416TH BOMBARDMENT WING IN LINE WITH AN AIR FORCE POLICY TO GIVE NEWER UNITS THE SAME DESIGNATION AS THOSE WHICH WON FAME IN WORLD II."

The 416 Bomb Group (L) were the first to fly A-20 aircraft in Europe and the first group to fly the A-26 there. The pioneering the group engaged in proved highly successful to assist ground forces in their advances toward Germany following D-Day. The group was called upon on numerous occasions, to attack specific targets hindering the advance of Allied Forces, and to blast enemy troop and equipment concentrations. Those missions elicited laudatory comments from both English and American High Command officials, including General Omar Bradley, General George Patton and Britian Air Commander, T. Leigh Mallory.

The complement of the group remained around 1200 with the addition of personnel as veteran personnel either completed their missions,. or may have been lost to enemy action.

A real close knit family developed which made bi-annual reunions, or kept together through annual newsletters, originated by and maintained by the late Dolph Whitten and his wife Marie. Wives and other family members of group personnel who have gone to the special heaven for fliers, attended these reunions to learn as much as they could about their 416th members no longer around. They excitedly listened and learned about the exploits of their husbands, fathers, or brothers. They also heard the reunion members win the war over and over again, at each gathering. The memories seem to explode when a few guys got together and started to reminisce about what went on 57 years ago. As one man put it, " I go to reunions to learn what happened long ago, because when I was there I was so engrossed in what I was supposed to do, that I didn't realize what was happening. Every reunion I go to, I find out more things I never knew occured."

Reunions started by various squadron personnel meeting in each others' homes starting in 1946. More and more members started to join those few, until it came time to expand the gatherings to full group reunions. It was then that Dolph Whitten took the reins and began organizing the group reunions, with the help of his wife, Marie. This is the listing of the Group gatherings:

1966 - Rome, NY (416th Wing Headquarters,
Griffis AFB)
1968 - Oklahoma City, OK
1970 - Stone Mountain, GA

1972 - Denver, CO
1974 - San Francisco, CA
1976 - Orlando, FL.
1978 - Biloxi, MI
1980 - San Antonio, TX
1982 - Huntington Beach, CA
1984 - Hot Springs, AR
1986 - Colorado Springs, CO
1988 - Kennewick, WA
1990 - Louisville, KY
1992 - Orange Beach, AL
1993 - Oklahoma City, OK (50th Anniversary of the Group formation at Will Rogers Field)
1994 - Oshkosh, WI
1996 - Tucson, AZ
1998 - San Antonio, TX
1999 - Kinston, NC
2000 - Hot Springs, AR.
2001 - Tulsa, OK

The group meets every year now, with the number of members attending declining due to age, illness, or passing. We are all in our 70s or 80s now, with memories fading, but as long as we are able, about 100 still assemble, including wives, and other family members. The cohesion, camaraderie and continuance still exists.

The annual newsletter still is published annually, with another editor, Bob Basnett, of Fulton, MO putting together the information members provide about their activities during the past year. Interesting reading! Always was, still is.!

ACKNOWLEDGEMENTS

The history of the 416th Bombardment Group (L) could not have been a reality were it not for the efforts of a certain few members of the group and their families to whom we extend our thanks and appreciation for their foresight and ability to gather important data included in this presentation.

Franklin Basford, a gunner on our A-20s from the 669th Squadron accumulated important details not previously assembled and without which this history would not be complete. His compilation of the names of all group members who were shot down, made prisoners of war, or lost their lives, whether in training or during combat, was the only place where this informtion had been compiled outside official documents. He chronicled the 285 missions the group flew, showing dates and destinations of each flight. He also assembled the names of each member of the group, by squadron assignment, identifying their Military Occupation Specialty (MOS) including the state from which they entered the service.

Basford's most memorable accomplishment was the design of, and distribution of, a memorial placque commemorating the 416th Bombardment Group. He was successful in having the placques set at the Arlington National Cemetery, Air Force Academy, Air Museum at Wright Patterson Field, March Field, Wethersfield, England Air Base, and EAA at Oshkosh, Wisconsin.

The 668th Squadron Executive Officer, Chester Wysocki, detailed 235 of the 285 missions the group flew, identifying the 668th squadron members participating in those forays. Rather unfortunately, his descriptive prose did not extend to the full number of missions we flew. However, all that he included was enormously helpful in this history.

Lowell Geffinger, Adjutant of the 670th, assembled monthly reports of that squadron's activities, starting with the formation of the group, identifying members as they joined or departed the group, plus naming the missions that the squadron's personnel became part of. His editorial comment highlighted important activities of the group as well of that of the squadron.

The 671st Squadron was fortunate to have had Gordon Russell among its members. Russell was a first year student of Journalism when he was called up for service and he practised what he was learning by keeping records of all missions the group flew, and most important, provided the loading list of all 671st members on those sorties.

The editorial comments on squadron, group and personal member activities provides interesting reading, and good references for this history. The photos and strike shots of bomb drops make a complete compilation of events. Each squadron member would like to have the loading list of missions they flew.

A very special tribute must be extended to the brother of Lieutenant Roland Enman, a Bombardier-Navigator for the 669th Squadron. Roland lost his life on a mission. Roland's brother, Doug, and his wife, Jane, decided to know more about Roland's role as a flier. They contacted members of the squadron and have attended a few group reunions, becoming acquainted and friendly with current members of the group. They went out of their way to research official documents of group and 669th squadron activities and compiled a book of facts not previously released to the public. They discovered a treasure of personal letters Roland had sent to his mother during his service, which Jane, a computer whiz, put together in a presentation worthy of praise. Their research documents of group goings-on are a part of this presentation.

Last, but by no means least, we must extend plaudits to the late Dolph Whitten , who was Adjutant of the 669th squadron, and his constant companion and wife, Marie, whose dedication and monumental efforts were extended to keep this group together by means of compiling an annual newsletter and arranging for bi-annual reunions all over the states. By these means, the group has maintained its identity and it has proven a strong catalyst in breeding strong friendships which have lasted through the past 57 years. Their recording secretary, Judy Beaty, has become an integral past of the group by typing up the annual newsletters, and remembering the details of the lives of contributors to the newsletters.

To the above special references, we extend our gratitude for their efforts and assistance in generating this history.

Thanks are extended to individuals who have been forthcoming with their experiences and information which turn out to be great reading.

Wayne Downing, a pilot who never quit, and flew 86 missions, signing up for a second tour while with the group, is the individual who insisted this history had to come to life for reference to living members of the 416th Bombardment Group, their families, their offsprings, and friends. You were right, Wayne, it had to be done! Too bad it did not come about many years ago when some of our boys who have departed this briefing for the special place in the blue, might have been interested in it.

DEDICATION

In memory of the young fliers, and the ever faithful and dependable ground crews and support groups who put the 416th light bombers in the air, day after day, under stressful conditions, we commend you and dedicate this history to you. Our casualties were relatively light, but their losses hung heavy in the hearts of loved ones at home. Those lost during the war and to those who made the trip to our special place in the blue, since,- we remember, - and want to emblazon your contribution to our efforts, - in our minds, for years to come.

Bantam Bombers vs. Heavyweights

The "Bantam" Bombers of the 9th Air Force, IX Bomber Command, 97th Combat Wing, were so proud to be part of the 416th Bomb Group (L) that made history in World War II, in what might be called, an insignificant, but at once, a significant way. Why would anybody say something like that? The reason is simple.

Compared to the experiences of the heavyweights of the 8th AirForce, we were a drop in the pond, but we did what we had to do, and did it right!

After reading the exploits of the 457th Bomb Group (H) in one of three books published by JM Press, covering that group, entitled FAIT ACCOMPLI, one could fathom the reasoning for this comparison. What the heavies endured would make what the 416th Bomb Group did seem like a picnic. Those members of the 416th who suffered injuries or the families of those who lost their lives with our little group, do not take too lightly to that remark, but the comparison is so vivid, and startling, it has to be said. Injury or death in heavies or lights is all the same. It hurts the same, and is also sad.

The bantam bombers flew as a group by itself on bombing missions, compared to the massing of a number of heavy bomber groups of the 8th Air Force, where six or more groups of B-17s and B-24s composed a mission.The bantams would zip through the sky at about 240 miles per hour, while the heavies lumbered along well under 200 MPH. Enemy fighters and flak gunners picked on the heavies because there were more of them and their destructive powers were more intense and immense. The losses of a heavy plane going down was three times more than that experienced by the lights, but losses were losses, only in degree. The lights flew three or four hour missions, while the heavies flew twice that time, more exasperating and more exposed to danger.

Our group was called upon to eradicate important targets and strong points at significant times. The bombing of the last remaining escape bridges over the Seine River at Oissel, the bombing out of the Mad Colonel at St. Malo, and the elimination of enemy forces hindering the advances of allied forces during their march toward Germany, after D-Day, were a few calls by higher Bomber Command, for the 416th to attack. They needed us, and we responded, as subsequent commendations reflect.

So, the bantam weights, carried their weight with aplomb!

GENERAL COMMENTS

The young men who enlisted in the Army Air Corps were within the range of 21 to 26 years old who assumed major leadership roles and grew to knowledgeable individuals in very short order. To see Colonels and even Generals at 26 to 30 years old was not an unusual occurrence especially for those who entered the service before the United States became engaged in World War II. It appeared that individuals in the Air Corps who had enlisted prior to our country became involved in conflict and who had learned to fly, would become flight leaders, and even Commanders of Groups rather quickly.

In the 416th Bomb Group, the four Squadron Commanders were all in the service before the Group organized, and had earned their wings early on. If any of them had learned to fly before entering the service, their experience prompted early rise in leadership roles.

The young enlistees volunteering for the flying corps, were first sent to classification centers for a short evaluation of their intellectual and physical abilities. They were all given an opportunity to ask for training in pilot, navigation, or bombardiering primary schools. It would be safe to assume that a majority of the boys would ask to become pilots, even though flying was not all the vogue in those days when a relatively few type war planes even existed.

One enlistee remembers having asked for pilot training. The officials told him he tested exceptionally well to be a navigator. He tried to convince them he would be happy being a pilot. They then sent him to Bombardier Primary training and then to Navigation School. Eventually he became a rated Bombardier-Navigator (BN).

Many Air Corps wannabees had never been in an airplane before, but being in the air cadet training program loomed high in their expectations. The drop out rate was not very high, but it was something they all feared during primary, secondary or final phases of training in either one of the three training disciplines.

In the 416th Bomb Group, a number of men who eventually became pilots were in the service during the bombing of Pearl Harbor on 7 December 1941. Having endured that catastrophe, they were given an opportunity to enroll in Air Cadet training, some without having to undergo the rigors of the entrance exams. Those exams were all encompassing in English, Math, History, and Reading/Comprehension abilities. At one time, the IQ (Intelligence Quotient) had to be over 130. It was open only to college graduates or at least two years of college training. It was eventually lowered to requiring an IQ of 115, and may have been lowered even further to 95. Then the rigorous physical exam known as the "64" had to be passed, with practically perfect 20/20 eyesight. The many healthy young men who surpassed all those trials, made up the successful Army Air Corps. This is not to demean the Navy and Marine Air Corps wannabees. some of whom had tougher flying assignments to overcome. Those boys landing on aircraft carriers, were the envy of many pilots who were happy landing on concrete runways.

When Air Cadet graduates had their wings pinned on and the brass Second Lieutenant's bars placed in their shoulders, they went to airfields to see for the first time, close up, the real warships they were destined to fly or to navigate. Pilots for the most part had already flown in the type planes to which they were assigned in Combat Groups. Navigators and Bombardiers had only experienced flying in AT-11s Beech planes where there was some room for mobility and contact with other crew members. When these BNs (Bombardier-Navigators) came to see their individual compartments in the twin engine A-20 attack bombers, it came as a surprise. They had to climb into the nose of the ship with only radio contact to the pilot, nor access to any other member of the crew. The gunners, also, were isolated from the pilot, although the gunners did have an open space for personal contact and mobility.

The pilots had the heavy responsibility of getting the plane ready for take off, getting it off the ground, loaded with bombs and other crew members, and then getting to form up in a well designed pattern to nuzzle up to his adjoining plane in his flight. Keeping in formation, maintaining control of the plane, releasing the bomb load at the right time, and returning to formation position to get back to base was full time work.

The leaders of a group formation on combat missions were normally squadron commanders or one of those pilots who had early flying training before the group was originated. If they were not formation, or box leaders, they became flight leaders of six planes within the boxes. As experience dictated, other than squadron commanders took lead positions on boxes (see box formations in later pages), or became flight leaders.

The lead navigator was responsible for getting the formation to the target, flying an assigned route, and trying to evade anti-aircraft gun emplacements. He could also dictate the evasive action paths the formation would take to avoid, as much as possible, flak bursts. Normally, the heavy concentrations of flak gun positions were known and plotted, from earlier mission experiences or photo reconnaissance. The evasive action was carefully monitored so the planes would get to their assigned target at the specified time, drop their loads, and leave. There were times when more than one group were assigned the same target but at different times, usually a 20 or 30 minute lapse between attacks. On a few missions, the heavy number of groups directed to the same target, had to do their thing, and get out of the way of the next group coming in at their specified time slot.

When the group reached the target area, the flights would spread out, and reach the initial point (IP) to start the bomb run, in groups of six. The lead plane was a glass nosed unit, with a BN aiming his Norden Bombsight on the MPI (Main Point of Impact). When his cross hairs clicked on the target, the bombs automatically dropped from the open bomb bay doors. When those bombs dropped, the other five planes would trip their bombs out to form a close pattern of bomb bursts on and near the target. This was one of the reasons for maintaining a close formation, to concentrate the bomb hits as close as possible to where they were aimed by the BN.

Gunners, were either turret gun operators or tunnel gunners, who held machine guns pointed toward the rear of the crafts. These young men were subject to weather because of the opening at the bottom of the plane from which the tunnel gunner operated. When the formations left England, going to France for their assigned mission, the gunners were required to test their guns while we flew over the open English Channel. They were the look-outs to warn of impending enemy fighter attackers, or other emergencies which may have occurred during flights. The tunnel gunner sometimes had a camera to photograph the bomb strikes. At least one photographer was flying to take the necessary picture of the bomb hits.

When the crews returned to base, they were immediately transported to de-briefing rooms, where each crew was interviewed to report any unusual sight they may have seen, or report on other emergencies which may have occured during the mission. Bomb strike reports were important to discuss. When the photographer's pictures were developed they were compared with the reports given by crew members. The photos were marked with the MPI (X) and the flight bomb patterns superimposed over the target area, to examine the damage done to the enemy positions plus to rate the bombing results, either fair, good, excellent, or superior, There also were designations as DND (Did NotDrop) or Unsatisfactory, or Not In Position.

The next step for the crews was to check out the next mission, to determine whether they were scheduled, with whom they would be flying and the position in the loading list. The target was not identified, that being done at the briefing prior to the mission take off time.

Briefings were another exciting time. Crews were awakened by the Operations designatee, perhaps taken to breakfast. (at 2:00 AM?), given the target for the mission, with the route plotted out, and showing the known heavy flak gun placements.

Photos of the target area were shown on the screen, with the BN's having to remember what the target looked like, the approach angle, the rendezvous point for the formation and the fighter escort, plus the route back to base. And don't forget where we were supposed to pick up our fighter escort on the way to the target.

Introduction to the History of the 416th Bombardment Group (L)

Being a part of the Greatest Generation was not exactly what we had in mind while doing our jobs for the 416th Bombardment Group (L) flying out of England and later from the European continent, France, Belgium, and Germany.

We were flying and servicing twin engine A-20 and eventually the upgraded A-26 bombers designated as light attack aircraft to bomb buzz-bomb launching sites in France as well as bridges, interdiction points to deter enemy actions, ammo dumps, air fields and troop concentrations of the German forces. The forward firing six guns on some of the planes of the A-20s and subsequently the 16 forward firing 50 caliber guns of the A-26s gave the planes the ability to strafe enemy targets after dropping bombs from higher altitudes. Pilots and gunners became excited about this possibility, but the reality of it did not materialize until well on during the war. Primary considerations were to drop bombs on the assigned enemy targets. The bombing of targets to help our advancing Allied troops after D-Day, 6 June 1944, was extremely important, for which we and the other Ninth Air Force Groups excelled.

These light bombers, carrying a pilot and two gunners, one handling an upper mechanized turret and another hand holding a 50 caliber gun, lying on his belly, and aiming out an opening underside the aircraft, constituted what was considered a Gun Ship, as differentiated from a flight leading glass nosed ship carrying a Pilot, Bombardier-Navigator and the two gunners, leading flights of six to bomb targets.

A formation of six planes, with one glass nosed ship and five gun ships, made up a flight. Three of these flights made up a box, and two or three boxes were a group formation. The usual formation to bomb included 36 aircraft, dropping bombs in flights of six at the target. The formation approached an Initial Point (IP), pealed off in flights of six and did their individual bomb-sighting with the exclusive Norden Bombsight operated by the Bombardier-Navigator (BN)

This is the story or the 416th Bombardment Group (L), its establishment as a fighting force in the European Theatre of Operation, as well as individual and group accomplishments which won praises of military commanders of the Air Force as well as Ground Forces leaders.

The Group was made up of four Squadrons, 668th, 669th, 670th, and 671st. It was ably supported by the 4th Service Group, 79th Station Complement, 199th Medical Detachment, 21st Weather Squadron, 1297th Military Police, and the ever present and dependable American Red Cross, during our operations.

FOREWORD

Wethersfield Airfield, the English base of the 416th Bomb Group, was one of the many bomber airfields built during 1942/1943. During the war my father worked for the British Air Ministry initially at Andrews Field and then in early 1944 at Wethersfield for the remainder of the war and beyond. The family lived, as I do now, in the nearby village of Gosfield which itself had an airfield which became the home of the 410th Bomb Group, also operating A-20 Havoc aircraft

My first contact with the 416th Bomb Group was on a summer evening in 1944 when as a young schoolboy, my father took me with him when he was called out to attend to an electrical problem that had occurred. Usually I was only taken when he was to visit non-operational areas, but this time it was out on the airfield beside the taxiway. I can recall to this day watching the Havocs landing and taxiing in on return from a mission. This was probably one of the main incidents which started the fascination I have for aviation. Many years later I decided to research the activities of the Essex based Light and Medium Bomber Groups and airfields from which they operated, which is an ongoing project.

The 416th Bomb Group came to England in early 1944, and the aircrews quickly had to acclimatise themselves to the flying procedures and the changeable weather conditions in England. After a few training missions, the 416th became operational against targets in France and Belgium. These ranged from flying bomb launching sites, airfields, gun sites, to road and rail targets in preparation for the forthcoming invasion of Europe on D-Day. The Havocs flew in box formations attacking at altitudes up to 12,000 feet. Most of the targets were heavily defended by German anti-aircraft guns (flak) and on many missions a high percentage of the attacking bombers were hit. Inevitably there were losses; on one day in August, the 416th lost four aircraft shot down in the target area while attacking a heavily defended target.

When the aircraft returned, the ground crews had to labour in the open throughout the night repairing the damage, ready for the next day's mission. Armours would load the bombs, often having to change the load later when an alternative target was selected and different types of bombs were required. The Group flew over a hundred operations from Wethersfield before moving to a new airfield in France in September 1944 as the targets moved farther into Germany.

Although a great deal has been written on the exploits of the Eighth Air Force, their brothers in arms in the Ninth Air Force have not to date received the same coverage, and this book written by the people who were actually involved will go a long way to recording how it was.

— Ian Mactaggart

Ian Mactaggart was a twelve year old who watched the 416th group assemble, take off and return from combat missions in 1944. His home is near our base in Wethersfield, a few miles away from Braintree which is located about 30 miles north and east from London.

Mactaggart has written a history of the airfields in England, principally from the County of Essex, where light and medium bombers were based. He attended two reunions of the 416th Bomb Group members here in the states, to accumulate first hand information to supplement his historical researches on his subject. He has supplied a substantial amount of the material he has uncovered to the Imperial War Museum, who are putting together a Roll of Honour of downed American fliers. In the late 60s, Mactaggart started researches of the many aircraft crashes that occurred in the County of Essex.

CHAPTER 1

Formation of the 416th Bomb Group
Headquarters Order #46 — Will Rogers Airfield
416th Bomb Group Special Order #1
1943 Group History
A-20 Development History
Specifications of the A-20G
A-20 and A-26 Planes
Specifications of the A-26C Douglas Invader
Formation Flying

Formation of 416th Bombardment Group (L)

The 416th Bombardment Group (L) was constituted on 25 January 1943 to be part of attack bombers envisioned as being capable of dropping loads of bombs on finite targets and then being able to go down to deck level and strafe areas held by enemy forces. Strafing capabilities became part of the designation for "light" bombers differentiating them from medium bombers such as the existing B-25 Mitchells and the B-26 Marauders.

The 416th Bomb Group was activated on 5 February 1943 at Will Rogers Field, Oklahoma City, Oklahoma, with no personnel or equipment assigned thereto. Ten days later, on 15 February 1943, Special Order #46 was issued from the Headquarters Army Base, Will Rogers Field, Oklahoma City, Oklahoma, naming 51 officers, ranking from Lieutenant Colonel to 2nd Lieutenants, and 241 enlisted men to be transferred to the newly formed 416th. Personnel from the then existing 46th Bomb Group at Will Rogers Field became the cadre for the 416th. Enlisted personnel from the 50th, 51st, 53rd, and 87th Bomb Squadrons were assigned to the 668th, 669th, 670th and 671st squadrons of the 416th (Copy of the Order attached). Lieutenant Colonel Richard D. Dick was named Group Commander.

On 15 February 1943, Headquarters of the 416th Bomb Group (L) issued its 1st Special Order, assigning Squadron Commanders and Officers to the four squadrons. The order was signed by Group Adjutant, Captain James W. Townsend. (Copy of the Order Attached).

Squadron Commanders began shaping up their various department heads, naming officers for the Armament, Engineering, Supply, Transportation, and Mess Hall, along with Tech Supply Sections. Actually, military equipment, such as airplanes, were in short supply, but training schedules were organized and carried out with whatever was available.

Training was, at best, becoming acquainted with your fellow workers and for flying personnel, establishing confidence in each other, and understanding what your job is, and doing the best that you can under the circumstances.

Flying training was not without their problems and ultimate fatalities. Flying personnel were required to walk around maintenance areas and watch mechanics service their planes or preparing equipment for installation. One particular instance saw a group of pilots and bombardier-navigators watch a mechanic immerse a bearing in a pail of oil. One of the pilots rolled up his sleeve and reached into the oil, elbow deep, and pulled out the bearing, examining it closely, remarking how well appearing the bearing seemed. It became apparent to the mechanic that someone was interested in what he was doing. A great sign of confidence in each other was the result. So it was, between crew chiefs and their assistants, that the pilots and bombardier navigators were a team who adopted each other, and their planes. Crew chiefs were particularly proud of their aircrafts. They seemed to be personally wounded when planes returned from missions bearing flak holes. Repairs were made with the utmost of care. On one occasion, the crew chief admonished the pilot, - in jest - when they returned from flight, asking, "What did you do to my plane?"

Heavy disciplines were exersized, including physical training in formation stances, parades and inspections, intersquadron competitions, all generally forming strong teams among themselves and the squadrons.

Shortages of planes in the formative stages of the group restricted the amount of flying training envisioned by higher ups, but good scheduling managed to right these inequities. For instance, when the group moved to Lake Charles, Louisiana from Will Rogers Field, each squadron had only five planes to spread out among the many pilots needing indoctrination.

At Will Rogers Field, Group formations and Saturday parades were formalized. Bivouacs were carried out and intersquadron competitions were organized with personnel doing their very best to out-do each other in inter-squadron drills. The Group parades and disciplines were proud accomplishments for all. A formal review by a visiting Brigadier General A. B. McDaniel resulted in a commendation of excellence, which was proudly passed around to the troops by Lt. Colonel Dick, following one of the parades.

HEADQUARTERS ARMY AIR BASE
WILL ROGERS FIELD, OKLAHOMA

NUMBER 46 EXTRACT February 15, 1943

---

23. The following named officers and EM of the 46th Bomb Group (L) are hereby trfd in gp to the 416th Bomb Group, (L), eff this date:

OFFICERS

Lt. Col. Richard D. Dick, 022569, AC, Group Commander
Capt. Griffin R. Beatty, 046509, AC
2nd Lt. William L. Kinney ,0568916, AC
Capt. James W. Townsend, 0351967, AC
Capt. Warren J. Cohen, 0400569, MC
1st. Lt. Chester C. Wysocki, 0402333, AC
1st. Lt. James R. Paisley, 0433253, AC
2nd Lt. Carl R. Holbert, 0572043, AC
Capt. Lewis C. Dull, 0354822, AC
2nd Lt. John E. Easterwood, 0857842, AC
2nd Lt. August T. Rini, 0512205, AC
2nd Lt. Gerald L. McCurry, 0857285, AC
W.O. William H. Moffeit, w2118789, AUS
2nd Lt. Reece Evans, 0857285, AC
2nd Lt. William L. Eubank, 0568073, AC
2nd Lt. Dana B. Horn, 0857294, AC
2nd Lt. Jay A. Adelblue, 0857261, AC
2nd Lt. Isreal J. Shikora, 0856139, AC
2nd Lt. Joseph R. Allen, 0509575, AC
2nd Lt. Carl. M. Singley, 0570272, AC
2nd Lt. Arthur A. Bliss, 0856659, AC
1st. Lt. Clayton W. Zesinger, 0365947, AC
Capt. William B. Cleves, 0495589, AC
Capt. William P. Thomas, 0496149, AC
1st. Lt. Maurice B, Sheridan, 0915759, AC
2nd Lt .Bernard P. Sweeney, 0649720, AC
2nd Lt. Bernard S. Metz, 0649679, AC
2nd Lt. Waymon D. Clark, 0736115, AC
2nd Lt George W. Cowgill, 0736127, AC
2nd Lt. Robert. M Cook, 0736122, AC
2nd Lt. Richard D. Cromwell, 0736131, AC
2nd Lt. Wilford J, Crutsinger, 0736134, AC
2nd Lt. William (NMI) Deanley, 0736147, AC
2nd Lt. Bernard F. Dotson, 0736153, AC
2nd Lt. Ray M. Cuberly, 0736135, AC
2nd Lt. Paul F. Curdy, 0736138
2nd Lt. John P. Downey, Jr., 0736154. AC
2nd Lt. Creston L. Drugan, Jr., 0736156, AC
2nd Lt. Robert J. Duthu, 0736160, AC
2nd Lt. John W. Holdaway, 0736216, AC
2nd Lt. Frederic E. Durland, 0736159
2nd Lt. Howard J. Hilderbrandt, 0736212, AC
2nd Lt. Elwin F. Howard , 0736218
2nd Lt. Meredith J. Huff, 0736220, AC
2nd Lt. David A. Hulse, 0736223, AC
2nd Lt. Eugene S. Hulette, 0736222. AC
2nd Lt. Chester R. Jackson, 0736226, AC

HEADQUARTERS ARMY AIR BASE
WILL ROGERS FIELD, OKLAHOMA

NUMBER 46 EXTRACT February 15, 1943

CO. 668th BOMB SQ
Capt. John G. Napier, 0431478 AC.
CO. 669th BOMB SQ.
Capt. Raymond T. Schlanser, 0431537, AC
CO. 670th BOMB SQ.
Capt. Robert F. Price, 0431508
CO. 671st BOMB SQ.
Capt. David L. Willetts, 0431583, AC

ENLISTED MEN
FROM HQ. 46th BOMB GP TO HQ 416TH BOMB GP

M/Sgt. Jack Miller,	6234516	M/Sgt. Joseph E. Holmgren,	R-1552008
Cpl. John D. Larimore	15019836	T/Sgt. John Laheta, Jr.	20544875
T/Sgt. Robert E. Burton	15063022	S/Sgt. Glen R. Hancock	18106885

Trfd fr 51st Bomb Sq., 46th Bomb Gp
Trfd fr 50th Bomb Sq., 46th Bomb Gp

FROM 50th BOMB SQ. TO 668TH BOMB SQ.

T/Sgt. Horace O. Edwards	6366328	Sgt. John A. Stevens	18037844
		Pvt. Fank C. Amend, Jr.	38127830
Cpl. Richard W. Neller	3913154	M/Sgt. Dennie B. Brosset	6920839
S/Sgt. Vernon E.Raines	35126242	S/Sgt. Nicholas J. Fish	35024434
T/Sgt. Frank L. Arens	14030226	T/Sgt. Charles F. Dike	18034967
T/Sgt. Roy E. Anderson	15016824	S/Sgt. Louis E. Taylor	35024984
S/Sgt. Stanley J. Buinski	15019627	Sgt. Veto H. Ketchin	11033371
Sgt. Booker B. Baker	35104799	Pfc. Joe C. Chapin	18060069
Pfc. James H. Medlock	14072470	Pvt. Owen R. Adkinson	39174761
Pvt. Lester G. Alsleben	37178365	Pvt. Claude N. Atkins	34267385
Pvt. Charles L. Ball	38150915	Pvt. Roy A. Chessmore	38128724
Pvt. Amos H. Clary	18120637	Pvt. John S. Craig	38161463
Pvt. Wilbur F. Crane	12043640	Pvt. Leo M. Delcriea	11042046
Pvt. Charlie J. Deutscher Jr.	38162476	Pvt. Roland E. Dullnig	18105729
Pvt. Robert M. Knight	18108891	Sgt. Everett O. Kline	15069175
Pvt. Charles S. Curtis, Jr.	38152259	Pvt. Russel D. Denner	39839641
T/Sgt. Paul S. Born	6395482	S/Sgt. Fred C. Geraghty Jr	35024306
Cpl. Wilbur S. Stanford, Jr.	35024348	T/Sgt. Jack H. Brown	18049661
S/Sgt. James P. Lewis	18004861	Cpl. Arthur F. Butler	12012624
Cpl. John F. Currioe, Jr.	20118661	Pvt. Alton F. Best	38203805
S/Sgt. Virgil A. Kuhlman	15019851	Cpl. Howard E. Meek	35026512
Sgt. Eldon R. Hoist	15069168	Pfc. William E. Nordhoff	33006766
Sgt. Gene J. Goldman	35024612	Cpl. Jonas D. Lanier	38146880
Sgt. Dominick S. BNrunetti	15019951	Sgt. David M. Halligan	35207829
Cpl. William T. Fryman	35033651	Pvt. Johnie A. Holy	38078651
Cpl. Gabriel J. Syobo, Jr.	39837048	Cpl. Ellis C. Acree	38094138
Pvt. Bailey East	35453650	Pvt. Ellis E. Hayes	15063110
Pvt. Ross Salimbene	15073670	Pfc. Edward R. Furtado	39090945
Pvt. Harold G. Winkler	39826848	Pvt. Emmet W. Drake	49840453
Cpl. Russel E. Brown	16006947	Pfc. Arthur Legg	35211318
S/Sgt. Carl A. Carter	35128235	Sgt. Jess A. Woodward	15063111
Pvt. Joseph E. Pisarski	13003412	Pfc. Edward A. Hampton	13050781
Pfc. William E. Duffield	35396316	Pfc. Herman C. Keebaugh	13053812

FROM 51st BOMB SQ TO 669th SQ

HEADQUARTERS ARMY AIR BASE
WILL ROGERS FIELD, OKLAHOMA

NUMBER 46 EXTRACT February 15, 1943

Name	Serial No.	Name	Serial No.
1st. Sgt. James E. Kiser	6257072	S/Sgt. Earl F. Rhodes	35034389
S/Sgt. Bernard F. Ahouse	15018865	Pvt. Albert W. Potts	37180316
S/Sgt. Audrey F. Martin	18047563	Cpl. Louis (NMI) Robert	37179943
S/Sgt. Leroy (NMI) Parker	35125156	Sgt. Jack R. Jablonsky	32178490
Pfc. Herman J. Bach	35255979	Pfc. Raymond J. Bode	36236984
T/Sgt. Keith Ozmore	7001280	Pvt. Edward C. Bergsma	39174180
Sgt. George C. Hobbs	7000405	Sgt. Kenneth R. Rogers	15019564
Pvt. Raymond W. Goughlan	36328349	Sgt. Carmin (NMI) Combs	35126207
Pvt. Gaylon B. Dunbar	38151471	Pfc. Max (NMI) Lawrence	38126704
Pvt. Robert C. Jaycox	35019128	S/Sgt. Earlan C. Johnson	15066564
Cpl. Doyle R. Miller	15069204	M/Sgt. Dwight E. Woods	6754181
T/Sgt. John N. Smith, Jr.	6983885	T/Sgt. John R. Yarbrough	14030363
T/Sgt. Connor N. Reed	6983844	S/Sgt Raymond M. Slieko	35024556
T.Sgt. Willie J. Proctor	14032518	S/Sgt.Eugene R.Nowaczewski	15063043
Sgt. Richard L. Haptonstall	35161441	Cpl. George (NMI) Wright	1807421[illegible]
Sgt. Stewart E. Mohler	35018986	Cpl. Elmer W. Mullins	18084385
S/Sgt. Charles W. Sturgeon	15069001	Cpl. Jennings C. Knutson	17033009
Cpl. Trafton E. Nossaman	38019540	S/Sgt. Raymond J. Mirka	15018864
Pvt. Thomas E. Melte	19066513	Pfc. Wilshire F. Mitchell	14025790
Cpl. Karl F. Dudding	15066573	Pvt. Clifford J. Durkin	39176459
Pvt. Buono A. Dyjak	36339929	Pvt. William H. Dyk	39606420
Pvt. Earl R. Easterday	39176663	Pvt. Coleman M. Elmore	14104402
T/Sgt. Charles A. Mann	18004884	Sgt. Dan Harlan	15019665
Cpl. Thomas M. Yarnell	15267950	Pvt. Myron C. Bethard	19084374
Pfc. James C. Bourland	19073232	Pvt. Kenneth S. Flaig	39242673
M/Sgt. Wm. J. F. Whittenhouse	6657824	S/Sgt. Bethel E. Ray	18035889
Cpl. Joseph C. Wysocki (DS)	15063140	Pvt. Edward C. Commyn	16103095
S/Sgt. William E. Biggs	18043645	Cpl. Kenneth Froelich	39842651
T/Sgt. Leroy T. Hancock	6971519	Sgt. Harold A. DeMoss	35035564
Pvt. Ronald C. Caylor	33209451	Cpl. Clayton W. Gobin	11023862
Pvt. Lawrence E. McCabe	35453164	Pvt. Russel(NMI)Dahlbeck	39179023
S/Sgt. Edward M. Anthony	18010826	S/Sgt. Theodore L. Heim	36027124
Cpl. William F. Entriken	15019999	Pvt. Wilbur E. Dyke	35340658
Pfc. Earl T. Conway	31096320	Pvt. Roy L. White	36434627

<u>FROM 53rd BOMB SQ TO 670th BOMB</u>

Name	Serial No.	Name	Serial No.
S/Sgt. Harry F. Coombs	15068712	S/Sgt. Clyde R. Perkins	15069235
Cpl. Lloyd E. Tracey	36221688	S/Sgt. Monroe C. Payton	18036057
Cpl. Robert M. Stephens	35125372	T/Sgt. Clarence R. Young	15062994
T/Sgt. James A. Trudeau	18032264	Pfc. Lawrence F. Bush	32244941
T/Sgt. George M. Black	6970991	Pfc. Milburn Chaplin	35162926
Pvt. Henry A. Vesely	35025698	M/Sgt. Ollie V. Shanks	6228680
S/Sgt. Lester E. Moydell	18004867	Cpl. William T. Casteen	3405666
Pvt. Joseph K. Brown	38107135	Pvt. Jas. F. Carney	17107876

Name	Serial No.	Name	Serial No.
Pvt. George E. Baldwin	16109161	Sgt. Herbert W. Wood	32081043
Pvt. Giles J. Starr	36232693	M/Sgt. Haller F. Keables	6914445
S/Sgt. Thurnan B. Strickland	14030225	Pfc. Zimmer L. Rape	14072510
Pfc. Harold H. Goodman	36216990	Sgt. William R. Reid	38078601
S/Sgt. Harold L. Garvin	35019041	S/Sgt. James T. Mobley	15085014
S/Sgt. William J. Donahue	17024222	Sgt. Virgil Reynolds	13035081
Sgt. Donald Levengood	15018771	Sgt. Francis X. Luke	32452858
T/Sgt. Donald C. Hoover	15018833	Sgt. Clifford D. Body	35035342
Pfc. Nathan D. Love	13033705	Pvt. John Trechock	15067227

HEADQUARTERS ARMY AIR BASE
WILL ROGERS FIELD, OKLAHOMA

NUMBER 46 EXTRACT February 15, 1943

Pfc. Harold F. Witmire	33023033	M/Sgt. Clayton Patric	6389968
M/Sgt. Ernest L. Horning	15042316	Pvt. M. G. Blair	19084154
T/Sgt. Noel E. Clark	18001494	S/Sgt. William Wenter	15019658
T/Sgt. Robert E. Atchison	17016264	S/Sgt. Leo H. Schwartz	18001374
Sgt. Leland L. Jones	35024803	Sgt. Paul L. Stewart	35002564
Sgt. Charles E. Gill	35208666	S/Sgt. Morris W. Burham	15063237
Cpl. Elmo W. Kline	35325458	Sgt. William H. Kidd	35152390
Sgt. Charles J. Mihalek	35024672	Pfc. Angelo F. Miranda	32244835
Sgt. Kenneth H. Hunt	35161384	Cpl. Horace R. Burch	38013710
Cpl. Charles G. Thompson	15019331	Pvt. Jameson Risser	15073529
Cpl. Edwin B. Saunders	15073544	Pvt. Gordon D. Gailbreath	14104462
Pvt. Raymond B. Hagerstrom	16030823	Sgt. Lynwood M.Robinson	13049808
Pvt. Lewis C. Bush	15019990	Pvt. John R. Foresman	39021323
Pvt. Hubert L. Click	14063685	Pfc. Newman G. Parker	15083880
Pvt. Richard Bos, Jr.	37121192	Pvt. Kenneth B. Gulley	38105454
Sgt. Adrian M. Howard	15019575	Pvt. Robert L. Stoy	33013981
FROM 87th BOMB SQ TO 671st BOMB SQ			
T/Sgt. John H. Tidwell	6926908	T/Sgt. James A. Skidmore	15016350
Pvt. Roswell F. Pogue	15046259	S/Sgt. Merl E. McClung	35162396
Sgt. Elmer W. Baxter	35161959	Cpl. Frank Fabic	33261478
Sgt. John W. McAfee	15068716	Pfc. Richard J. Olmer	37256118
S/Sgt. Richard L. Humphrey	15019819	S/Sgt. Philip D. Graves	16028318
S/Sgt. Lawrence A. West	11023925	Sgt. Theodore V. Elmore	6931117
Cpl. Bernard J. Conner	20510687	Pvt. Marvin J. Culwell	39251450
Pvt. Charles W. Ehrhardt	18103989	S/Sgt. Harry L. Meadows	15069181
Cpl. Paul E. Murphy	13050698	Sgt. Warren R. Peters	15069078
Cpl. Edward G. Pochatko	13041060	Cpl. Eugene M. Lowe	14055909
Sgt. Lonnie O. Bays	35208627	Sgt. James L. France	35208573
Pfc. Jewell F. Irwin	34280065	Pfc. William C. Emery	34203731
M/Sgt. Alvin W.Prey	6794104	M/Sgt. Elmer W. Gillet	6680201
M/Sgt. George L. Zeanah	20443166	T/Sgt. Hosea H. Farrow	6397293
S/Sgt. Alec E. Moore	35126142	S/Sgt. Goodman Goldberg	35105247
Sgt. Anthony Baginski	35162965	S/Sgt. Irwin H. Faur	37041025
Sgt. Max F. Weatherford	15066585	Sgt. Alton D. Blackford	35163257

THIS IS A TRUE EXACT COPY

FRANK M. HOPPE, (Group Historical Officer0
1st LT. AIR CORPS

HEADQUARTERS
416TH BOMBARDMENT GROUP (L)
WILL ROGERS FIELD

SPECIAL ORDERS
NUMBER 1

Oklahoma City, Okla.
February 15, 1943

1. Capt. Raymond T. Schlanser 0-431537, is reld fr assd to 669th Bomb Sq (L) and is assd to 670th Bomb Sq (L) and aptd Sq Comdr. (Vice Capt Robert F. Price 0-431508 AC reld)

2. Capt. Robert F. Price, 0-431508 AC, is reld fr assd to 670th Bomb Sq (L) and is assd to 669th Bomb Sq (L) and aptd Sq Cmdr. (Vice Capt. Raymond T. Schlanser 0-431537 AC reld)

3. The following named Officers, Hdqr. 416th Bomb Sq (L), are attached to the 669th Bomb Sq for administration:

Capt. Griffin R. Beatty, 046309, AC
Capt. Warren J. Conan, 0400569 MC
Capt. William P.Thomas, 0496149, AC
Capt. James W. Townsend, 0351967, AC
2nd Lt. William L. Kinney, 0568916, AC

4. The following named Officers, Hdqr., 416th Bomb Sq (L) are assigned duties as indicated:

Capt.Griffin R. Beatty, 046309, AC	Group Operations
Capt. Warren J. Conan, 0400569, MC	Group Surgeon
Capt. William P. Thomas, 0496149, AC	Group Intelligence
Capt. James W. Townsend, 0351967, AC	Group Adjutant
2nd Lt. William L. Kinney, 0568916, AC	Group Material

5. The following named Officers having been asgd to the 416th Bomb Group (L) per Par 23, 80 46, Hq WRF, Okla., dated Feb.15th, 1943 are asgd to duties as indicated:

<u>668th BOMB SQ (L)</u>

1st Lt. James R. Paisley, 0433253
1st Lt. Chester C. Wysocki, 0402333, AC
1st Lt. Clayton Z. Zesiger, 0365947, AC
2nd Lt. George W. Cowgill, 0736127, AC
2nd Lt. John P.Donney, Jr., 0736154, AC
2nd Lt. John R. Easterwood, 0857842
2nd Lt. Reese Evans, 0857285, AC
2nd Lt. John W. Holdaway, 0736216, AC
2nd Lt. David A. Hulse, 0736223, AC
2nd Lt. Chester R. Jackson, 0736226, AC
2nd Lt. Israel J. Shikora, 0356135, AC

<u>669th BOMB SQ (L)</u>

Captain William B. Cleves, 0495589, AC
Capt.Lewis C. Dull, 0354822, AC
2nd Lt. Joseph R. Allen, 0509575, AC
2nd Robert M. Cosk, 0736122, AC

HEADQUARTERS
416TH BOMBARDMENT GROUP (L)
WILL ROGERS FIELD

2nd Lt. Ray Cuberly, 0736135, AC
2nd Lt. William (NMI) Branley, 0736147, CA
2nd Lt. William L,.Ewbank, 0568073, AC
2nd Lt. Carl N. Nolbert, 0572043, AC
2nd Lt. Meredith J. Huff, 0736221
2nd Lt. August T.Rini, 0512205, AC

670th BOMB SQ (L)

1st Lt.Maurice B. Sheridan, 0915759, AC
2nd Lt. Paul J.Curdy, 0736138, AC
2nd Lt. Richard D.Cromwell, 0736131, AC
2nd Lt. Robert J. Duthu, 0736160, AC
2nd Lt. Dana B. Horn, 0857294, AC
2nd Lt. Elwin F. Howard, 0736218, AC
2nd Lt. Eugene S. Hulletts, 0736232, AC
2nd Lt. Gerald L. McCurry, 0867270, AC
2nd Lt. Carl W. Singley, 0570272, AC
2nd Lt. Bernard F. STanley, 0649720,AC

671st BOMB SQ (L)

2nd Lt. Jay A. Ailsblue, 0857361
2nd Lt. Arthur L. Bliss, 0856639, AC
2nd Lt. Waylon D. Clark, 0736115, AC
2nd Lt. Wilford J. Crutsinger, 0738134, AC
2nd Lt. Bernard F. Dotson, 0736153, AC
2nd Lt. Crehton L. Drugan, 0736156, AC
2nd Lt. Fredrick F. Rupland, 0736157, AC
2nd Lt. Bernard S. Metz, 0-649679, AC
W.O. William H. Moffett, W2116789, AUS.

6. The following named enl men, Hq 416th Bomb Grp (L) are attached to 668th Bomb Sq (L) for Rat. Qtrs and Adm;

M/Sgt. Joseph E. Holmgren, R.-1552008
M/Sgt. Jack Miller, 6234516
T/Sgt. Robert E. Burton, 15063022
T/Sgt. John Laheta, Jr., 20544875
S/Sgt. Glen R. Hancock,18106885
Corp. John D. Larimore, 15019835

By order of Lt.Col Dick:

James W. Townsend
Captain, Air Corps,
Adjutant

A TRUE COPY
Frank M. Hoppe, 1st., AC Group Historical Officer

1943 Group History
Group Formations

The Four Hundred and Sixteenth (416th) Bombardment Group (L) was activated on 5 February, 1943, without personnel, at Will Rogers Field, Oklahoma City, Oklahoma. The authority for the organization of this Group was contained in General Orders #3, Headquarters Army Air Base, Will Rogers Field, Oklahoma, dated 4 February, 1943. The components making up the Group were the 668th, 669th, 670th, and 671st Bombardment Squadrons Light.

The original transfer of fifty-one (51) Officers and two hundred and forty one (241) Enlisted Men was made on 15 February 1943. The source of the cadre was the 46th Bombardment Group and units from Will Rogers Field; from Blythe, Calif., from Barksdale Field, La., and a number of men with considerable overseas experience from the Third Air Force Replacement Center, Plant Park, Florida. These key personnel were in most cases, soldiers of valuable experience, and their contributions were especially large.

Until 15 February, all personnel were attached to their parent organization for duty, rations, and quarters. However, on that date, the 46th Bombardment Group Light moved to the North side of Will Rogers Field, leaving the South side to the 416th Bombardment Group (further references will call it the 416th Bomb Group (L).

The Group originally operated as an Operational Training Unit under the III Air Support Command. Under the leadership of its young and energetic Commanding Officer, Lt. Col. Richard D. Dick, the Group began to lay the foundation to cope with the administative and operational problems it would soon face. The following Officers were assigned to the duties indicated:

Capt. Griffin R. Beatty.........................Group Operations Officer
Capt. Warren J. Conan.........................Group Surgeon Officer
Capt. William P. Thomas.....................Group IntelligenceOfficer

Capt. James W. Townsend.................... Group Adjutant Officer
2nd Lt. William L. Kinney...................................Group Materiel

The four men who were selected to be Commanding Officers of thc four Squadrons had been together ever since their graduation from Flying School. They had gained valuable experience while on Desert Maneuvers in California. They were:

Capt. John G. Napier...CO 668th
Capt. Robert F. Price...CO 669th
Captain Raymond T. Schlanser.....................................CO 670th
Captain David L. Willetts...CO 671st

The Group fell back on the parent Group, the 46th, for assistance with its training. Pilots were attached to the 46 Bomb Group for transition flying during the first three months of our existence. On 11 May, the first eight (8) planes were assigned to the 416th Group. One B-25 C and one A-20-B was given to each of the 668th and 669th Squadrons. Two A-20-Bs were assigned to each of the 670th and 671st Squadrons.

Classes in all military occupational specialties were conducted by the 46th Bomb Group until 1 June1943. The Pilots attended Ground School, for five hours a day, in the following subjects: code, link trainer, aircraft recognition, operation and maintenance of the A-20 and B-25, air navigation, radio, instrument procedure, etc. The Intelligence personnel attended classes for one hour a day. Training films were shown, such as DIVIDE AND CONQUER, which all personnel saw on 21 and 24 May.

The training of the mind was important, but the training and conditioning of the body was just as important to produce the type of soldier that Col. Dick wanted. Therefore, a physical training program was set up. Both Officers and Enlisted Men participated in the program of Calisthenics and games. The men took physical fitness tests during the third week of May. The Group experience of the bivouac was important,. The men pitched shelter halves They were instruced in how to camouflage and in camouflage discipline. After supper, the Group returned to the Base.

Ceremonial Reviews were held on Saturday mornings, in which all available men paraded.

Moral during this period while at Will Rogers Field was high. Military courtesy and discipline was commendable.

The enlisted personnel enjoyed the recreational activities and entertainment prepared for them. Typical of the recreation available to them were these events taken from a copy of FUN DIAL, an announcement paper:

Recreation on the Base

Sunday - - - - - - - - - - - Radio Broadcast
All-Girl Show
Mystery Show
Monday - - - - - - - - - - -Stag and Stunt
Tuesday - - - - - - - - - - -Dance
Wednesday - - - - - - - - -Dance
Thursday - - - - - - - - - - Dance
Friday - - - - - - - - - - - - Grab Bag Nite
Saturday - - - - - - - - - - -Dance

These papers were designed by an Enlisted man of the Group and posted weekly in the Squadron Barracks. Stories and pictures of personnel and activities were featured in two pages of Field News, the Base Weekly Newspaper.

Typical of the competitive spirit that had already arisen between the Squadrons of the Group was the interest shown in the Field Day planned by Lt. John Flummerfelt, Group Athletic Officer. Squadrons sent its representatives into events of all kinds from a horseshoe tournament to a mile relay. No less interest was shown in the Officer's Softball League that started on May 20.

Despite the apparently full schedule of activities, the social life of the Group was not neglected. Dances were held at the Base Recreation Hall for the Enlisted Men.

For every man you know who has ever tried to defy the laws of gravity, you will find one who faced death. There are some who lose out on the struggle. On April 15, 2nd Lt. Eugene S. Hulette, while on temporaty duty at Amarillo, Texas was killed on a routine training mission.

It was about the beginning of April when the Group began to function quite smoothly. On April 4, the Group was assigned to the 56th Bombardment Training Wing, General Order #8, III Air Support Command. Throughout that month and the next, the Group progressed appreciably. On May 13, approval was received for Aircraft Marking for the 671st Squadron.

SO Published 1 June, transferred the Group to Lake Charles, Louisiana, thus beginning the second phase of training for the History of the Group.

A-20 Development History

Two booklets published by Squadron/Signal Publications from Carrolton, Texas,with Jim Mesko as editor, covers the evolution of the A-20 twin engine light attack bomber. The plane. which became the A-20, was not the original concept or design of the United States Air Corps. Mesko writes that Douglas Aircraft Company Engineers envisioned the need for a fast flying twin engine bomber to replace the only single engine Northrup A-17 attack aircraft then in existence. Jack Northrup and Ed Heinemann, with Douglas, began designing the twin engine fast flying bomber in 1936. They designated the aircraft, 7A, and had thoughts to develop it to fly at 250 miles per hour, carrying a crew of three, and weighing about 9500 pounds.

The Northrup-Heinemann design was not entirely complete when in 1937 the U. S. Army realized the need for a twin engine fast flying bomber, and set parameters for a 200 mile per hour, 1200 mile range plane capable of carrying 1200 pounds of bombs. Heinemann undertook the design of the plane by himself when Northrup left the Douglas Company to start his own company. The designer changed the name to the 7-B to meet the Army's specifications. Two designs were required, with one being equipped with a glass or plexiglass nose so a Bombardier could ride there. The other planes would have to be solid nose with either four or six guns to protrude, shooting forward. These gun ships would be used to strafe enemy positions after dropping their bomb loads from higher altitudes. The glass nosed planes would be equipped with forward firing high caliber machine guns, located near the bottom of the plane, straddling the bombardier's compartment. Both models would have a top mounted mechanized turret with twin 50 caliber guns and a "tunnel" gunner position, for a man to be laying on the floor at the bottom of the plane, aiming a gun toward the rear of the plane.

The French Government was in the throes of upgrading their military capabilities and noted the test flights of the 7-B. Being impressed with their performance, they immediately ordered 100 of the new planes. They eventually revised that number to 270 units. The British became interested in this attack model fast plane and ordered hundreds, in 1940, to be used as night fighters. They named this exciting addition to their RAF as the "Boston." The British began using their Boston B-7s as daylight bombers with a high degree of success. This practice may have been the precursor of precision daylight bombers envisioned by the U.S. Air Corps. The DB-7 designation was adopted by the U. S., as an acronym for Douglas Bomber- 7. This model was upgraded to include 1100 HP Pratt and Whitney R-1830 radial engines, which improved performance in bomb loads and speeds. It first flew in 1938.

It was not until 1939 that the U. S. Army Air Corps placed orders with Douglas for the DB-7s. They asked for superchargers to be added and a new designation became the A-20, powered with Wright R-2600, 1600 HP engines. When test flights showed the superchargers would not be used at high altitude missions, they were eliminated, resulting in improved performance.

Subsequent modifications in armament, glass nosed compartments, and engine cowlings, brought designations to A-20-J and K models. The A-20 J and K were the glass nosed type for the Bombardier-Navigator position and the Norden Bombsight. The G designation included six 50 caliber nose guns, plus two 50 caliber turret guns, and the tunnel gun.

The Bombardier-Navigator entered his compartment from a bottom dropping hinged door. This position was isolated from the pilot's cockpit. There was no armor plated protection for the man in the glass nose. An escape hatch at the top of the compartment was the emergency exit. Gunners in the center of the plane were also isolated from the pilot.

Specifications of the A-20 G

Length : 48' 0"
Height: 17' 7"
Wingspan: 61' 4"
Maximuim Speed: 340 MPH
Engine: Two R-2600-23 1600 HP
Armament
- Six .50 Caliber Nose Guns (Pilot Controlled)
- Two .50 Caliber Turret Guns
- One .30 Caliber Hand Held Tunnel Gun

Combat Range: 1000 Miles
Service Ceiling: 25,800 Feet

Pilots assigned to fly the A-20s were extremely pleased with the ease of handling in flight, confidence in emergencies with capabilities of flying on single engine, roomy, comfortable cockpit with easy access to all required controls, and handy instrument panel read-outs.

New Super Havocs Blasting at Germany

London, May 20 (AP).—Two new versions of the A-20 Havoc light bomber, each capable of carrying a ton of high explosives, now are flying against Germans from British bases, Lieut. Gen. Brereton, commander of the U. S. 9th Air Force, announced today.

The Douglas Havoc A-20 in flight.

One was described as a bombardier version with transparent nose and the other as an attack type with solid nose and six forward machine-guns.

The sister ships have been flying and bombing together during the pre-invasion offensive. The attack version releases its bombs in synchronization with the glass-nosed craft which does the aiming.

Boasting a speed in excess of 320 miles an hour and a tactical radius of more than 350 miles, the new Havoc's power-operated turrets with pairs of 50 caliber machine-guns can fire 'round the clock."

With nine machine-guns, the solid-nosed Havoc is the most powerfully-armed A-20 ever produced. Its six nose guns make it an excellent low-altitude strafing plane, also.

The bombardier version carries a crew of four while the attack ship has three, the pilot releasing the bombs.

German Ace Killed

London, May 20 (AP).—A Berlin broadcast today reported the death of a German air ace, Rudolf Frank, in a night fighter action after 45 air victories.

N.Y. Daily News - Sunday - May 21st and

A-20 and A-26 Planes

Pilots who were fortunate enough to be assigned to the A-20 aircraft have laudatory comments on the benefits of flying these bombers, which were the fastest at that time. They said they handled like fighter planes. Pilots were comfortable in keeping their planes in tight formations with visual acuity from both the left and right side, due to the relatively narrow cockpit, with no obstructions. The engine nacelles gave planty of side view clearance and the forward visibility was exceptional. The speed and maneuverability was exciting for pilots.

The 416th Bomb Group were the first to fly the A-20 planes in combat in the European Theatre of Operations starting in early March, 1944. The 409th and 410th Bomb Groups were activated a few months later, to become part of the Ninth Bomber Command of the Ninth Air Force.

Damaged A-20 planes were not dangerous to fly, even on single engine with one engine prop feathered.

Normal bombing missions were flown at 12,000 feet altitude, sometimes up to 15,000 feet. The planes were not outfitted with heaters, or oxygen equipment. During winter flying months, crew members had to improvise their own clothing to overcome the sub-zero temperatures they had to fly in. The normal foot protection was to don a pair of silk socks, then a pair of woolen socks, covered with paper wrappings, usual GI shoes and then fur-lined flying boots. Fur lined over pants and jackets were standard gear, also.

Hand protection consisted of silk gloves and fur-lined over-gloves. The two gunners were exposed to the outside temperatures because of the opening at the bottom of the hatch so their clothing had to be better insulated, according to their ingenuity. In spite of these minor inconveniences, everything worked out rather well.

Formations for bombing usually consisted of 36 aircraft, made up of two boxes, with three flights and six planes in each flight. The lead bombardier-navigator was responsible to navigate the formation to the target Initial Point (IP), when each of the flights of six planes would separate to make the bomb run. Each flight was headed up by a glass nosed ship with the Bombardier-Navigator (BN) having to sight the target on the bomb run, synchronizing the aiming point and dropping the bombs. When his bombs were released, the other five planes in the flight were required to toggle their bombs out. The tightness of the formation would make for a good concentration of bombs on the aiming point.

When we talk about forward firing gun ships, capable of strafing enemy targets, the bomb-strafe missions did not take place until the 416th were equipped with A-26 planes, in November of 1944. These planes offered up to 16 forward firing 50 caliber guns. In addition, they were capable of carrying eight 500 pound bombs in the bomb bay as well as two on under wing shackles. The 416th Group were the first to fly A-26 planes in combat, as a group.

The strafing capabilities of these planes caught the attention of General Pete Quesada, the then Commanding General of the Tactical Air Command of the 9th Air Force. He learned of the extraordinary capabilities of the A-26.

Richard V. Wheeler, a West Point Graduate, then a Captain in the 671st Squadron of the 416th Bomb Group tells this story:

> I had completed 65 missions and a few more, so I was assigned temporary duty to J. Lawton Collins' Division, the Jayhawk Division, at the front in late 1944, just before the Battle of the Bulge. General Collins was quite a Commander. He was the father of the Astronaut Collins, who was the third member of the astronauts with the Aldren and Armstrong team. This assignment was a few weeks before the Battle of the Bulge erupted, which caught everyone by surprise. The Army had drawn a battle line along the Rhine River, building them up. The war had kind of stabilized and they were lining up for the final big push, through the Ardennes and on into Berlin. They had apparently requested from the Air Corps, representatives to advise them on what were logical targets, light, medium, and heavy bombers, with fighters, would be better able to concentrate upon. We were advising Collins' Staff what were typical targets for fighters to go for, or light, or heavies to hit. We had representatives from fighter, light and medium, plus heavy bomber groups on the advisory staff.
>
> I was assigned to the ground troops, but I went up to talk to Three Star General Pete Quesada, who was the Commanding General of the Tactical Air Command of the 9th Air Force. He was a well known General of the fighter outfits. Word came down that General Quesada had heard about the A-26s our group was flying as a new aircraft in the the-

ater. The A-26s had replaced the A-20s we flew. The 416th was the first group flying the 26s. I went up to talk to General Quesada since he was always interested in forward firing fifty caliber guns the A-26s had. The fighters might have six 50 caliber guns on the P-47s and they could do a heck of a job in strafing railroad cars, etc., but to have 16 - 50 caliber guns, got Quesada's attention. He wanted to know whether or not it was feasible for some of the fighter pilots who knew strafing better than we did, to try strafing with our planes. He asked if his pilots could use our planes to advantage.

The A-26 designation meant attack, so I thought the plane should be used for its designed purpose. The A-26s without the bombardier noses, had eight 50s in the nose and six under the wings. In addition, the two top turret guns could be directed by the pilot. There was also a turret underneath. With that firing power, Quesada envisioned massive destruction could be dealt out. Fighter pilots knew how to strafe trains, and with those 50s on the 26s, they could blow a train right off the tracks rather than explode it.

Finally, word came down from Bomber Command, through General Quesada, that he wanted to have six of our Group's A-26s on loan to fighter pilots. Six fighter pilots checked into our group and after flying indoctrination in a minimum of time, they were eager to go. With two flights of three planes, they took off for targets unknown to us. They were to nose down and strafe it. They thought that was fabulous, with all that gun power, they could desecrate anything.

However, when they attacked a well defended target, they had to pull up with their fighters to escape the flak. Any bomber would lose speed fast going up quickly, and they would become good targets for the good flak gunners on the ground. Fighter pilots could climb practically as fast as they went down, but not bombers, which could go up at 200 to 250 MPH.

There were no German fighters in the area. We had air superiority.The fighters were staying pretty close to defend Berlin.

When the flak started to burst around the fighter pilots on the upward climb with our bombers, it was a new experience for them since during bombing missions, fighters always got way away from flak, and they hardly ever experienced that. They didn't like flak around them.

After a period of a couple of weeks, these fighter pilots decided they were better off with their own aircraft, so they returned the A-26s to our Group.

The planes underwent careful inspection when we got them back, and it was determined that the diving maneuver stressed the wings which were literally bent out of shape. They had pulled too many G's and the planes were declared unairworthy and were scrapped.

Our Group did eventually utilize the A-26s on bomb-strafe missions, with our pilots and crews, with some modicum of success. Those missions are covered in later chapters.

Specifications of the A-26C Douglas Invader

	Attack Bombers
Wingspan	70 feet (21.34 m)
Length	51 feet 3 inches (15.62 m)
Height	18 feet 6 inches (5.64 m)
Cruise Speed	284 mph (457 km/h)
Maximum Speed	355 mph (571 km/h)
Range	1400 miles (2253 km)
Ceiling	22,100 feet (6736 m)
Engines	Two Wright R-2800-79, rated 2000 hp
or	Two Pratt-Whitney R-2800, rated 2C00
Armament (B Models)	Eight 50 cal. (nose guns) Six 50 cal. (wing mounted) Up to 4000 pounds of bombs
Crew	2 on B Models (Gun Ships) 3 on C Models

Formation Flying

BOX I (A)

			A-1-1			
		A-1-3		A-1-2		
			A-1-4			
		A-1-6		A-1-5		
	A-3-1				A-2-1	
A-3-3		A-3-2		A-2-3		A-2-2
	A-3-4				A-2-4	
A-3-6		A-3-5		A-2-6		A-2-5

BOX II (B)

			B-1-1			
		B-I-3		B-1-2		
			B-1-4			
		B-1-6		B-1-5		
	B-3-1				B-2-1	
B-3-3		B-3-2		B-2-3		B-2-2
	B-3-4				B-2-4	
B-3-6		B-3-5		B-2-6		B-2-5

BOX III (C)

			C-1-1			
		C-1-3		C-1-2		
			C-1-4			
		C-1-6		C-1-5		
	C-3-1				C-2-1	
C-3-3		C-3-2		C-2-3		C-2-2
	C-3-4				C-2-4	
C-3-6		C-3-5		C-2-6		C-2-5

Forming The Boxes:

When the tower controllers fired a signal, engines were started.

Each flight of six lined up on the runway, two by two.

Each plane took off in 10 second intervals, after the go signal.

Thereby, each flight took off in one minute, flying a designated time and then making a predetermined angle or turn to join their leader

Each box was off in three minutes.

Entire formation of two boxes was formed in six minutes.

1st Box A	Lead Flight #1
2nd Box B	Right Flight #2
3rd Box C	Left Flight #3

Third Number—position in flight

Chapter 2

Lake Charles Training
Laurel Training Sessions
On the Ocean to Action
Wethersfield, England
15th February Occurrences 1944

Lake Charles Training

On 3 June 1943, the 416th Bomb Group advance echelon departed Will Rogers Field, Oklahoma City for their new training base at Lake Charles, Louisiana. The air echelon leaving on 4 June.

The new base was a welcome sight with seemingly new barracks buildings, flower gardens, expansive hangers, and sun - sun - sun and warm weather. The only thing missing at this point were more planes to fly, but we all knew they would be there some time in the future.

Training, training, training - with formation flying being emphasized as more flying equipment made their appearance. Additional personnel kept reporting for duty, including a large group of newly trained navigators who had basic training as bombardiers. They would be known as Bombardier-Navigators (BN). These dual rated men were to become leaders of flights of six aircraft, with three flights to a box, and two or three boxes to make up a group formation. The BN leading the formation would be responsible for navigating the group to the Initial Point (IP) where the flights would peel off and make the bomb run from the IP to the target, flying straight and level, with the BN in charge of flying the plane. In the meantime, he was lining up the sights on the Norden Bombsight until the cross hairs intersected to automatically release the bombs. The five other planes in the flight would drop their bombs when the flight leader let his go. So, the planes being in close formation would permit a concentration of bombs to blanket the aiming point of the target.

During the month of June, the War Department, Headquarters of the Army Air Force, Washington, D. C. approved the individual squadron insignia.

On June 15, two planes from our group collided, taking the lives of six men, including Lt. Paul Curdy, S/Sgt. R. L. Wentling, Sgt. L. E. Zelley, and Pvt. T. F. Riley. On July 4, another mishap claimed the life of Lt.R. Scully. These were tragic losses for the squadrons.

New Personnel kept arriving to each squadron and surprisingly, other prior members of the squadrons were being transferred to other groups. During September, 16 new graduates of the West Point Military Academy joined the group from flying school. Each of the squadrons received four of these men as permanent personnel.

An emergency evacuation of some planes came about on 16 September due to a hurricane alert, threatening the base. Flight ready planes were sent to Will Rogers Field in Oklahoma City. Those unable to take to the air were harnessed down in the hangers. The threat ceased in 24 hours with all planes returning to the station to renew the training schedules.

In addition to flight training, personnel were required to participate in physical exercise, running, and just plain calisthenics. Colonel Dick would circulate among the exercise formations, providing encouragement and insuring that everybody was doing their thing. Inter squadron competition was encouraged and enjoyed.

Another crash in October took the life of a newly assigned Bombardier-Navigator, Lt. Herman C. Jones. He was flying with Lt. Robert Duthu, and gunner Sgt. Robert E. Lee. They were coming in for a landing in fog and smoke, but didn't make it. The pilot and gunner were not seriously injured, although Duthu required hospitalization.

On 30 October, word came down for the group to prepare for a move to Laurel Air Base, in Mississippi. Everything was to move the next day, requiring feverish activities. At 0400 on 1 November, a 99 truck convoy moved out to make the 345 mile trip to Laurel. At 1915 that evening, we reached the new base with everybody scrambling for bunk space.

Lowell Geffinger reports that on 5 November Captain William J. Meng joined the 670th Squadron as CO, having served as Assistant Ground-Air Support Officer from Group Headquarters, relieving Capt. MacGillivray. Meng joined the group in July 1943, having spent two years in the Canal Zone and Caribbean area with the 59th Bomb Squadron in a successful anti-submarine campaign.

Laurel Training Sessions

It didn't take too long to realize the intensity of training planned for the group while at Laurel, Mississippi. Upon awakening the first day at the new base, November 2nd, 1943,orders came down for the group to engage in maneuvers taking place in Pollock, Louisiana, These were real war games, assimilating air raids over enemy territories, with crews dropping flour sacks on targets instead of bombs. Some live bombs, probably 100 pounders, were used on occasion. Missions were planned for day and night bombing, with ground crews exchanging places with air crews and vice versa, so all could feel the effects of what real war might be like. Medium altitude missions, including skip bombing were practiced. Skip bombing was not the favorite sport since on occasion, a bomb dropped would skim along the water surface and bounce up pretty close to the plane dropping it.

On November 6th crews from all squadrons took off for demonstration tours of five Army Bases in Fort Benning, Fort Knox, Fort Riley, Fort Sill, and Camp Hood. Maintenance personnel accompanied the crews to be certain of the service required by our planes. Demonstrations at each visited camp included formation flying, low altitude tactics, and general possible support for ground troops. The demonstration tour lasted until November 25th.

While those crews and personnel were making the tour, the remainder of the group were called out for a one week bivouac not too far from the base camp. Assimilating field living conditions were an important training for everyone involved, including a field mess arrangement, which turned out to be most satisfactory, they even having the wherewithall to serve ice cream, a rarity under any circumstance. This bivouac lasted from 9 November til 16 November . This was a for- real bivouac with every one sleeping in tents. Engineering, Intelligence, Operations, Communication, and Tech Supply remained in the field while other personnel returned to their BOQs.

The intensity of the training was extended to other areas, with personnel attending Cook's and Baker's training, Camouflage Schools, Administrative Inspector's School, Chemical Warfare School, First Aid Training, and Intelligence. Ordnance and Communication Sections operated in the bivouac field area while others attended Base Drivers' School. It appeared a well rounded training was taking place for the group.

Inspections by various groups were taking place during the month. The group was part of the 3rd Air Force, since inspectors from that group checked us out on the 7th of October. October 22nd to 25th III Bomber Command made detailed inspections which required many modifications to our operation, requiring upgrading.

During December 13th and 14th, IIIrd Bomber Command again appeared for an inspection and the next inspection was the POM (Preparation for Overseas Movement) team on December 16th through the 19th. If the group did not pass these rigid inspections, the groups would have to revert to training again, passing up the opportunity of going overseas. With a great sigh of relief, the group found it had passed the POM going - over.

Not one day went by without some training, or inspection, taking place, all in preparation for what we expected to face overseas. Formation flying at medium high altitudes was stressed, and navigation expertise was emphasized. Pilots were most diligent in slotting their planes in for tight formations

Starting December 28th all personnel were restricted to base. No personal phone calls could be made from the base. No visitors were permitted on base.

New Year's Day saw the group boarding a train while visitors, and family members waved their goodbyes amid the Laurel Air Force Base Band Strains; we were headed for Camp Shanks, New York, north of New York City. We left Laurel at about 1400 and after a two and a half day ride, arrived at Camp Shanks at 0300, on 3 January, amid a snow storm with three inches of the white stuff on the ground. Imagine the surprises of many southern boys who had never been in a snow storm before, slogging through slush to our quarters at the Camp. These same country boys were to have high level experiences on visits to New York City with 12 hour passes.

Training and continued inspections, with training for off loading ships was practiced, climbing down rope ladders, and abandon ship procedures, All mail was censored. Enlisted personnel were escorted by officers to mess halls and back to barracks, to movies and other gatherings.

January 17th, 1944, with full back packs, personnel boarded a train, departing Camp Shanks for a Port of Embarkation, Weehawken, New Jersey. We boarded a ferry boat to board a converted passenger Liner, SS COLOMBE and we were on our way on 18 January at 1230 for a ten day cruise, to an unknown destination.

On the Ocean to Action

After a short train ride from Camp Shanks, New York on January 17, 1944, we marched on to a ferry boat, docked at Weehawken, New Jersey, another first for youngsters from land locked states. We docked at a harbor on the North River in New York City. We loaded aboard the converted French Passenger Liner SS COLOMBE. Meal tickets were distributed and cabins were available on a first come, making your own choice of roommates basis, for officers. Double deck beds were the vogue. Anywhere from four to eight men to a cabin.

Enlisted personnel were bedded down on pipe rack type cots, stacked three high with relatively narrow passageways between tiers, in the lower levels of the ship. These pipe rack type accommodations were reminiscent of the type used in steerage compartments which brought immigrants to this country from foreign shores around the turn of the century. The biggest differences were the sanitary facilities were much better for our soldiers, and the two a day delicious meals to enjoy. Compared to bivouac fare, there is no comparison.

The COLOMBE left dockside about 1230 PM on 18 January, sailing down the river, under the Manhattan and then the Brooklyn Bridges, past Ellis Island and a final farewell to the Statue of Liberty. We waved goodbyes to Staten Island citizens and out of New York Harbor to the Atlantic Ocean. Our ship became part of a 150 ship convoy, with our vessel on the outside rear of the convoy. Not a very safe place to be. However, destroyer escorts were always in sight, scooting back and forth. Way out in the ocean, destroyers would belch smoke screens, and sometimes, general alarm gongs were heard, making for exciting moments. With smoke screens and gongs sounding, it meant enemy submarines were in the area

As we made our way into open seas, rough weather was encountered occasionally, while we watched other smaller vessels bobbing up and down, sometimes out of sight below the high billowing waves, and then riding the crest of the waves, with a sickening feeling, just watching them. Needless to say, sea sickness was not an unusual occurence among our passengers. Some poor souls experienced Mal de Mer during the entire ten days aboard.

Between meals, keeping fit was a necessity with exercise and instruction classes helping to pass the time of day. Leisure time was always watching the convoy ships, and just looking at the wake of our boat. It was amusing to hear people trying to figure out our ultimate destination, with some boys having us near Labrador, and others as far south as the Bahamas. No one ever told us where we were heading. Getting top side during gunnery practise for all the Navy destroyers and other military vessels in the convoy was interesting, along with watching our crew members test firing their guns mounted on the fore and aft of the ship in gun emplacements.

On 28 January, following ten days at sea, land was sighted and identified as Scotland. The SS COLOMBE moored at Gourock, Scotland and anchored over-night. The next day we sailed down to Glasgow. As many as could, crowded the deck railings when we moored, and the first Scottish words we heard, with, of course a heavy Scottish brogue, was "UP A WEE BIT" from longshoremen starting to unload our cargo. Was that thrilling, or what? Then children started to crowd the docks, craning their necks upward to GIs, begging for chocolate or gum. It appeared the boys were delighted to share their goodies with these youngsters, bringing laughter, hoots and hollers as the kids gathered up and made off with their loot.

Wethersfield, England

We were all packed up, ready to disembark while the baggage and military equipment was being off-loaded from the ship. When personnel were permitted off the SS COLOMBE on 31 January, we boarded the elite type English railtrains. Six people to each compartment, plus all our carry-ons. About one half of the contingent left dockside as 2300 on the 31st, with the remainder of the group leaving at 0200 February 1st.

The narrow rails and speedy engines, with their shrill different type whistles amused us. We passed lovely clean, countryside and hamlets. Late the afternoon of 1 February we arrived at Wethersfield, Essex County, about 30 miles northeast of London. Squadron personnel were directed to assigned areas entering Quonset Huts, which were neat and clean, looking practically brand new. The roof was of corrugated metal with no insulation, and one pot bellied stove in the center of the room. Ten men to a hut. Those who bedded near the doors, one on each end of the huts, quite a distance from the center hot pot bellied stove, had to find ways to keep warm. One building standing among the group of Quonset Huts had a door sign reading ABLUTION, a strange word indeed, for Yanks. The explanation came as a washroom, cold water only, if you please. At least we had running water, better than the basins we had to fill during bivouac times. Some of the boys could not wait to bathe themselves and they found old fashioned wash tubs, which they managed to fill with tepid water, with the heated water coming from pots on the pot bellied stoves. They squatted in the tubs, with their knees tucked practically under their chins. At least they were bathing.

Another set of buildings set apart from the living quarters, contained real bath tubs. Each squadron had turns using the bath tubs, with the strong admonition not to use more water in the bottom of the tub than the Queen of England was using - that is no more than two inches of water per person for each ablution. The shortage of coal was the reason, which was understandable, and the hot water was not available every day, only designated times. There were no monitors around to watch how much water was being used by individuals, but we were on the honor system. Too much usage caused the hot water to cease flowing. However, with whatever level of water was used, we did have hot water occasionally. A real nice treat for wartime.

Training intensified as our planes began to arrive. Formation flying was emphasized again, and again, with cross country missions being run over the beautiful countryside. Tight formations were the talk of the time with pilots sticking their wing tips nearly in the sides of their flight partners. Navigators were indoctinated to war type maps in flying their missions. Bombardiers were practicing bomb dropping techniques on a moving platform in hangers, where a doodle bug was scooting around the floor with a target ring on it. A pilot steered the platform and the BN had to zero in on the target, dropping a plunger on the target, assimiliating a hit. As corny as this may sound, this practise was helpful in keeping up the techniques of using the Norden Bombsight. Team work between the pilot and the BN also developed.

The early training of flight crews in the states continued in England at our first base in Wethersfield. This training was not without unfortunate accidents, taking the life of one of the pilots of the 671st squadron. The morning of 14 February, 2nd Lt. William Minnicks, making his first flight on foreign soil, piloting an A-20 G plane, took off at about 0910. He was flying into an overcast at a steep climbing angle, and disappeared. He was supposed to have two gunners with him, but lacking parachutes, they did not join him. While no one could see what happened to him, the best guess was that the plane stalled in the steep climb, and he was not able to pull out of the stall. The plane was located, resting on its back, a total wreck.

Another training mission on 21 February with a plane piloted by Lt. Francis DeMand, proved to be a thrilling experience for a Bombardier-Navigator, Lt. Al Jedinak, who was riding at the tunnel gunner's position at the bottom of the plane. Lt.

DeMand went into a slight dive and pulled up suddenly, causing Jedinak to slide out the open hatch. Fortunately, he had his chute on, and floated down about 40 miles from our base, much to the surprise of not only himself, but the Englishmen in the area. When Jedinak returned to base, be remarked, "These airplanes ain't safe."

The few fatalities experienced stateside during training were stressful, but knowing we made it overseas and having an accident befall a member before meeting the enemy, made for uncomfortable feelings, and brought our mission dangers closer.

Crew chiefs and flight line mechanics took extraordinary means to care for their individual aircraft, since they considered the plane assigned to them as practically personal property, and that wasn't a bad thing to happen. This was exhibited many times in the future when the possessiveness of their charges was discussed. If their planes came backfrom a mission shot up, you could see the hurt they felt, even taking offense that someone would do that to their plane. Administration, Engineering, Ordnance, Maintenance, Transportation and Mess Hall personnel worked their tails off to make everything just right, in keeping within the concept of what we were there for. Everything had to be done just right to excel in the assuredly rigid inspections known to be coming.

A-20s peeling off to land.
Wethersfield, England

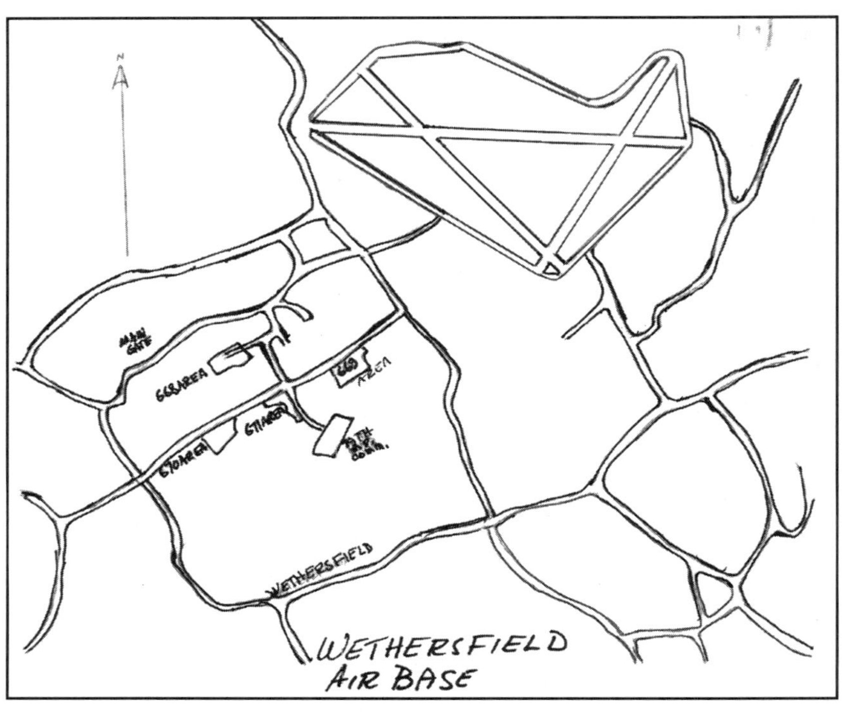
N
MAIN GATE
668AREA
669 AREA
671AREA
670AREA
WETHERSFIELD
WETHERSFIELD
AIR BASE

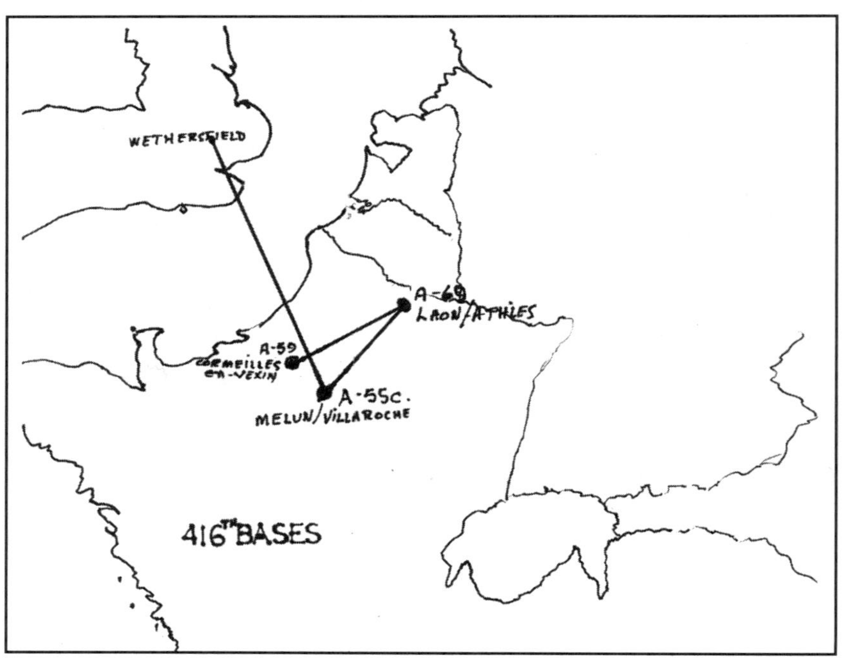
WETHERSFIELD
A-69
LAON/ATHIES
A-59
CORMEILLES
EN-VEXIN
A-55C.
MELUN/VILLAROCHE
416TH BASES

15th February Occurrences 1944

Was this a "getting to know you" month at our new base in Wethersfield? It had to be, for various serious and excitng instances.

Our group had been tagged as an attack light bomber outfit and designated within the 9th Air Force as a Tactical Air Force. Other members of the Tactical Air Force, a P-47 and a P-38, buzzed our airfield on the same day, perhaps wanting us to know what they looked like because they were probably going to be our protectors during missions over enemy territory. Their antics were thrilling to watch, a private air show.

On a not so exciting time, Lt. "Gee" Meredith took an A-20-G up on a training flight. When he tried to land, he found his hydraulic and emergency systems had failed making the landing a hot one, causing him to overrun the landing strip, winding up in a ditch at the end of the runway. Meredith nor his gunners, Sgts. Leroy R. Shaw and Clarence M. Gray were injured. This could not have been said about the plane which wound up with its nose tucked in the ditch and its tail in the air. A complete wash out !

Major Towles left his post as 668th Squadron Command Officer to move to Wing headquarters. The new C.O. would be Major Robert F. Price.

Snow and lousy weather prevented training flying, but as the clouds disappeared, a group of new A-20 aircraft arrived, being ferried in from the states. One pilot, bringing in the new planes, Lt. Wayne Downing would be assigned to the 668th Squadron. His love of flying would be measured by the fact he completed his tour of 65 missions and then re-enlisted for a second tour. The war ended, with he having piled up 86 missions, but Downing kept flying, remained in the service and saw additional duty in Korea.

For an unknown reason, a B-17 landed at our base, perhaps for refueling. The shiny aluminum plane was a good tourist attraction for our boys. Our planes were over-painted GI brown.

When the B-17 took off, the pilot made a 180 sweeping turn with the wings perpendicular to the ground, and then buzzed the field, to the delight of watchers.

Other flying elements, this time of the enemy, wanted us to know they were aware of our presence, caused an air raid alarm, with our boys scrambling for the fox holes and air raid shelters. The planes seemed to be right overhead on the February 15 night, with their droning for about an hour, our boys, in skivies, watching the bright search lights highlighting them and seeing flak burst around them, made us forget the cold. Perhaps the apprehensive feeling of being attacked was more important. Bombs were dropped, missing our facility, but landing on other fields not too far from ours. We had experienced four other air raid alerts since we arrived here a bare few weeks ago.

The STARS AND STRIPES military newspaper broke the news that the 9th Air Force Tactical Air Command existed in England. They wrote:

> Supreme Headquarters, Allied Expeditionary Force, disclosed last night that elements of the Ninth U. S. Air Force had been incorporated with the Allied Air Force controlled by Air Chief Marshall, Sir Trafford-Leigh Mallory.
>
> It was the first Allied acknowledgment of the Ninth's presence in this theater, although its aircraft have been operating from British bases for sometime.
>
> Maj. Gen. Louis H. Brewerton, who was its commander in the Middle East and in North Africa before the force moved here to form a team with the Eighth and the RAF, is in command, the announcement said.
>
> As a tactical air force, the Ninth will show its full strength with medium bombers, fighter-bombers, attack-bombers,, and fighters, the announcement said.

It pointed out that a pattern for entry into Europe calls for air superiority before the land battle commences, and that Gen. Montgomery has always insisted that the enemy's air forces be neutralized before the ground forces went into battle.

Action toward this goal would be the first assignment of the Ninth, Headquarters said.

A second assignment, it continued, would be systematic attack on the railroads, marshalling yards, and truck convoy routes leading to the enemy's replacement depots behind the lines. Still a third assignment, after the landings had been affected, would be to bomb selected targets in the battle area along with other elements of the U. S. British and Allied Air Forces.

The 416th took up this assignment of Attack Bombers, with eagerness and anticipation.

Wethersfield, England 1944
Standing (L. to R.) Pilots, 668th Sq.
R.G. Meredith, Gus Ebenstein, L.G. Peede, R.K. Cruze.
Front (L. to R.) BNs B.H. Bradford, R.T. McBrien

CHAPTER 3

Early Missions
April Showers
April Ending 1944
McGlohn Mission

Early Missions

Mission #1 - 3 March 1944 - Poix Airfield - The thrill of the first mission to enemy territory was an event in the minds of the participants selected to make this baptism of fire. It was a relatively small formation of only 18 planes. Major Harold Radetsky was the lead pilot. The fighter escort was planned to rendezvous with our group over the channel, before it reached the French Coast, but something went awry when they did not show up, so the mission was recalled.

It would be desirable to name each crew member participating on the missions and to have the loading lists of each foray, but that would be a book all its own. Consequently, the name of the lead flight and box leaders will be identified, as they are mentioned in official documents available for viewing.We have a representative group of loading listings later in this presention for about 30 missions, identifying all participants.

Mission #2 - 4 March - Berney-St.Martin Airfield, France - Major Farmer led the formation of 21 aircraft. Major Meng with Lt. Powell as Bombardier-Navigator (BN) - Lt. Hulse with Lt. Conte BN - Captain Dunn with Lt.Royalty BN and Lt. Platter with Lt.Arrington led flights. A 100 percent (10/10) cloud cover prevented the sighting of the target, so no bombs were dropped. The formation returned to base. Returning over the channel, some of the pilots jettisoned their bombs, probably feeling that landing with live bombs could create risk. They later found this problem would not exist, so bombs were brought back to base on future missions, when weather or aborts of missions occured.

One of the planes, piloted by Lt. Ostrander, lost its hydraulic fluid which would have prevented the pilot from lowering his landing gear. As he approached the base, he called the tower to report his problem. Group Commander, Colonel Mace, one of the tower spectators, instructed Ostrander to return to the channel, drop his bombs and return to base and crash land between the runways. Ostrander reported back to Colonel Mace he only had about 20 gallons of fuel left and wouldn't be able to fly to the channel and back to base.

Jimmy Wilson, one of Ostrander's gunners, said, "I heard the Colonel tell Ostrander that he was probably frightened and just go do as you were told. Before we got to the base, on the first run, the emergency gong was going and the pilot could not contact us in the back. I was in the turret, and in the excitement of what was going on, I hooked my chest chute on and noticed the pull cord was on the left side, and here I was, right handed. I managed to get the chute off, switched it around and got down from the turret.

"The other gunner, Sgt. Binney, was ready to jump, but he must have pulled his rip cord and the parachute came undone in the plane. I gathered up the shrounds of the chute, pointed Binney toward the opening on the bottom of the plane, and told Binney he had to go. I pushed him out and he came down on land near Ipswich. I jumped and landed on a haystack."

When Wilson hit the ground, a few English children ran toward him yelling, "Hi Yank, got any gum?" Wilson thought that was the last straw.

Ostrander jettisoned his canopy and jumped out over the channel when he ran out of gas. He had called Air-Sea Rescue and they picked him up in short order. He was returned to base, as were his two gunners.

For those not familiar with Air-Sea Rescue, a number of boats were constantly patrolling in the channel to assist downed air crew members who had to parachute from planes, or had to be rescued from splash-down planes. It was very successful, having saved many crewmen.

Mission #3 - Conches Airdrome. This was another miscue of the rendezvous with our fighter escort, so the mission was aborted, and everyone returned to base with their bombs. The formation leader in Box I was Lt. Colonel T. R. Ford, with Lt. W.L.Smith, BN - Major J. G. Napier with Lt. Lytle, BN - Major

M. W. Campbell and Lt. J. Kupits, BN - Major R. F. Price with Lt. A. R. Hand, BN, led flights.

During the briefing, the flyers were told that while the number of missions they were expected to fly to complete their tours was 50, that did not necessarily mean their tours would be over. Whether this was a precursor of things to come was not clear, -but eventually pilots and bombardier-navigators would be required to complete 65 missions before looking forward to returning to the states. Gunners were to complete 50 missions, and many of them did that in short order.

Mission # 4 - 7 March - Conches Airdrome. Major C. S. Towles with Lt. William Smith, BN led this mission. Captain Loyd Dunn and Lt. Pete Royalty BN - Major David Willetts and Lt. Albert Jedinak, BN, led flights. Twenty aircraft took part. At the target, one of the bombardiers had a problem with his bomb-sight and therefore did not drop his bombs, nor did the other planes in his flight. Otherwise, the demolition bombs dropped by the other flights, wreaked havoc (no pun intended) on the run-ways and taxi strips of the airfield.

Lt. Chester Jackson, flying at the tail end of a flight, banked his plane to see the bombs bursting on the target, his first view of bombs on enemy targets. In actuality, pilots could not see bomb hits, as they were flying in formation, keeping their attention on their position. The bombardier had to lean over his bomb-sight and stretch his head over the bottom glass to see his efforts. Tunnel gunners at the open hatch at the bottom of the plane also had a good view, and some planes carried pohotographers to take pictures of the burst, for record purposes. Some gunners acted as photographers.

Mission #5 - 18 March - Vacqueriette NoBall site. These NoBalls were launching pads for self-propelled motorized bombs aimed at England. The pads were located on the coast of France, pointed across the channel toward England, with no particular target in mind. While the motor was running, it was not a threat. When the motor quit, it glided down in silence, exploding with tremendous force. Many English Spitfire pilots were able to get alongside the motorized V-1 bombs, as they were called, and fly up to the unit, tipping their wing under the wing of the bomb, upsetting it, dropping it into the channel.

This formation was led by Major W. W. Farmer with Lt. M. A. Pape BN. Major Price and Lt. Hand, BN with Captain W. Battersby and Lt.W. Lytle BN led flights.. On approaching the target, when Major Price opened his bomb bay doors, his bombs dropped, causing the following planes in his flight to drop their load, all falling short of the target. This might be classified a learning experience to enforce discipline for the proper shackling up of bombs to prevent pre-release with no bombsight being used. Some flak damaged a few planes.

Mission #6 - 19 March - Wisques NoBall site. Our attack bombers, flying at lower altitudes than heavy bombers, could have better aiming possibilities on these well concealed and camouflaged targets.

Major Towles led the formation of 36 aircraft on what turned out to be a real baptism of fire. Flak was everywhere around the target. Fire and smoke obscured the target for the first box, but the second box was able to make out the aiming point and dropped their load. The first box came around and made a second run, while the anti-aircraft gunners had plenty of time to reload and re-aim, making the second bomb run dangerous. A third pass on the target was made by other flights. This got the attention of the gunners and they peppered everything in the sky.

Major Meng and Lt. Vernon Powell, BN - Major Willetts and Lt. Robert Basnett, BN - Major M.W.Campbell and Lt. W.H.Palin, BN -Captain R.A.Clark with Lt.C.W.Jones BN - and Major Radetsky with Lt. W.L.Smith BN led flights. Lt. Powell had a large piece of flak crash against his helmet, knocking him cold.

As our formation neared this heavily defended target, our boys saw a B-17 tumbling out of the sky in front of them, with some seeing parachutes blossoming out. A B-26 was seen without its tail section spinning out of control. A P-47 fighter took a hit, crashing. One of our planes, piloted by Lt. Horace F. Pair was pretty well shot up, causing him to leave the formation heading back to base. He just about made it to the English Coast, when he crash landed. His gunners, staying with him, jumped out and with the help of onlookers, managed to pull Lt. Pair out of his wrecked ship.

Captain Hiram Conant had a harrowing experience when a bomb from another plane dropped on his right wing, damaging the aileron. He managed to bring the plane back.

With each squadron having only ten planes in their inventory, having every one of them damaged in any one mission was something to shake up morale. The ever faithful crew chiefs and line mechanics wasted no time putting everything back to working order, ready for the next thrilling rides by the crews.

Mission #7 - 20 March - Foret Nationale de Tourneben NoBall. Major Towles with Lt. Pape BN and Lt. Smith, flying experimentally in a piggy-back position as Bombardier Navigator on a new A-20-J glass nosed plane made this run. The Bombardier-Navigator compartment was not very roomy, and squeezing two men into that space was quite unusual. Major Radetsky flew as Deputy, to take over in the event the leader was unable to complete the bomb run or have trouble on the mission,. A deputy flew with each first box leader, as backup.

The formation lost the Initial Point (IP), the starting point for a straight and level bomb run where planes did not take evasive action, but flew a level flight. Having missed the IP, they did not attack the target. The formation flew past the target, made right turns instead of left, which is the heading they were supposed to take. They came up to the Seine River, near Paris, and turned 180 degrees to back track. Flak greeted them on their excursion, but evasive action helped diminish damage, although all but five planes received flak hits. Major Willetts and Lt. Basnett BN led a flight.

Mission #9 - 26 March - Vacqueriette NoBall. Lt. Col.T.R.Ford with Lts. Royalty and Arrington as a BN team led the first box. Major Campbell with Lt. Palin flew deputy. Major Meng and Lt. Powell, BN - Captain Jackson and Lt. Conte BN led flights. The bombing proceeded with no problem, since no flak or fighters threatened the group. Aerial photos showed smoke and fire coming up from the target area.

This was the last mission of the month, the group having completed only nine since the first one on the 3rd of March. A combination of inclement weather, coupled with the "learning" experience of bombardier-navigators and pilots had to endure, plus malfunctioning bombing equipment, all contributed to the low number of successful trips over enemy territory.

The Commanding General of the IX Bomber Command sent congratulations to the 416th for "having arrived" following this first month of operation. They also said, "successful."

Group Commanding Officer, Colonel Harold L.Mace, gathered the crews together for a "pep" talk, pointing out that all mechanics, crew chiefs, armament, and ordnance personnel should maintain a high degree of readiness and proficiency in order for the group to succeed and be prepared for the eventual invasion and a quick trip home.

The first month of operation saw 229 planes on sorties, having dropped 287 tons of bombs in combat. No planes or personnel were lost over enemy territory. Eight men were awarded Purple Heart Medals for wounds received in action.

On March 17, IX Bomber Command conducted an inspection of the group base and came away with a gratifying report on what they saw.

670th Squad, Bombardier Navigators, March 1944.
L. to R.— Lt. R.Conte, Lt. F.Burseil, Lt. V.Powell, Lt. W.Forna

The Group strength was reported as:

668th Squadron	35 Officers	264 Enlisted Men
669th Squadron	37 Officers	266 Enlisted Men
670th Squardron	41 Officers	267 Enlisted Men
671st Squadron	38 Officers	264 Enlisted Men
Hdqs. 416th Group	36 Officers	59 Enlisted Men
Totals	187 Officers	1120 Enlisted Men

Mission #10 - 10 April - AM - Bois de Ruit Rues Noball. This mission came after 15 days of bad weather, during which time we had a few false starts. On two occasions planes had taken off and were recalled - frustrating, to say the least, with everybody anxious for action. When this tenth mission did get off , it proved to be quite costly for the group. Very intense accurate flak met the formation at the target, with three planes being shot out of the sky. The enemy gunners seemed to concentrate on individual flights rather than a blanket of flak bursts popping all around the group. Some flights did not receive hits, while others paid well for the mispleasure. Lt. Arthur Raines from the 669th squadron with gunners S/Sgts Glenn Bender and Jack Neilsen were last seen losing altitude, giving out distress calls. All three were listed as missing in action.

The second plane hit was piloted by Lt. William F. Cramsie from the 671st with gunners S/Sgts Charles Henshaw and Jack Steward. They were headed down toward the channel, asking for a bearing to base; they were all listed as MIA. The third plane piloted by Lt. Marion (Scotty) Street from the 669th squadron was badly shot up. Street gave the order to his gunners to bail out, and they did, splashing down in the channel and then being picked up by air-sea rescue teams.

Lt. Street, having lost an engine, nurtured his plane with skill and belly landed on the English coast. He walked away, uninjured. Maybe his discipline from West Point training gave him the foresight to do the right thing to protect himself.

Captain Loyd Dunn of the 671st squadron had his hydraulic line shot out, causing him to wash out the plane without brakes on landing. It wound up in a ditch at the end of the runway. His gunner, S/Sgt Worden was injured on the crash landing.

The bombing results were way off, dropping quite a way away from the target. Poor weather conditions contributed to the faulty bombsighting. The only damage incurred on this mission was that inflicted on a number of planes.

10 April: Listed as Mission #11. A group of our A-20 aircraft were flown to a B-26 Bomb Base with no prior knowledge as to why we were there. At the briefing, the A-20 crews were told they were to preceed the B-26 formation over the most heavily defended target in LeHavre, France, where the really big guns were protecting the harbor. The B-26s took off and formed up. The A-20s then took off, and flew 2000 feet below the B-26s, with tunnel gunners dropping "window" which were aluminum strips. This window provided a fake target for radar controlled guns on the ground. It worked well, with the A-20s scooting by at high speeds, with the gunners not able to track them successfully. The flak bursts all exploded into the layer of aluminum strips, well below the B-26s who dropped their bombs successfully. No planes were hit. Window mission a success.

Captain Chester Jackson with Lt. Ralph Conte, BN, led the window flights. The A-20 crews flew back to the B-26 base, where we were hailed as heroes for protecting them from the deadly flak. B-26 pilots were all inquiring about the flying capabilities of the A-20 compared to the lumbering take-offs and their hot landing B-26s.

When Jackson parked at a revetment, dignitaries of the B-26 Group were there with General Dwight D. Eisenhower. "Ike" questioned our crew on the mission we flew and inspected our A-20, never having seen one before. He and Captain Jackson stooped low to look up into the bombbay, and Jackson knocked Ike's hat off his head. Everybody had a good laugh about it, except Jackson, whose face remained red for quite a while.

That evening, the A-20 crews visited the Officer's Club where a rousing crap game was in progress. One of the shooters was Hollywood Actor Robert Preston, who was very friendly, even though he was losing. None of our crews could buy a drink, as everything was paid for by the grateful crews of the guys who were on the mission that day. We all returned to Wethersfield the next morning, feeling good for the mission we helped succeed.

The success of the window screens became standard procedures for missions of light and medium bombers of the IX Bomber Command.

Mission #12 -10 April - Lingham Noball. Major Meng and Lt. Powell, BN led Box I with Major Willetts and Lts. Henry Arrington and Pete Royalty, as bombardier and navigator, leading the second box. After the first box made two runs on the target, the BN was unable to pick up the target and did not drop his bombs. The second box was more successful and hit the target squarely. Considerable flak greeted the formation, but all planes returned to base safely.

Mission #13 and 14 - 11 April - Bonniers and Beauvoir NoBall targets. Each of the two boxes were assigned different targets although both taking off in normal fashion and split up at the target area. Major Meng and Lt. Powell, BN went for one Noball and Major Willetts and Lt. Basnett went after the other. Both bombardiers hit their assigned aiming points, after which the two boxes re-assembled and flew back to base. Moderate flak met both boxes but with little damage. The major problem meeting the group was a heavy cloud bank prevented normal landing patterns. Descending through the clouds caused planes to scatter, fortunately, not into each other. They made it back to base in pairs, or trios and various times, but with no casualties.

Mission #15 - 12 April - Vacqueriette Noball. Colonel Farmer and Captain Huff with Lt. Kupits, BN led the boxes. Cloud cover over the target made it necessary for some boxes to make two bomb runs and even though this was necessary, only 20 planes were able to drop, doing considerable damage. Captain Dunn and Lt. Jedinak BN, participated.

Mission #16 - 13 April - Noball target not identified.

Mission #17 and 18 - 13 April - Yvrench Bois Carre and Petite Bois Tillencourt Noball sites. Major Willetts and Lt. Royalty, BN and Major Meng and Lt. Powell, BN led boxes. Here again, the two boxes split up near the target sites and individually bombed separate targets with good results. Lts. Platter and Jedinak participated. Window dropping planes were led by Lts. Osborne, Meagher and Lesher. Moderate flak caused some damage to ships, but all returned to base safely. Bombing results were rated excellent and good.

Usual lousy weather kept all planes grounded. On 16 April, the anticipation of preparation for movements came to reality with an order came down, requiring a practice move to take place. Eager and quick packing and boxing up of documents took place and on the 17th at 0900 every squadron was ready to go. Trucks, loaded with gear, and personnel all packed with personal gear, lined up and the early echolon left the base. The second echelon left at 1000, all in an orderly manner, prepared for possible enemy action on the way. Things went pretty smoothly, included a "pit" stop after two hours, and all of a sudden the commanders realized no one made arrangements for chow. One of the most demoralizing situations for GIs is to not fortify their energy with good food. The usual K rations were issued, but not appreciated as much as a chow line feed.

Both echelons returned to base at 1430 and 1530 for the second group. In all, it showed that preparations for quick moves and actual movements, could be made when the time comes.

April Showers

April showers kept planes grounded , but not to cause too much leisure to our group, orders came down to the squadrons as reported by Lowell Geffinger, Adjutant of the 670th Squadron. He reported:

> A group mobility exercise was held on April 17 to practice for possible future moves. The Field Order was received on April 16th and there followed a great deal of activity preparing for the move the following morning. All equipment was packed and loaded on trucks. Personnel were equipped and armed, and everything was ready to move by 0900 on the 17th. The advance echelon commanded by Captain Sheridan departed at 1000. The second echelon commanded by Lt. Geffinger departed at 1100. Both echelons followed a prepared route, and ready to act against any enemy attack., The advanced echelon returned to base at 1430 and the rear at 1540. Much was learned from this practice move which would be of help in any future move that might come about., A few minor delays along the route were encountered, possibly caused by insufficient briefing before the trip and also possibly inexperience.

Mission #19 - 18 April - Charloi - St. Martin. The weather cleared on April 18th, when 38 planes took off to bomb a different target from NoBalls, a marshalling yard at Charloi-St.

April 18, Mission #19. Combat Crew (L. to R.) R.Conte-BN, G. McNulty-Pilot, R.Addleman-Gunner, H.White-Gunner

Martin, in Belgium. Major Meng and Lt. Powell, BN led the first box with Major Price and Lt. Hand, BN the second box leader. Bomb bursts on an engine repair shed and a power house, along with marshalling yard tracks made for a successful attack. The second box was unable to pick up the target, so did not drop their load. Flights led by Captain McNulty and Lt.Conte, BN, and Captain Dunn,and Lt. Sutliffe, BN, participated. Considerable damage was done to the facility, with little or inaccurate flak being encountered. No plane received battle damage.

Mission #20 - 19 April - Bois de Huit Rue NoBall. We were back on going for destruction of NoBall sites again. This one had been attacked before. Colonel Ford and Lt. Royalty, BN led Box I with Major Price and Lt. Hand, BN leading Box II. Thirty-five planes dropped 138 x 500 pound bombs right over the aiming point, Captain Dunn amd Lt. Arrington, BN led a flight.

Mission #21 - 20 April - AM - Gorenflos NoBall. Major Meng with Lt. Powell, BN led Box I with Captain Jackson and Lt. Conte, BN leading Box II. Lt. Osborne and Lt. Maltby, BN plus

Captain Dunn and Lt. Arrington, BN led flights. Take off was at 1300. On reaching the French Coast, a heavy cloud cover obscured the ground, making the target invisible. Hence, no bombs were dropped. Light inaccurate flak caused no damage to planes.

Mission #22 - 20 April - PM - Yvrench/Bois Carre NoBall. The 38 planes had hardly cooled down from the morning flight when they were reloaded for a second mission. As on the morning mission, clouds and haze obscured the ground and no bombs were dropped. Those bombs had to be tired, hanging there on shackles all day long,. Flak along the route was heavy with damage sustained by a number of our planes. A B-26 outfit was flying to the right of our formation, and they seemed to be the target for the gunners, as flak bursts enveloped the group. One parachute was seen blossomed out, and another chute dropped over the channel. Major Willetts and Lt. Royalty BN led this group.

The STARS AND STRIPES gave the 416th front page coverage citing the successes the group enjoyed since starting their medium, level bombing a little over a month ago,. The article mentioned the problems encountered by Ostrander and his two gunners, Wilson and Binney on the group's first mission.

Mission #23 - 21 April - Yvrench/Bois Carre NoBall. Again - These people keep rebuilding what we knock down, so they must be pretty important targets. Major Willetts and Lt. Royalty BN led Box I with Major Price and Lt. Hand BN leading Box II. Captain Hulse and Lt. Conte, BN led a flight. The first box came in over the target area too wide and did not drop. The second box did, however, made up for that by plastering the target. No enemy opposition was experienced.

Mission #24 - 22 April - AM - Behen NoBall. Major Campbell and Lt. Palin BN led Box I with Major Price and Lt. Hand leading Box II. Captain Hulse and Lt. Conte, BN and Lt.Stockwell with Lt. Jedinak BN led flights. This target was in the Pas de Calais area, making it a short run for the group. Flak was accurate on the bomb run with no serious damage to the planes or personnel.

Mission #25 - 22 April - PM - Linghem NoBall. Major Willetts with Lt.Royalty, BN led Box I with Captain Hulse and Lt. Conte BN, leading Box II. As the formation crossed the French Coast, near Dunkurque, heavy flak greeted them with considerable damage. After bombs away, on the way out of France, extreme heavy flak blasts greeted our boys, with heavy damage, but all planes being able to make it back to base safely. Bombing results were excellent.

Mission #26 - 23 April - Bonniereres NoBall. We've been here before and were not too happy with the greeting we got back then. Today, Sunday, the experts were manning the antiaircraft guns. Major Price with Lt. Hand, BN, led Box I with Major Campbell and Lt. Palin, BN leading Box II, The second box took an unusually long bomb run giving the gunners good time to cut their fuses. Lt. Joseph T. Shouten, with gunners S/Sgt. Robert Williamson and Sgt. Feistl were flying in slot #4 on the lead flight of Box II. This slot is directly behind and below the Box leader in position #1. A flak burst hit Shouten's right engine. He remained in his slot,. but another burst hit them amid ships, splitting the plane in half, causing a flat spin down. No parachutes were seen coming out. When the flak hit Shouten's plane amidships, the bombs dropped out, causing the planes behind him to think the drop was following a legitimate bomb run, so they dropped their load, well short of the assigned aiming point. Other planes came back with multiple flak holes, one with 38 shots and another with 29 hits.

April 24 - A mission scheduled for today did not get too far from base, getting a recall before reaching the English Channel. The weather was cloudy, requiring ascents and descents through a hazy mixture. Lt. A. A. McDonald of the 669th Squadron, lost control of his plane and started a dive, causing a wing to break. He managed to pull the plane out of the dive, but knew he was going to crash. He saw he was heading for a housing area and managed to maneuver the plane to an open space and crash landed, exploding the bombs. His heroic effort probably saved many civilian lives. Gunners with McDonald included S/Sgt. Leroy Barard and S/Sgt. Joseph J. Shields .All three crew members perished. Their remains were interred in the American Military Cemetery at Cambridge, England. No other planes were lost.

Mission #27 - 25 April - AM - Bois D'Enfer. The 37 planes led by Major Willetts with Lt. Royalty, BN on Box I with Captain Hulse and Lt. Conte leading Box II, headed for this noball site which was heavily defended. The first box got to drop their bombs with good results. Low clouds and shadows prevented the second box from seeing the target, so no drop was made. Lt. Siracuse with Lt. McBrien, BN took a direct hit on a wing and an engine. Gas and oil were streaming out the the hit areas, but Siracusa managed to get the plane to English soil, even though losing altitude very fast.

Mission #28 - 25 April - PM - St. Pierre de Mont Coastal Guns . Major Meng with Lt. Battersby and Captain Dunn each led boxes. A strong concentration blanketed the gun emplacements. No enemy flak or fighters bothered the crews.

Mission #29 - 26 April - Louvain Railroad Junction. The formation was being threatened by enemy fighters, but our P-47 escorts convinced them to stay away from our boys. Major Willetts and Lt. Royalty, BN and Captain Battersby with Lt. Lytle, BN led boxes. The first box got out of position so did not drop, but the second box zeroed in rather well, causing explosions and fire.

Mission #30 - 27 April - AM - Monceau sur Sambre Marshalling Yard. Captain Dunn and Lt. Arrington, BN led boxes. Captain Hulse and Lt. Conte, BN and Lt. Platter with Lt. Basnett, BN led flights. Cloud cover obscured the target so no drop was attempted. No flak was encountered on the way in, but during a break in the clouds on the way back to the coast, some inaccurate flak came up - but no damage resulted.

Mission #31 - 27 April - PM - Arras Marshalling Yard. Major Price and Lt. Hand, BN with Captain Dunn and Lt.Arrington, BN led boxes. This was the first mission with bombs shackled under the wings. As expected, some speed was lost and maneuverability was impaired somewhat, but they worked. Lt. Marzolf and Jedinak participated in blasting the aiming point. The main engine shed in this large marshalling yard was demolished and the extra bombs on all planes created a good strike pattern, with planes in close position. RAF Spitfires escorted our bombers, and kept enemy attackers away from the formation.

Bad weather grounded all planes, although the group took off early on 28 April but got recalled before they got too far due to inclement weather over Europe. Bad weather the next day kept everybody busy at the base, including more training, no missions.

Mission #32 - 30 April - Bonnieres NoBall. Major Price with Lt. Hand BN, Captain Battersby with Lt. Lytle, BN, and Major Campbell with Lt. Palin each led a box for a total of 39 planes, dropping bombs with good results. Lt. Platter and Lt.Basnett participated on this mission. No opposition met the formation. This was a three box mission, but bombing results were not too favorable.

Wethersfield, England 1944
Two 668th Sq. Pilots
Joe Meagher (seated) reading mail from home, and Wayne Downing (standing).

April Ending 1944

Lowell Geffinger's 670th Squadron history reports that on April 27th, large scale chemical warfare exercises were held, to prepare everyone for the possibility of a mustard gas attack. Chemical warfare training was held during the entire month of April, but the large scale exercise really used mustard gas, from which everyone seemed well protected and trained. Weekly lectures by the chemical warfare section had been given to squadron personnel in addition to literature and practical maneuvers. Also, a station defense school was set up early in April for all personnel, which included a week's course given to each man. Ground officers were trained and lectured on map reading, and tours were held.

The April 30th mission was another experiment, with three boxes of 12 planes going over a target with the thought that three bomb aimers would give a better probability of coverage of the target area. It did not seem to go well on this particular mission, with only one of the three boxes hitting the target.

Lt. George Cowgill, flying with the 671st squadron had a thrill to talk about. Evidently flak was pretty accurate, since one 88 mm shell entered the bottom of his plane and went right through the top of the plane, exploding well above him with no other visible damage or interruption to his flying. A rather unusual bit of luck here, but any type of luck on the good side is worth wishing for. Not many of the planes received damage.

Mission #33 - 30 April - PM - Busigny Marshalling Yard, North of St. Quentin, France. This was another unusual trip in that our group was to follow the 409th Bomb Group in, providing 72 aircarft in total to eliminate this target. Major Meng with Lt. Powell, BN led Box I and Captain Dunn and Lt. Arrington BN, leading Box II. Approaching the French coast, the 409th entered over a heavily defended area, which was not the assigned entry point on the coast. Major Meng turned his box toward the assigned entry point, and proceeded toward the target. Lt. Powell and Lt. Arrington strung their bombs on a 400 yard stretch, prac-

JUNCTION JOLTED

(Official U. S. Army Air Forces foto from A. P.)

ON THE NOSE. Huge column of smoke rises from Nazi rail junction at Busigny, in northern France, as Yank bomber of 9th Air Force gets direct hit. Yesterday nearly 1,750 U. S. bombers and fighters smashed into Germany for fifth time this week to pound an aircraft assembly plant at Tutow and rail yards at Osnabruck.

—Story on page 2

tically destroying everything in the marshalling yard. Lt. Marzolf and Lt. Basnett, BN, and Captain Hulse with Lt. Conte, BN, Lt.Stockwell and Lt. Jedinak,BN led flights. Excellent results were recorded by all flights.

A congratulatory telegram from General Anderson of the IX Bomber Command was sent to the group for their success.

One plane, piloted by West Point Graduate Lt. Ed Renth relates this story experienced on the Busigny mission:

> We dropped our bomb load after the lead bombardier released his, while flak was popping all around us. Suddenly, as though Thor's hammer struck the bottom of my plane, it jumped about two feet. The shock was indescribable. I experienced every bit of emotion, including fear, shear horror, terror, panic, and an icy fist squeezing my heart. I saw fluid oozing down and back on the inside of the left engine nacelle. I feathered the prop and cut off the full flow to the engine. It was absolutely dead.

The formation kept on their path, and when Renth looked up, he was truly alone, the formation disappeared in the murk. His right engine started to sputter. The Spitfire escorts left the formation.

> While we were attending to our problems, the formation kept going on their way, and suddenly we were alone. Our Spitfire escorts had left and all I thought about was that the ground forces would be radioing their fighters to come after us. A B-26 Maurauder group was about 1000 feet above us with their bomb bay doors open. In a few minutes they loosed 288 bombs which passed within a hairbreadth from us. At the same time, five fighters were approaching us at 4 o'clock high, we couldn't tell whose they were, until the unmistakable outline of the P-38s came into view and chased the intruders away. I instructed my gunners to watch for the yellow nosed ME-109s, and if they saw them, the boys were to bail out. I had to concentrate on navigating back toward base.
>
> We were losing altitude fast, and were down to about 1500 feet with 20mm, 40mm, and 88mm shells popping all around us. We needed more speed so I instructed the gunners to throw everything out that was loose while we were over the channel. I even fired my 50 caliber nose guns to lighten the load.
>
> We were down to about 100 feet and the English Channel was in sight, and I saw an airfield runway right ahead of me. Just before touch down I saw a group of poles and fences at the end of the runway. The left wing struck a pole, the left landing gear collapsed and we went screeching down on our belly. When we stopped, we scrambled out and sat away from the plane, and lit a cigarette. A tweedy looking

Englishman came toward them and said, "Bloody good show, chaps."

During April, the group participated in 24 missions with 774 sorties, dropping 534-1/2 tons of bombs. Group strength for April was:

668th BS	39 Officers	264 Enlisted Men
669th	37 Officers	262 Enlisted Men
670th	41 Officers	268 Enlisted Men
671st	35 Officers	261 Enlisted Men
Grp Hqs	35 Officers	59 Enlisted Men
Totals	187 Officers	1114 Enlisted Men

On the 15th of April, the American Flag was raised for the first time at the Headquarters Building, in Wethersfield, replacing the R. A. F. Flag. The base was officially turned over to the USAAF by the RAF Commander, Squadron Leader Newman.

9th Air Force planes caught this Nazi train over the Moselle River.

McGlohn Mission

Captain Dave Hulse with Lt.Ralph Conte, BN, were leading a flight on a mission to Bonnieres and Beauvoir NoBall site, on 11 April. Hulse was the officer detailed to write up awards recommendations for fliers. Hulse related this story:

> Charles McGlohn was flying on our wing,. We were going into the Pas de Calais area, and he caught a piece of flak that wounded his leg or arm. The shot knocked out his complete instrument panel, destroying it. He made the bomb run with us, ignoring the pain. When the bombardier dropped his bombs, McGlohn dropped his load. When we started back to base, the cloud cover was from 2,000 to 10,000 feet thick. We had to go down through 10,000 feet of overcast. As our flight dropped down, McGlohn tried to stay in formation with us, but the clouds were so thick and dense, he lost sight of me and he became very concerned that he may get lost in midstream and would not be able to tell which was up or down without instruments to go by. He was also concerned about hitting another plane.
>
> He left the formation. He had not gone too deeply into the fog, so he went back up, well above the clouds, cut back on the throttle, trimmed up the ship to where it was flying in a slight dive, and started to descend. But first, he asked his gunners to bail out, but they stayed with him. As he started down, he thought he was going down about 1000 feet a minute, which meant it would take him about ten minutes through the cloud bank. He had to sit there without moving, holding the controls steady. He came out of the bottom of the clouds. He was moving at a high velocity, which he could not tell for sure without any instruments, and pulled back on

the steering column and got the ship under control. He saw a field nearby, underneath, and went in to land. The crew all scrambled out of the plane. He was taken to a hospital.

When I talked to him after he was released from the hospital, he told me what he had done. I thought he deserved some kind of an award, since he probably saved flying into another ship in the clouds on the way down and he took steps to prevent such a mishap. At that time there was some kind of a rule on awards, that if you were injured and bleeding before you went into the target, and dropped your bombs and came back, that was considered an heroic thing. If you got hit on the way back coming to base, that was not considered heroic. In the first case, maybe a Silver Star, in the second place, maybe a DFC.

The Awards and Decorations Offcer, John T. S. Morris, wrote up the mission and his prose was excellent, but his description lacked substance. Since he was not a flier, he could not know what danger must be, in the air. I felt he deserved at least a DFC, so I re-wrote the citation request on a borrowed old typewriter which hardly worked. I mounted the machine on a discarded K-rations box. I had to overcome a problem of the keys on the machine striking twice, so I tied an old coke bottle on a string, and held the carriage in place. I had to make three copies, all originals, no erasures, which General Vanderberg read. He erased DFC and put in for a Silver Star to Charlie. He got what he deserved.

McGlohn's daughter-in-law contacted members of the 416th and asked about Charlie's missions, wanting to know more about his association with the group members.

This is one of the reasons this History is prepared, for those who want to know what these Attack Bombers and their crews endured during that time of our lives.

Synchronizing watches at briefing.
Lt. Roy Van Rope, Lt. R. Hackley, Lt. R. Conte, Cpt. D. Hulse

Arriving at plane.
Lt. R. Conte, SS F. Allred, SS D. Stevens, Cpt. D. Hulse

Checking route with crew.
Hulse, Stevens, Conte, Allred

Donning flak jackets.

CHAPTER 4

May 1944 Missions
Continuing May Ending

May 1944 Missions

The general feeling that the invasion was not too far off seemed to occupy the minds of all group personnel. After all, we had been in business of knocking on the door of the German Forces for almost two months now, with a high degree of confidence. Certainly, our efforts were felt "over there" and the enthusiasm of our flyers was high. With May rolling around, it was felt the weather had to be a little better than we had been experiencing since March, so things looked brighter from that end.

Our ground personnel, mechanics, crew chiefs, armament, ordnance, all displayed a great deal of confidence in their assignments as they kept aircraft in tip-top condition and being on the job super early in the mornings, and late at night to be sure the very best equipment was ready for crews to do their assigned tasks. A tremendous amount of respect for those people was displayed by the crews. We were ready to show our stuff starting in May.

We had also been informed that two other A-20 Groups, the 409th and the 410th, would be activated in England to combine with our efforts.

Mission #34 -1 May - AM Charleroi Montignies Marshalling Yard. This target had been scheduled twice before but never reached due to recall once and a cloud cover preventing bombing the second time. Things looked good for this one. Major Willetts and Lt. Royalty, BN with Captain Clark and Lt. Jones leading boxes, took off with 37 planes to reach this target. It was a long flight, but no planes ran out of gas. Flak was light and no fighters threatened us with Spitfires providing our protective screen. It was always so comforting to see those "little friends" to be circling around us about 2000 feet up. Lts. Marzolf and Basnett, BN led flights. Bombing results were classified as good. All returned safely.

Mission #34, 1 May. Charleroi Montignies Marshalling Yard.

Mission #35 - 1 May PM - Blanc Misseron Marshalling Yard. The second group of 37 planes took off about 1700 to undo another marshalling yard to prevent movement of troops and equipment designed to hurt Americans. We were on double daylight savings time, so it remained light until about 2300 hours, making flying a little easier than doing so in darkness. Major Campbell and Lt. Palin, BN led the first box with Captain Battersby and Lt. Lytle, BN on the second box. Lt. Stockwell and Lt. Jedinak BN, and Captain Hulse with Lt. Conte, BN, led flights. Bombing was rated Good with plenty of damage. Flak was encountered over the Ostend area on the way to and from the target. Our escort service was provided by our little friends, so no enemy fighters came close. Captain Hulse did not realize his plane had been hit so badly until he tried to land. The nose wheel collapsed and the plane slid down the runway with Lt. Conte watching sparks fly high, under, and around him, with his bombardier cage scraping the runway, until the plane ran off the runway. Conte made his way out the upper escape hatch. The pilot or gunners were not injured.

Mission #36 - 2 May - Blanc Misseron Marshalling Yard Again. This was a large marshalling yard, requiring extensive attention by our bombers. Major Meng, and Lt. Powell, BN and Captain Dunn and Lt. Arrington, BN led boxes. Flights were led by Lts. Marzolf and Basnett, BN, and Captain Jackson and Lt. Conte, BN and Lt. Shaefer, his BN was not listed. Our group attacked this target with the 409th Group, but the timing was a little off. As the second box, led by Dunn and Arrington,were making their bomb run, Arrington saw that the first box of the 409th was right above them. He moved his box aside and watched the bombs from the 409th fall right over the spot he just left. Something go wrong here? Arrington then made a second bomb run and dropped his missiles. When strike photos were developed, it determined that the second box made excellent hits on a target not planned to be attacked. It was Valecciennes

Mission #36, 2 May. Blanc Misseron Marshalling Yard.

Marshalling Yard, (after all they all look alike from 12,000 feet), 6 and 1/2 miles away from Blanc Misseron, which was a B-26 target for that day, but evidently at a different time. The 416th first box results were rated as good.

Inclement weather caused stand-downs with no missions flown for four days.

This was not counted as a mission, but on 4 May, various crews were awakened early and told they were going on a secret mission. They took off at 0500 and returned at 0700. Everything was hush-hush, so very few people knew what went on, although results were termed as being satisfactory. Six crews from the 671st were part of this mission, led by Captain Dunn and Lt. Arrington, BN.

More crews were coming in from replacement centers and some changes within the squadrons were made, so that a better balance of crews could be counted in squadrons. Bombardier-Navigator/Pilot teams were exchanged to give all squadrons better balance with more lead teams. Promotions were being received by crews who were with the group from the start. New Gunners were received to relieve the strain from the number of missions many of the older gunners were flying. These older gunners were away up there in age, about 20 on average.

Another "treat" was arranged by Colonel Mace to conduct a make-believe briefing, so that all ground personnel could experience what went on during regular briefings. The guys enjoyed learning what went on behind closed doors at the normal briefings. The mock up briefing gave the men the intricacies of what goes on in the planning and execution of missions.

Mission #37 - 7 May - AM - Blanc Misseron Marshalling Yard. Again?!? The luck of this target was shown again when a cloud cover prevented the boys from dropping their loads. Major Willetts and Lt. Royalty, BN with Lts. Marzolf and Basnett, BN participating.

Mission #38 - 7 May - PM - Behen Noball. The weather did not improve this afternoon since the target was protected by cloud cover. However, the ack-ack gunners knew where the formation was and they did considerable damage. All ships received flak of some size or another. Lt. Wysocki reports that:

> A large piece of flak, followed by smaller pieces, hit Lt. Ritchie's plane amid-ships, and raised quite some havoc (no pun intended). A piece of steel, wedged between Hibbs (gunner) and his tunnel gun, setting off a few rounds. Had it been a few inches closer, it would have seriously injured him. Upon landing, the ship was in such bad shape, that it had to be sent to the 4th Service Group for battle damage. No one suffered any injuries, but all suffered moments of anxiety.

Mission #39 - 8 May - AM - Aerschot Marshalling Yard.- We thought the weather here in May would be better than that we experienced in prior months. But, it seems weather closes in faster than the weather forecasters can keep up with them. This mission was not effective for a cloud cover over the target, so all bombs were brought back for reuse. Lts. Stockwell and Jedinak led flights on this mission.

Mission #40 - 8 May - PM - Ailly L'Haut Cloches Noball. As just reported, the weather clears up as fast as it clouds up. This target was available for sighting and it was done with precision. Major Willetts and Lt. Royalty, BN, led Box I with Captain Hulse and Lt. Conte, BN, leading Box II, Lts. Stockwell and Jedinak led flights. Bombing was done in flights of six, providing a better chance of hits with six flights making a stab at hitting the aiming point. It worked well, with great results. Flak was severe, however, and considerable damage was experienced. Lt. Scott Ritchie, a West Pointer had a narrow escape yesterday, but somebody was after him because another flak burst hit his plane, knocking out his right engine, and slightly wounding his gunners S/Sgts Newkirk and Anderson. He managed to bring the ship back to base, landing on only two wheels, with the nose wheel collapsing, but he did so successfully. It never ceases to amaze, how 20 year old youngsters, gunners, and other crew members can retain their composure and determination to undergo trials and rough conditions on a daily basis and always come back for more.

Mission #41 - May 9 - AM - Aerschot Marshalling Yard - Three boxes let by Major Campbell and Lt. Palin, BN, Captain Hulse with Lt. Conte, BN, and Captain Battersby with Lt. Lytle, BN. Lt.Stockwell and Lt. Jedinak, BN led a flight. A total of 41 planes dropped on this target, destroying a turntable, a 3-bay building and a 3-bay workshop. In addition, 45 boxcars were destroyed and the tracks to the turntable wore torn up.

A real sad entry here, to report that Captain Battersby, 668th Operations Officer, after returning from the morning mission, his 18th, took a newly arrived plane up for a test flight. On these test flights, evidently other that regular crew members are permitted to ride with them. PFC Charles W. Coleman, a parachute rigger, went up with Battersby. When they tried to land, for some unknown reason, the plane nose-dived, plunged to earth and exploded, killing both occupants. Battersby, a proud parent, a superb pilot, and an excellent officer, died in the line of duty. Chester Wysocki wrote:

> A reason cannot be given for this tragedy. An expert pilot and a good ship, but fate deemed it not to be a "happy landing." It will be hard to forget this man, who was more of a father, than a superior officer. Who always had time to listen to your troubles, and give a hand when needed. Who bolstered morale, when it was low. Who fought for the rights of his "boys" when the going was rough. We won't forget.
>
> There is a place "in the blue" where all eagles go to rest when their time is up. Hope they are now sitting in the front row with the best of them.

Yes, Bat, you will be with us when we break a bottle in Berlin, and when we drink a toast in Tokyo. When it is over, and we are home, America won't forget you breed of men, who made the supreme sacrifice for her freedom and democracy.

We are proud of you, each and every one of us, to have served with you, and now, humbly in comradeship, - we salute you.

Mission #42 - PM - 9 May - Bois d'enfer Noball. Again, three boxes with a total of 40 planes went after this important Noball target. Major Meng, Captain McNulty, and Captain Dunn led the boxes The first two boxes had good bombing results reported. The third box did not pick up the target, so no drop. Lts. Stockwell and Jedinak, BN and Captain Hulse with Lt. Conte, led flights, with good drops.

Mission #43 - AM - 11 May - Corneille eu Vexin Airdrome. Two boxes of 18 aircraft each went after this target which was heavily defended. The first box led by Major Willetts and Lt. Royalty, BN hit the target with fair results. For no explainable reason, the second box led by Captain Dunn and Lt. Arrington, BN, lost sight of the lead box, so they returned to base. Fortunately, the fighter escort went in to the target area with the first box. Nine of the 18 planes in that first box received flak inflicted battle damage. Since the second box sort of aborted the mission, the crews in that box, were not credited with a mission.

Mission #44 - PM - 11 May - Aerschot Marshalling Yard. Major Meng with Lt. Powell, BN led box I and Captain Clark with Lt. Jones BN, led box II. When Powell dropped his bombs, the fire and smoke was so intense that it obscured the aiming point for Lt. Jones who could not drop without knowing where his bombs were going, so they returned with their load. The flak increased its intensity, resulting in 14 planes being damaged severely.

Members of the 668th squadron traveled to Cambridge Military Cemetery to attend the burial service for Captain Battersby and PFC Coleman. It was a mass service with about 25 flag draped coffins ready for internment. Roll call was given, and individuals present saluted their friends for the last time. Then four chaplains gave a short sermon, and a rifle salute was fired. Taps were blown and re-echoed. It was a stirring ceremony and we shall all remember it. Officers and enlisted men were buried side by side there, the democratic way. Rows on Rows of white crosses and Stars of David, are there, giving testimony to American bravery and valor.

Mission # 45 - 12 May - AM - Monchy-Breton Airdrome. Major Price with Lt. Hand, BN, and Captain Dunn and Lt.Arrington, BN led boxes. Lts. Marzolf and Basnett led a flight. The report from the 668th squadron history states that "for some reason, the bombsight and apparatus malfunctioned, and no bombs were dropped. There was no flak, and P-47s provided escort. All ships returned in good shape. "

Mission #46 - 12 May - PM - Beauvoir Noball. The route to this target was through what was known as "flak-alley" and it lived up to its name. Many planes suffered severe damage. One plane, piloted by Lt. Robert Stockwell with Lt. Albert Jedinak, BN, leading a flight, received a direct hit in the open bomb bay, and another shot in the tail section. The bombbay exploded and photos of this flaming injured plane is on exhibit at the Dayton Air Museum and has been shown in many Air Force periodicals. From the severity of the flames, it was thought no one could possibly escape from it, but the bombardier, Jedinak, and one gunner, Sgt. Egan W. Rust did manage to parachute out to be taken prisoner and eventually returned to freedom. Rust was the tunnel gunner who hand held a machine gun out the open hatch at the bottom of the plane, so it would have been easy for him to slide out by pushing himself into the air, which he did. Jedinak said he had just released his bombs, following the lead bombardier's drop, when his plane lifted from the hit in the bombbay.

Mission #46. Al Jedinak.

The plane side-slipped out of the formation and was in a flat spin, He tried to contact Stockwell, but got no response. Then the emergency gong rang twice, not the usual three times which meant everybody out! Jedinak was pinned to the bottom of his small compartment, facing toward the pilot's cockpit. Centrifugal force kept him pinned down.

Before the plane started spinning, he evidently unknowingly, released the emergency hatch handle at the bottom of the plane. He tried to lift himself up but seemed to have been pinned down. He tried to kick the escape door open by banging down on it, but it did not budge either. He laid back and felt a quietness as the plane flat spinned downward. Looking around he saw the dinghy ring on his parachute had caught between the side of the plane and the bulkhead. He finally worked it free and another kick at the hatch, dropped it out.

He tumbled down after it, wondering if the whirling props would cut him up as he flew by them under the plane. He did bump his head against the underside of the burning craft, but freed himself, with the chute not yet opened. In his descent, he was falling with his head lower than his feet , he yanked the pull cord and the chute blossomed open but the shround came up between his legs, the chute failing to open. A violent tug got the chute in proper position, and down he went the way chutes are supposed to operate. Looking around, he saw the plane off in the distance with the canopy still in place, not being able to see Stockwell. Ground fire was shooting at him.

Jedinak landed in a bomb crater, where he pulled off his flying suit, insignia, Mae West, and rolled up the chute, covering it all with clods of dirt. He kept his flying jacket. Making his way to a wooded thicket, he saw another chute coming down, and also saw flames of the plane burning in the distance. In short order three Germans approached him, ordered him out, and pointing a Luger and rifles at him, marched him toward the gun emplacements they had been monitoring, The Germans also cornered the gunner, Egan Rust, and the two of them were frisked, leaving only their uniforms and jackets.

Looking around, Jedinak saw a battery of anti-aircraft guns, mulling over in his mind that our A-2 Intelligence were right by saying this area was a hot bed of anti-aircraft fire. He was amazed at the number of guns in such a small confined area.

The two Americans were treated well, given food, but interrogated intensely, but neither gave more than their rank, name, and serial number although having been pressured to give them other information about their units, their targets, and other military information.

Stalags were visited, having been moved four times. Jedinak was liberated from Moosberg by Patton's Third Army on 27 April, 1945.

When he was repatriated, Jedinak visited Stockwell's widow, telling about their last mission and his experiences with Stockwell before the mission. A good friendship blossomed and they eventually married. Jedinak passed away in 1994.

Mission #47 - 13 May - Beauvais-Tille Airdrome. This was a three box mission with 42 aircraft, with boxes led by Major

Campbell and Lt. Palin, BN, Captain McNulty and Lt. Burseil, BN, and Lt. Osborne and Lt. Forma, BN. The first box rated an excellent in their aim, the other two were not as fortunate. However, a huge hanger was hit as were several other buildings. Although heavy flak greeted the formation, no serious damage was inflicted on the planes, all returning safely. P-47s escorted them in and out.

Practice missions were planned due to weather preventing bombing attacks. The only excitement, if you want to call it that, was that Captain Hiram Conant, and that spark-plug, Lt. Gus Ebenstein, lost their 48 hours passes because they retracted up their wheels too soon after take-off. Thats a no-no, the authorities wanted those wheels down longer. Seems nobody can have any fun anymore, but the only person they could talk to were the Chaplain, because their story fell on other deaf ears.

Mission #48 - 15 May - Creil Airdrome. Major Meng and Lt. Powell, BN led Box I with Captain Hulse and Lt. Conte, BN leading Box II. Clouds started to accumulate and Lt. Powell was able to find an opening in the clouds, enabling him to drop his bombs. Conte could not see the target due to clouds, and only made one pass at the target, and returned to base. Spitfires covered us from enemy aircraft, and little flak was seen.

Mission #49 - 19 May - Beauville Fille Coastal Guns. Major Price and Lt. Hand led Box I with Captain Conant and Lt. McBrien, BN as deputy. Captain Clark and Lt. Jones, BN, led Box II. Late in the afternoon, 38 planes took off for this flight. Cloud cover prevented the first box from dropping their bombs, but the second box got a glimpse of the target and dropped, with fair results. Coming back, the formation flew into a thick overcast, and Lt. Crispino from the 670th squadron's plane suddenly went into a spin. Crispino called for his gunners to bail out, but they didn't, but he did. The two gunners, veterans from the activitation of the squadron, went down with the ship and perished. Crispino was injured in his parachute descent and was hospitalized.

Mission #50 - 20 May AM - Beauvais-Tolle Airdrome. This was a costly mission for the group, with 38 planes taking off, 26 returned with heavy damage. Major Willetts and Captain Dunn with BNs Lt.Royalty and Arrington led boxes. The target area was known to be heavily defended. The lead navigator became confused and became lost. He wound up bombing the airfield at Montidier, which wasn't such a bad deal after all. The major problem was the loss of three planes, and of course, their crews. Lt. Bradford with gunners S/Sgt Vern E. McIver and S/Sgt Clarence Gray, and Lt. Mitchell E. Keopfel (who was promoted to 1st Lt. today), with his gunners S/Sgt. Ray Bankston and Leroy R. Shaw, all went down in France. A total of only three chutes were seen to come down. Lt. F. W. Henderson with gunners Sgts. P.E. Colombe and R. M. Griswold crash landed in England. Neither he nor his gunners were injured. Lt. Joseph Meager with gunners Damico and Hantake brought their badly damaged ship back to England and another crash landing without injury. Lt. Merchant came back on single engine. He had received cuts about the face when his instrument panel was shot out. Lt. York and Wipperman landed in some open fields, with damage to their gas tanks.

Mission #51 - 20 May - PM - Cormeilles-eu-Vexin Airdrome. Major Campbell and Lt. Palin, BN led Box I and Captain Clark and Lt. Jones, BN led Box II. Captain Hulse and Lt. Conte, BN led a flight. Thirty-five planes took off for what turned out to be a happy mission. There were no flak bursts, no losses, casualties, or battle damage, while achieving excellent results in the bombing. Concentration of the bombs blanketed five blast shelters, destroying three, two others received near misses or direct hits.

Mission #52 - 22 May - Carmeille-eu-Vixen. This was a three box formation with Major Meng and Lt. Powell BN, on the first Box, Captain Jackson and Lt. Maltby BN on Box II and Captain Huff and Lt. Kupits BN, leading Box III. The formation took off and ten minutes from take-off they ran into a solid mass of clouds, requiring a climb through the mess. The group had a policy on "Ascent Through Clouds" and this was it. Going up thousands of feet demanded the expertise of instrument flying while remaining somewhat in formation. One box - the third box - became lost and returned to base. That left 24 planes to go to the target. On Popping out of the top of the cloud bank, one may be reminded of watching a pot of porridge on a hot stove, with pops of air jumping out the top of the porridge, so it is with planes coming out of a thick cloud cover. Captain Hulse and Lt. Conte BN, and Captain Prentiss and Lt. Lytle, BN led flights. Excellent bombing was reported. Enemy fighters threatened the formation but our trusted "little friends" shooed them away. The long climb through the cloud bank, a five minute bomb run, and the distance of the target from the base, made fuel dangerously low. Two A-20s from another group were seen in the area, one afire, and the other making its way across the channel, splash-crashed in. Two boxes of B-26s had bombed the same target as did the 416th, with excellent results, also.

Mission #53 - 24 May -AM - Beaumont le Roger Airfield near Paris. - (a long distance from base) -led by Major Willetts and Lt.Royalty, BN with Captain Conant and Lt.McBrien, BN in the second box. Bombing results were not reported to be very good. The first box dropped 600 feet short and the second box dropped 2000 feet short. Lt. Marzolf and Lt. Basnett, BN, Captain Hulse with Lt.Conte, BN, led flights. Captain McNulty and Lt. Burseil flew as deputy to take over in the event the leader was not able to continue. Coming off the target, the formation had to descend through a heavy cloud layer at speeds reported to be 300 feet per minute descent, which assimilates fighter tactics or dive bombers. Scary! The experience while exhilarating, came out successfully, with no problems.

Mission #54 - 24 May - PM - Abbeyville-Drucat Airfield. This is the home of the dangerous yellow nose painted ME-109s. Major Price, Lt. Hand, BN, led Box I with Captain Clark and Lt. Jones, BN on Box II and Lt. Osborne, and Lt.Forma leading Box III. Lt. Marzolf and Lt. Basnett, BN participated. Bomb results were not too good. Boxes I and II were wide and short respectively, with Box III slightly short and right of the aiming point. No flak was encountered, much to the surprise of everyone. Window planes preceeded the boxes because of the expected heavy barrages coming up. Was someone asleep down there? P-47s accompanied the formation, but they did not have to work either.

Mission #55 - 25 May - Monchy/Breton Airfield. Major Meng and Lt. Powell BN, took Box I in with Captain Hulse and Lt.Conte, BN, led Box II. The first box dropped prematurely, about eight miles short, which is most unusual for this experienced bombardier. Something had to go wrong with his equipment. The second box hit the aiming point, destroying the hanger and adjoining buildings. Lts. Marzolf and Basnett, BN led flights. The crews started wondering whether the Germans were running out of ack-ack shells. This is the third mission, over usually heavily defended territory where blankets of flak bursts met bombers.

Mission #56 - 26 May - Beauville-Tille Airdrome. Major Willetts and Captain Dunn with Lts. Royalty and Arrington, BNs in Boxes I and II. Box III was led by Lts. Osborne and Forma, BN. The formation crossed the coast of France and flew in about 20 miles, but missed their rendezvous with fighters, so were recalled. No flak or fighters bothered the group.

Mission #57 - May 27 - AM -Amiens Marshalling Yard. Our group were scheduled to fall behind the 409th Bomb Group and go into this target with boxes from both groups. The first box leader, and his deputy (of the 409th) were both knocked out of the air. This is what flak gunners shoot for, the leaders, and for the first time they did it well. The remainder of the formation strayed off course. Major Campbell decided to abandon the mission. His BN - Lt. Palin decided the two groups needed a leader to get everybody back to base, so he arranged to take the lead, and navigated everybody back to base. The 409th strays, tagged along behind to get to their home, also. Captain Clark and Lt. Jones, BN led our second Box. Lts. Marzolf and Basnett, BN led flights.

Mission #58 - May 27 - PM - Amiens Marshalling Yard. The records do not show who led this formation in. The reports show that the pilot flying No. 4 slot of the first box took a flak burst, which caused his bombs to drop out, making the planes behind him to jettison their bombs. This was ten seconds before the leader was to drop his load. Some of the bombs did hit the target with fair results. Lt. A. W. Gullion of the 669th with gunners S/Sgts. Grady F. Cope and Gerald Coffey, and Lt. Lucien Siracusa with gunners, S/Sgts. James Hume and Floyd Brown were all hit by flak causing them all to parachute out with their planes crashing near the target area. Lt. Thomas J. Sims caught flak going on the bomb run, but he continued on to drop his bombs. He moved away from the flight, losing speed, feeling faint, he called to his gunners, Sgts. Harry W. Larsen and Julius J. Williamson, Jr. to bail out, which they did. Simms kept going and crash landed on the coast of England nursing his badly damaged ship and himself bleeding and hardly conscious. Upon landing, he passed out, was retrieved from the plane and carried to a nearby hospital. Siracusa was a POW, and returned to duty. Lt. H. E. Hewes took a hit over the target and also went down. He evidently made it back to friendly territory since he was returned to the states carrying the designation SWA (Seriously Wounded in Action).

10 May 1944. D.Stephens, left gunner F. Allred, right gunner Pilot not identified

Continuing May Ending

Mission #59 - 28 May - AM -Bruges/St. Michel Radar Station, Belgium. This was a three box mission, led by Major Meng and Lt. Powell, BN, Captain Jackson amd Lt. Maltby, BN, and Captain Dunn with Lt. Arrington, BN. Bombing results were categorized as only fair, bombing with boxes of 14 planes each. P-47s escorted the formation, and no flak was experienced Lts. Marzolf and Basnett, BN participated.

Mission #60 - 28 May - PM - Vacqueriette Noball. This was a mission where two boxes were to bomb individual targets. One box, led by Major Willetts and Lt. Royalty, BN were assigned the Vacqueriette Noball. This box was to lead a box of planes from the 409th to the target. A good concentration of hits on the target was reported. Captain Hulse and Lt. Conte, BN led a flight.

There was mild flak to contend with which gave a new gunner S/Sgt Francis L. Flacks, something to remind him what may be in store for him and the group in the future. He got hit with a shot of flak, causing serious enough injuries to require hospitalization. Some mild humor came of this when "Flacks caught flak" evolved. You can imagine who didn't think it was so funny, lying in bed, all bandaged up.

Mission #61 - 28 May - PM - Behen Noball. The second box of planes of the 416th, leading a box of planes from the 409th , with Major Campbell and Lt. Palin, BN leading our box did an excellent job of creaming this site.

Mission #62 - 29 May - Achiet Airdrome. Major Price and Lt. Hand, BN and Lts. Osborne and Forma led boxes. Lts. Marzolf and Basnett, BN and Captain Hulse with Lt. Conte, BN, led flights with excellent results reported. P-47s circled the formations and no flak was reported.

Mission #63 - 30 May - Denain Prouvy Airdrome. Major Willetts and Lt. Royalty, BN and Captain Conant and Lt.

McBrien, BN led boxes. . Captain Hulse and Lt.Conte, BN, and Lts. Matzolf and Basnett, BN led flights. Lts. Sommers and McQuade flew deputy. Bombing results were rated excellent. P-47s provided cover for the group. No flak.

The month of May was a pretty hectic one for the group with 30 missions flown. Their successes were noted by higher ups, including a commendation for the IX bomber Command from the Air Commander-in-Chief of the Allied Expeditionary Force, T. LEIGH -MALLORY which read:

> Now that full reports have come in relating to the recent concentrated effort against special targets in Northern France, it is apparent that of all Bomber Forces involved, those of Ninth Air Force proved to be by far the most efficacious in knocking out these difficult and well defended tagets.
>
> 2. I have also watched the results of the Ninth Air Force operations against coastal defense batteries, and here again have been impressed with the accuracy of the bombing.
>
> The concentrated, determined, and highly skilled manner in which these Groups have operated augurs well for the future, and I shall be glad if you will convey my congratulations to all those air and ground crews which have been involved in these operations.

Major General L. H. Brereton, Commanding the IX Bomber Command endorsed Mallory's commendation thusly:

> It is with genuine pride and satisfaction in your accomplishments that I forward this letter on to you and every member of your command. You have had keen competition in your relentless assaults against the enemy and the statement of the Air Commander-

in-Chief that you have proved to be by far the most efficacious in knocking out these difficult and well defended targets' is in itself great praise.

I have full faith and confidence in your ability and determination to maintain your most commendable record in the approaching invasion of the Continent. I wish you every success.

Brigadier General Samuel E. Anderson, Commanding the IX Comber Command sent the following to all Commanding Officers of the Combat Wings, IX Bomber Command, and Commanding Officers of All Stations, IX Bomber Command:

1. The above letter from the Commanding General Ninth Air Force, expressing his pride and satisfaction in the accomplishments of IX Bomber Command and his faith and confidence in IX Bomber Command's ability and determination to operate efficiently and effectively in the coming invasion of the continent and this endorsement will be:

a. read to all combat crew members at briefing.

b. posted on all Squadron bulletin boards on your station for a period of three days in order that all station personnel may be informed of the high regard the Air Commander-in-Chief, Allied Expeditionary Air Force, and the Commanding General, Ninth Air Force, have for IX Bomber Command and its accomplishments and of my great pride in IX Bomber Command.

2. I dictate the above steps to inform all personnel of this letter because I am fully aware that the present scale of operations and the excellent bombing results being obtained are possible only because each officer and enlisted man in IX Bomber Command is doing his assigned task in the most

efficient and loyal way possible. Combat crews deliver the bombs, the work of the ground personnel makes it possible for them to do so. Any credit due IX Bomber Command belongs to the command as a whole -- not to any individuals.

3. General Brereton's expression of faith and confidence in IX Bomber Command is most gratifying. It is also a challenge to us all. I am fully confident that no unit or individual of IX Bomber Command will fail to do his utmost to make the approaching invasion of the Continent the greatest success in military history. Your utmost efforts will be necessary, but I am confident they will be sufficient for victory. You have been tested and found worthy of the great part you will take in the supreme effort to crush our enemies. I am proud of you and confident of your success.

These accolades go a long way for the morale of all personnel who are proud recipients of these words,

A-26 flight turning into formation. A-20 in the lead.

Chapter 5

June 1944 Operations
D-Day and Beyond
Mission #73

June 1944 Operations

The month of June is a most important month for our group, considering the greatest military operation on record took place. Writing about it after it occured is easy, knowing what was coming was only a matter of conjecture, but we in the 416th Bomb Group knew what we were leading up to, knew that the invasion was coming, but not when, knew we had to continue to play the cards being dealt to us, and knew we had to do our best to meet any challenge presented to us.

The 1st of June was not one of the days we would call cooperative as far as weather was concerned. So, other practice and training missions seemed to be the procedures to follow. Chet Wysocki, in his usual exemplary means of prose documentation wrote:

> Today, the beginning of the month, proved to be a 'mission-less' day. This attributed to the fact, that typical English inclement weather provided. One of those days where it rains, then clears up, then rains.
>
> During one of these lulls, an incident occured, which makes writing this log a treat. Two of our

"Sweating out" returning planes from combat zone. June 1944.

experienced 'pride & joys' namely, Capt. Conant and Lt. Osborne, decided to fly that basic training plane, the AT-6. We have one here, used mainly for navigation flights. Now this type of plane is one of the first a fledgling flies, during training days. Hiram (with nearly 2000 hours) and 'Drop Dead' (with nearly 700 hours), both with much combat experience, took up this lovely, charming, delightful, AT-6.

After watching them 'shoot' several landings, we tired of it. Then some inner urge prompted us to look out the window. Have you ever seen a ruptured duck? Well, we saw the nearest thing to it. For there was the AT-6, props digging the ground, left wing on the ground, and one landing gear buckled.

That was something never expected, but the best part was yet to come. Let me describe the ensuing scene. These two gentlemen returned to Operations, where they received ovations of sarcasm, 'cracks' etc. It brings to memory, the practice of two boys caught stealing cookies from the cookie jar. Very Sheepish!

Here are some sentences of conversation that followed:

'You call him and tell him about it!'

'Naw, you call him, maybe he isn't there!'

'But, Hiram, after all ________________'

'Oh, alright, I'll call him' (Who were they about to call? Right, - the Colonel).

The above description is very brief, and doesn't do justice to the actual scene that took place. It is best to draw the curtain now, and leave the rest to your imagination."

Mission #64 - 2 June - Gorenflos Noball. Major Campbell with Lt. Palin, BN led Box I, with Captain Hulse and Lt. Conte BN, flying deputy. Box II was led by Captain Dunn and Lt.Arrington, BN. Bombing results were good, with light inaccurate flak experienced. P-47s provided escorts. Lt. McBride of the 670th squadron showed the mettle of which these pilots were cast. He noticed the manifold pressure for his left engine dropped to zero. Continuing on single engine, he kept on the path to the target, but he had fallen behind the flight. Watching the formation way ahead of him dropping their bombs, he flew up to where he thought they dropped their bombs and let his load go after counting five. Pictures of the strikes showed his bombs hit the target squarely. Who needs a bombardier? Turning off the target, he tagged way behind the formation which was taking flak. He was not threatened. Fighters escorted him back over the channel, where he landed at the base, none the least for wear.

Mission #65 - 3 June - Chartres Airdrome, France. This mission took off in the afternoon on one of the deepest penetrations this group undertook over enemy territory. Major Price and Lt. Hand, BN led the first Box with Captain Conant and Lt.McBrien, BN leading second box. Major Napier and Lt. W. L. Smith flew deputy. Captain Hulse and Lt.Conte, BN led a flight. As soon as the formation entered the French coast, heavy flak came up, hitting Lt.Gus Ebenstein severely, causing him to turn back to base. This requires the spare who flies along, to take up the space left vacant by Ebenstein. Lt. Meredith filled this void. Lt. A. P. Nikas received flak hits at the coast, also, but he continued on with the group. At the target, Lt. Nikas took more shots, causing his plane to go down with gunners, S/Sgt A. W. Newkirk and Sgt. G. W. Scott. They all managed to bail out since they were listed as POWs and returned. Bombing results were good.

Lt. Nikas was a new pilot to the 668th squadron, a native of Chicago. He had a reputation as an experienced football player both at high school and college. He had flown six prior missions. Sgt. Scott had flown eight sorties.

Mission #65, 3 June. Chartres Airdrome.
Combat Crew (L. to R.) F.Allred, D.Hulse, R.Conte, D.Stevens

S/Sgt. Arlington Newkirk a 20 year old, was one of those talented artists, whose favorite character was Bugs Bunny, which was painted on his flight jacket and also on the plane he flew. His drawings were also on display at the Aero Club. He had earned a Purple Heart from previous missions, and the Air Medal, having 33 missions to his credit.

Mission #66 - 4 June - St. Pierre du Mont Coastal Guns. Major Meng and Lt. Powell, BN led Box I and Captain Conant and Lt. McBrien, BN. led Box II Captain Hulse and Lt.Conte, BN, plus Lts. Marzolf and Basnett, BN led flights. While flak was considered light, it managed to hit a few of our planes. Major Radetsky had one engine shot out. When he climbed out of his cockpit, he noticed three flak holes very near to where he was sitting. Near misses, are sometimes okay. Captain Conant had dropped their bombs and then they took a flak shot. His radio and VHF equipment caught fire, giving his gunners a hard time putting out the blaze, but they managed to do so. One engine was out, and his hydraulic lines were damaged severely. In addition, one wing bomb did not release, leaving it hanging from its shackle. Lt. McBrien, in the nose of the ship called to say he was bleeding, but the wound was found to be minor. Conant had a problem lowering his wheels, but managed a safe landing

June 5 was a stand down day due to weather, but the planes were all being painted in three alternate black and white stripes on the wings and the fuselage. All personnel were called back to base, and no passes were available. Something big was coming, but nothing specific.

A-26, 669th Squadron.

22 June 1944.
G. McNulty (standing left), R. Addleman (standing right), F.Burseil (kneeling left), H.White (kneeling right).

D-Day and Beyond

The big day finally arrived. INVASION of EUROPE by the Allied forces. Could they not have picked a better day?? The answer was no, but with all the preparation ready to go, delays were probably more devastating than this stormy day. With the hundreds of thousands of troops and millions of tons of equipment and hundreds of planes, all primed, waiting was not the answer. The 416th was ready!

All during the night, it seemed the sky was full of planes for the drone of engines seemed endless. These, we learned later were the transport planes, pulling gliders to the beaches of Normandy, with paratroopers, so many miles away. Everyone, including the German High Command, expected the invasion to take place at the Pas de Calais, a scant 22 miles from the English coast. But to cross the entire English Channel to get to Normandy, was quite an accomplishment, considering the low hanging clouds. But, that was the mission. Just wait, you flyers, we're going to do it!

Lead crews of pilots and Bombardier-Navigators were awakened at an unusual hour on 6 June, hustled into a briefing room and the doors were locked behind them, with shades drawn - nobody more allowed in, and nobody allowed to go out. The briefing announcement was exciting, our land forces were broaching the French Coast Line at that hour, and we were scheduled to go in to help them. But, what lousy weather for flying! Low flung clouds, thousands of feet thick, which would normally call for a stand-down. But not today! If there was any sky in which to fly, we had to go up. The lead crews were briefed, and we were going, weather or not

Mission #67 - 6 June - PM - Argentan Cross Roads. At 1300 fifty-six planes lined up for take-off, three boxes of six plane flights. Major Willetts, and Lt.Royalty, BN led Box I with Lt. Col. Farmer and Lt. Pape, BN, as deputy. The second flight in Box I was Lts. Marzolf and Basnett, BN. Third flight led by Lt. Cole. The Second box was led by Major Price and Lt. Hand, BN.

Deputy was Lts. Sommers and McQuade, BN. Flight II led by Captain Hulse and Lt.Conte, BN. Flight III of Box II was Lt. Ebenstein. Box III led by Lts. Osborne and Forma, BN, with Captain Huff and Lt. Kupits, BN as deputy. Flight II of this third box was Lt. King and Lt. Morton, BN, and Box III was Captain Jackson and Lt. Maltby, BN

The formation flew over the channel under a cloud bank 2000 feet off the surface, making the awesome sight of the thousands of boats, battleships, destroyers, LSTs, CSTs, and any other ocean going vessel available, visible to the crews. Crossing the beachhead was another awesome sight, with men and equipment strewn all over the beaches We were flying so low that fighter escort could not have covered us, so they weren't there. No flak was encountered, but small arms fire with tracer bullets were flying by the formation with little accuracy. Evidently the big gunners didn't feel any fools would be flying in this weather, so they must have taken some time off.

The target was a major crossroads which was in heavy use by German ground forces to bring men and equipment up to the beaches. Bombing at low level without the use of the Norden Bombsight was different for the bombardiers, but they managed to get their bombs down to destroy the intended target. Rather unfortunately, there were many French civilians in or near the crossroads, waving their welcomes to our planes, but, eventually, practically the entire town was blown off the map. Bombing was at 1700 feet.

All personnel and planes returned to base without damage.

Mission #68 - 6 June - Late PM - Serquex Marshalling Yard. Again, 39 aircraft took off at 2007 with Major Meng, and Lt. Powell, BN leading the formation. Captain McNulty and Lt. Burseil BN were deputy. Available records are not available to identify all the other box leaders, but Major Campbell and Lt. Palin, BN, were probably Box II leaders. The Mission Summary states that only 34 planes dropped their bombs, 164 x 500

General Purpose bombs on the primary target. Two aircraft failed to drop; one, a leader, because of personnel error and the other because leader did not drop. Three aircraft landed away from base unaccounted for.

Three aircraft and 10 crew members are missing, presumably due to enemy action. 25 ships sustained flak battle damage and 2 crew members are wounded. Bombing was by twelves from 3000 to 3500 feet. Three boxes were dispatched.

One story has to be told, regarding the heroics of Major Meng. As he, the leader of the formation, neared the target, a flak burst knocked out his left engine and it started to burn. With the possibility of the engine blowing up momentarily, he continued on the bomb run. Intense, heavy flak was experienced, knocking three planes out of the air. Major Meng, turned away from the target, heading toward base, when he dropped out of the lead position, trying to douse the engine fire. He managed to bring the plane back to base on one engine. The entire formation suffered some damage, some worse than others.

Major Campbell of the 669th squadron was shot down. Lt. R. A. Wipperman with gunners Sgt. L.C.Mazza and S/Sgt. H. S.Ahrens went down over the target. All three were listed as MIA, but made POWs. Major Campbell was also made a POW, but all returned for repatriation.

Mission #69 - 7 June - AM - Lessay Bridge. Major Willetts and Lt.Royalty, BN led Box I and Lts. Marzolf and Basnett, BN led Box II Captain Huff and Lt. Kupits flew as deputy to Marzolf. Bombing results were reported as being good, with no enemy reaction by flak or fighters.

Mission #70 - 7 June - PM - Balleroy Road Junction. Major Price and Lt. Hand, BN led Box I with Lts. Osborne and Forma, BN leading Box II. Each box was assigned a different target, with the second box going for a Nazi Field Headquarters at Littry, France. Both boxes scored well, destroying their targets. Again, no flak or fighters bothered the group. All returned safely.

Mission #71 - 8 June - Vitre RR Bridge. Major Meng and Lt. Powell, BN led Box I with Captain Hulse and Lt. Conte, BN as deputy. The formation took off in what was reasonably fair weather, got up to 11,000 feet until they approached the south side of the channel, when a heavy cloud bank met them. The formation went down to practically ground level, where they ran into fog, requiring them to break up for safety. They all managed to return to base. Later that afternoon, another group took off but were recalled after being air borne a half hour.

On 9 June, word came down that enemy troops were dropping paratroops in England, intent to attack airbases. All personnel were issued ammunition for their guns, and intense patrols were established. Gas masks, steel helmets were worn constantly. This alert lasted for two days, when everything returned to normal.

On 10 June, the 97th Bomb Wing General Backus visited our group to compliment us on the excellent bombing missions the group completed.

Mission #72 - 11 June - Falaise Railroad Junction. The allied ground forces were making remarkably good headway following the invasion. Aircrews were beside themselves because they could not help as much as they possibly could. Major Willetts and Lt.Royalty BN led Box I. Captain Hulse and Lt. Conte, BN led a Box. Lts. Marzolf and Basnett, BN and Lts. Rudisill and Joost, BN participated. Clouds covered the target area, so no bombs were dropped. P-47s circled the formation, light flak came up but no damage was experienced.

Mission #73

Mission #73 - 12 June - Epernon Railroad Embankment. Three boxes took off for this target, with the first box led by Major Price and Lt. Hand, BN, Lts. Osborne and Forma, BN, and Captain Dunn and Arrington, BN leading the other two boxes. The sleek P-51s provided escort and only light flak met the group. The first two boxes ran into some difficulty with their bombing results rated as "Gross." The third box with Arrington bombing, covered the target and earned an excellent rating. No damage to any planes.

Mission #74 - 13 June - St. Sauveur Le Vicomte Railway junction. Major Meng and Lt. Powell, BN led this mission Lts. Marzolf and Basnett, BN flew deputy. Lts. Cole and Beck, BN and Lts. Shaefer and Burg, BN led boxes. This mission was classified as uneventful, the first and third box bombs were way off while the second box scored an excellent. Fighter cover was great, and little flak was encountered. In typical English weather, the group took off in clear skies at 0530. When they returned at 0830, the ceiling got down to visibility of 1/2 mile.

Mission #75 - 14 June - AM -Aunay-Sur-Odon Railway Junction. Captain Conant, Lt. Shaefer and Lt. Osborne flew as box leaders and deputies. Lt. DeMand and Lt. Hanlon, BN also participated. Bombing was done in box formations, with excellents being scored.

The most thrilling thing about this mission was experienced by Captain Bailey, Intelligence Officer of the 668th Squadron. He rode in the nose of the plane piloted by Captain Prentiss. Its always exciting for regular flyers to witness ground officers or men experiencing the pleasures of doing missions, expecially Intelligence Officers who brief the men after each mission. This makes them understand what the crews may be talking about when they are de-briefed.

Mission #76 - 14 June - PM - St. Hilaire du Harcourt Railroad Junction. Major Willetts and Lt.Royalty, BN and Captain Dunn with Lt. Arrington, BN led boxes. Each box was assigned a different target. The second box scored well on a railroad bridge while the first box did not rate well on a highway bridge. The group took off at 1800, having been held up by inclement and clearing weather on a regular cycle. It doesn't happen very often with the excellence ground crews, mechanics, and crew chiefs look after their planes, but maybe it was the weather to cause Lt. Cruze to have trouble getting off the ground, with throttles not cooperating as they should. Lt. Mish took his position in the flight, but had problems 45 minutes after take off, with an overheating engine. The cowl flaps froze, eliminating their operation. Rather than continue for the three hour flight with hot engines, he turned back, which was the safe thing to do, leaving only four ships in this flight. Lt. Colonel Farmer and Lt. Pape as BN participated on this mission. All aircraft returned unharmed.

Misstion #77 - 15 June - AM - Lessay Bridge. Major Price and Lt. Hand, BN led Box I and Lts. Osborne and Forma, BN led Box II. Captain Conant and Lt. McBrien, BN flew deputy to Major Price. Flights were led by Lts. Morton and Madenfort, BN, - Captain Huff and Lt. Kupits, BN, Captain Rudisill and Joost, BN, and Lts. Marzolf and Basnett, BN. Bombing was by flights of six with good results over-all. Take off was in good weather, but on the way over the channel, they had to get down to about 500 feet over water. Fortunately, the clouds disappeared over the target area, allowing bombing at about 6000 feet. No flak was met, nor fighters. On the return to base, Major Price kept the formation in position and buzzed the field with all 36 planes, an exciting display of precision, but not everybody is happy over events of that magnitude.

Mission #78 - 15 June PM - Domfront Fuel Depot. Major Meng and Lt. Powell, BN led this mission with Captain Hulse and Lt. Conte BN on Box II. Other flights were led by Lt.Shaefer and Lt. Burn, BN, Captain Dunn and Lt.Arrington, BN. Bombing had to be done by flights at 3000 feet altitude due to lowering clouds, but results were excellent. The fuel depot was aflame when the formation left. No flak or fighters bothered the group. Don't you think the fighter escort are happy that the Luftwaff do not make hits on our group? Perhaps our speed of up to 250 MPH may confuse them. But, we're happy with the outcome.

On this day, June 15, Lt. McGlohn received his Silver Star Medal for his heroic efforts on a previous mission. Well deserved!

16 June - Weather kept all scheduled crews on hold all day long, with almost start-ups, but cancellations due to closing in clouds and rain. C'e l'vie.

Mission #78, 15 June. Domfront Fuel Depot.

Mission #79 - 18 June - Foret de Conches Fuel Depot. Captain Conant and Lt. McBrien, BN, Lts. Osborne and Forma, BN, Captain Dunn and Lt. Arrington, BN, Lts. Cole and Beck, BN, and Captain Hulse and Lt. Conte, BN led flights. Take-off was in reasonably good weather, but the closer the group got to the target, clouds moved in, with a 100 percent cloud cover at 12,000 feet. No bombs were dropped, so back they came fully loaded. No flak or fighters. Another Intelligence Officer, Lt. Mazanec rode with Captain Conant for "experience." This was his first combat mission, but he didn't get to see much more than clouds.

Mission #80 - 20 June - AM - Ligescourt Noball. Captain Dunn and Lt.Arrington, BN, led Box I with Lts. Marzolf and Basnett, BN leading Box II. Flights were led by Captain Hulse and Lt. Conte, BN, Lts. Morton and Madenfort, BN, and Lt. Shaefer and Lt. Burg, BN. This target required the formation to fly over heavily defended areas, where the 1st sergeants manned the anti-aircraft guns, so window planes preceeded the group. Window dropping planes were led by Lts. Sommers and McQuade, BN. Very little flak bothered the group. Bombing was classifed from good to fair.

Mission #81 - 20 June - PM - LeGrand Rossegnol Noball site. - Major Price and Lt. Hand, BN led Box I. Captain Conant and Lt. McBrien, BN led Box II - Captain Huff and Lt. Kupits, BN, Lts. Morton and Madenfort, BN, Lts. DeMand and Hanlon, led flights. The 409th Bomb Group had targeted this aiming point in the morning, and we had to do the same in the afternoon. This target was about a mile away from the Ligescourt Noball we hit yesterday, which we knew was heavily defended, but to everyone's surprise, no flak came up. Bombing was rated from good to excellent. All planes returned safely.

The group was visited by inspection teams, known as POM (Preparation for Overseas Movement). These guys come along with more than the white glove treatment, not over-looking anything. Our readiness for another movement was approved, with the group earning an "excellent" for their equipment and records.

Mission #82 - 21 June - Middel Straits. Major Meng and Lt. Powell, BN led Box I with Lt. Col. Aylesworth and Lt. Lytle, BN as deputy. Lt. Col. Farmer and Major Thomas, a visitor also flew behind Meng. Lts. DeMand and Hanlon, BN, led a flight. Cloud cover at the target area required Pathfinder Bombing, or PFF, following B-26s which use electronic equipment to zero in on the target, they drop their bombs, and our formations, release theirs. Bombing was in groups of 15 planes, another unusual manner experiment. Evidently everything went as planned as the target was photoed as being washed out. No flak or fighters were a problem. All returned safely.

Mission #83 - 22 June - Cherbourg Heavy Gun Emplacement. - This target had to be destroyed since it was in the way of advancing allied troops. The IX Bomber Command, with medium and light bombers attacking it, as well as fighter strafes. Since there were so many groups assigned to wipe out this annoyance, the timing of the separate bombing groups had to be precise. Window dropping ships helped disperse flak bursts, but two planes did incur hits requiring a forced landing on an allied held airstrip in France for one plane. The other flew single engine back to England, landing on another emergency strip. Lt.Shea with gunners S/Sgts. Lee and Falk was one of the two planes hit over the target. With one engine out and his hydraulic lines inoperative due to having been cut, required Shea to overrun the end of the runway, shearing off the nose wheel and the right wheel, and skidded another 75 yards. The gunners lay prone on the floor of their compartment, escaping injury. That emergency landing strip was in the right place, having just been completed three hours earlier than Shea's landing. One other plane had already used it, so it came in handy. The three occupants of Shea's plane had an opportunity to visit a bombed out chateau, which had been a German Headquarters. Many souvenirs were gathered before they were transported back to base on a C-47. Lts. DeMand and Hanlon, BN -Lts. Shaefer and Burg, BN led flights. The mission was led by Captain Jackson with Lt. Maltby, BN and Captain Hulse and Lt. Conte, BN as deputy. With 37 planes attacking, ll were battle damaged.

Our base must have been a safe haven for other planes, since a B-24, Liberator, a British Halifax, and a B-26 made emergency landings here. It was interesting for our men to scrutinize these foreign ships.

Mission #84 -24 June - AM - Middel Straete Noball. Two boxes of 15 planes in each were to bomb at 12,000 feet with PFF Pathfinder B-26 planes ahead of our group. Results were not available. No flak or fighters. Captain Dunn and Lt.Arrington, BN were on this mission.

Mission #85 - 24 June - PM - Bagnoles de Lorne Fuel Dump. Lt. Osborne and Lt. Forma, BN led Box I and Major Price with Lt. Hand, BN led Box II. Lts. DeMand and Hanlon, BN, and Captain Hulse and Lt. Conte, BN led flights. Bombing results

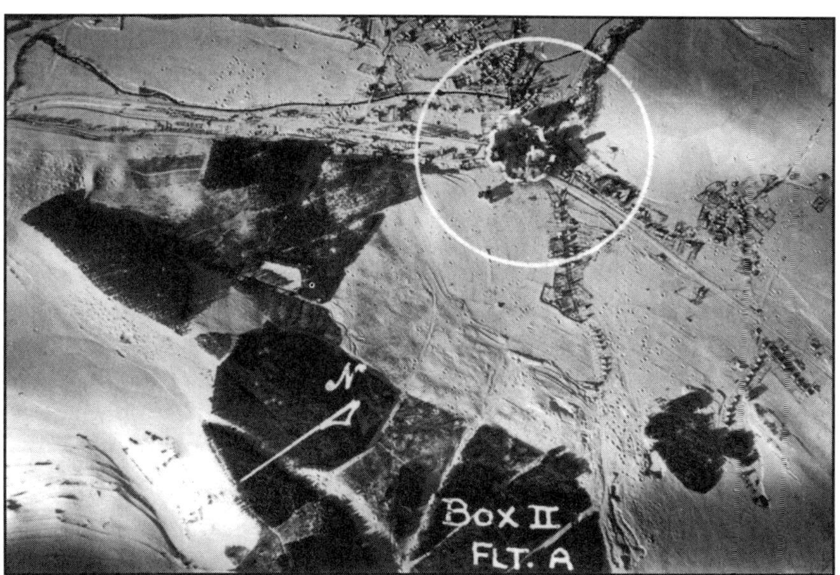

Mission #85, 24 June. Bagnoles de Lorne Fuel Dump.

were termed fair. No harm to ships. This was a relatively short mission, but a good baptism for crews flying their first missions, including Lt. Anderson and gunners Ruga and Schafer, Lt. Kenny and gunners Spadoni and Noteriani, Lt.Colquit and gunners Giesy and Cherry, and Lt. Harris with gunners Ernstrom and Potter.

Mission #86 - 25 June - Foret D'Andaine Fuel Dump. There isn't much written up about this mission, but it was termed successful. Captain Dunn and Lt.Arrington, BN, with Lts. Cole and Beck, BN, and Captain Hulse and Lt.Conte, BN led flights. Again two more crews from the 668th flew on their first mission, being Lt. Walsh and gunners, Wright and Novak, plus Lt. Clausen and gunners Fetko and Brown. All ships returned unharmed.

During non-mission days, crews from each squadron take to the air in training sessions, sharpening formation flying, bombing and navigational techniques, and generally making the most of idle time, all resulting in better missions.

Mission #87 - 29 June - St. Hillaire-Vitre Railroad Junction. - Major Willetts and Lt.Royalty, BN led this mission. Lts. Shaefer and Burg, BN led Box II. Lts. Cole and Beck, BN and Captain Hulse and Lt. Conte, BN led flights. Each box of six flights had separate targets to zero in on, with excellent results. The ack-ack gunners cut their fuses and aimed for one particular box and that contained a first mission pilot, F/O Baxter, who had with him gunners Enstrom and Potter, both on their second mission. Flak burst amid ships, bursting in flame. No one saw chutes open, although Potter did turn up as an escapee from a POW camp. Engstrom and Baxter were not accounted for. Other heavy damage occured to Lts. Shaefer and Downing, both of whom had to return to the English coast with forced landings. Captain Conant's plane was severely damaged, but he managed to coax it back to base.

Mission #88 - 30 June - Thury-Harcourt Railroad Junction. Captain Dunn and Lt. Arrington, BN, Lts. DeMand and Hanlon, BN, Lts. Cole and Beck, BN, Captain Prentiss and Lt. McBrien, BN, and Lt. Meagher and Lt. Burg, BN, led flights. The usual "little Friends" were with the mission, and little flak came up. Bombing results were termed from fair to good.

Thus ended 25 missions for the month, some rather rough, others, like we'll take them any day in the week. Some transfers of personnel were made between squadrons, and two members of the group jumped up to Wing Headquarters.

A 668th pilot, West Point Grad lst Lt. Scott Ritchie was dispatched to fly a "smoke" mission with the RAF. He had gunners Anderson and Smith with him. For unexplained reasons, the plane disappeared from its spot and the next thing others noticed was a pile of rubble on the ground, snuffing out these great boys. Ritchie was a well experienced pilot, having brought in damaged craft before, including bringing in a plane on fire during training in Lake Charles, Louisiana. The two gunners were 20 and 21 years old, a sad loss.

F-6, 670th Squadron, 416th Bomb Group. Melun, France.

Chapter 6

July 1944 Missions
Ninth Bomber Command Press Release

July 1944 Missions

July started with rain - rain and so much so on 3 July that flooding of barracks and other buildings occured. Even training missions didn't take place. The only exciting thing - exciting?? - the buzz bombs are becoming more frequent, and more important, closer. But, as the saying goes, as long as we can hear that unusual motor going, you're safe. When that noise stops, the glide path and the resultant boom when it hits, is frightening enough. It is estimated the explosives in the buzz bomb is equivalent to a ton of TNT. It sure makes a big hole, and having seen the destruction on buildings in London, when we were there on 48 hour passes, really makes an impression.

There's one thing that was always impressive, is the fortitude and resolve of the English people to have lived through the many years of German Bombers devastating their homes, office buildings, and anything you can name, without complaining. Sure, they wonder when it will all come to an end, but in the meantime, they did their utmost to help their cause, abide by their air raid alerts, and sleeping in the subways, night after night, whole families of them, just living with something they could do very little about, but make the best of what they could endure.

Mission #89 - 4 July - La Morintiere Defended Area. Leading Box I were Lts. Osborne and Forma, BN with Major Price and Lt. Hand heading up the second box. Captain Prentiss and Lt. McBrien, BN, Captain McNulty with Lt. Burseil, BN flew as deputies to the boxes. Lts. DeMand and Hanlon, BN flew as flight leaders. Cloud cover over the target required B-26 PFF Pathfinders to signal the bomb drops. Results were unobserved. No flak or fighters threatened the group.

Mission #90 - 5 July - Merlemont Headquarters Buildings. Captain Jackson and Lt. Maltby, BN led Box I with Captain Prentiss and Lt. McBrien, BN as deputy. Lts. Sommers and McQuade led Box II with Captain McNulty and Lt. Burseil as deputy. Captain Huff and Lt. Kupits led a flight. This was an unusual arrangements of flights and boxes. Only four planes to a flight and four flights to a box. Bombing was by box, so 16 planes had to drop when the lead bombardier of each box sighted and released his bombs.

This target was the German Noball Headquarters which means it had to be heavily defended, as our pilots soon found out. The first box zeroed in on the target for an excellent rating, while the second box earned a "poor" score. Captain Jackson took a flak hit which killed his left engine, damaging it to the extent he could not feather the prop, which remained flat, causing a difficult flying status. Speed was lost and the plane always wanted to turn to the left, so the pilot had to fight that continuously. He had to leave the formation, dropping altitude fast, so much so that he could barely make the English coast. His bombardier, Maltby was wounded. Before Jackson attempted a crash landing, he gave the bail-out signal to the crew to bail out. Only one man riding with him, a photographer PFC Byron K. Allen, from the 4th Combat Camera Unit, decided to jump. He did, but his chute did not open, resulting in his demise. Jackson sought any place to land and saw an abandoned RAF field so he crash landed successfully, with no further injury to his bombardier and remaining gunner. When the crew exited the ship, they found themselves being peppered by bullet shells falling out of the sky. It appeared a Spitfire was gunning at a Buzz-Bomb flying overhead. Many other planes in the formation suffered flak damage, but all were able to return to base.

Mission #91 - 6 July - AM - Epernon Railroad Embankment. Lts. Marzolf and Basnett, BN led Box I with Major Willetts and Lt. Royalty, BN heading up Box II. The formations were back to three flights to a box, with six ships in a flight, Other flight leaders were, Lts. Rudisill and Joost, BN, Lts. Osborne and Forma, BN, Captain Huff and Lt. Kupits, BN, and Lts. Demun and W. L. Smith, BN. Each of the six flights had a different target assigned to them, such as bridges and railroad junctions. After dropping, they were to re-assemble behind Marzolf's flight back to base. This was a four hour flight, longer than the normal ones, but the boys came through well enough.

On 6 July, the first Silver Oak Leaf Clusters, signifying 30 missions completed were pinned on Major Meng, Captains Hulse, Jackson, and Rudisill, Lts. Conte, Ostrander, and Harrold. Those officers were the first in the 670th squadron to have flown that many missions. All were part of the original group formed in Lake Charles, Louisiana.

Mission #92 - 6 July - PM - Verneuil-LaLoupe Railroad. Box I was led by Major Price and Lt. Hand, BN with the second box led by Lts. Osborne and Forma, BN. Lts. Cole and Beck, BN and Lts. Marzolf and Basnett, BN led flights. Here again, we were back to six ship flights and three flights to a box. Also, again, each flight had separate targets to attack, such as bridges, railroad, and highway crossings. Lt. Forma didn't pick up his target, so went on to drop a bridge into the water. In spite of his excellent drop, he was awarded a "poor" since he didn't get to his assigned target.

Four pilots of the 668th completed their 40th mission, they being Lts. Downing, Hill, Peede, and Lesher.

Mission #93 - 7 July - St. Pierre-Sur Dives Bridge. Major Willetts and Lt.Royalty BN led Box I with Captain Rudisill and Lt. Joost, BN leading Box II. (Rudisill was made Captain a few days ago). Congratulations to a swell guy! Captain Prentiss and Lt. McBrien, BN flew deputy to Box I leader and Captain Huff and Lt. Kupits, BN flew deputy to Box II leader. Lt. Sommers and McQuade led a flight. Take off was at 2000, by the time the formation got to the target, a combination of darkness, and haze guarded the target. Bombs went away, but results could not be determined, since the developed photos taken after the bomb drop could not be distinguished. The planes all made it back okay,. and landed about midnight, again, the four hour mission really taxed the gas supply of the planes.

Mission #94 - 8 July - AM - Caen Strong Point - Lts. Osborne and Forma, BN were in front of Box I with Major Price and Lt. Hand, on Box II. Lts. Cole and Basnett, BN and Lts. Marzolf and Beck, BN led flights. This target was important since it was in direct support of ground troops. Bombing results were scored excellent. Little flak didn't bother the group, and air cover by "little friends" kept the formation safe.

Mission #95 - 8 July - PM - Combourg and Avranches Railheads. Two boxes had different targets to hit. The first box went for Combourg and the second box hit Avranches. Lt. DeMand and Hanlon led a flight. Box leaders names were not available. Bombing results were rated excellent, with no damage to planes from fighters or flak.

Mission #96 - 11 July - Bourth Railway Bridge. The leader of the first box on this mission is not chronicled and the only information available on the mission is related by Chet Wysocki who gives the best information. Weather was threatening in the morning, but things cleared up in the afternoon and the boys took off. When we are told B-26 Pathfinders would lead us in, we knew clouds would hide the target . The second box was led by Lts. Osborne and Forma, BN with Lt. Meagher and Lt. Burg, BN as deputy. The formation was again a queer one with only four planes to a flight and four flights to a box. What were the brass experimenting with? When 16 planes drop bombs from one box leader, it would seem that the odds of hitting are not too good if the leader ran into trouble. If the leader went far off the target, and that does happen, nobody gets to put their bombs where they are supposed to go. It would seem that the best attack would be to have flights of six bomb, increasing the possibility of success by many-fold. In any event, on this mission, with PFF techniques utilized, bombing results were not recorded due to the cloud cover. No flak or fighters interferred with the formation, so all returned safely.

Today, 36 enlisted men were pinned with the Good Conduct Medals.

Mission #97 - 12 July - Foret D'Andaine Fuel Depot. - Here again, accurate records are not available, and the only information comes from the 668th's Chet Wysocki. He reports that the crews were awakened at 0400 and after breakfast and briefing, took off at 0730. We do know that Major Willetts and Lt. Royalty, BN were listed as being on this one , but no information as to whether or not they led it. They probably did. Lts. Marzolf and Beck, BN are also listed as are Lt. Meagher with Lt. Burg. BN. No damage was incurred on the planes. Pathfinders again gave us the lead with bombing through the clouds, so no results recorded. Another Milk-Run? We'll take it every time.

Mission #98 - 14 July -- Bourth Railroad Embankment. Late this afternoon this formatin of two Boxes with four flights in each box and four planes in each flight took off. The box leader is not mentioned in the history of the 668th, 670th, or 671st squadrons, so we must assume the leaders were from the 669th squadron. No detailed information about the 669th squadron is available, and whatever has been recorded was difficult to read from the official documents available at Boling AFB and Maxwell AFB. The transciptions cannot be reproduced, and for that reason many of the 669th squadron activities are missing from this dissertation. On this 98th mission, Lts. Osborne and Forma, BN led Box II with Captain Jackson and Maltby BN as deputy. Major Dunn and Arrington BN also listed as being on the trip. B-26 PFF Pathfinders led the group over the target to bomb through the clouds. No results were recorded. No flak or fighters were seen. .

Mission #99 - 16 July - St. Hillaire Du Harcourt Railroad RR embankment. Following two delays in the morning, this mission took off in the afternoon. Bombing was done through clouds following B-26 Pathfinder planes. Captain McNulty and Lt. Burseil, BN and Captain Hulse and Lt. Conte, BN led flights. This mission was 3:45 hours with results of the bomb drops unavailable.

Mission #100 - 18 July - AM -Giberville Strong Point. Records show that over 2000 planes dumped 8000 tons of bombs on this area, where German hordes are located near Caen. This makes it a very important target to defend and the Germans did that very well. Heavy intense flak caused major damage to planes. Captain McNulty and Lt. Burseil, BN led Box I with Captain Prentiss and Lt. McBrien as deputy. The German gunners zeroed in on the box leader, hitting the bombardier's compartment, destroying the Norden Bombsight. The BN, Lt. Burseil was hit in the face; with no bombsight, and a confusion of smoke at the target, the lead plane did not drop its bombs. The following planes, therefore, did not unload their bombs, either.

On July 19, the STARS AND STRIPES wrote:

> Spearheading the great onslaught on the continent, was a dawn attack by Havocs and Marauders against German armor amassed ahead of the British east flank in Normandy.

Mission #101 -18 July - PM - Gles-Sur-Risle Railroad Junction - Pontautou. This target was again heavily defended resulting in a number of injuries to personnel and planes. Six members of the 670th were wounded on this trip, including Lts. Rooney, Sommers, and Conte. S/Sgts. McCleary, DiNapoli, and Stephens were also hit. Lt. Pat Rooney was leading a window mission when his right engine was hit, rendering it useless. A second burst hit his interphone and hydraulic lines. A third burst also hit the plane, and the two gunners could not communicate except through lip reading and pointing. McCleary motioned to his fellow gunner, DiNapoli that he was badly wounded. DiNapoli came down from his turret position, tore away part of McCleary's flying gear, applied a tournaquet and administered a shot of morphine to ease the pain. Lt Rooney, being hit badly, and realizing his plane was pretty well shot up and no way to talk to his gunners, thought he had better try to land for assistance to

Mission #101, 18 July. Railroad choke point. View from 12,500 feet.

everybody on board. He left the formation and headed back to base - salvoed his bombs in a field, and reached an airfield in Ford, England for an emergency landing. As he touched down, a Spitfire was taking off on the same runway, headed right for Rooney. The Spitfire got off the ground and raised his wheels, just missing Rooney. With no hydraulics, and only one wheel down, a belly landing was made. Rooney was so badly shot up he could not get out of his cockpit, and was extracted by ground personnel. He and McCleary were transported to a nearby hospital for treatment. McCreary's arm bore a bad compound fracture, necessitating his recuperation back to the states. Rooney's plane was a total wreck. The scoring on the bombing was rated as excellent. Flights were led by Lts. Marzolf and Beck,BN Lts. Cole and Basnett BN, and Captain Hulse and Lt. Conte, BN.

On this same mission, Lt. Hall took a flak hit just as the formation crossed the French Coast toward the target. He stayed in formation and got to drop his bombs with the rest of the flight. His air speed indicator and altimeter were not registering. He called back to his gunners to check if they were wounded. He also asked them to check to see if any hydraulic lines were broken. They determined that hydraulic and other lines were ruptured. S/Sgt Burger cut off the jagged edges of damaged tubing, flared open the flattened parts, took rubber tubing from his Mae West and improvised a repair which got the instruments in the pilot's instrument panel to begin registering again. Lt. Hall headed back to base, where their Crew Chief T/Sgt Spillett said the repair was so professional that it could last a long time.

Another sad occurence on this mission, relates to Lt. R.K. Cruze of the 668th squadron.

His ship was so badly damaged that he had to ditch in the channel. His two gunners, Sgts. Geisy and Cherry were with Cruze. Air-Sea Rescue was ready to pick them up as Lt. Cruze was swimming toward them. His Mae West was either damaged or he did not have it on. Cruze went under before he got to the rescue boat and drowned. Sgt. Cherry was picked up but the rescue team worked on him for hours, but could not bring him around. He also passed away. Sgt. Giesy's wounds required him to be hospitalized.

All other ships landed, badly shot up.

Not all fatalities occur on bombing missions. A group of our boys were on their way to a railroad station, in a jeep. Their jeep cracked up and S/Sgt William H. Coe, a gunner with 47 missions, only 19 or 20 years old injured in the accident was hospitalized and passed away after many days of attention.

Mission #102 - 19 July - Bruz Fuel Depot. Lts. Marzolf and Beck, BN, and Lts. Cole and Basnett, BN led flights from the 671st squadron. Prior to take-off, Captain Prentiss of the 668th was preflighting his plane when his radio set and Gee bombing equipment caught fire. The crew scrambled around and climbed into another plane and took off with the mission. Clouds and shadows covered the target so no bombs were dropped by some flights. Some did get their bombs away. After bombs away, F/O Byrne's plane was severely damaged by flak. His turret gunner, Sgt. Cummings saw his partner in the tunnel position, Sgt. Cochran, motionless. Cummings left his post and found Cochran could not be helped. He notified F/O Byrne who left the formation and landed on a fighter strip in Normandy. Sgt. Cochran was buried in Dlosville, France.

Mission #103 - 22 July - Bourth Bridge. Major Price and Lt. Hand, BN took the lead of Box I with Captain McNulty and Lt. Burseil, BN leading Box II. Lts. Marzolf and Beck, BN participated. Pathfinder B-26s led the group in for bombing through a cloud cover. After this four hour mission, all planes returned to base safely.

Mission #104 -23 July - AM - Evreaux Railroad Embankment. Bombing results were not available due to the formation having to bomb through clouds, following B-26 Pathfinder leaders. Lts. DeMand and Hanlon, BN led a flight.

Technical Inspectors of the IX Bomber Command made an inspection of the entire Group resulting in an EXCELLENT rating. Colonel Mace, CO of the 416th called all personnel in a hanger to congratulate everyone on the manner in which the group passed such a rigid inspection.

Mission #105 - 25 July - St. Giles France. Major Meng and Lt. Powell BN led this mission with Captain McNulty and Lt. Burseil, BN flying as deputy. The second Box was led by Captain Rudisill and Lt. Joost, BN and Lts. DeMand and Hanlon, BN as deputy. Captain Hulse and Lt. Conte, BN led a flight. Precision bombing was not what this mission was all about. It was termed as area bombing, with bombs plastering an area supporting our ground troops. The results of the bombing was reported in percentages of bombs hitting the assigned area. The first box received 75% effectiveness with the second box receiving a 90% rating. Little flak was seen. All ships returned with no damage.

Mission #106 - 26 July - Marigny Strong Point. This was another area bombing attack in support of allied ground forces. Lts. Meagher and Burg, BN and Major Dunn and Lt. Arrington, BN, plus Lts. Marzolf and Beck BN, participated. Weather and visibility made bombing results impossible to measure. No Planes were hit, all returning safely.

Mission #107 - 28 July - La Gouesniere Fuel Depot. Captain McNulty and Lt. Burseil, BN led Box I. Captain Hulse and Lt. Conte, BN led Box II, Bombing was through clouds with PFF B-26s leading the group. Colonel Mace flew this mission. No flak came up, all returned to base safely.

Mission #108 - 30 July - Caumont Area. Major Price and Lt. Hand, BN took Box I with Lts. Osborne and Forma leading Box II. Captain Huff and Lt. Kupits BN flew deputy to Box II leader. The field order came through at midnight, requesting flights to assist allied forces moving in a pivotal area. The request was for fragmentation bombs. Armament personnel went to work at 0200 and a briefing was called for 0500 and take off at 0730. As the missions neared the target, clouds moved in requiring bomb drops through the clouds. Higher offices advised the group that their bombs fell in the right area, permitting British troops to advance further inland. Caumont was not far from the original beachhead. Other IX bomber Command groups also hit this area, enabling Allied troops to move safely on a wide front.

Mission #109 - 31 July - AM - Liseaux Marshalling Yard. Major Clark, Lt. Jones, BN led Box I. Captain Hulse and Lt.Conte, BN, Lt. Meagher and Lt. Burg, BN, Lt. DeMand and Lt. Hanlon led flights. As they approached the target they found it cloud covered, so they proceeded to the secondary target and found that pretty well cloud covered. The first box dropped with what we termed as "fair" results. The second box did not see the target, so they held their bombs. This was a milk run-no flak or fighters.

Mission #110 - 31 July - PM - Mantes-Gassicourt Railroad Bridge. Major Willetts and Lt. Royalty, BN, Lts. Demand and Hanlon, BN, Lts. Osborne and Forma, BN, and Lts. Meagher and Burg, led flights. Lts. Cole and Basnett, BN led Box II. Bombing results were classified from good to excellent. No enemy action.

Ninth Bomber Command Press Release

The Public Relations Release of the July month-end summary by Ninth Bomber Command relates to the 416th operations and our other group operations.

D-Plus 55 - July 31st, sees the German war machine reeling backward from the shank of the Cherbourg Peninsula under the sledge-hammer impact of the American offensive there; while in the center of the Normandy line the British front has exploded into action and Rommell's defenses are being rolled slowly backward onto the heels of a bulky and badly pounded support system; and still further east the Canadians have anchored the bloody line on Caen and have refused to budge in spite of murderous counter assaults.

This, in a paragraph, is the picture which Marauder and Havoc crewmen see on the ground thousands of feet below them as the sum-total of a difficult month of invasion warfare.

If the pre-invasion month of May could be described as a “softening-up-period,” and the invasion month of June labeled a “close-in-support month” - then July might well be a month devoted to strangulation of the enemy's life-lines, choking off the battle front from reserves and supplies, confusing and disrupting his movements, forcing him to expend vital fuel and equipment, and generally “tripping him up” where the fall would hurt him most. Perhaps, in a sense, the month of July was a combination of the strategy and tactics of both June and May before it.

July has been a month in which the first feverish surges of the invasion battle settled into a more estabilized situation; in which both invader and defender more or less retarded tempo in order to catch a second wind. Battle lines straightened and solidified and ground progress was at first slow, while supplies and re-inforcements came up and the generals marshalled their forces for the all-out fight that now appears to be in development.

For medium and light bombers of the Ninth Air Force, here was a special task. While Montgomery arrayed his forces on the ground, their job was to make life miserable for Rommel - disrupt -delay - destroy - wear him down.

In a summer month which Britons declare to be one of the filthiest weather in nearly half a century, the Marauders and Havocs went at it, day after day, from early morning missions to those which saw them swarming their home fields in partial darkness; flying in weather so bad that not many months ago they would not have ventured off the ground; bombing through heavy clouds - and all the while maintaining a remarkable record of accomplishment.

Now, thirty one days later, it is obvious that without this agressive type of operations, the present ground drive doubtless could not have been mounted.

In the early part of July, Ninth medium and light bombers began operations with a series of attacks on bridges, railheads, communications, and fuel dumps, climaxing this on July 6 with assaults on 44 targets - more than any single day in the Ninth's history in the ETO. The Marauders and Havocs already had smashed the bridges over the Seine and wrecked or rendered useless most of those over the Loire. The Germans were frantically attempting to repair the broken spans or swing temporary structures over the valleys. But, meantime they were being forced to funnel troops and supplies through the Paris area, except on those remaining bridges which had been temporarily erected or could be temporarily repaired. With the enemy transport thus bottled up, the Ninth Bombers aimed at further blocking their movements, and struck at six important rail links in the area west of Paris serving the battle front. The lines were blasted at 36 points in all, and embankments, fills and spurs were severely damaged. As a result of this round of pummeling a crack Panzer Division moving toward the front was completely blocked and subsequent pounding of road and junction points in the area still further delayed its movement. To date, intelligence indicates, this division has not yet reached an area of effective employment.

This was all part of the program to force the Germans to movement by road, compelling them to transfer troops and equipment from rail to highway, throwing an added burden on already overstrained motor transport, forcing a high rate of fuel expenditure and shortening the limited life of tanks and heavy tracked vehicles whose normal life-spans range from 600 to 700 hours. Thus, time and gasoline wasted on the backroads of the war theater were just that much the enemy could not use in the battle lines. At the same time, these tactics jammed the highways with vehicles which laid open to strafing or drove them to slow and costly night movements.

On July 7, the Ninth bombers went out to polish off the last of the principal bridges spanning the Loire. Three of the four bridges attacked were temporarily destroyed. To accomplish this, the Marauders flew w ith full bomb load at extreme range - more than 750 miles for the round trip.

During the middle portion of the month, the Marauder-Havoc team continued its attacks on communications and fuel dumps, and also went after P-Plane launching sites, troop and equipment concentrations, and targets in the battle area.

Flexibility, which characterized this month's operations was demonstrated in repeated switches from strategical to close-in tactical targets. On July 9, the bombers joined in a combined assault on the Caen area which resulted in driving the enemy from its positions in the easterly section of this strong-point, an operation which was described by the Army as "decisive."

Between the combined hammering of inland refineries by the heavies, and the constant beating being given to road and rail arteries in western France, intelligence reports of organizations raiding each other's fuel supplies to meet their own need, came in and it was indicated that Rommel was hard pressed for fuel. Seizing upon this, the Marauder-Havoc team went into play against large fuel concentration points in the feeder area behind the front. In spite of bad weather and heavy clouds these missions were run, mostly using Pathfinder techniques, and remarkably satisfactory results were reported.

Again in the middle of the month, Marauders and Havocs switched to close-in support and this time went ahead of American ground forces in the St.Lo area. Similar support was again given in the latter part of the month ahead of ground troops when they pushed through St. Lo and began their current drive to the Southwest beyond the bitterly contested town. The joint operation has been described as "paving the way for the most successful offensive on the Normandy front since Cherbourg."

July 23 was the biggest single day in the history of the Ninth bombers' blind activities. Eleven separate group attacks were made on ten targets - nine bridges, and a fuel dump - all employing Pathfinder technique.

A review of statistics for the month reveals that the total bomb-tonnage dropped was not as large as in previous months, due in part to the consistently bad weather which restricted flying and to some degree by the nature and extent of targets attacked.

For those who like the figures, the Ninth bombers flew a total of more than 6400 sorties involving a gross bomb tonnage well over 9,000 tons against a total of some 150 targets. Losses for the period totaled 30 ships, 24 Marauders and 6 Havocs. The figures, in themselves, are less significant than the fact that these operations were carried out in the face of unfavorable flying conditions and a majority of the missions were on blind bombing.

The real essence of this Month's activities lies in the fact that at all odds, the mediums and lights carried the air war forward during a vital period when the Allied situation was being compressed for the drive that is now so evidently in progress.

CHAPTER 7

August 1944 Missions
Oissel Bridge Operation
Mission #117
Distinguished Unit Citation

August 1944 Missions

The early part of the month saw some personnel being switched around for various good reasons. The 416th Bomb Group Commanding Officer, Colonel Harold L. Mace flew up (that's how the Cub Scouts term it when they move up to being Tenderfoot Boy Scouts), to assume command of the 98th Combat Wing of the Ninth Bombardment Command. Colonel Mace assumed command of the 416th in October 1943, while we were at Lake Charles, Louisiana, relieving Lt.Colonel Richard D. Dick who was the original CO of the group since February 1943. Command of the 416th was assumed by Lt. Colonel Theodore R.Aylesworth. Rumors had it that Colonel Mace would soon be wearing a star. That's what he said our group was going to do for him at a group assemblage early during our operations.

On 4 August, many group personnel watched a wounded B-17 flying toward our base and saw it explode in flight. Nine parachutes were seen opening and the plane crashed about three miles from our base.

Transfers of pilots Captains Hulse and Moore plus Lt. Conte, BN and Lt.Greene, A West Point Graduate pilot, from the 670th squadron to the 669th squadron to strengthen it. The 670th had a strong group of personnel, so they were spread around. The 670th gained Captain Hiram F. Conant, Operations Officer and F/O Jay R. Warren and Lt. Warren Musgrove, pilots. F/O Byrne received his promotion to 2nd Lieutenant.

On to our missions for the month of August.

Mission #111 - 2 August - Caudebeck Airdrome. Major Meng with Lt. Powell BN, led Box I. Lts. Demand and Hanlon from the 671 squadron, led a flight. Flak greeted the formation as they approached the target but that did not deter the bombing flights. Lt. DeMand's Bombardier did not pick up the target on the first run, so asked Major Meng for permission to take his flight in for a second run. Major Meng gave his okay so the flight turned off the Initial Point but the anti-aircraft gunners had taken a second look and re-adjusted their sights, peppering the flight, causing some damage, but no personnel were affected. The group bombing results were rated from fair to good. Lt. Cannon's plane had his right engine shot out, forcing him to land at an emergency base in Ford, England. His gunners, Sgts. Robinson and Brzenski were not injured. All other planes made it safely back to base.

Mission #112 - 4 August - Beauvais Marshalling Yard. Major Price with Lt. Hand, BN led Box I with Captain McNulty and Lt. Burseil, BN leading Box II. Lts. DeMand and Hanlon, BN plus Lts. Cole and Basnett, BN led flights. Flak greeted the formation near the target, but all flights got their bombs away. Evasive action by the lead plane prevented damage to the planes, with all returning to base with little or no damage. Bombing results were rated good.

Regarding evasive action, it was the lead navigator to direct the pilot and the entire formation on what some may consider zig-zag turns, but very gently. The leader had to estimate the time between bursts from the gun nozzles and the time it would take for that shell to explode at their flying level. Usually, at 12,000 feet flying altitude, we figured it would take about 12 seconds for the flak to explode after it left the gun, so the lead man would have to time his directional flights one way or the other, changing compass directions , every 10 or twelve seconds, but at the same time not losing the route designed to take the formation to the target. Flying straight and level during a flak attack was risky, since gunners would anticipate your direction and shoot for it before you got there, so we had to change paths to evade the bursts. It didn't work all the time, but it was effective most of the time. Evasive action was never taken on the bomb run since the sighting of the target with the Norden Bombsight had to be true on a straight approach. This is where the bombers were at more risk since the AA gunners knew what they had to do to score hits on the planes. It worked well for them.

Mission #113 - 5 August - AM - Marigny-Compiegne Marshalling Yard. This was a three and a half hour flight, with our formation taking off as 1245. Major Willetts and Lt. Royalty, BN headed up Box I. Flights were led by Lts. Osborne and Burg, BN. With no flak, the bombing runs were smooth with four flights scoring excellents and two good. All crews returned with no damage. Another milk-run?

Mission #114 - 5 August - PM - Laigle Railroad Bridge. Within three hours of the planes returning from the first mission, the Crew Chiefs and their line mechanics, plus armament, had the ships reloaded and serviced, ready to go. And that they did for this important assignment. Flights were led by Major Dunn and Lt. Arrington, BN - Lts.DeMand and Hanlon, BN - Lts. Meagher and Burg, BN, plus Captain Prentiss and Lt. McBrien, BN. The bombing was in flights of six and excellent results were recorded. Lt. DeMand had to make a second run on the target when his flight was sqeezed out of the formation on the first run. After dropping, the flights moved away from the formation and flew over a heavily defended area, resulting in all planes suffering damage. Lt.R. D. Perkins with gunners S/Sgts. Sherry and Linneman had their right engine knocked out and his wing gas tank ruptured, losing enough gas requiring him to make an emergency landing on the Normandy beachhead, completely destroying the ship.

Oissel Bridge Operation

Mission #115 - 6 August - Oissel Bridge. This mission was one of the most important for the group to fly. The 409th Bomb Group of A-20s had attacked this bridge this morning but did not knock it out. The Commanding General of the IX Bomber Command, Brigadier General Anderson specifically asked the 416th to destroy this bridge.

The official record on this mission states that this is a double track bridge in two sections over the Seine River. Each bridge had three spans of steel girders and was 620 feet long. Beginning on 10 May 44, these two bridges have been attacked,

Mission #116, 6 August. Oissel Bridge. Closing Falaise Gap escape. Last bridge over Seine River.

repaired in part and reattacked with varying degrees of damage. About June 1st, a single track diversion bridge was completed immediately to the East of the south bridge (30' away from the original bridge), was knocked out and rebuilt several times. On August 3rd, in 48 hours, this diversion bridge was again rebuilt and connects with the regular tracks at the North end of the island. A light foot bridge spans the river between the diversion bridge and the original bridge, probably used by repair crews.

The new diversion bridge is of light steel or heavy timber construction. This is the only complete railroad bridge across the Seine River.

One, and possibly three German Divisions are moving by the route to the battle area.

The 410th was dispatched yesterday but did not attack due to 10/10 cloud cover.

The reason the target is so important is that it was the last remaining bridge over the Seine River used to transport German forces trapped in the Falaise Gap, numbering around 200,000 troops, being pushed ahead by General Patton in his easterly charge from the Cherbourg area. With this bridge out of commission, the Germans had no place to make their get-away from the envelope they were caught in. Four Nazi Panzer Divisions were ready to cross the bridge., The importance of this bridge was also realized by the anti-aircraft gunners, protecting it for miles around and in front of it by the Germans.

Our group took off in the morning at 1000, with 40 planes, including three window dropping aircraft. When we reached the target area, clouds had completely enveloped it, requiring the group to return to base after a four and a half hour of flight. Back at the base, the weather cleared, and the planes were gassed up again, and the crews took off at 1800.

Mission #116 - 6 August - Oissel Bridge. Again, 41 planes took off with Lts. Osborne and Forma, BN leading. Major Napier and Lt. Madenfort BN on the second box. Captain Hulse and Lt. Conte BN led flight #2 to the first flight. The German gunners having seen us this morning, were now quite ready to see us again. They must have readjusted their sights and fuses. The bombing was to be done in flights of six, and a four minute bomb run was started. This is an unusually long bomb run for such a well defended target, but the importance of wiping out the target was more important than anything. All flights, except one, were able to zero in on the aiming points, there being two spans required to be put out of service. The one flight with BN Lt. Madenfort riding with Major Napier did not drop because the bombardier received a severe flak hit and could not very well operate his bombsight.

Four planes were lost on the bomb run, including Lt. Douglas T. Sommers with Sgts. John L. Johnson and Stanley R. Zakliskewicz and Lt. Thomas W.McManus with gunners Sgt. John H.LaPorte and Gerald A. Hart. Lt. Sommers tried to crash land on an emergency airstrip but was unsuccessful. All his crew were reported as MIA. Lt. McManus and his crew are also listed as MIA. Lt Colonel Farmer, Group Operations Officer with Sgts. J. E. Hay and J. A. Buskirk and Lt. A. J. Welsh with gunners Sgts. R.E.Wright and S. G. Novack are all listed as Missing In Action. Lt. Osborne, leading the formation had to leave his position due to flak damage, making an emergency landing at the Normandy beachhead. His gunner S/Sgt. E. E. Kelly was injured.

Other flight leaders included Captain Jackson and Lt. Maltby, BN, - Major Napier with Lt. Madenfort BN, -Lts. Marzolf and Beck, BN, and Captain Huff with Lt.Kupits, BN.

Every plane on the mission was damaged, but the objective was accomplished. The bridge was wiped out. Of the six flights bombing, four scored excellent, one good, and one did not bomb due to the bombardier being injured. Many of the planes landed on emergency airfield due to the damage they received.

When Lt. Osborne, leading the mission went down, Captain Hulse and Lt. Conte assumed the lead to navigate the group back to base, without further incident.

Colonel Backus, CO of the 97th Bomb Wing flew with the 416th Group in the Second Flight of the First Box.

The mission was termed a complete success and earned a commendation from the Commanding General of the IX bomber Command, who was reported to have remarked, "It wasn't good bombing, it wasn't excellent bombing, it was perfect bombing."

The group received the Distinguished Unit Citation for this mission.

FROM 97TH COMBAT BOMB WING
TO; CO 416TH BOMB GROUP (L)
PRIORITY CONFIDENTIAL

FOLLOWING MESSAGE RECEIVED FROM COMMANDING GENERAL IX BOMBER COMMAND, QUOTE, MY REQUEST THAT YOU ASSIGN THE 416TH BOMB GROUP OF YOUR COMMAND TO ATTACK THE OISSEL BRIDGE WAS PROMPTED BY MY GREAT CONFIDENCE IN THE GROUP'S ABILITY AND COURAGE. THE BOMBING OF THE BRIDGE ON 6 AUGUST FULLY JUSTIFIED MY CONFIDENCE. IN

SPITE OF INTENSE OPPOSITION AT THE TARGET, THE ACCURACY OF THE BOMBING WOULD REFLECT CREDIT ON A GROUP BOMBING ON A PRACTICE RANGE. AS A RESULT A TROUBLESOME AND IMPORTANT TARGET WHICH HAD ALREADY COST IX BOMBER COMMAND FOUR PLANES LOST AND MANY DAMAGED WAS ALMOST CERTAINLY DESTROYED. PLEASE INFORM THE GROUP OF MY ADMIRATION FOR THE COURAGE AND BOMBING ACCURACY DISPLAYED. OISSEL WAS AN IMPORTANT AND DIFFICULT ASSIGNMENT SUPERBLY ACCOMPLISHED. ANDERSON QUOTE.

TO THIS COMMENDATION, I WISH TO ADD THAT I AM INDEED PROUD TO BE THE COMMANDING OFFICER OF THE WING IN WHICH THE 416TH BOMB GROUP (L) IS SUCH AN EFFICIENT AND OUTSTANDING NUMBER.

DEEPLY REGRET THE LOSSES IN YESTERDAY AFTER-NOON'S MISSION, BUT AT THE SAME TIME, I WISH TO COMMEND YOU HIGHLY FOR THE SUPERB BOMBING ATTACKS CARRIED OUT AGAINST YESTERDAY'S TARGET. THE OISSEL BRIDGES AND UPON THE COMPEIGNE MARIGNY MARSHALLING YARDS ON 5 JULY 1944 YOUR DESTRUCTION OF THESE TARGETS WAS OF GREAT MILITARY VALUE AND IMPORTANCE .

SIGNED
BACKUS

A Certified True copy
/s/ Harold L. Sommers
HAROLD L. SOMMERS
Captain, Air Corps
Operations Officer
669th Bombardment Group (L)
416th Bombardment Group (L)

This was transmitted personally, and typed originally for Lt. Ralph Conte

Mission #116. Oissel Bridge over Seine River, France. 6 August 1944. 416th Group bombing results closing Falaise Gap escape route of Germans.

Bombs from Allied planes wrecked this Nazi retreat bridge across the Rhone River at Arles, France.

On August 7, Lt. Ronald Perkins and his two gunners, S/Sgts. Sherry and Linneman who made a forced landing at Normandy Beach of 5 August, returned to the 416th. He went down on the 5th when one engine was knocked out and a hole was blown in a gas tank. He completely washed out the ship. His landing must have appeared spectacular to on-lookers, since he came down on one engine and one wheel, the other wheel having been knocked out of service. He said they spun around several times and when it stopped , they exited it fast, with surprisingly no injuries. The next day, the crew went on the August 8th PM mission.

Mission #117 - 8 August - AM - Frevent Railroad Junction. Major Clark and Lt. Jones BN, and Captain Rudisill with Lt. Joost led Boxes. Lts. Marzolf and Beck, BN and Lt. Wheeler and Arrington, BN led, Captain McNulty and Lt. Burseil, BN and Lt. Meagher and Lt. Burg, BN led flights. This was a hot target, having been there before, and they did not move their big guns away, so we found out. Lt. Norman Shainberg with gunners Sgts. J. D. Dugan and L. B. Curtis received a direct hit and was seen going down in flames. One wing was sheared off and then the plane exploded. Lt. Peter Dontas with S/Sgts. A. L. Nielsen and W. E. Fields also went down. All were listed as MIA Shainberg, Dugan, Curtis and Fields were POWs and freed. Lt. Dontas and S/Sgt. Nielsen were listed as KIA. Bombing results were excellent, with tracks, with box cars, and buildings seen to burst in flames. Lt. "Gee" Meredith noticed other pilots signalling to him that something was hanging from a wing. He determined it was one of his bombs that did not unshackle. The bomb was armed, and Meredith had to nurse it back to base and land as softly as he could, which he did. As soon as the plane rolled to a stop, all crew members scrambled away.

Mission #118 - 8 August - PM - Bois De Pierre Chateau Radar. Leading the first box was Major Price and Lt. Hand, BN, Captain Prentiss and Lt. McBrien, BN, Lts. Wheeler and Arrington, BN led flights. Bombing was rated as excellent with a blanketting of the Chateau. Some flak was experienced, but with little damage. The formation was attacked by ME-109s, but our P-38s intercepted them with success. One gunner said he saw a new German Jet fighter shoot down a P-38. An ME-109 dove toward a P-38 and knocked one engine off its mount. The P-38 pilot straightened out, and asked for a bearing home and headed there. The other P-38s took after the ME-109 and shot it up, with the pilot bailing out, but his chute was not seen to have opened.

Two new bombardiers joined the 670th squadron, Lts. Dale G. Ackerson amd William E. Brewer.

Mission #119 - 9 August - AM - Bois De Pierre Chateau Radar. Evidently the previous day's bombing was not sufficient to exterminate this installation. Major Willetts, and Lt. Royalty, BN. Lts. Marzolf and Beck, BN, Captain McNulty and Burseil, BN, and Lts. Meagher and Burg, BN, and Captain Hulse and Lt. Conte, BN led flights. Bombing results were scored excellent again, with about 50 craters all around the building. One string of bombs stretched from in front of the chateau and continued on right past it, for excellent results. Some flak was experienced.

New pilots were added to the 670th, being Lt. Harry Popeney and F/O Elizabeth O. Turner on 9 August.

Mission #120 - 9August - PM - Chauny Railroad Bridge. Captain Prentiss and Lt. McBrien, BN, Lts.Wheeler and Arrington, BN, Captain Hulse and Lt. Conte, BN, Lt. Meagher, and Lt. Burg, all led flights. The first box leader, not identified, evidently missed identifying the primary target and went on to the secondary target, a highway bridge at Apilly. The scoring was not scored. No flak or fighters came near the formation, all returned safely.

Second Lieutenant James R. Nichols joined the squadron as a bombardier-navigator, starting to fly with Lt. William Greene as a new team.

On 10 August, Major Meng moved up to Deputy Group Commander, with Major Lloyd F. Dunn assuming command of the 670th.

Captain Clark of the 669th left the squadron to become Assistant Group Operations Officer. He had been Squadron Operations Officer, which title passed on to Captain Sommers. Lt. Behlmer was named Assistant Operations Officer.

Mission #121- 10 August - AM - Foret de Romare Ammunition Dump. Leading the boxes were Major Price and Lt. Hand, BN, Box I with Captain McNulty and Lt. Burseil, BN, on Box II. Lts. Wheeler and Arrington, BN, Lts. Marzolf and Beck, BN and Captain Hulse and Lt. Conte, BN led flights. - Clouds moved in over the target, the mission was recalled.

Mission #122 - 10 August - PM - Le Lande de Louge - Ammo Dump. Captain Huff and Lt. Kupits, BN led Box I. Captain Morton Lt. Moore, BN led Box II. Lts. Wheeler and Arrington, BN, Lts. Marzolf and Beck, BN, Lts. Meagher and Burg, BN led flights. - On take-off Lt. Kenny of the 668th with gunners Sgts. Spadoni and Natoriani experienced engine failure, causing the plane to crash not far from the end of the runway. Lt. Kenny walked away uninjured. Sgt.. Notariani ws injured rather seriously, requiring hospitalization and eventually returned to the states for serious wounds received in action, for recuperation. Sgt.Spadoni suffered a broken jaw and other minor injuries.

The evening of 10 August, the group were treated to what was explained as being a spectaculare sight, at least it was impressive. Looking up, just prior to midnight, there must have been 1000 or more RAF four engine bombers, with night lights on, making the sky appear to be a moving carpet, heading for the southern coast of England for their usual carpet bombing of German cities. It must have taken 15 minutes for them all to pass over. In addition to the plane lights, massive search sky lights were scanning the sky for foreign planes that may have invaded the area. In all, the Brits put on a great show, not to lessen the engine noises drowning out conversation.

Mission #123 - 11 August - AM - Foret du Romare Ammo Dump. Captain McNulty and Lt. Burseil, BN led Box I with

Captain Hulse and Lt.Conte, BN as deputy. Lts. Marzolf and Beck, BN, and Lts. Greeley and Mitchell, BN led flights. Bombing for Box I did not score well, dropping well off the target. Box II bombs enveloped the target with good results. Our bombardiers let their bombs go on the B-26 PFF Pathfinder plane signal, over the cloud bank.

Mission #124 - 11 August - PM - St. Malo Gun Defenses. The Mad Colonel of St. Malo had to be taken out of his castle. Their guns were holding back the Allied forces which were up to 1500 yards of the castle. The 416th -SUPER BOMBARDIERS were called upon to hit this castle but be sure not to hurt any of our ground crews, less that a half mile away. Captain Hulse and Lt. Conte, BN, Captain Morton and Lt. Moore, BN, Lt.Wheeler and Lt. Arrington, BN, Captain McNulty with Lt. Burseil, BN. The official report stated: "That afternoon Captain Hulse and Captain Morton led two flights of a formation that attacked the St. Malo

Mission #124, 11 August. Bombing out the Mad Colonel. Holding up advancing Allied troops 1500 yards away.

gun defenses. Lt. Conte, Captain Hulse's BN did a superior job of bombing with a circular error of a little more than 100 feet. The infantry sent congratulations on the splendid aid we had given them." The scoring of all the flights were two excellents, one good, three fair. Conte's bombs started dropping just off shore, walked up to the castle and made direct hits on the building.

Mission #125 - 12 August - La Ferte Mace Ecouche Highway. This target was just ahead of our advancing allied ground forces, near Argentan and an area where German forces were trying to escape from the Failaise Gap. Over 150 bombers from the Ninth Bomber Command had been dispatched to this choke point, involving six other bomber groups. The 416th were rated to have done the best bombing, with three flights scoring excellents. A convoy of German vehicles trying to make their getaway were hit on the roadways, with tremendous explosions and fires testifying to the great bombing. Captain McNulty and Lt. Burseil, BN, led Box I with Lts. Osborne, and Forma, leading Box II. Captain Morton and Lt. Moore, BN., Lts.Wheeler and Arrington, BN, Lts. Cole and Basnett, BN led flights. Of the six flights, three scored excellent, two good and one poor. No flak or fighters were seen, all returning safely. On the way back to base, Lt.Sparlng of the 670th squadron ran out of gas near the home base. Trying to crash land, the tail section of the plane broke off, causing the two gunners S/Sgts. Bryan and Shaw, to fall out, and be seriously injured with compound fractures requiring hospitalization and eventual return to the states for treatment. Prior to their departure, S/Sgt. Bryan was awarded the Soldier's Medal for pulling his gunner partner Shaw from the tail section of the broken-up plane, in spite of his own injuries.

Mission #126 - 13 August - Pont D'Eveque in the Lisieux area. These again,were choke points to close up for the German troops trying to make their way back to the Fatherland. Major Willetts and Lt. Royalty, BN led Box I with Captain Hulse and Lt. Conte, BN leading Box II. Lts. Osborne and Forma BN, and

Lt. Demun and Lt. McQuade, BN led flights. Bombing was effective, cutting off the road escapes. Excellent bombing was reported along with good and fair scores. While flak was reported as being light, it was quite accurate, hitting six planes, but no losses were reported.

On August 14, Brigadier General Anderson sent commendations to S/Sgts. Blackford and Burger for their ingenious repairs to the altimeter and air speed lines of Lt. Hall's plane on the mission to Glos Sur Risle on 18 July, enabling the plane to fly right.

Mission #127 - 15 August - Foret De Chantilly Fuel Depot. Captain Hulse and Lt.Conte, BN led Box I with Major Napier and Lt. Jones, BN leading Box II. Lt.Greene and Lt. Nichols, flew deputy on Captain Hulse. Lts. Adams and Hanlon, BN and Lts. Cole and Basnett, BN led flights. A cloud bank with slightly broken cloud layers moved into the target area. Lt. Conte, instructed his pilot to descend from an altitude of 12,000 feet to about 8000 feet, through cloud layers, readjusting his bomb sight settings as he went down. The bomb load was fragmentation bombs, and when Conte caught sight of the target, he zeroed in and dropped the box load with 95 percent of the bombs landing in the fuel dump, scoring an excellent.

Mission #128 - 17 August - Montfort Sur Risle Bridge. Captain McNulty and Lt. Burseil, BN led Box I, Captain Morton and Lt. Moore, BN, Lts. Greeley and Mitchell, BN, and Lts. Bartmus and Hardy, BN led flights. B-26 PFF Pathfinder planes led the formation in, dropping from 11,700 feet. Results were unobserved due to the clouds. No losses, casualties, or damage was sustained.

A combination of inclement weather - so what else is new? - and the preparation for a move of the group, caused a lapse in bombing missions. Training, Training, including close order drill was ordered, individuals packing up, and squadron officials making ready for the evacuation of Wethersfield was paramount.

On August 22, a surprise visit by Sergeant Potter, who was shot down with F/O Baxter on 29 June, walked into the squadron area. His tale may have sounded fabricated, but it did come true. Sgt. Potter had parachuted from the plane which was flat spinning down after taking a direct hit. He did not see F/O Baxter or Sgt. Ernstrom parachute out. While Potter was floating down, German soldiers were shooting at him, He was captured and made prisoner. During his first six weeks there, he became friendly with an Australian pilot, concocting an escape plan. They executed it and made their way in France, becoming friendly with a French family in an area overrun by Germans. They lived there, in civilian clothing. One morning they awoke to find that the town they were in was liberated by American forces. They visited the CO of the outfit, and following intense interrogation and able to convince everybody they were legitimate allied personnel, they were sent back to England. He had lost 15 pound in the short time he was POW and with the French people, he looked palid, but happy to be back. He was returned to the states.

Mission #129 - 25 August - Brest/Kerviniou Coastal Defense Battery. Major Price and Lt. Hand, BN led Box I. Major Napier Lt. Jones, BN,- Lts. Greeley and Mitchell, BN,- Lts. Adams and Hanlon, BN, -Captain Marzolf and Lt. Beck, BN, -Lt. Demun and Lt. McQuade, BN led flights. This flight was one of the longest for the group, to protect this important port. The entire Ninth Bomber Command were attacking this port, with Naval vessels bombarding it from the seas. The formation took off at 1300, dropped their bombs and had to land at a refueling depot at St. Mawgen on the southern part of England. They landed there at 1630 and got back to base at 2100. An extremely long mission for these type planes, but the boys did it! Scoring fared from excellent to fair, measured as a success.

Mission #130 - 26 August - AM -Champiegne-Clairox Fuel Depot. Flights were led by Lts. Osborne and Forma, BN,- Lts. Meagher and Burg, BN, -Captain Huff and Lt. Kupits, BN, -

Lts.Adams and Hanlon, BN, and Lts.Greeley and Mitchell, BN. Violent explosions and fires proved bombing excellence. No flak or enemy planes bothered the formation.

Mission #131 - 26 August - PM - Roeun troop, transports and tank concentrations. These were part of the German forces trying to cross the Seine, waiting to be shuttled across the wide span since there were no suitable bridges to cross. Major Willetts and Lt. Royalty, BN led Box I. Captain Morton and Lt. Moore, BN, - Lts. Demun and McQuade, BN, - Lts. Cole and Basnett, BN led flights. Each of the six flights were assigned different targets in this area, with fragmentation bombs, but only one flight managed to get their bombs away. Other flights were bothered by a combination of clouds, haze, and smoke, so they all brought their load back to base. Some flak was effective. Lt. A. J. Vleghels was wounded slightly,

Mission #132 - 27 August - Roeun Area. Major Price and Lt. Hand, BN took the lead of Box I with Lts. Osborne and Forma leading Box II. Captain Marzolf and Beck, BN led a flight. The 416th was one of seven Ninth Bomber Command Groups attacking this concentraion of vehicles, tanks, and personnel, waiting to cross the Seine in boats. Again fragmentation bombs from our group, dropped through a thick haze, managed to destroy hundreds of vehicles .

Mission #133 - 28 August - Doulens Fuel Depot. Captain Huff and Lt. Kupits led Box I with Captain Morton and Lt. Moore, BN, leading Box II. Captain McNulty and Lt. Burseil, BN, - Captain Marzolf and Lt. Beck, BN and Lts. DeMand and Burns, BN led flights. Bombing was scored as three excellents, two goods, and one fair. No enemy fighters or flak bothered the formation.

30 August - On a training mission, Lt. John D. Smith, assigned to the 669th squadron was on a training mission with Lt. E. L. Miller. Lt. Smith was on Miller's right wing and in trying to cross under Lt. Miller's plane, hit, cutting off the tail of

Miller's plane, at the turret. Miller jettisoned his hatch giving his gunner the bail out signal, both jumped with opened parachutes. Lt. Smith had joined the outfit only eight days earlier, and now is being buried at Cambridge Military Cemetery.

Distinguished Unit Citation

RESTRICTED
HEADQUARTERS
NINTH AIR FORCE
GENERAL ORDERS — APO 696. U S ARMY
Number 144 — 25 July 1945

BATTLE HONORS - Citation on Unit — Section I

I—BATTLE HONORS - Under the provisions of Section IV, Circular NO. 333, War Department, 1943, the following-named unit of the Ninth Air Force is cited for extraordinary heroism, in action against the enemy. The citation reads as follows:

> The 416th Bombardment Group. For extraordinary heroism in armed conflict with the enemy from 6 August to 9 August 1944. During the withdrawal of the beleaguered German ground forces from the Falaise Gap the 416th Bombardment Group launched a series of determined attacks upon strategic strongly defended enemy positions in an attempt to turn the enemy retreat into a rout. On the afternoon of 6 August the group dispatched forty aircraft in an attack against the key bridge at Oissel, the last escape route for the enemy across the Seine River. In anticipation of attack the enemy had concentrated a large number of anticraft installations in this area. The withering barrage of fire which was thrown up took a toll of 3 Havocs destroyed and 26 damaged. Fighting through the intense resistance, with the wounded still at their posts, the flak ridden forma-

tion released the bombs with devastating effect upon the bridge. Maintenance crews worked feverishly to repair the battle damage, and on 8 August a full strength formation was dispatched to attack the railway junction at Frebent, France. Although two planes were shot down over the target area and eight were severely damaged the airmen demonstrated extraordinary skill and determination in destroying a large quantity of vitally needed enemy equipment and rolling stock. Both air and ground crews toiled ceaselessly to repair the crippled aircraft, and on the following day the group had launched two additional attacks, inflicting heavy damage on a German Radar establishment at Bois du Pierre and destroyed the enemy railroad bridge at Clauny, France. The aggressive flying tactics and courage displayed by the airmen in attacking these vital targets, and the determined efforts and technical skill exhibited by the ground personnel during this critical period of operations in Northern France distinguish the 416th Bombardment Group above others engaged in similar action, and are in keeping with the finest tradition of the Army Air Forces.

CHAPTER 8

September 1944 Missions
Move to Melun, France

September 1944 Missions

Expectations for the month of September were anxious ones, since we knew our group had to get closer to the action as the front lines were moving further and further into France and in an easterly direction. Flights from Wethersfield were getting beynd our comfortable range, and besides, we had been going through many preparations for movements,- and the inspections we underwent meant something, but in any event we were ready.

Some good news developed around the base. Sgt. A. W. Newkirk from the 668th squadron who had been reported as MIA, made his escape from a POW Camp and made his way to France. He, somehow, got to some French underground organizations and joined forces with them after establishing his identity as a former American flyer. Newkirk reported that in his exploits with the "Maquis" he is credited with killing six German soldiers and knocking out some gun emplacements.

Also, from the 669th squadron, Sgt. J. E. Ray, Lt. Palin, S/Sgt. Boyer and S/Sgt. J. D. Dugan, all of whom had been listed as MIA, were returned and sent back to the States. Also, it was learned that Major Murdock W.Campbell, S/Sgt. Peter P. Masiulewics, S/Sgt. Herbert E. Shatzer, and S/Sgt. James B. Thompson were all now POWs.

On September 24th, Technical Sergeant Richard L. Haptonstall, a crew chief, was removing an engine from a plane for an overhaul. The engine fell on him, crushing him, and he died with in a short time.

On September 1st, orders issued by the High Command, General Dwight D. Eisenhower that the port of Brest had to be bombed until they surrendered to Allied Forces. The Ninth Bomber Command took this to heart, besides, it was an order from "Ike" so they put the wheels in motion.

Mission #134 - 1 September - Brest stronghold. Wake up call was at 0400 with take off at 0730 with flights led by Captain Hulse and Lt.Conte, BN,- Major Napier and Lt. Jones. BN.,- Captain Cole and Lt. Basnett, BN, -Lts. Osborne and Forma, BN, and Captain McNulty and Lt. Burseil, BN. After a two hour flight to Brest, they found a complete cloud cover, so no bombing took place. No flak or fighters bothered the group.

After our group left the target area, four B-26 groups reached Brest and were able to drop their bombs with great results. These were not enough, since more flights were to be made there, we were told.

Another mission took off later that day, but were recalled when weather informed that clouds had still hidden the target of Brest.

Mission #135 - 3 September - AM -Brest Stronghold. Another early wake up call, with the group taking off at 0600 in total darkness. Major Willets and Lt.Royalty, BN led the formation. Captain Huff and Lt. Kupits, BN, - Captain Hulse and Lt.Conte, BN,- Captain McNulty and Lt. Burseil, BN, and Lts. DeMand and Burn BN. led flights. Lts. Bartmus and Hardy flew deputy. Again, clouds moved in as the 416th neared Brest, so they turned back without dropping. A few hours later, six IX Bomber Command groups were able to bomb the target with the clouds rolling away. They succeeded to practically demolish their aiming points.

Mission #136 - 3 September - PM - Brest Stronghold. Major Price and Lt. Hand, BN, and Captain McNulty and Lt.Burseil, BN led Boxes. Captain Peck and Lt. Madenfort, BN, - Lts. Greenley and Mitchell, BN and Lts.Adams and Hanlon, led flights. Trying to bomb by flights, only two flights were able to release their bombs, with only fair results due to poor visibility. The other flights returned with their bombs. It was surprising that such an important target did not call for heavy anti-aircraft guns. No damage was encountered by our planes. One full flight had to land in the south of England to refuel before getting back to Wethersfield.

Our targets in France were getting too far away from Wethersfield, so the move to the continent had to come pretty soon.

Mission #137 - 5 September - Brest Stronghold. Captain Hulse and Lt. Conte, BN and Captain Huff and Lt. Kupits, BN led boxes. Major Price and Lt. Hand, BN,- Captain Cole and Lt. Basnett, BN, -Captain Marzolf and Lt. Beck, BN, and Lts. Hand and Burns BN, led flights. The box leaders scored excellent bombing with their bombs destroying the building and causing severe damage to the strongpoint. The 416th Group were the first in over the target this day, followed by so many other groups, that one pilot quipped that they had to take numbers and get in line to bomb. A group of heavies came over the target right behind our group. Devastation was the word of the day for this target. Evidently all groups took "Ike" at his word to bomb until the Brest Port gave in. They're getting close to doing just that! Our flights scored either excellents or goods.

Mission #138 - 6 September - AM - Brest Stronghold. Another 0630 take-off for this group to be part of over 300 other planes to attack this place. Out of six flights of the 416th, five scored excellents, the only Ninth Bomber Command to score that well. Among the flight leaders were Captain Morton and Lt. Moore, BN,- Captain McNulty and Lt. Burseil, BN, -Major Price and Lt. Hand, BN,- Lts. DeMand and Burns, BN, and Lts. Adams and Hanlon, BN. Clear weather gave our bomb aimers a good read on the target and they showed their expertise.

Mission #139 - 6 September - PM - Brest Stronghold. The planes hadn't had time to cool off when they were refueled, re-armed and ready to go again within three hours of getting back to base. Weather closed in again, but the boys got down below the heavy cloud layer and bombed at about 2000 feet. Only three flights were able to drop their bombs. Captain Huff and Lt. Kupits, BN, leading a flight made six bomb runs on the target but gave up when they could not see the aiming point. Lts.Greene and Nichols, BN scored a "good" on their run, this being their first bombing mission as a team. Good for them! Major Willetts and Lt.Royalty, BN led the group in. Captain Marzolf and Lt. Beck, BN, -Lts. Bartmus and Hardy, BN led flights.

Lining up to hit buzz bomb sites. Bomb racks in front unloaded. Wethersfield, England 1944. 416th Bomb Group (L), 670th Squadron.

The STARS AND STRIPES daily newspaper of the armed forces, printed that an A-20 was missing after the afternoon mission at Brest. It developed that Lt. Merchant had taken a hit from the small arms fire and light flak at that low altitude. In about 1000 sorties our group made over Brest, this was the first downed aircraft.

This is a good story in itself. Lt. W.A. Merchant was flying in No. 3 slot in a flight when his right engine flamed out and a cylinder broke away. Merchant salvoed his bombs which landed in a farm area, pulling away from the formation. He gave the bail-out order to his gunners, S/Sgts. C. J. Harp and K. P. Brown. These gunners had flown 48 missions with Merchant. They were in plane No. 221 which had 86 white bombs painted on it, a real veteran of combat! The two gunners jumped and floated down, landing on a small peninsula. Merchant had feathered his disabled engine and headed toward Brest. The two gunners found each other and were picked up by some Artillery Soldiers. Sgt. Harp had sprained his ankle, having landed without his flying boots, losing them during his descent, causing him to hit the ground in bare feet. He received medical treatment and were put up in a chateau until the morning.

The next morning, they were taken to XII Army headquarters by jeep and then to Morlaix, a small town northeast of Brest. They saw an A-20 parked in the mud off a runway - it was their plane! A mechanic told them the pilot was okay and had walked away. His whereabouts were not known. The gunners hopped a ride on a C-47 and were returned to England.

Merchant's story went thusly:

> With the engine feathered, the fire died out. I was at about 1400 feet altitude, losing about 50 feet a minute and going 150 MPH, looking for a place to land. I spotted this little field, and approached it at 90 degrees, put down on the runway, hit the air bottle about 1/3 down, and both tires blew out. We kept going straight. When we stopped, I threw the hatch and jumped out, running away thinking it might blow. I managed to meet an American Red Cross girl who invited me to her mobile unit, where she fixed me a fried egg sandwich at 0130. The next morning I got to Gael and in an L4-B, but there was no transportation to get me out of there.

He got back to the French coast and hitched a ride on a C-47 to London.

Mission #140 - 10 September - Foret de Haye, near Nancy. General Patton was forging his way east toward Germany. Bomber Command ordered the 416th along with the 410th, a sister group, to pin point and demolish a strong point and ammunition depot. Five Medium bombers, B-26s, were assigned to area bomb around the targets we had. The A-20s were reported to have done more damage with their attacks than did the B-26 planes. Major Price and Lt. Hand, BN, and Captain Osborne and Lt. Forma, BN led boxes. Lt. Greenley and Lt. Mitchell, BN led a flight. Of the six flights dropping bombs, four of them scored excellents, which is one of the reasons the 416th is called upon regularly to hit finite targets. Not that we're proud or something!?! No opposition was met, No damage to aircraft was experienced.

Mission #141 - 11 September - St. Julian les Metz. This mission was pretty close to the Border of Germany, a communication center for the full sector of the battle front for the Germans. Captain Hulse and Lt. Conte, BN led Box I with Major Napier and Lt. Jones, leading Box II. Captain Osborne and Lt. Forma, BN,- Captain Wheeler and Lt. Arrington, BN, and Lts. DeMand and Burns, BN, led flights. Some light, accurate flak came up near the target, but not much damage was inflicted on our planes. Bombing scored two excellents, two "good" one fair, and one flight did not bomb due to haze over the target. Eight ships sustained flak hits, but all returned to base with no personal injuries.

Mission #142 - 12 September -AM - St. Wendel Marshalling Yard. For the first time, our group would be bombing in Germany, in front of the Siegfried line, 25 miles inside Germany. This gave the crews some internal excitement. Rather unexpectedly, no flak or fighters bothered the formation. The only thing detrimental to the success of the mission was weather closing in. Of six flights, only two were able to see and drop their bombs. Lt. Greene and Lt. Nichols, BN hit nearby marshalling yards. After making two bomb runs, Lts. Adams and Hanlon, BN could not drop due to cloud cover. All planes returned to base at 1200.

Mission #143 - 12 September - PM - Foret de Haye, West of Nancy. General George Patton was halted for a short time in his drive to Germany, and he called on some precision bombing by Attack Bombers to clear his path. Ninth Bomber Command called on the 416th and three B-26 groups to hit this German Artillery position. At 1550, our group took off after a short respite from the morning mission. Major Willetts and Lt. Royalty, BN led Box I and for the first time, Captain Wheeler and Lt.Arrington, BM were to lead the second Box. Captains Morton, and Peck,BN and Lt. Meagher and Lt. Burg, BN, led flights. Can you call this a perfect mission, or what, when six flights each score an "Excellent"? It appeared so, since a statement from GHQ news summary printed, "Ground units report the bombing of the 9th Bombardment Division on the Foret de Haye on 12 September was so effective that Germans in the area marched out with their hands in the air and surrended, American ground troops had to fire practically no shots to effect the surrender." Quite a success!

An interesting sidelight occured on this mission. Captain Wheeler, leading the second box, lost communication with his bombardier, Lt. Arrington. Arrington could talk to Wheeler, but Wheeler couldn't respond. They managed to understand each other by having Arrington talk, or ask questions, and Wheeler would blink the call light, with one blink meaning yes, and two blinks meaning no. With this innovative manner, they reached the Initial Point of the bomb run, dropped their bombs, with satisfactory results, and got back to base with no further problem. Hollywood?!?

Mission #144 - 14 September - Brest. Captain Osborne and Lt. Forma, BN leading Box I with Captain McNulty and Lt. Burseil, BN on Box II. Captain Cole and Lt. Basnett,BN led a flight. Thirty six aircraft made the "milk-run" to Brest, with no flak or fighters bothering the group. Reaching the target area, cloud cover prevented dropping bombs, so they returned to base. Crossing the channel toward England, planes were running low on petrol, having to get down below the overcast. Captain Cole got down to 300 feet altitude, Six planes had to set down on landing strips in Cherbourg to gas up. Lt. Gary landed on an air strip in the Cherbourg area. All got back to base safely. Lt. Downing lost oil pressure and had to land in Normandy, without problems.

Move To Melun, France

The order came down from headquarters to move the group to A-55 - Villa Rouche, Melun, France, 15 miles from Paris. One half of the group were scheduled to move on the 15th of September, very early, like at 0330. Trucks with crews and gear left Wethersfield at 0630 to reach Sybil Hedingham where a train waited, heading for Southampton, which was reached at 1430. The lush country side was interesting for the American boys to see and enjoy, giving English citizens, mainly the gals, the usual whistles and waves. Field rations - K- rations - were served during the trip. At Southampton, trucks awaited the troops for transportation to a marshalling area, all fenced in, with empty tents already standing. No hot meals, canned rations again - no running water, no wood for heating. The night was spent in cool circumstances, the next day and night were the same. No fires nor hot meals.

On 17 September, everybody had packed up and left for a two mile hike to dockside. For soldiers not accustomed to long hikes, this was an exhausting trip, but it was done. Marching through town, making friends and waving on the way, giving kids treats like gum and candy made the trip happy. Red Cross personnel greeted the boys before they boarded a ferry boat, the LADY OF MAN, with the usual tasty doughnuts, and hot coffee.

Everybody was on board by 1700 and made to find berths for overnight rest. Some entertainment was put on by our boys, and the gals from the Red Cross. In the 18th, the LADY OF MAN ferryboat slipped out and headed across the channel. At 1340 the ferry met and tied up with LSTs which took the troops to the beachhead, much as the ground warriors did on D-Day, 6 June. Unloading on shore, they treked across the Utah Beach, witnessing the devastation created on that great day, plus German pillboxes, and German Prisoners-of-War cleaning up the beaches, none of whom looked very happy. Some were just kids and others looked like old men to our 20 year olds.

Our boys hoisted their packs and began a march toward a bivouc area passing French homes, with French people not pay-ing much attention to our boys, they having witnessed enough in the past, we supposed.

The first bivouac area didn't seem to be just right, so everyone packed up again and after another two mile hike, fully loaded, found what they felt was better. So tents were pitched - in the dark - with rain falling. The pup tents at least kept the rain off their heads during the night. On 19 September, everyone loaded on to trucks for about another hour, rough ride, passing through Carenton, which was practically torn apart. German prisoners were working on roadways, and generally cleaning up debris. Other towns suffered the ravages of war, were observed during the truck ride. What could have been going through the minds of these young fellows, seeing the ravages of war, which they helped create, and wondering how the local citizenry could feel friendly toward those boys who create the devastation? This was war, and whomsever were the victors were welcome, but the underlying feeling of not having a home or town to go to, had to be uppermost in their minds. The convoy reached another selected bivouac area, four miles from Insigny, near the town of Catz, France.

On 20 September, orders barked to get ready to move out, so all packed up again to wait for transportation, which never came. The boys unpacked again, and found some squad tents unoccupied, which they took over. Again, no running water, slit trenches did their duty.

The 21st of September two trucks and trailers showed up; all personnel were packed in rather tightly to reach a simplified airfield where C-47s were parked. Troops were loaded on them, which took off and returned in about a half hour, losing no time to load and unload. The flight to the new permanent (?) base was about an hour and a quarter away, a recently Luftwaffe occupied airfield. Plenty of bombing ruts all around it, and on it. Waiting trucks took the boys to their squadron areas, where pup tents were again pitched. The next day, rain again greeted the awakening troops who fell in for roll-call, and work details. The Germans tried very hard to ruin everything in sight before they left. Civilian personnel, French, Polish, and some Italians started conversations with our troops. We learned that the Germans did indeed want to ruin everything, and when they took off, in whatever bombers and fighters they had left, they strafed and bombed the area with everything they could throw out. Booby traps, and land mines were everywhere, and extreme caution was necessary for everyone to think about, constantly.

The first building to be set up was the Mess Hall, where for the first time in over a week, a hot meal was served, and continued to be served, each lunch and dinner. Breakfast, too! Ten-member tents were erected as were "outhouses" and headquarters, medical facilities, etc.

While this was going on, getting this echelon of ground personnel situated, the war was still going on from Wethersfield.

Mission #145 - 16 September - Bergen op Zoom, Holland. This mission would help Allied troops block avenues of escape for German Forces, and we were called upon to bomb out a viaduct, a railroad, and a road over Bergen op Zoom. The Germans seemed to work to establish a fortress at Walcheren Island which would guard the entrance to Antwerp Harbor. Four other IX Airforce groups and the 416th were called upon to prevent this from happening. A B-26 Group and the 410th, A-20 Group went in first to bomb the dike at Arnemuiden which connected the Walcheren and the Zuid Beveland Isthmus. Our target was the Bath dike which connected the mainland and the isthmus.

It was a relatively short flight, but not without extreme danger, since, as we found out, barges and land guns protected these areas, with efficiency. The first box led by Captain Huff and Lt. Kupits, BN seemed to have been the center of attention of the anti-craft gunners, since they knocked out two of the six planes in that first flight of the first box, all 669th squadron planes. One plane went down over the target and one crash landed in France. Captain Morton led Box II with Lts. Greenley and

Mitchell, BN, Lts. Adams and Hanlon, BN, and Lts. DeMand and Burns, leading flights.

Lt. Vleghels took a direct hit on the bomb run. His gunners, S/Sgts. Rice and Young parachuted out and were seen dropping toward the shore line. Vleghel evidently drowned, as was determined from records uncovered by his step-daughter, Deborah Smith. When Vleghels did not return, his wife married, and Debby is the result of that marriage. Debby did an extensive research on the accident which took Lt. Vleghel, even obtaining a picture of his bier, and burying place. Debby contacted members of the 669th squadron and attended two re-unions the 416th group held in Kinston, NC and Hot Springs, AR to talk to members of the 669th and to learn as much as she could about missions, and the history of the squadron and the group. She is writing a book about this mission and other information about her mother's first husband, Vleghel.

Sgt Rice was listed as KIA and Sgt. Young listed as MIA.

The second ship of the 669th which was hit, piloted by Lt. Clark had an engine knocked out. He ordered his gunners to bail out, which they did succesfully, and he continued flying the plane southerly, crash landing near Caen, with no injury to himself.

The second box of this formation did not attract the attention of the flak gunners, so no damage became them. The bombing was successful, with Lt. Mitchell hitting the assigned target area, hitting a bridge and cutting a major highway.

This was the last mission flown from Wethersfield by the 416th. All the remaining troops in Wethersfield boarded trucks, then boats, and crews flew their planes to Melun, thankfully, all without mishap. Crews flew over the City of Paris, and right over and close to the Eiffel Tower. One gunner riding at the bottom open hatch of the A-20 tried to grab the flag which flew on top of the Tower as their plane flew over it at too close a range.

The move took place from 16 September, when the advance echelon left Wethersfield, and the rear echelons and air crews left on 23 September. The last echelon left Wethersfield on 27 September.

At Melun, all the squadrons were assigned areas of occupancy at the new airfield, and were given the chores of getting everything in ship-shape, as soon as possible. Ten men tents were erected by the occupants, with officers in tents at one end and enlisted personnel at the other end of the squadron sections. Alongside each tent, the occupants were required to dig and reinforce bomb shelters for obvious reasons. As time went on, each tent became more home like, with wooden platform floors, if enterprenours were able to scround enough material together. A big pot belly stove sat in the center of the tent, with the guys whose cots were close to center always were too hot, and those at the ends of the tent, wanted more heat, too cold to be comfortable. Who was going to guarantee anybody they were going to be comfortable in a war?

One main addition to the 669th squadron area was a hot shower installation. You cannot imagine what this meant to the squadron personnel and what a job it was to keep other squadron guys away from this luxury, with plenty of water, and hot at that! One pilot, Lt. Leo Poundstone, evidently had construction experience and he was able to round up an old bathtub, and lots of pipe to carry water, connecting up to a water supply, and found lots of wood to fire up for the water. The tub was mounted about eight feet overhead, and shower heads, and pull strings made things the best they could be under the circumstances. He had to rig up a safe and reliable fire place to heat the water overhead, and that didn't seem to be a problem. Mixing valves and controls made things just dandy!

Other parts of the abandoned base were explored as time permitted, being ever watchful for booby traps, land mines, or even live ammunition. One man found a cache of parachute bombs, with frag explosives at the leading edge. He thought he would retrieve the silk from the parachute section and send the goods to his wife to make silk blouses. He started to dissassemble the bomb, but incorrectly, started taking the live ammunition end apart first, when he was suddenluy stopped and reminded what he was getting close to, like hitting the striking pin of the bomb. Everything was delayed until better judgement abounded, and the silk was eventually retrieved without further incident. WHEW!

The airfield in itself was massive, requiring hours to make a car tour of the entire area. It enveloped a few towns. The Lufftwafte left many of their bombs at the plane revetments, and Nazi propoganda leaflets were everywhere.

All personnel were occupied putting up temporary buildings with whatever scrap lumber could be found, even taking down something that looked like a building, and reassembling it to house an operation of some kind, pup tents gave way to larger quarters, also tents, but ten men units. The remains of the Germans were cleared out little by little and the base became honorable.

September 26 saw the first mission from A-55 briefed, but it didn't get off due to inclement weather.

Mission #146 - 27 September - Foret de Parroy Fuel Depot. Major Dunn, the new 670th squadron commander led this first mission. Flight leaders included Lts. Meagher and Burg, BN, Lts. Bartmus and Hardy, BN, Lts. DeMand and Burns, BN. As the formation approached the target area, clouds moved in and no bomb runs were attempted. All returned to base, until the next time!

> Speaking about flying from an airfield in France, we must report that our new airfield previously occupied by the Lufftwafte for a long time, meant that some of the German aviators had to make friends with the French populace, whether in friendly circumstances or in enforced companionship. In any event, it was not very long after our planes began flying missions from that base A-55 in Melun, we had to return from missions in dusk or many times in darkness. As our formation

Nazi propaganda leaflet

Five questions for the American soldier:

1. Are you certain of finding a job if you have the good luck to get back to the States safe and sound from the war?
2. Won't the best jobs be held by those who were wiser than you and avoided taking part in the war?
3. What security have you for your existence if you come back from the war sick, wounded, minus a limb or even blinded?
4. Is your family sufficiently provided for if you are one of the many who will never see America again?
5. Are your savings secure against the inflation which is threatening the USA as a result of the absurdly high war loans, or will you and your family be reduced to beggars after the war?

Nazi propaganda leaflet

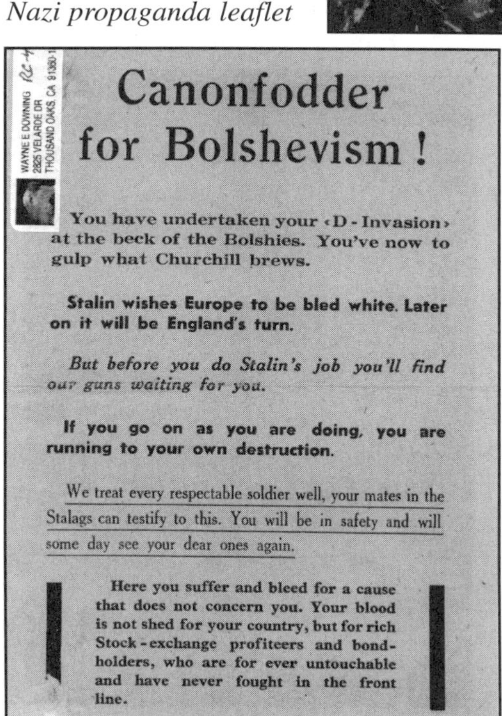

Canonfodder for Bolshevism !

You have undertaken your ‹D - Invasion› at the beck of the Bolshies. You've now to gulp what Churchill brews.

Stalin wishes Europe to be bled white. Later on it will be England's turn.

But before you do Stalin's job you'll find our guns waiting for you.

If you go on as you are doing, you are running to your own destruction.

We treat every respectable soldier well, your mates in the Stalags can testify to this. You will be in safety and will some day see your dear ones again.

Here you suffer and bleed for a cause that does not concern you. Your blood is not shed for your country, but for rich Stock - exchange profiteers and bond-holders, who are for ever untouchable and have never fought in the front line.

approached the field for landing, crews could see lights from windows in houses, covered by shades, and the shades would be raised and lowered, undoubtedly as some form of a signal to Germans who the people may have thought were returning to Melun. The signals were definitely not intended to be guiding lights for our returning flights from the front. So, we figured the collaborateurs were still trying to maintain their friendship with the former occupants of the airbase. To our knowledge, those providing the signals were not apprehended.

When the planes returned from their first trip toward the front, the group had the remainder of the day off, giving crew chiefs time to really examine their planes and do whatever maintenance was required. For the first night after the first mission, passes into town were available to those who could be spared from details and to whomever were entitled to them. Visiting local cafes, restaurants, and the French madamoiselles, was a treat for many boys. The town was a short ride from the base. Very quaint to visit, with many restful areas to enjoy. The citizens were friendly and receptive to Yanks. Bars were packed with GIs who started to learn what "voule vou" meant.

Mission #147 - 28 September - Foret de Parroy, near Nancy. Major Willetts and Lt.Royalty BN led Box I. Lts. Pair and Corum BN, Captain Marzolf and Lt. Beck BN, Captain Bartmus and Lt. Hardy BN led flights. Today, incidentally, Bartmus was made Captain, Congrats! Only one flight was able to drop their bombs, since clouds moved in hiding the target from the bombsights of other BNs. The bombing had to be carefully maneuvered since our Allied ground troops were in the vicinity of this area, and we could not risk dropping our bombs near them, so the BNs held their loads.

It was a thrill for crews to take off from an airfield on the continent to reach the front lines.

Mission #148 - 29 September - AM - Bitburg Marshalling Yard, Germany. Major Price with Lt. Hand, BN, led Box I with Captain Osborne and Lt.Forma,. BN on Box II. Lts. Adams and Hanlon BN, and Lts. Pair and Corum BN led flights. This target was well protected by anti-aircraft gunners, and manned by experts. At least eight gun emplacements were firing at the group, with shots hitting the planes as they formed up for the IP (Initial Point of the Bomb Run when all planes fly straight and level without evasive action). Lt. Nordstrom of the 670th squadron with gunners S/Sgts. Gossett and Miller, took a direct hit and the airplane exploded, breaking in half. Only one chute emerged, that of S/Sgt Gossett. Lt. Boukamp of the 669th squadron and his gunners were lost when their plane's both engines caught fire and glided away from the formation. His gunners, S/Sgts R. J. Colosimo and Joeng S. Wing got out and made POWs. Boukamp was lost. All other planes returned to base with flak shots, so no one escaped the fury of the gunners.

Mission #149 - 29 September - PM - Julich Marshalling Yard. These marshalling yard attacks were meant to prevent much needed ammo, equipment, and troops from reaching the front lines, and shoring up the Siegfried Line, designed to defend Germany from attack. The Germans must have felt these yards were important too, since they were very well defended by top gunners, as the 416th found out on this second mission of the day. Captain Huff and Lt. Kupits BN, and Major Napier with Lt. Jones BN led the boxes. Lts. Demand and Corum BN, Lts. Adams and Hanlon BN, Lts. Meagher and Burg BN, Lts. Anderson and Babbage BN, and Lt. Miracle and F/O McCartney BN and Captain Jackson and Lt. Maltby BN, led flights. Only 20 of the 36 planes got to drop their bombs due to weather closing in. Flak was severe, causing three planes to go down.

The bombardiers were instructed to drop their bombs one minute after passing over the aiming point in the event they could not see the primary target, which they did but the results were undetermined.

Captain Jackson from the 670th squadron had his plane pretty well shot up. His tunnel gunner, S/Sgt.W. J. Daniel received a direct hit on one leg, severing an artery, causing excessive bleeding. Jackson gunned his plane in an effort to get the injured man to medical care, but the bleeding was so profuse, and unstoppable, the young man died before the plane could land. This was the first crew member of the group to expire during a mission.

Lt. F. W. DeMand of the 671st squadron received a direct flak burst, and his flight dispersed amid air by the number of hits they received. DeMand got a direct hit to a gas tank, exploding it, causing his BN, A. C. Burns, and gunners, S/Sgts. R. J. Troyer and C. W. Middleton to go down. Lt. R. W.York with gunners S/Sgts.L. A. Ashton and H. J. Wilds and Lt. R. C. Morehouse and gunners, S/Sgts. L. A. Zygiel and A. J. Burgess, all went down. Lts. Greenley and Mitchell, BN, were leading one of the flights. This was, indeed, one of the costliest missions for the group with so many losses. Five planes and crews were lost, and one fatality makes for a serious loss to the group.

The last word in fast light bombers, the new A-26 planes arrived at our group today. They will begin training flights for indoctrination with check outs being conducted with the pilots who had experience in them, who led the new planes to Melun.Those A-26 pilots will become members of the 416th Group. For a period, the glass nosed A-20s will lead all flights, with the A-26 planes forming up the remaining five planes of the flights.

The A-26 "gun" ships had forward firing 50 caliber guns, 16 of them, with two more in the top turret being capable of firing forward. These planes were designed to drop bombs at higher altitudes, and be able to go down to strafe targets, much the same as the A-20s were designed to do, but never got around to it. There is no question in the minds of the pilots that the strafing missions would be a thing of the future. The speed of the planes and the increased bomb load capabilities make these zippy units a thing of envy .

670th members. Melun, France 1944.
L. to R. Donald J. Reichert, Flight Surgeon,
William E. Brewer, BN, Theron S. Merritt, Pilot

Living Quarters
Melun, France 1944

CHAPTER 9

October-November 1944
Transition Time, November 1944

October-November, 1944

The transition training of pilots and Bombardier-Navigators for the shiny aluminum A-26s continued, with all crews anxious to get into them and fly missions. The lack of glass nosed, - Model C - A-26s were not available yet, so as stated, A-20 glass nosed planes would carry the BNs to missions, with the A-26 gun ships behind them in flight formations. Speed was increased and the tripled bomb load of the 26s over the A-20s made these planes the desire of pilots and BNs. However, since the A-20 still had not expanded their range of operation, the type of missions flown had to co-incide with that lead plane's ability.

Mission #150 - 2 October - Urbach area, close to Aachen. After three attempts on bomb runs to hit this target, all planes had to return to base with their bombs still shackled up..Flight leaders included Captain Cole and Lt. Basnett BN, Captain Bartmus and Lt. Hardy BN, and Captain Osborne and Lt. Forma, BN. This had to be an important target since four different Ninth Bombardment Groups were assigned to destroy it, but it didn't happen due to cloud cover. Air crews felt they were not doing what they were capable of doing in helping ground forces advance on German positions, all related to weather.

Mission #151 - 3 October - Duren Marshalling Yard. Major Willetts and Lt. Royalty BN led this formation with Captain Cole and Lt. Basnett BN on the second box. Lt. Pair and Lt. Corum BN, flew as deputy. Flight leaders included Lts. Meagher and Burg, BN, and Lt. Miracle and F/O McCartney, a new BN. It was a three hour flight with no interference from fighters or flak, but again, no bombs were dropped due to cloud cover. When is the sun going to shine again so we can help those foot sloggers in rain and mud, do their jobs better? Lt. Pair, who flew deputy to Major Willetts, left the formation and went down to 6000 feet to determine if the cloud cover would lighten up, but since it didn't he again joined the formation and they all returned to base, loaded with bombs once more.

On 3 October the Associated Press reported

> NINTH AIR FORCE ALL ON CONTINENT.
>
> All planes of the American Ninth Air Force largest tactical Air Force in the World, are operating now from bases on the Continent, it was disclosed today.
>
> Marauder, medium bombers, some of the last to be shifted from England, are included in the Ninth Air Force, along with Havoc dive bombers, fighter bombers, Black Widow night fighters, and Mustang, Lightning and Thunderbolt fighters.
>
> Flying their first operation from the continent fields exclusively, Marauders and Havocs joined fighter bombers yesterday in attacking German strong points ahead of the new push by the American First Army.
>
> The tremendous job of moving was accomplished with a minimum loss of operational time. Most of the ground personnel and all heavy equipment crossed the channel in LSTS. Skeleton crews remained behind to help with the last missions from English bases.
>
> Airstrips constructed early in the invasion now are far behind the front. Most bombers and fighters are operating from French airfields captured from the Germans, although facilities are limited by bombings which some of the present airmen administered.

Ninth Bomber Divison Headquarters issued a statement that in the September offensive, Marauders and Havocs had flown over 1300 sorties over Germany, bombing in close support of Allied Ground Forces. September 12th was the first time medium and light bombers flew against the heavily defended Siegfried Line defenses It was the first time these bombers crossed the German border's aerial frontier and dropped bombs on German soil. Enemy damage to the enemy's tank traps resulted.

The Ninth Bombardment Divison attacked the heavily defended and difficult to capture, Brest, taking eight straight days of bombardment by B-26s and A-20s to permit Allied forces to take this strong point. The post surrendered the later part of the month of September. General Eisenhower had issued orders to "keep bombing until its garrison surrenders." We did our part!

Mission (none) 5 October - Duren Marshalling Yard. The formation took off and flew for about an hour, but were recalled due to the usual inclement weather. No bombing today.

Mission #152 - 6 October - Duren Marshalling Yard. Major Price and Lt. Hand, BN and Captain Osborne with Lt. Forma, BN led boxes. Lts.Adams,- Hanlon, BN, Lts. Pair and Corum,. BN, and Lts. Greeley and Mitchell, BN, Captain Peck and Lt. Madenfort, BN, led flights. This important target assisted Lt.General Hodges' troops gain possession of an extensive marshalling area for Germans, readying troops and ammo to reach front lines. Cutting off those supplies helped Hodges do their job. Flak met the group, causing extensive damage to some planes. Window strips helped the higher flying flights, but as the strips floated down they assumed the altitude of the following lower flying boys, our groups, so they suffered the hits from moderate flak. Bombing results rated from excellent to fair, with one flight not dropping due to the bombsight gyro tilting in the wrong direction.

Mission #153 - 7 October - Trier Supply Dump. Captain Huff and Lt. Kupits BN and Captain Morton and Lt. Moore, BN led boxes. Flight leaders included Lts. Meagher and Burg, BN, Captain Marzolf and Lt. Beck, BN, Lts. Pair and Corum, BN.

Flak met the boys over the target, causing one plane piloted by Lt. Saidla with gunners Sgts. Cavanaugh and Harris to go down. Three chutes blossomed with the crews ultimately reported as POWs and released after the war ended. Bombing results were scored as excellent for a majority of the flights. Two flights overshot the target due to incorrect operation of the bombsights. Their bombs did considerable damage where they fell, wiping out bridges and buildings bordering the marshalling yard. Brigadier General Backus from 97 Bomb Wing flew with our group on this trip.

Mission #154 - 8 October - Linnich Town. The intent of this mission was to block travel through it to battle areas for the enemy and we were called upon to saturate bomb the major roadways through it. Major Dunn led Box I. Other flights were led by Captain Bartmus and Lt. Hardy, BN, Lts. Meagher and Burg, BN, and Lts. Greeley and Mitchell, BN plus Major Napier and Lt. Jones, BN. Results were recorded as excellent for the first flight bombs. Other flights had trouble picking up the aiming point due to haze and managed to drop their bombs effectively outside the main target, following previous instructions to bomb German territory if there were reasons to not bomb the aiming point. Light inaccurate flak came up, but you could not get Lt. Kreh and his gunners Sgts Shelton and Schenck to say that it was inaccurate. They took a direct hit, causing Kreh to nurture the plane as best he could, about ten minutes away from the target, when he had to crash land it 18 miles north of Reims, doing a good job by not hurting himself or the two gunners. They were picked up and returned to base. The plane was washed out.

Continuous rain for the next few days kept planes grounded. Personnel were assigned to"policing" work around the base and general cleanup. Many new crew members reported to the 416th, since a few original crews were nearing the magic “65” missions and back to the States category.

The 670th squadron was placed on "training" status for conversion to A-26 planes and transition They were non-operational for a few days.

Mission #155 - 12 October - Langerwehe town. This was another town categorized as a key transportation center in the way of advancing Allied troops heading toward Aachen. Major Willetts and Lt.Royalty BN,, Captain Cole and Lt. Basnett, BN, led the boxes. Lts. Meagher and Burg, BN. and Captain Osborne and Lt.Forma BN managed to hit the target, the only two flights able to bomb. Other flights flew over cloud cover and were unable to view the aiming point.

Mission #156 - 13 October - Langerwehe town again. Since cloud cover prevented bombing of all flights yesterday, this was another try and weather cooperated. Major Price and Lt. Hand, BN with Captain Osborne and Lt. Forma, BN leading boxes. Captain Wheeler and Lt.Arrington, BN, plus Lts. Pair and Corum, BN, and Lts Greene and Nichols BN, Captain Huff and Lt. Kupits, BN led flights. Bombing was successful with excellents being scored. The enemy had 12 gun emplacements around this area but all planes returned without damage.

Mission #157 - 14 October - Mayen Railroad Bridge. This bridge permitted German troops to cross the river toward Aachen, and it had to be taken out. Weather prevented that from happening, again. Captain Prentiss and Lt. Burseil, BN, Captain Bartmus and Lt. Hardy, BN, Lts. Greeley and Mitchell, BN, and Lts. Pair and Corum, BN led flights. No enemy action, so all planes returned to base safely.

A training mission of six planes from the 671st squadron resulted in tragedy for some, since they inadvertently flew over Dunkirk on a training mission. This area was held by the Germans yet and they let the planes overhead know it. Six relatively new pilots and one new bombardier-navigator were being trained by Lt. Royalty, a seasoned BN. Lt. J.J. Lackovich would be flying with Lt. E. C. Francis as a new BN. Approaching Dunkirk, the gunners let go, hitting Lt. G. L. Milhorn, in No. 6 slot of the six plane flight. An engine caught fire and the pilot lost altitude fast. The two gunners, Sgt. D. Chest and Cpl. W. J. Doran bailed out. Before starting back to base, the formation checked the spot where the plane was seen, aflame, alongside a road. Other pilots of the flight thought that the pilot did not make it. A few days later Captain Shaefer and Captain Moore flew to an airfield close to where Milhorn's plane went down to gather information about the crash and find out where Milhorn's body might be. They met Lt. Milhorn there slightly injured with burn scars on his face and neck. Milhorn related that when he saw his engine on fire, he instructed the gunners to go, and he straightened the plane up. The fire in the bomb bay was getting worse, so he pulled the emergency hatch release but it didn't work. He knocked the hatch off and stood up, facing the tail of the ship, and the slip stream took him back, fortunately, clearing the vertical stabilizer tail piece. He was at about 4000 feet, parachuted down and met up with his two gunners, who landed about five miles from his landing spot. French people picked them up, took them to an RAF field, where they received exceptional treatment. Sgt. Chest and Lt. Milhorn returned to our base. Cpl. Doran had to be hospitalized due to flak injury to his leg.

If this was training, what would combat be like?

On October 15, newly arrived pilots were being trained for combat mission flights. The 670th Squadron had a flight of six up for formation flying, when bad weather closed in. Pilot, Lieutenant Samuel P. Leishman with gunners Sgts. Eugene Shempren and Joseph Siracusa lost their lives trying to get under the cloud bank. His plane was in a thirty degree dive and struck a large tree on top of a hill, wiping out the plane and crew.

One plane piloted by Lt. Sheley lost his position in the flight and became disoriented. He tried to find an airfield to land. He saw an open field and went in. His nose wheel twisted when it hit a bump in the field, badly damaging the plane. The crew escaped unhurt.

Captain Dunn, leading the training flight landed near Paris and another made it to Brussels. Others made it to England safely.

Mission #158 - 17 October - Trier Railroad Bridge. After three days of rain, this mission took off but cloud cover required PFF Pathfinder leading the formation. Major Willetts and Lt. Royalty, BN led our group. Lts. Meagher and Burg, BN, Captain Cole and Lt. Basnett, BN and Lt. Miracle with F/O McCartney, BN led flights. No reason was given, but the B-26 PFF planes did not drop their bombs, nor did our group, returning to base, loaded as heavily as they went up, less the gas used.

No further missions would be flown until all pilots had completed transition flying in the new A-26 planes provided for our group, we being the first one to fly them in combat in Europe as a group.

Transition Time
November 1944

The arrival of the sleek, aluminum shiny A-26s with a training crew in a mobile trailer made for exciting times among crew members, crew chiefs, and mechanics. The 416th were to be the first group to fly these zippy attack bombers in combat. Training and transition had to take place, with perhaps only four A-26s available, the squadrons had to switch them around and schedule the crews for familiarization of the new planes.

During October, the 670th squadron were placed on stand-down while as many of their crews as possible trained on the A-26s. Gunners had to learn new mechanical procedures to operate the turret guns. Bombardier-Navigators and pilots had to learn a few new tactics also. Pilots would have to be aware that with wider cockpits, for a "co-Pilot" seat next to them, (although there were no controls there), meant their visibility to the right changed from the single compartment of the A-20. That meant, keeping in tight formations might be a little more difficult, but certainly possible. The speed increased a little from the Havocs, and the bomb load practically tripled, so weight in take-off and landing, made a little difference, also.

With each squadron taking turns flying with the small number of planes available, it appeared the group would be ready for missions by the middle of November. More new planes kept coming in, with our pilots flying the comfortable A-20s to England, and returning with the A-26s, weather permitting, of course. Glass nosed Invaders were not available in quantity yet, so the A-20 J and Ks still were used to lead flights of A-26 gun ships.

Eventually, the A-26 Cs did show up and all squadrons were so equipped.

The 26 Cs had more spacious accommodations for the Bombardier-Navigators to operate in, so a new technique was initiated, by having two such men fly in the nose, with one being responsible to do the navigation, and the other to manipulate the bomb sight. While this split the responsibility, it seemed to the most seasoned BNs that their skills and abilities were being questioned, but being good soldiers, they accepted their roles and went on to battle.

During the month of October, an A-20 of the 670th Squadron, #224 -was the first such plane to complete 100 combat missions without ever having to abort a mission due to mechanical failure of any type. The plane had flown the Group's first combat mission on 3 March and the engines which powered the plane then, still carried the crews on its 100th mission. The plane carried the identification on the nose as MISS LAID.

The Crew Chief who nurtured this plane, Technical Sergeant Royal S. Everts, was honored with a medal, and accompanied the pilot, Lt. Hugh Monroe and his two gunners, Sgts. Risko and Kidd to a ceremony in Paris where the unity of the French Government and the Allied Forces was performed. The name MISS LAID would hardly be appropriate for this impressive ceremony before dignitaries of both governments, so the plane was renamed "LA FRANCE LIBRE." Ninth Air Force Chief of Staff, Brigadier General Strahm dedicated the future missions of the plane to the new French Government. General Martial Valin, French Air Force Commanding General, and Charles Tillon, French Minister of Air for France accepted the dedication for the French Government. MME Monique Rolland, the beautiful French Actress christened the A-20, LA FRANCE LIBRE. Representing the Ninth Air Command were General Duncan and General Backus. The Group's C.O., Colonel Aylesworth attended

Lt. Monroe had flown almost all of his 65 combat missions on the plane, as did his two gunners.

A new combat crew was assigned to the 671 squadron on 8 November, consisting of 2nd Lt. R. C. Miles, pilot with 2nd Lt. W. G. Kelley, BN and gunners Morrissy and Pepe. On their first transition flight of A-26s, the plane was seen coming out of an overcast upside down and in a spin, crashing. All four crew members died on 11 November. One of the gunners had bailed out but evidently did not attach his parachute properly, dropping him without opening.

Mission #159 - 17 November - Haguenau Supply Depot. The first mission with 28 A-26 gun ships, led in flights of six by A-20s. Captain Huff and Lt. Kupits, BN and Captain Hulse and Lt. Conte, BN led boxes. Captain Wheeler and Lt. Arrington, BN and Captain Cole and Lt. Basnett, BN led flights. Kupits and Conte scored excellents on their bombing. Others scored fair and two as unsatisfactory Weather was closing in and the formation went down to 8000 feet to make their bomb run. The newness of the A-26 planes for the pilots resulted in other than a tight formation, they not being accustomed to the vision from the wider cockpit, causing apprehension on getting too close to their formation partners. Practice will make things better as time goes on.

Mission #160 - 18 November - Breisach Railroad Bridge. Lt. Col. Willetts and Lt.Royalty BN led Box I with Captain Wheeler and Lt. Arrington, BN on Box II. Captain Peck and Lt. Madenfort, BN, Captain Osborne and Lt. Forma, BN and Lts. Lackovich and Francis, BN led flights. Results were excellent for the two box leaders as well as for two of the other flight leaders. No enemy fighters or flak were encountered.

Mission #161 - 19 November - Merzig Troop Concentration. Three boxes were assigned this important target to open the way for ground forces to advance. The results were excellent, with commendations received from Commmanding General of the XIX TAC Corps and General Anderson of Ninth Bomber Command, congratulating the group for its assistance in ground troop advances. Major Price and Lt. Hand, BN and Captain Osborne with Lt.Forma BN and Captain Hulse with Lt. Conte, BN led the boxes. Conte had to make three runs at the target due to cloud cover, but finally zeroed in on the aiming point, as did the other BNs. Lts. Pair and Corum BN and Captain Cole and Lt. Basnett, BN led flights successfully. No flak or fighters bothered the group, making this a “milk-run.”

Lieutenant General Patton wrote a congratulatory letter to Ninth Air Force, as follows:

> The splendid bombing on the German Town of Merzig on the morning of November 19 by over 160 medium bombers of your command is producing excellent results. This bombing, coupled with your afternoon effort on the ordnance depot at Pirmasens, I am certain will materially assist this Army in cracking the Siegfried Line and defeating the German Nation.
>
> The willingness of your airmen to go in against heavily defended targets is an inspiration to this Army.
>
> For all of the officers and men of the 3rd USARMY, I wish to express to you our admiration for your magnificient efforts and we express our appreciation for your cooperation.

This letter was endorsed by Lieutenant General Bradley, Major General Vandenberg, Commanding General of the Ninth AirForce, and Major General Anderson wrote:

> It is a great pleasure for me to add to the above message my own commendation to each combat crew and all ground personnel who have in any way contributed to this offensive for their courage, loyalty and efficient performance in a most hazardous task.

Mission #162 - 19 November -PM - Landau Airdrome. Captain Huff and Lt. Kupits, BN and Captain Peck and Lt. Madenfort BN, led boxes. Lts. Greenley and Mitchell, BN, Captain Bartmus and Lt. Hardy, BN and Lts. Meagher and Burg, BN led flights. A heavy cloud bank moved in over the target causing all planes to return to base, loaded. The formation made three attempts to drop their bombs, but the clouds did not part long enough for the BNs to zero their bombsights in on the aiming point. Captain Bartmus and Lt. "Gus" Ebenstein got reprieved from future missions, since this was their 65th, and thankfully, it was another "Milk-Run?" This was the second mission of the day with some of the crews not being able to grab dinner between flights. The usual experienced and helpful crew chiefs and their mechanics, along with armament and engineering, were able to re-load and refuel the planes to take on this hurried second trip. With the intense overcast which moved in, the flights dispersed and required some of them to land at bases other than the home base. Fortunately, this was done with no losses or mishaps.

Mission #163 - 29 November - Mariamweiler. Captain Hulse and Lt. Conte, BN led Box I. Flight leaders were Captain Osborne and Lt. Forma, BN and Captain Prentiss and Lt. Burseil, BN, and Lts. Pair and Corum, BN. Modern and intense flak en route and Moderate over the target caused damage to many planes. Lt. McBride of the 670th received a direct hit over the target, exploding the plane. The gunner, S/Sgt. Eutsler and McBride managed to bail out and land in friendly territory. The plane went down aflame as a total loss.

Due to the transition training of pilots and bombardier-navigators and gunners, to the new A-26s, in combination with lousy weather, only five missions were flown in November. On A-26s, there is only one gunner on each plane

Chapter 10

December 1944 Missions
Ninth Bomber Division Press Release

December 1944 Missions

Mission #164 - 2 December - Saarlautern,Germany. Lt. Col. Willetts, and Lt. Royalty, BN led Box I - Captain Marzolf and Lt. Beck took over Box II. Captain Meagher and Lt. Burg BN, flew deputy to Box I. Lts. Miracle and McCartney, BN led a flight. Heavy cloud cover required bombing with PFF help. Up to the target area, it was considered a Milk Run, but the skies opened up with accurate heavy flak, causing damage to 21 aircraft. Bombing was rated Superior for one flight, dropping their load within 1000 feet of the main aiming point. This mission was one in which other IX Bomber Command Marauders, and Havocs were called upon to hinder German Forces from amassing troops and equipment. Anti-tank positions, gun emplacements, and dug in tanks were aiming at advancing allied forces. The area bombing technique worked very well, helping Patton's boys advance. One of the flights released their bombs prematurely due to a malfunction.

This mission is one that a then 22 year old pilot said he would never forget.

> Joe Meagher, flying deputy to a Box leader, approaching the target felt a burst of flak lifting his plane, an A-20K, up 15 feet, when he felt a numbing sensation on his right ankle. His manifold pressure went to zero on his right engine. He turned right out of the formation, feathering his dead engine and noticing his left engine smoking. He quickly enumerated six decisions he knew he would have to contend with including
>
> 1. having his crew bail out to safety
> 2. try to make it to friendly territory and bail out himself
> 3. stay with the plane and belly in

4. (his intercom was out so he could not communicate with his crew}

5. Fly the damaged ship to safety with a painful injury

He decided to go down under the overcast and look for a flat spot to belly in "What about my bombardier, up in the nose of the ship? He doesn't have much protection. I can't talk to my crew."

He trimmed up and started through the clouds, 240 MPH with one engine smoking

He got down to 800 feet, skipped hedgerows, and God answering his prayers, gave him a flat surface being worked on by Caterpillar tractors. He knew he was in friendly territory, he thought, because Germans don't use yellow Cats. He buzzed the field 20 feet over the tractors, hoping they would pull the tractors off the flat surface. He pulled up into the clouds and dropped the plane nose sharply to force the wheels down since hydraulics were out. He heard the THUG and felt he was safe going in. On landing, and coming to a screeching halt, everybody scrambled out of the plane. Gunner McCreary gave Meagher a shot of morphine to ease the pain. His ankle was broken, requiring an eight month hospital stay. His BN, Burg was assigned to another pilot, Lt. Miracle, both of whom were shot down on Christmas Day during the Battle of the Bulge. Meagher says his prayers to God were answered for his crew.

This was Captain Meagher's 65th mission, along with his gunner, McCreary. On this mission, Lt. Renth,West Pointer, was knocked out of the formation, but he managed to land without injury to himself or his gunners. His plane was last seen going down, rapidly - from the formation.

December 3rd and 4th were "rain" days, with no missions. Lt. Miracle received his Captain bars. Lts H.D.Andrews and R. H. Smith, W. E. Downing, completed their 65th missions. But, ironically, it seems, the 65th missions are sometimes shakey. Lt. Andrews had his plane's rudder seriously damaged by flak bursts, but he was able to coax his way to safety. Downing signed up for a second tour and was transferred to the 670th squadron. New pilots keep coming in to replace those of the original group who are completing their tours and leaving for stateside rest and re-assignments. West Point Graduate, Richard V. Miracle received his promotion to Captain.

On December 1, Lt. Vernon Powell, the No. 1 Bombardier of the group was assigned as Group Bombardier-Navigator, transferring from the 670th Squadron to Group HDQS.

Mission #165 - 5 December - Kall, Germany. Another cloudy overcast mission resulting in PFF bombing by flights led by Captain Osborne, with Lt.Forma, BN. Other flights were led by Captain Prentiss with Lt. Burseil, BN,- Lts. Brown and Kerns, BN and Lts. Pair and Corum, BN. Flying window was Captain Cole with Lt. Basnett, BN. Bombing was rated as good in adverse bombing conditions, flying over 13,000 feet altitude on this rigid cloudy, cold day. No flak or fighters were seen.

Mission #166 - 6 December - Erkelenz, Germany. Pathfinder B-26s had to lead the boxes due to cloud cover, which is becoming an everyday occurrence, but bombs were dropped anyway with unobserved results. Flights were led by Captain Hulse and Lt. Conte, BN, - Lts. Brown and Kerns, BN,- Lts. Buskirk and Hanna, BN and Lt.Stanley with F/O Blount, BN. Bombing was at 13,000 feet - no flak or fighters bothered the group. Captain Cole of the 671st squadron wound up his 65th mission by flying a window dropping ship. S/Sgt. Horace Wellin, also of the 671st flew his 65th mission today.

Sometimes its difficult to understand everything that goes on. New pilots were being transferred to our group and some pilots were leaving the 416th to go to the 410th group.

The STARS AND STRIPES carried an item in their 8 December issue about the newest addition to our group, the A-26, and repeating Lt. McGlohn's description as it being "a dream ship."

Mission #167 - 8 December - Sinzig Railroad Bridge. Major Dunn and Lt. Maltby, BN, led Box I and Captain Atkinson with Lt. Ackerson, BN on Box II. Flights were led by Lts. Anderson and Babbage, BN, - Lts. Buskirk and Hanna, BN, plus Lts. Brown and Kerns, BN. A new bomb dropping technique was being introduced, called GEE equipment. This uses coordinates of geographic dimensions to line up the bombsight pointers together, when bombing through cloud layers. It appears successful and will be used on future bombing missions. No flak or fighters were encountered on this mission. On the way back, however, flak greeted the formation as it was descending from the 13,000 foot bombing altitude. One plane was hit and had its engine knocked out, but the pilot Lt. Grunig, made it back okay.

Mission #168 - 9 December - AM -Saarwellengen Supply Depot. This area was well equipped with heavy artillery and means to deter any Allied Forces, situated a little over a mile away, from advancing. Unfortunately, a heavy cloud cover prevented eye contact with the target, so bombing was done by PFF Pathfinders. The weather was extremely cold, with some icing forming on our planes, interfering with flying under ideal conditions. Not long after our formation took off from A-55, an armada of heavies flew over our base on the way to Germany. The temperature up there must have been well below zero temperature, since condensation trails followed the big boys, in an illustrious pattern against the blue sky. A treat to see, but the German flak gunners could also see them and gave a good aiming point for their experienced men to cut their fuses with accuracy. The formation of heavies was so great, it took over 20 minutes for all the planes to pass overhead. On our mission our bombers let their bombs go through clouds, with unobserved results. Lt. Col.

Willetts and Lt. Royalty BN led this mission with Captain Marzolf and Lt. Beck, BN leading a flight.

Mission #169 - 9 December - PM - Dilsburg. A heavily defended village - Take off was at 1400 in what looked like turbulent clouds. Captain Osborne, on his 65th mission, with Lt.Forma, BN led Box I. Captain Prentiss and Lt. Burseil led Box II. The cloud cover required PFF Pathfinders to lead us in, but an undetermined problem developed and no bombs were dropped. No enemy action greeted the group. All returned safely, landing after dark.

Adverse weather prevented missions for the next two days. However, on 11 December a group of Congressmen and women of the House Military Affairs Committee visited our base. Either the bad weather or other more important assignments awaited them, because they didn't even get out of their cars, but sped through our compound. Their mission was to determine problems any of our soldiers were experiencing, and with the idea of improving conditions. We hope they found ways to make war better.

More and more of our original crews were being sent back to the states after completing their 65 missions. Replacements were coming in just as fast. These new boys were well trained and really eager to do a good job. Some of the A-26 transition training crews were assigned to the 416th as permanent members. Lt. Claude Brown and Lt. John Buskirk with BN Lt. Hanna became attached to the 671st squadron. Lt. Jim Kerns was assigned as BN to Lt. Brown and they made up a great team, eventually leading missions.

Three BNs from the 671st squadron were transferred to the 410th Bomb Group, including Lts. Francis, Mitchell and Hansen. Captain Wheeler and Lt.Arrington, his BN, were sent up to the front lines to help evaluate the type of targets each of the heavy, medium or light bombers could better attack. Wheeler was given the task of explaining how missions were planned and executed.

Mission #170 - 12 December - Schleiden, Germany. Uncertain weather delayed take off until noon with our planes following the B-26 Pathfinders. Trouble again took over with the PFF equipment, preventing the group from dropping their bombs. Flights were led by Lts. Mish and Shaft, BN, Lts. Brown and Kerns, BN, and Lts. Buskirk and Hanna, BN. Lts. Anderson with Babbage, BN, leading a flight, had to return to base after flying for about 45 minutes, since their nose wheel did not retract. When he got over the field, he snapped the plane nose up and down a few times to ensure it would not collapse, locking it in place. The touch-down was made with no further problems. No battle damage was incurred for the formation and all returned to base safely.

The Ninth Bombardment Division Inspector General paid a visit to our group on 13 December. A complete administrative inspection took place, resulting in a superior rating being posted.

Mission #171 - 13 December - Germund, Germany. Major Dunn and Lt. Maltby, BN led Box I with Captain Harrold and Lt. Brewer, BN leading Box II. Other flights led by Lts. Buskirk and Hanna, BN,- Lts. Mish and Shaft, BN, - Lts. Stanley and Blount, BN - Lts. Miracle and McCartney, BN. Another snafu on the PFF equipment prevented our group from dropping on the primary target. The Pathfinders turned to Blankenheim as a secondary target and dropped on GEE technique. The second box picked the village of Schultz to hit, with success. No enemy action deterred the missions.

Mission #172 - 15 December - Heimbach, Germany. Lt.Col. Willetts and Lt. Royalty, BN with Captain Marzolf and Lt. Beck, BN leading boxes. Lts. Miracle and McCartney BN and Lts., Stanley and Blount, BN led flights. Another bombing through clouds with no results determined. No interference from flak or fighters, either.

The surprise attack by German forces against St. Vith, Malmedy, and Bastogne started on 16 December and the weather closed in, preventing allied planes from taking off to assist ground troops. Even our base received an alert, causing a doubling of the guards, and all personnel being armed. Rumors of enemy paratroopers being dropped near our base persisted, causing itchy fingers on our guards, causing them to shoot at any shadow, or whatever moved. German planes were droning overhead, and we got to wonder how and why they could fly and we couldn't. Our crews were ever so anxious to get up in the air to drop frags on enemy concentrations, but weather kept all planes grounded.

On 20 December we were routed out of bed at 0400 with the information that enemy were close to attack our base by paratroopers. Guards were multiplied, and on extreme alert. Our luck held out and no problems developed.

Mission #173 - 23 December -AM - Saarburg Bridge. The enemy were using this bridge to get their tanks, ammo and troops near our forces, so it had to be taken out. Weather was clear enough for the bombardiers to get a good sighting on the target. Bombing results were two superiors, three excellents, Major Price and Lt. Hand, BN leading Box I could not pick up the target and did not bomb on their first run. Captain Prentiss and Lt. Burseil, BN leading Box II dropped right down the pickle barrel, as the saying goes, rating a superior, since all the planes were in tight enough to blanket the bridge. Other flight leaders were, Lts. Buskirk and Hanna, BN- Lts. Pair and Corum, BN.. Major Price and Lt. Hand BN made a second run on the target, scoring one of the excellent ratings. No enemy counterfire or fighters threatened the group.

Mission #174 - 23 December - PM - Waxweiler Marshalling Yard. Captain Morton and Lt. Moore, BN of the 669th squadron were assigned to lead Box I, with Captain Hulse and Lt. Conte, BN to lead Box II. Moore was being indoctrinated to become a box leader and the assignment was for Lt. Conte to take over in the event Lt. Moore got in trouble. Other flight leaders were Lts. Miracle and Burg, BN, Lts. Greeley and Basnett, BN, Lts. Brown and Kerns, BN, Lts. Lackovich and Muir,BN, and Lts. Estes and Hlivko, BN

When Box I approached the Initial Point, they took off in the wrong direction, toward a marshalling yard being held by allied forces. Conte tried to contact Moore to have him bring his box behind Box II but Moore kept going, dropping his bombs on our equipment and gasoline supply. It happened to be some of General Patton's gas for his tanks.

Conte turned his box toward the assigned target, blanketing it . He then got Box I to fall in behind his, and they returned to base.

On the way to de-briefing, Major Napier summoned Conte and Hulse into his tent. Napier was on the phone with General Backus of the IX Bomber Command and said that Backus wanted to talk to Conte. Backus wanted to know what happened up there. Conte explained he saw Moore going off- target, so turned his box toward the assigned one and dropped. Backus tore a little into Conte for breaking formation, but then congratulated him for doing the right thing. General Backus told Conte he was coming to our squadron in a few days and wanted Conte to navigate a mission with him. This was done on 27 December.

The more experienced bombardiers on other flights were aware that the first box was heading in the wrong direction, so they did not drop. Lt. Claude Brown, with Lt. Jim Kerns as BN, relates this story:

> Jim and I were assigned to fly flight 2 on the first box, this is the flight to the right of the leader. At the IP, we broke off into flights to do our individual bombing.
>
> At the IP, I didn't hear anything from my bombardier
>
> I said, 'Jim, they called the IP.'
>
> Jim said, 'I'm sorry Brownie, I don't see a damn thing I recognize.'

So I'm following the leader down the trail maybe thirty seconds or a minute, and they open their bomb doors. Again, there is silence. 'Jim, they opened their bomb bay doors.'

'Brownie, I'm sorry, just don't see anything I recognize.' said Jim.

Another few seconds go by and the leader announced, 'Bombs Away' I said with considerable emotion, 'they dropped their bombs.'

So we closed the bomb doors. As we left the target it was customary to put the aircraft into a slight dive to pick up about 300 MPH and scoot out of area as quickly as possible. On this occasion, I called the leader and asked him for permission to re-attack the target. That request was denied and I was told to take the bombs home.

I got on poor Jim's back all the way home. Said a lot of ugly things to him for the next two hundred miles. 'Jim, we practiced all winter, and the first time we have an opportunity to make a name for ourselves you screwed up.' I felt we were going to be in big trouble.

We landed without incident with our four thousand pound bomb load. We taxied to our area and our hardstand. Who should be waiting for us but the Squadron Commander. Oh brother, I thought, here it comes. I was sure a courts martial was coming our way. As I climbed out of the airplane he was all smiles, approached us and put an arm around me and said, 'Great job, Brownie'

I said, 'Sir, you don't understand, we've still got our bombs.' He said, 'Yeah, we know' then went and shook Jim's hand. By this time, the crew truck has come around to take us to debriefing. I'm in a quandry. I don't know what's happening. When we get to debriefing, there was a lot of hell raising

> going on. The leader's navigator mistook the city he was supposed to bomb, and he bombed on our side of the bomb line. The bombs struck a jump off point that General Patton was establishing. It contained a large reserve of fuel and supplies. As I understood it, he lost most of his gasoline reserves. The lead bombardier was court martialed.

First Lieutenant "Punchy" Moore was demoted.

Mission #175 - 24 December - Zulpich, Germany. Christmas Eve, but the mission has to be run. Forty-three aircraft took off early afternoon to hit this important military target. Flights were led by Lts. Anderson and Babbage, BN, - Captain Marzolf and Lt. Beck, BN, and Lt. Evans with McCartney, BN. Heavy flak was thrown up at the target site. One A-26, piloted by Lt. Reece B. Robertson with Staff Sgt. M. W. Cheney, took a direct hit on the bomb run, but he continued on and dropped their bombs, after which it went down. Bombing scores were rated three excellents, two superior, one no attack and one unsatisfactory. Captain Marzolf was on his last (65th) mission. Christman Eve back at the base meant guard duty for many, but the usual Midnight Mass was held with many Catholics as well as Non-Catholics attending.

Mission #176 - 25 December - MERRY CHRISTMAS - AM - Munstereifel, Germany. A real sad day for such a joyous celebration. At 0900, the formation took off to bomb an important communication center. As the planes neared Malmedy and Munstereifel, heavy flak greeted them. Colonel Willetts and Lt. Royalty, BN led Box I. Other flights led by Captain Miracle, Lt. Burg, BN- Captain Prentiss, Lt. Burseil, BN, -and Lts. Pair and Corum, BN. On the straight and narrow bomb run, direct hits downed Captain Miracle's plane, he on his 65th mission. Lt. Kehoe of the 669th squadron took another hit, causing his plane to catch fire and go down. One chute was seen to open. In all, the main target was not rendered useless, since flak bursts obscured visibility. Bombardiers selected targets nearby, bridges, and roads, with effect. One plane piloted by Lt. Mooney lost his flight in the clouds, so he tacked on to another flight going in to bomb. Of the seven planes in that flight, only three were still together. Mooney's ship caught 74 flak holes in it. Lt.Greene of the 669th, on his 65th mission, was hit, but he did manage to get back. Mooney landed with a flat tire, but came out okay. Bombing scored one superior. Two did not bomb the primary and one - no attack.

Mission #177 - 25 December - PM -Hillshelm. Captain Prentiss and Lt. Burseil, BN led Box I with Major Price and Lt. Hand, BN leading Box II. Price was scheduled to lead this formation, but had a problem taking off. Prentiss took the lead. Other flight leaders were Lts. Brown and Kerns, BN, Lt. Svenson was flying deputy to Box I leader. Reaching the target, heavy accurate flak hit Prentiss' ship as well as his right wing man and his deputy. All planes went down with no chutes seen opening. They crashed with none escaping. Flak damaged almost all the planes. The gunner in Prentiss' ship S/Sgt Brown was on his last mission and was slated to return to the states. Major Price and Lt. Buchunan had to land away from base. Our fighter escorts held Luftwaffe planes from attackimg our formation. Christmas 1944 was not a good day for the group. We lost four ships and crews and 39 aircraft were severely damaged. Like Captain Miracle, Lt. Zubon a West Point Grad. flew his 65th mission the morning of Christmas.

Early in the morning of 27 December, at 0100 an air raid alert sounded. Everybody who could hear, or awaken, jumped in the fox holes. After thirty minutes with no action, all returned to their sacks. About five minutes later, machine gun fire and cannon shots were heard, and everybody jumped back into the foxholes, in their underwear, covering themselves up as a strafing job by German fighters, raked the field for about ten minutes. No casualties nor damage was reported. It was determined that someone had lit a flare near one runway, luring the planes toward our field, and the strafing began.

Plans were drawn up in the event of an emergency evacuation. The group stands on strict alert, with doubling of the guards. Also, foxholes were manicured and cleaned out, just in case. All personnel were confined to base for a two week period.

Mission #178 - 27 December - Eller Bridge. General Backus, Commander of the IX Bomber Command elected to lead this mission with Lt. Conte, as BN . Flight leaders were Lts. Brown and Kerns, BN, - Lt. Lackovich and Lt. Muir, BN, . With 29 aircraft loaded with 1000 pound bombs, we were after a main bridge and tunnel used extensively by German Forces. The bombing scored three superior, and two excellents. This pleased General Backus tremendously. Aerial reconnaissance showed the bridge intact but the approaching tunnel was rendered unserviceable. No enemy fighters or flak was encountered. Enemy troop trains were stalled and damaged in the tunnel entrance.

Mission #178, 27 December. Eller Bridge.

Mission #179 - 29 December - Keuchinger Bridge. Thirty-four planes took off but were unable to drop their bombs due to weather closing in. Lts. Stanley and Blount, BN, - Lts. Brown and Kerns, BN - and Lts. Greeley and Basnett, BN, led flights. Two attempted bomb runs, which netted nothing. All planes returned safely with no damage.

No missions was flown 30 or 31 December. New Year's was pretty quiet until the air raid sirens went off again. Foxholes were filled up. Each tent had its own foxhole, large enough to accommodate all tent mates. No running water, or heaters, though.

It was not long after the air raid siren sounded that an enemy plane dropped bombs, missing everything on the base, hitting a field apart from our area.

Quite a bit of snow dropped during the month of December, meaning keeping the runways clear for take-offs and landings. Jury rigged snow plows were put together by a few astute and talented GIs, which served the purpose intended.

Ninth Bomber Division Press Release

The activities of the Ninth Bomber Command for 1944 is detailed as follows:

> News reports continued to emphasize the seriousness of the German counter offensive on the Western Front, but fog covered battle areas kept the B-26 Marauders, A-20 Havocs and A-26 Invaders of the Ninth Bombardment Division tied to the ground.
>
> The airmen wanted to help the foot sloggers who were reeling backward under the weight of Von Rundstedt's counter attack. They were eager to give support like that at Cherbourg, Caen, St. Lo, Falaise and the Rouen loop. Now, if ever, was the time when tactical air power was needed.
>
> But the weather favored the enemy whose counter attack, launched Dec 16 in a blanket of fog, had punched swiftly into western Belgium under soupy skies.
>
> For seven days airmen "sweated out" a break in the weather. Then, on Dec 23, the skies cleared over the snow swept front lines, permitting air support to go to the rescue of embattled Allied ground forces. :
>
> Major General Samuel E. Anderson, commanding the Ninth Bombardment Division, put 657 medium bombers over the western front on the first clear weather day, dispatching Marauders, Havocs and Invaders to attack bridges, road junctions and villages within the communications network supplying the German counter offensive.
>
> Determination of crewmen to aid ground forces was so great that one group elected to carry out its attack without fighter escort rather than abandon its mission. The group was jumped by more than 75

ME 109s and FW 190s, but completed its attack despite loss of 16 bombers out of a formation of 36.

Four groups, in all, were jumped by German fighters as the division engaged in its biggest aerial battle with the Luftwaffe. Thirty-two enemy fighters were shot down, 12 probably destroyed and 33 more reported damaged at a cost of 36 bombers.

The weather, which earlier in the month had been so much in the enemy's favor, now had turned against him.

For five days, from Dec 23 through Dec 27, Marauders, Havocs and Invaders, flying 2554 sorties, roared over battle areas striking at communications centers, bridges, defended villages and other strong points within or immediately behind the central sector of the western front where the counter attack had been launched.

Coming as it did at the fag end of December, the five-day assault provided a smashing climax to a year's operations for the division.

Not a big month as figures go, December, however, saw the medium bombers once again delivering the punch which months before had made them famous in paving the way for the invasion and sealing off the Normandy battle area to enemy troop and supply movements.

Nearing the 100,000 ton mark in total bombs dropped, the division poured 90,410 tons of high explosives on enemy installations in 1944 switching from round-the-clock attacks on flying bomb launching sights, marshalling yards, bridges and gun emplacements in the first six months of the year to direct support of the Invasion after June 6.

Mid-year provided the busiest period for the division's bombers. Flying two and sometimes three missions a day, Marauders, and Havocs completed

11,270 sorties in May and added 10,538 more in June, droppng nearly 30,000 tons of bombs in the two-month period.

The record month of May produced the opening of the "bridge busting"campaign along the Seine and Loire Rivers which marked one of the most successful phases of the year's operations. Records disclosed of 17 principal bridges spanning the Seine alone, medium bombers of Ninth Bombardment Division destroyed 13 of these and shared credit for destruction of three others with fighter bombers.

Bridges remained high on the priority list of targets after June 6, but to provide close support to the invasion forces, they had led onto the Normandy beaches, medium bombers stepped up their offensives to include attacks on fuel, ammunition and supply dumps, transportation lines, road junctions and troop concentrations.

With allied armies poised on the outskirts of the Siegfried line in August, Marauder and Havoc groups moved their bases from England to France to remain within range of the ground forces they were supporting. Operating as the first Allied bombers to fly from French soil since 1940, the Marauders and Havocs were joined by the new, fast A-26 Invaders as they started pounding at the Siegfried line and communications and supply targets in Western Gemany.

As the German armies withdrew toward the Rhine, establishing strong points in each town along the way, the medium bombers directed saturation attacks at defended villages, clearing out strongly-fortified positions in the path of advancing Allied ground forces.

Throughout October, November and the early part of December, the Ninth's twin engine bombers struck at fortress towns all along the western front, centering the weight of their attacks on villages in the Duren area where fighting was the bitterest.

Meanwhile, they continued hammering the enemy's communications and supply lines, attacking bridges, railheads, fuel and ammunition dumps to round out the year's operation with a toal of 70,268 sorties. Against 288 losses for the year, the divison posted claims of 52 enemy planes destroyed, 21 probably destroyed and 59 damaged.

Chapter 11

January 1945 Missions

January 1945 Missions

What will the new year bring for the 416th? Predictions of victory for the allies was encouraging, but no matter what actually happened, the group has to continue doing what it came over here to do. Attack the enemy positions to weaken their efforts, was the cry.

Visions of returning to the states came true for another large group of crewmembers, mostly all of whom came over with the group in January last year. With those going, continued training and evaluation of replacement crews brought out great promise for the future of our purpose in being here. Lead crews were efficiently carrying out their assignments and the ever present and dependable, crew chiefs, ordnance, engineering, and administrative personnel continuted unabated. What would the flyers do without these great friends? A great deal of respect was on going for every person doing what they were trained to do. The chefs were especially appreciated because of their limited access to mainstay meals, and their ability to present meals in the best manner with whatever they had. Rationing was not the case, rather availability of basic ingredients to prepare wholesome meals was paramount.

A new policy instituted late January gave flight leading pilots and bombardier-navigators additional credit of one quarter mission for each formation or flight they led. This means that for every four missions led, they would receive credit for five missions. This would shorten their stay with the group. Ground personnel got no special credit for all they did for the group. Equality??

Major Collins H. Ferris was assigned Group Air Inspector, relieving Lt. Col. Meng who was now Deputy Group Commander.

Mission #180 - 1 January 1945 - Mont le Ban Command Post and Headquarters. This was an experimental mission, testing the attack bombers for missions envisioned from their concept. - The ability to drop bombs from higher elevations and then go down to ground level and strafe enemy positions. Six crews from the 670th squadron were chosen to do this. Captain H. J. Harrold, a West Pointer, with Lt.William E. Brewer, BN in an A-20 leading five A-26 gun ships, which had 16 forward firing 50 caliber machine guns, operated by the pilot. The turret gunner had two more guns which could be facing forward, making a total of 18 guns aiming at the targets. The planes were loaded with 260 pound fragmentation bombs . P-47 Thunderbolt fighter planes were supposed to drop smoke bombs on the target area, while the flight of six bombers were to drop their loads from 8000 feet altitude. On the first bomb run, sighting by the bombsight was not accomplished; the second run was not synchronized with the smoke bomb drops, and the third run was made after the smoke bomb markers dissipated, so no real bomb run was made. Heavy, accurate intense flak from 28 permanent ground guns managed to damage planes knocking one out of the sky. It was flown by Lt. T. A. Murphy with gunner S/Sgt. L. W.O'Connell. Murphy jettisoned his 20 bombs in the target area, but his plane was seen gliding down with only one chute popped open.

Another crew left for the front lines to experience a different war perspective. Major Dunn, C. O. of the 670th squadron and Lt. A. Maltby, BN with gunner S/Sgt Majeski received the privilege of this observation trip.

Mission #181 - 2 January - Simmern Bridge 26 miles north of Coblenz. Lt.Col. Willetts and Lt. Royalty, BN led Box I - Lt. Pair and Lt. Corum led Box II. Other flights were led by Lt.Stanley and F/O Blount, BN - Lt.Evans and Lt. McCartney, BN - Lts. Lackovich and Muir, BN. The field was covered with ice and snow and a haze covered the runway. A few ships did not make it to the runway due to poor visibility, but those that did, met with disasterous results. The first A-26 piloted by Lt. H. P.Clark with gunner S/Sgt. J. W. Sabadosh took off and crashed not far from the end of the runway. The plane, loaded with 1000 pound bombs exploded, killing both men. A second plane with Lt. R. J. Lackner at the controls, with gunner Sgt. A. J. Musserre crashed about a mile from the runway end, just about where the first plane exploded.

The crew of the second plane ran from the downed plane and sought safety, just as their bombs exploded, not harming them. The explosion knocked out windows of the squadron headquarters building. Lt.Rooney of the 670th squadron, was edging his plane down the runway for takeoff but something malfunctioned and he pulled up right off the end of the runway. Another plane behind Rooney took off and made it off the end of the runway, but didn't get more than a few feet off the ground and it went down. Rooney left his plane and when a third plane hit, he started to run toward them to help, if he could. The crew came running away from the plane and Rooney and his gunner took cover just as the 1000 pounders exploded, causing damage to Rooney's plane sitting at the end of the runway. The reasons for the failure to get off rested with icing on the wings and possibly in the carburetors. Lt. Roberts with gunner Windisch were in the third plane. Windisch was able to extricate Roberts from the plane before it exploded, too. With all that confusion to watch as other planes took off, they continued to form up and head for the target, all 27 of them. Scoring was superior and excellent, but the bridge still stood, requiring a few more mission to do it in. Flak was not too significant although ME-0109s attempted a pass at the formation, but were driven away by our fighter escorts.

Mission #182 - 5 January - Simmern Bridge. Major Price and Lt. Hand, BN led Box I with Captain McNulty and Lt. Forma BN leading Box II. Lts.Brown and Kerns, BN led flights. The target was cloud covered, PFF B-26s led but the first leader was off course. Second Box dropped on PFF but results were not obtained. All returned safely with only one aircraft having been hit by flak.

Mission #183 - 11 January - Simmern Bridge Again. Captain Hulse and Lt. Conte, BN led Box I with Captain Stebbins and Lt.Calloway, BN on Box II. Flight leaders were Lts. Brown and Kerns, BN,= Lts. Greenley and Basnett, BN and Lts. Lackovich and Muir, BN. PFF pathfinder equipment failed so lead BNs used GEE equipment to bomb secondary targets at Alsey, Germany, severing a major highway. The cold temperatures were evident to the crews, getting down to 27 degrees below zero. Did we say that no heaters were normal equipment for the A-20s? Frost bite was the next thing to worry about. The silk gloves, paper wrapping in our shoes, and fur lined boots, helped just a little. Cold is cold at 27 below!

Mission #184 - 13 January - Steinbruck Rail Bridge. Major Price, Lt. Hand, BN led Box I. Lts. Lackovich and Muir, BN led a flight. Lt. Roberts with gunner Sgt. Windisch crashed on take off, having just cleared the runway as the plane mushed and settled. This is the same crew that crash landed on take off earlier this month. Lt. Nathanson, with gunner Sgt. Kaminski had to abort since the nose wheel did not retract.. This left 19 planes to carry on the mission behind a PFF Pathfinder B-26. Heavy flak tracked the formation on a long bomb run with minor damage to planes. Results could not be photographed. Captain Sears and M/Sgt. Wells suffered damage to their plane, found they could not lower their landing gear when attempting to land, so had to belly land in at another air base, A-69. Two other planes landed at A-69 since our field closed in due to weather. All other planes found different airfields to take them in.

Mission #185 - 14 January - Schleiden Strong Point. Captain Hulse and Lt. Conte, BN led Box I. Captain Tutt and Lt. Beck, BN and Lt. Buskirk with Lt. Hanna, BN led other flights. The A-26 piloted by Lt. G. C. Van Meter and gunner Sgt. C. M. Kiker could not gain altitude and crashed just north of the runway, exploding, killing both crewmembers. The mission took off behind PFF Pathfinder B-26s. When reaching the target area, the lead BN took over the lead from the PFF leaders and went down the bomb run visually, his bombs blanketing the aiming point. The bombs blasted roads and buildings, severing a railroad line in four places. All north-south roads were blocked by the results of the bomb craters. The group received an excellent report.

Many of the planes had to land at alternate airfields since A-55, our field, was closed in due to weather. Three planes experienced problems with landing gears which collapsed on landing. They had been hit with heavy flak. Lts. L.E. Cannon, J.W. Blevins, and F/O H. J.Wilson were not injured on their landings. F/O Wilson from the 671st squadron on his first flight, showed the results of his good training, when he found his engines cutting in and out due to icing. He lost his position in the flight, but kept going in the direction of the formation. The engines began purring correctly, so he tagged on to the end of another group (409th) on their bomb run. Heavy flak greeted the flight. Returning, Wilson left the flight as it neared A-55 but he lost sight of it. He headed toward Paris and went in to land. He checked indicators and saw all wheels were down and locked. As he landed, the wheels collapsed, causing his plane to skid off the runway into a snowbank. He suffered a broken leg. His gunner, Cpl. Stypenski, was uninjured.

Mission #186 - 15 January - Simmern Bridge. For some unknown reason, the 416th was the only Ninth Bombardment Division Group to fly a mission today with 45 planes, led by Lt. Col. Willetts and Lt.Royalty, BN. Captain Pair and Lt. Corum BN led Box II. Lt. Mish and BN Lt. Shaft led a flight. GEE equipment had to be used because of complete cloud cover at the target. The second box did not drop due to some malfunction of the bombsight. Results of other flights were undetermined due to the clouds. Previous bombings of this bridge showed the approaches around the bridge destroyed, but the structure still stands. If vehicles could not get to it due to the approaches destroyed, the bridge had limited usage. No flak, so all returned safely after this four hour trip. The base is still on an alert status, with guards being doubled up.

Mission #187 - 16 January - Sinzig Bridge. Captain McNulty and Lt. Forma BN, headed up Box I with Captain Evans and F/O McCartney, BN. Captain Monroe and Lt. Kirk, BN plus Captain Tutt and Lt. Peck, BN plus Lts. Brown and Kerns, BN leading flights. En route to the target, light accurate flak came up. At the target, moderate, more accurate flak met the boys. Bombing scored a superior for the Box II BN and Excellent for the Box I BN. The bombs destroyed an approach to the bridge and cut the tracks leading to the bridge, but the bridge still remained in tact. Extensive damage was reported on the marshalling yard adjacent to the bridge approaches. Ten aircraft suffered damage from flak, but no personnel injuries

First Sergeant Combs of the 670th Squadron received a letter from the mother of S/Sgt Gossett who was shot down in October, 1944, stating that her son wrote from a prison camp and is a POW. That sounds like good news, but also not so good. At least, he's alive.

Another pilot and his gunner were sent up to the front lines as Air Liaison Officer. Captain Harrold, West Point Grad and his gunner, S/Sgt. Burns made the trip. Real lousy weather consisting of ice and snow kept all planes grounded for five days. More of our crews were assigned to the front lines for experience and liaison. They all appeared glad to be in the flying corps, compared with the fighting ground forces. When we had ground forces with us, flying missions, they all never felt safe up in the air, and preferred to be on the ground. They said they had no place to hide when the firing started.

A group of P-51 fighter pilots stayed with our group for a few days since they could not get to their bases in England. Ours was a diversionary airfield for them. Needless to say, friendships resulted, and when they left our base, they put on a BUZZ Job which were at once thrilling, and at the same time, wondering why would they be so wild. The show was a great enjoyment to onlookers , they barely topped haystacks and building roofs, but they must have known what they were doing.

Mission #188 - 21 January - Euskirchken Railroad Bridge. Major Dunn and Lt. Brewer, BN led Box I with Captain Monroe and Lt. Kirk, BN leading Box II. Lt. Stanley and F/O Blount, BN Captain Greenley and Lt.Basnett, BN led flights. B-26s had attacked this bridge before, but the Germans had rebuilt it with railroad tracks. Our bombs hit the bridge and bombs tore up an attached marshalling yard. Window dropping preceeded the formation, but heavy flak got through to the planes, causing damage on a few planes. No injuries. Bombing was on PFF which the first box followed. The second box did not see the PFF signal, so did not drop. The results of flight bombings were rated two superior and one excellent. Two did not drop. Captain Greenley and Lt. Basnett, BN leading a flight, had their elevator trim tab freeze up, causing the plane to slip away from the formation. They attemped to join up other flights but did not make it properly, dropping their bombs away from the target.

Mission #189 -22 January - AM - Simmern Bridge. Again ! Lt.Col. Willetts and Lt.Royalty, BN led Box I with Captain Pair and Lt. Corum, BN leading Box II. Lts.Evans and McCartney, BN led flights. Lt.Colquitt flew a window dropping ship. Pathfinder B-26s led the formation. Weak inaccurate flak came up on the way to the target, but none was at the target. One plane received minor damage. Bombing was done following the PFF drops and results were not determined. This was another four hour flight, but the A-26s were capable of this longer range, while the A-20s were not.

Mission #190 - 22 January - PM - Dasburg Area. No sooner had the morning mission planes got to their revetments, a call came down from Ninth Bomber Command Headquarters to have a flight of six planes prepared for a strafing mission on a long column of enemy army vehicles. We were to meet escorting P-47s into the target area, but unfortunately, no rendezvous took place. The long line of vehicles were held up at a bridge which had been knocked out of service by B-26s. The column was fleeing eastward. Six A-26s were loaded with 50 caliber ammunition on each of the 16 forward firing guns, which would have made a major impact if they had gotten to do their job. Howevr, GHQ recalled the flight. Captain McNulty, Lt. Forma BN with Lts.

Jackson and Winn BN were on this special attack mission which did not materialize.

Mission #191 - 23 January AM - Dasburg Area. This was a six plane flight designed to bomb at a lower level than usual and then drop down to ground level and strafe targets of opportunity. They selected a target near Arzfeld in the vicinity of Dasburg. Captain Paul Atkinson with Lt. Dale Ackerson, BN led a formation of six planes, they being an A-20 leading five A-26 gun ships. Weather was bad, cloudy, cold, and the six planes did not form up as a flight, not able to get together. They were in touch with each other by radio. The rendezvous with fighter escort was made and Atkinson proceeded to the target.

Extreme heavy flak peppered his plane. The bombardier, Ackerson, sitting in the glass nose took a bad hit, causing his left leg to be practically severed above the ankle. Pilot Atkinson was hit in the face, The plane was on fire and one engine was shot out of commission. With a smoke filled cockpit, Atkinson jettisoned his over-head hatch, but continued on the bomb run and peeled off to strafe. The elevator controls were unusable so Atkinson relied on the elevator trim tabs. They dropped their bombs in the target area, went down and strafed. Paul felt the plane vibrating and assumed his gunner was firing his guns. The gunner saw the red light flash, which meant jettisoning or bailing out. It was determined that the gunner who saw the pilot's hatch blow away thought it was time for him to go, and he did, probably landing in German held territory.

After strafing, Atkinson searched for a homing beam. At about this time he knew he had to get the plane and his BN to friendly territory. Ackerson, in all his misery, called Atkinson, giving his position and telling Atkinson to correct direction toward friendly lines. Ackerson was trying to stem the excessive bleeding.

They were flying on one engine, doing about 260 MPH with Atkinson anxiously seeking a landing spot, somewhere in friendly territory. As they crossed the bomb line, Atkinson was wounded in the leg. He was flying without aid from his air speed indicator. Ackerson, interphoned back to Atkinson that they were now in friendly territory. Atkinson tried to contact fighter control for protection, but was unable to get them to respond. He found a relatively flat spot and crash landed, knowing he had to do something before his bombardier bled to death. With a wheels up landing, flaps down, the plane skidded into a tree, stopping in a gully after cresting a hill. Ackerson was thrown out of his harness and struggled for about five minutes when some infantrymen came running up and helped him leave the plane, which fortunately was not afire. First aid was administered at the site, and both crewmembers were rushed to a field hospital. Atkinson suffered a broken ankle and hand. They were transferred to a General Hospital.

Gunner J. L. Collier was listed as MIA, no one knew where he bailed out, but he did so, following instructions dictating that the last resort signal in the event the electrical signal went out, was for him to hit the silk.

Ackerson's both legs were almost shot off below the knees. He survived.

The other five planes in Atkinson's flight did get down to strafe without being in formation. They dropped their bombs on a town where a large group of vehicles were moving. One tunnel gunner, S/Sgt. Raymond J.Gatti, strafed gun emplacements. The pilot landed at A-68, with a few hits on his plane.

Mission #192 - 23 January PM - Blankenheim Area. Six plane bombing-strafing mission -Six A-26s took off in early afternoon, led by Captain Tutt and Lt. Beck as BN. Lt. Beck was riding in the jump seat beside the pilot. Bad weather prevented the planes from joining up as a formation or flight. At the target area, heavy flak came up, with a chunk hitting Lt. Beck on the leg. Flak knocked out the intercom system and the plane's hydraulics. Captain Tutt continued to the target area but was unable to bomb or strafe. He found a landing strip at Laon and went in. Other pilots did not fare so well, either. F/O Wilson, who crash landed on his first mission about a week ago, did not form up with the flight shortly after take off. He did, however, continue on to the target area and dropped his 260 pound bombs on a railroad junction in Blankenheim. He went down from his 3000 feet bombing altitude and strafed a column of vehicles, causing one to catch fire and severely damaging three more. His plane was badly flak damaged and he continued on to land at Juvincourt.

Captain Nielsen volunteered for low level missions. The flight he was in broke up into two ship attack mode. He took a flak burst at the storm window which hit him in the face, knocking him out. Unconscious, the plane zoomed down until he came out of his stupor at about 1000 feet. He managed to pull out, and headed toward a landing at Juvincourt. He did not strafe since his gun sight was damaged, impairing his sighting.

Lts. Murray and Herman separated from their flight lead plane. They did not find a suitable target to hit, so returned to land at friendly bases. The sixth plane, piloted by Lt. Gary, to make up this flight of six did not get too far from the take off field. His landing gear would not retract. He returned to base but the landing gear collapsed. With a full load of bombs and ammunition, they were grateful that nothing ignited.

In a combination of weather or other reason, the six ship bomb-strafe missions didn't do too much to build up any confidence in that endeavor. It must be understood that all pilots who undertook these type missions, were volunteers.

Mission #193 - 24 January - Schleiden. Major Price and Lt. Hand, BN led Box I. Only 21 planes were able to be suited up for this mission. Three planes dropped window strips ahead of the formation. Only three flights dropped, with two scoring excellents. One flight leader's bombsight malfunctioned, preventing a drop. Little, inaccurate flak was experienced. All Planes returned safely.

Mission #194 - 25 January - Kall Railroad Junction. Captain Hulse and Lt. Conte, BN led Box I Captain Stebbins and Lt. Calloway, BN led Box II . Captain McNulty and Lt. Forma, BN and Captain Greenley and Lt. Basnett, BN led flights. On the bomb run, Captain McNulty's bombs fell out of the plane when the bomb bay doors opened, causing the bombs to fall way short of the target. Superior rating for the first box and three excellents were also scored.. A convoy of enemy vehicles were on the road near the target and they were blanketed in a cloud of smoke and fire from the bombs being dropped.-

Mission #195 - 29 January - Nonweiller Railway Bridge. Major Dunn and Lt. Brewer, BN led Box I with Captain Evans and F/O McCartney, BN on Box II. McCartney was promoted to 2nd Lt. for well deserved bombing performed during his short assignment with the group. Lt. Bill Lytle, Group Bombardier received his Captain's bars.

Group strength for the Group at the end of January stood at:

668th Squadron	57 Officers	299 Enlisted Men
669th Squadron	59 Officers	300 Enlisted Men
670th Squadron	60 Officers	301 Enlisted Men
671st Squadron	59 Officers	297 Enlisted Men
Hqs.	34 Officers	58 Enlisted Men
Totals	269 Officers	1255 Enlisted Men

CHAPTER 12

February 1945 Missions

February 1945 Missions

As our ground forces kept forging ahead toward Germany, targets for our group were being pushed further and further away from us at Melun, so the obvious decision was to locate our type bombing groups closer to the front lines. Early in February a group of our officers and enlisted men visited A-69, a former medium bomber station near Laon/Athies. The field had been home for Luftwaffe bombers not too long ago. The condition of the operations were deplorable, with only four of the five hangers being suitable for occupancy. Of three runways, only one was servicable, one of them having over 100 bomb craters, and the other only having been partially repaired. Taxi ways were pock marked with holes making them unusable.. No one ever explained how the 323rd Bomb Group could have operated from there in its deplorable condition, even though they were supposedly having to occupy the base for a few days before they moved out somewhere else.

The four usable hangers were set up for mess halls for each of our four squadrons. The fifth was designated for a photo lab and gunnery training equipment.

In wasn't too long before we were able to employ French workmen to make the repairs necessary to make something out of this apparent choas. All the roadways and runways were made somewhat serviceable, and the future looked promising.

The group started moving from A-55, Villa Rouche, Melun, with two squadrons piling into 40 and 8 freight cars used on World War I, making for an uncomfortable voyage, with men and equipment stacked in these relatively small cars. But, things like this had to be endured, and everyone made the best of it. Fortunately, the weather abated a little, with cold, nasty cold days not bothering movement. Tents of the 668th and 670th squadrons were taken down and moved to A-69. The other two squadrons made the move on the 14th of February. Before departing A-55, a general clean up was conducted and team from the Inspector General's office of the Ninth Bombardment Division checked out the old field and rated our efforts as Superior.

The new field - A-69 was a diversionary field used by allied planes needing emergency landings; as a matter of fact, many of our boys had used it not too long ago. A-69 was only about 100 miles from the front, so access to targets to assist advancing allied forces was paramount. The proximity to the action would permit two missions a day for the group.

Whatever shacks or small buildings left behind by the previous occupants gave operations and other departments the ability to set up their needs without too many problems. Quite a bit of usable lumber was also available for enterprising individuals to put up other quarters and recreation areas, as the need arose. Living for all crews and service personnel was still in tents, but large enough for somewhat near comfortable conditions.

With the able assistance and guidance of the Engineering personnel, the new base was shaping up to be a real nice place to be, better than those we had at Melun, A-55. While all this work was going on to reestablish this base as a point of comfort, the American Red Cross gals - and guys - were nearby with their welcome coffee and doughnut. Did they make them up right on the spot? They were always there nice and warm and juicy. The doughnuts, that is!

Some changes in personnel and their assignments took place this month. Lieutenant Colonel William Meng, the pleasant, knowledgeable, experienced, pilot and administrator, was promoted up to 9th Bombardment Division as Air Inspector. He was almost a permanent fixture for the group and the 670th squadron which he commanded for so many months, with great accomplishments.

Major Collin Ferris, left his post as Group Inspector to take command of the 670th squadron.

Major Dunn left his post as CO of the 670th and transferred to become Group Operations Officer.

Lieutenant Colonel Harold Radetsky was moved up to Deputy Group Commander and Air Inspector.

Captain William H. Naier transferred to the Zone of the Interior from having been Group Ordnance Officer. His spot was taken over by First Lieutanant Carl J. Norris

Captain Richard V. Wheeler transferred to Group Operations from the 671 squadron.

Major R.A. Clark was appointed A-3 Controller in charge of night diversions.

Mission #196 - 1 February - Schleiden. Colonel Willetts and Lt. Royalty, BN lined up to take two boxes on this mission. Prior to take off, however, Headquarters called down to cancel the take off of the second box. Captain Greenley with Lt. Basnett, BN = Lts. Herman and Graeber BN and Captain Hulse and Lt. Conte, BN led flights. Perhaps higher ups felt that since the cloud cover at the target, it would not be sensible to send all those planes over with the possibility that they would not be able to hit the target. In any event, the three flights of the first box did drop their bombs through clouds, following PFF Pathfinder leaders. Results were unobserved. No damage was incurred on the planes since no flak or fighters showed up.

Mission #197 - 2 February - Euskirchen Communication Center. Captain Price with Lt. Hand, BN plus Captain McNulty and Lt. Forma, BN led boxes. Lts. Brown and Kerns, BN led a flight. They made two runs at the target, placing their bombs squarely on the aiming point, scoring an excellent rating. As soon as the formation crossed the bomb line, intense, accurate flak greeted our planes. Twenty-two planes suffered damage. Window planes preceeded the group dropping aluminum strips but the flak came through the window strips. Bombing was registered as two excellents and two others as good. One plane piloted by Lt. D. E. Smith, while flying window, suffered a loud explosion in the rear of the plane. He tried to contact his gunners but got no response. He landed the plane safely at A-76 airfield and found one gunner S/Sgt. D. R.Abriola, must have bailed out over enemy territory and the other, Sergeant R. DeStafano, dead on the floor of the compartment. There was only a relatively small hole in the side of the plane, but the bulkhead must have buckled in from the force of an unexplained explosion, hitting the gunner, his body badly broken up.

One other plane was reported as having a wing shot off and the plane spun in without parachutes having been seen. Names of the crew are not available

Mission #198 - 3 February - Berg/Gladbach Storage and Repair Depot. Cloud cover required PFF Pathfinder leaders taking the formation in. Only one box made the mission, led by Captain Stebbins and Lt. Calloway BN. Captain Greenley and Lt. Basnett, BN led a flight. This target just east of Cologne was heavily protected with 24 flak guns, causing moderate, accurate bursts around the formation. Four planes suffered battle damage. One flight got separated from the formation due to bad weather. They formed behind the 409th Bomb Group and dropped their bombs when they did. So, it shouldn't be a loss!
Four groups were assigned to attack this target but weather did not cooperate, covering the aiming point with clouds.

4 February - plans were released calling for the group to move to another base - A-69 at Laon, France. Everybody available was busy packing with the first echelon leaving A-55 on 5 February by truck convoy, arriving the next morning, the 6th. to make preparation for the remainder of the group. On 9 February, all ground personnel were loaded on the famed 40/8 box cars and started to Laon a 110 mile ride. A truck convoy left at 0130 of 10 February, arriving at Laon at 1000. Rain and cold weather made the trip uncomfortable. The air echelon arrived on the 10th, also. In the mean time, missions were being flown from A-55.

Mission #199 - 6 February - Berg/Gladbach Depot again, but weather prevented visual bombing, with PFF Pathfinders leading the formation in. Major Dunn, Lt. Brewer, BN led Box I and Captain Evans and Lt. McCartney, BN on Box II. Lts. Buskirk and Hanna, BN, Lts.Anderson and Babbage, BN with Captain Greenley and Lt. Basnett, BN led flights. Weak inaccurate flak was encountered, in spite of the supposedly heavy artillery at this site. Recon photos showed a factory and three large building, plus a double track railroad took direct hits. Two planes received minor damage.

Mission #200 - 8 February - Nutterden-Crannenberg, Holland. Colonel Willetts and Lt.Royalty, BN and Captain Pair, Lt. Corum, BN led boxes. Captain Hulse and Lt. Conte BN led a flight. The group has now been outfitted with glass nosed A-26s, releasing the popular A-20s, for leading flights. The concept of two BNs riding in the nose of the A-26s started, with one man responsible for the navigation and the other to be the bombardier. Lt. Muir rode with Lt.Royalty as the combination BN team. Clouds obscured the target again. The secondary targets were hit with good results. Lt. Stead reported he was low on gas, but then there was no further communication from him. His plane had crashed, killing him and seriously injuring his gunner, Sgt. C. E. Transhina who died the next day.

The Canadian and British ground forces were scheduled for a big push toward Dusseldorf, and aerial bombardment was called to clear some of the path for them. The Canadian First Army stepped off on an offensive to reach the Rhine River. While weather was bad our bombing helped since we received a letter of commendation for the excellent bombing accomplished.

Mission #201 - 9 February - Kempen, Germany. Captain Stebbins with Lt.Calloway BN and Captain Evans with Lt. McCartney, BN led boxes. Captain Greenley and Lt. Basnett, BN, Lts. Chalmers and Eckard as a new BN team, led flights. For some unknown reason the formation separated, -got lost - so the primary target was not bombed . The PFF equipment failed to function, and the GEE techniques didn't work. The first box leader made a second run at the target, but did not drop because of a foul up malfunction of the bomb rack releases, so eight planes did not drop. The second box went on to a secondary target, dropping their bombs on Lingen, using GEE equipment. Three planes dropped their load on Lichenare, 19 planes dropped on Scherfede. Two planes had to make emergency landings, Lt.Cannon with S/S Robinson in Holland and Lt. Montrose with S/S Felkel at A-89 airfield. Lt.Cannon's plane was totally destroyed, while Montrose made a safe landing, returning to our base the next day, with his plane. None of the crews of either plane were injured. Captain Borman with gunner Sgt. R.J. Perujo had taken a shot in the gas tank, depleting his fuel, requiring him to land emergency at A-54 in Belgium.

Mission #202 - 10 February Munstereifel. Major Price and Lt.Forma with F/O Harvest as combination bombardier-navigator were on Box I. Captain Hulse with Lt.Conte and Lt. Kupits as the BN team were leading Box II. Lts. Buskirk and Hanna, BN and Lts. Lachovich/Muir BN led flights. Excellent results were obtained by the use of PFF technique. This target was the one flown by our group on Christmas morning when two crews were lost over the target. Since most of the squadron personnel were on the road to the new base at Laon, the flyers were operating on a skeleton basis, including ground personnel. But, the job got done.

Mission #203 - 13 February - Iserlohn. With only one box scheduled to make this mission, Major Dunn and Lt. Brewer, BN led. Lts. Buskirk and Hanna, BN led a flight as did Lts. Evans and McCartney, BN. This was the first official mission from our new base A-69. The rendezvous with our fighter escort did not materialize so the formation did not get to bomb the primary target, cloud cover contributing to the problem. Bombs were dropped on a secondary target, Wittlich, using GEE equipment. No enemy fighters or flak hindered the operation. Results were unobserved.

Mission #204 - 14 February - AM -Mechornish Motor Transport Repair Depot. Colonel Willetts, Lts. Royalty and Basnett as the BN team in Box I, with Captain Pair with Lts.

Corum and Muir in Box II. - Lt.Colonel Napier with Lts. Conte and Kupits as BNs, and Lts.Anderson and Babbage, BN,- Lt. Chalmers with Lt. Eckard, BN, led flights with Lts.Stanley and Blount, BN flew deputy. Heavy, accurate flak at the target met the group. The first box leader dropped their bombs on PFF. Captain Pair's ship experienced mechanical failure, so they didn't drop. He turned away from the formation, with the deputy taking over and trying to bomb a secondary target. He led the box toward the Rhine River, then made a wide turn toward our lines, crossing over some heavy anti-aircraft guns, damaging ten planes flying in his box. Lt. Chalmers, Lt. Eckard, BN and gunner S/Sgt. E. Fortuner took a direct hit and went down in flames. One chute, believed to be Lt. Chalmers, was seen to open. Eckard and Fortuner were listed as MIA. Photo recon showed the target was pretty well damaged, with a large freight station severely damaged, and two smaller building being hit. Baggage cars were badly damaged and burned out, three rail lines were knocked out. At least two hits were scored on the roof of a well camouflaged concrete building. So, bombing through PFF is not all that bad! This was Lt. Conte's 65th mission, feeling lucky not to have been injured on this last combat sortie.

Mission #205 - 14 February - PM - Rheinbach Ammunition Dump. Major Price, Lt. Forma and Lt. Babbage as BN team, with Captain Evans Lt. McCartney and F/O Harvest as BN in Box II. Flights were headed up by Lts. Buskirk and Hanna, BN plus Lts. Lackovich and Muir, BN. Bombing was through a thick cloud layer. A pathfinder plane was scheduled to lead the formation, but he could not contact his base station, the bombing was then done visually, with excellent results. The bright flashes, explosion and smoke spoke well of the aiming. One flight leader did not receive the message that they were to go in as box bombing. They went off and bombed the town of Ludendorf. Moderate flak came up, but no serious damage was experienced, although 20 planes of the group were hit. The planes landed at base after dusk.

Mission #206 - 16 February - Unna Ordnance Depot. Captain Stebbins and Lt. Calloway BN and Captain Sommers with Lt. Kupits, BN led boxes. Captain Tutt with BN Lt. Beck, and Lts. Lackovich and Muir, BN,- Lts. Mish and Shaft, BN and Lts. Jacobsen and F/O Harvest BN, led flights. The PFF plane took a hit losing his sighting on the primary target and bombed the town of Kamen with excellent results. Other flights hit alternate targets. Intense flak hit planes. F/ O W. D. Wilson and Sgt. E. F. Berkes went down after their plane nosed up. No chutes were seen to blossom, although Sgt. Berkes was listed as having been returned to military command. This was Wilson's eighth mission. He had encountered bad luck on previous missions, and performed exceedingly well under trying circumstances in the past. Lt. Beck, BN, figured out the lead planes were not hitting the primary targets, so he turned toward the town of Kid Kaiseran and dropped his bombs there with good results.

Lt. J. F. Allen had one engine knocked out of service, but he continued on to the target, droppng his bombs. He then headed west, asking for a homing. He received a message that he was over friendly territory and to continue on. He flew right into a heavy concentrated barrage from 20 flak guns. He almost landed at an airfield, which he thought was in allied hands. He heard a German accent on the transmission and realized that was the wrong place to go. A radio contact from a British Air Field gave him a heading to safety. When he landed at that field, he was told he flew into one of the most heavily defended flak emplacements in the area where he was lured to go. Luckily, he made it out okay.

Mission #207 - 19 February - Weisbaden Ammunition Depot. Major Dunn and Lt. Brewer, Col. Napier and Lt. Moore, BN led boxes. Captain Tutt and Lt. Beck BN, and Lt. Buskirk and Hanna, BN,- Lts. Anderson and Babbage, BN, and Lts.Evans and McCartney, BN led flights. This was a four hour flight deep into Germany. Clouds, however, required PFF Pathfinders to lead the mission in. Little flak came up, with no casualties or injuries.

Mision #208 - 21 February - AM - Geldern Communication Center. The mission report from the 668th squadron states that one half of our mission group would assemble with one half of the formation from the 410th Bomb Group and the other half would form up with the other half of the 410th Bomb Group. No mention is made of which group led the boxes. Captain Stebbins and F/O Blount led one flight of the 416th as did Lts. Singletary and Rosenquist. Stebbins made two runs at the target but the BN did not synchronize. The same thing happened to the other BN after two runs. They both then chose a casual target in Nieukerk. A cloud cover over the target may have been the cause of not being able to zero in.

Mission #209 - 21 February - PM - Lage Bridge. Colonel Willetts and Lt. Royalty and Basnett as BN team and Captain Pair with Lts. Muir and Corum as BN team led boxes. Bombing was through clouds and flak barrages. Bombing results were a concentration of craters east of the bridge and on an embankment. The track was probably cut. Two planes suffered severe damage. A third plane piloted by Lt. R. K. Johnson of the 669th squadron had an engine shot out. Feathering it, he returned to base on single engine and attempted to land. He didn't think he would make it on the first run, so pulled up, but turned into his dead engine. He had no pulling power, the plane stalled and headed toward the tents in the 670th squadron area. Some pilots were watching the landings, saw Johnson's plane coming toward them, and ran. They did not get clear enough. The plane struck a wooden building. The three pilots were hit, being Lt. John Cook, Lt. V. S. Merritt and Lt. Sheley. Lt. Cook suffered a fractured skull, hips, and legs, causing him to lose his life. Merritt suffered a fractured leg and Sheley had a foot bone broken. Pilot Johnson was trapped in his wreckage for about an hour, and was dragged out, suffering a broken collar bone and cuts about the face. His gunner, Sgt. Brandt escaped injury. The fuselage bent double at

Mission #209, 21 February 1945. Checking flak holes on A-26. L. to R. Wayne Downing - Pilot, A. Gomez - Crew Chief, T.H. Goss - BN.

Mission #209, 21 February 1945. 669th Pilot Lt. R.K. Johnson. Crash landing on one engine in 670th Sq. living area. Lt. John Cook killed, Lt. S. Shelley and Lt. V. S. Merritt injured.

about the middle of the bomb bay, causing Johnson to be thrown back toward the wheel well, jamming him in. The metal around him had to be cut out in order to free him..

Mission #210 -and #211 - 22 February - Miltenberg -Hochost - Munster - Bombing Strafing Mission. A massive offensive was planned for this day to have the 8th Air Force and 9th Air Force help the ground forces in their advances in Germany by disrupting their communications network. The 9th Air Force was assigned the job of bombing out three bridges and railroad sidings. Bombing was to be done at 10,000 feet and then the formations were to break up into two ship elements and go down to strafing altitudes to wipe out the bridges and railroad sidings. This was, indeed, going to be a thrilling and knowingly dangerous missions and was met with much enthusiasm. Major Price with Lt. Forma and F/O Harvest as BN team leading Box I with three flights to attack the Miltenberg target. Captain Evans and Lt. McCartney and F/O Blount as BNs, were to take out the Hochost target with two flights and Lt. Brunig and Lt. Morris BN to attack Munster with one flight.

Another target was assigned to Lt. Rooney and Lt. Kirk, as BN to wipe out the Simmern Bridge with the seventh flight and this was to count as mission #211.

The bombing attacks on Miltenberg and Hochost were successful. The Munster attack was hindered by haze preventing proper sighting of the target. This flight flew south about 43 miles and picked up a bridge at Mochesheim and knocked it out of commission.

The strafing crews succeeded with tremendous results, including one tank train destroyed and left burning, one horse drawn vehicle destroyed, four heavy motor transports destroyed, one railroad station damaged, 15 buildings damaged severely, one light motor transport left burning, five barges damaged, 16 goods wagons damaged. At Simmern, 15 barracks damaged and oil tanks damaged. Photos showed 11 craters on railroad crossings, cutting at least seven damaged lines and destroying six wagons.

A total of 63,605 rounds of ammunition were spent and 55 tons of bombs dropped. With each A-26 spitting 50 caliber bullets out of 16 guns, must have been quite a sight to experience. There is no way to describe the elation of the crews participating in this exciting adventure.

Mission #212 - 23 February - Golzheim Railroad Junction. Colonel Napier, Lts. Brewer and Maltby, BN team in Box I led flights headed up by Lts. Mish and Shaft, BN,- Lts. Buskirk and Hanna, BN,- Lts. Lackovich and Muir, BN, and Lts.Gary and Castle, BN. Lt.Stanley and F/O Blount flew deputy. A B-26 PFF Pathfinder led the formation, bombing at 13,500 feet with bombing rated as excellent. No flak or fighters were seen.

Mission #213 - 24 February - Vierson Communication Center. Major Dunn, Lts. Brewer and Maltby, BNs and Lts. Rooney with Kirk and Koch, BNs on Boxes. Captain Tutt and Lt. Beck, BN,- Lts. Lackovich and Muir, BN, -Captain Evans and Lt. McCartney, BN plus Lts.Anderson and Babbage, BN all led flights. The 416th and five other groups participated in the bombing to help advancing troops in close support for their advance toward Cologne. The 410th group bombed first with excellent results. Our group met a cloud cover, requiring GEE equipment bombing. Accurate flak bursts came up on the last minute of the bomb run, injuring ten aircraft. All planes returned safely to base.

Mission #214 - 25 February - Kerpen CommunicationCenter. Colonel Willetts with Lts. Royalty and Basnett, BNs and Captain Pair with Lts.Corum and Muir, BNs, led boxes. Lts.STanley and Blount, BN and Lts. Mish and Shaft, BN led flights. The first box sighted the target without PFF leading and scored an excellent. The second box followed PFF in and dropped on their lead. Lt. J.J. Farley, flying deputy on Col. Willetts took a direct hit on his left engine, knocking it out of the nacelle. Control was lost and the plane spun down. No chutes were seen. Sgt. E.R. Hardesty was the gunner with Farley. Other crew members reported the plane exploded. A piece of the engine struck Lt. Graeber's plane, but he was able to straighten it out and stay with the formation. Flak bursts blossomed out in front of the formation as it neared the target area, and continued on until they crossed the bomb line going home. Eight aircraft were pretty badly damaged, but they all managed to get back to base. The crews counted 27 guns firing at them near the target and 50 east of the target. A formidable concentration of firepower! On take-off, Colonel Willetts could not get his wheels up and did not access the lead. Lt. Mish was supposed to have taken the lead position, but the flights formed up on the deputy, Lt. Farley, instead. One flight from the second box formed up with the first box leaving Captain Pair with only one flight in his box. Colonel Willetts eventually caught up with the formation and assumed the Box I lead. Another first was experienced on the mission, with two newcomers to the 668th squadron flying in the jump seat of the A-26s, "to see how things are done." Lt.Tank and F/O Gunkel flew with Lts. Jacobsen and McCready. Their enthusiasm and excitement was expressed all over the base.

Mission #215 - 25 February - PM Norvenish (Munstereifel Town). As Captain Hulse said so often, "The planes can hardly catch their breath when the have to get going again." So it was on this day, again. The planes had not cooled down from the morning mission, when they were refueled and re-armed, even though the weather was threatening. Major Price and Lts. Forma and McCartney, BNs and Captain Anderson with BNs Lts., - Babbage and Shaft leading boxes. Captain Tutt and Lt. Beck BN and Lts. Buskirk and Hanna BN led flights. At 1400 the planes took off and arrived at the target cloud covered, requiring bombing with PFF pathfinders. Again, a new replacement pilot was riding shotgun with another pilot on our A-26s to see what the war was all about. Lt. Evarts rode with Lt. Kenny, which got Evarts all excited about what to expect when he got to ride the left seat.

Mission #216 - 26 February - Sindorf Communication Center. Colonel Napier with Lts.Moore and McQuade BNs with Captain Stebbins and Lts. Calloway and Johnson, BNs led boxes. This is the fourth straight day that we were called upon to bomb ahead of IX and I Armies. Captain Evans and Lt. McCartney, BN, Lts. Mish and Shaft, BN, Captain Tutt with Lt. Beck, BN and Lts. Buskirk and Hanna, BN led flights. The PFF plane could not drop his bombs. Col. Napier contacted "Roselee" because their GEE devices were not working. Roselee directed them to hit Munstereifel. When they arrived over that target, they found that the second box had selected that same target on its own. Results were not determined due to cloud cover. One plane had to drop out of its spot in the formation due to engine trouble. He joined up with the 410th group hitting Wickrath Communication Center. No flak was encountered.

Mission #217 - 28 February - Unna Communication Center. Major Dunn with Lts. Brewer and Maltby, BNs - Lt. Rooney with Lts. Kirk and Koch BNs led boxes. Lts. Stanley and Blount, BN, Lts. Anderson and Babbage, BN, Captain Tutt and Lt. Beck, BN with Lts. Lackovich and Muir, BN, led flights - Cloud cover required PFF pathfinders to lead the formation. The PFF unit ran into some difficulty and did not signal a drop, but the BN box leader, using his own GEE equipment went on to bomb a marshalling yard at Seigen with good results. The second box got to drop with their PFF leader, dropping incendiary bombs on the primary target. This facility included two dozen large buildings and barracks which were demolished. This was another milk-run - No fighters or flak.

With only 28 days in February, our group flew 22 missions on 17 days, inclement weather preventing our filling up every calender day. We assisted the ground troops in their race to Germany, with excellent results. The bombing/strafing missions were by far the most exhilarating for our crews, even though they spelled danger every time they went out. The big move closer to the front lines was equally exciting, even though living conditions were not the best, but what can you expect in a war zone? We did the best we could with whatever little we had, which is the same thing other groups are going through as we get closer to the Fatherland.

A press release from the Ninth Bombardment Division Headquarters highlighted what the 416 Bomb Group did along with other A-20 and A-26 groups, and the ever reliable B-26 groups. We should never leave out our respect and admiration for the wonderful escort protective services provided by the fighters, P-38s, P-47s and P-51s. It was a warm feeling looking up to see these little birds circling our formations during our raids. We felt somebody cared about our good happenings. The press release said our 9th Division

> attacks left Germany's communication network along the western front a jig-saw of broken and damaged bridges, leveled towns and severed rail lines. . . . The 24 day offensive saw the medium and light bombers, flying more than 7,000 sorties, roar over front line ground forces to batter Germany's transportation system in an area extending from Hanover south to the Saar Valley. They rained 11,000 tons of bombs on 59 communication centers.

CHAPTER 13

March 1945 Missions
It Happened at the Front
Rooney's Sad Mission
Ninth Bomb Division Has Record Month

March 1945 Missions

The strength of the group at the end of February was 253 Officers and 1221 Enlisted men. At the end of March, the group strength was:

668th Squadron	52 Officers	268 Enlisted Men
669th "	59 Officers	291 Enlisted Men
670th "	63 Officers	294 Enlisted Men
671st "	65 Officers	284 Enlisted Men
HQ. 416th	33 Officers	55 Enlisted Men
Totals	272 Officers	1192 Enlisted Men

Personnel changes made during March would be:

Major McNulty became Commanding Officer of 668th Bomb Squadron
Lt. Colonel Willetts named Operations Officer for the Group
Major Dunn became Commanding Officer of the 671st from C.O. of the 670th
Major Ferris became Commanding Officer of the 670th Bomb Squadron
Lt. Royalty, BN transferred to 670 as Assistant Operations Officer
Lt. Forma, BN transferred to 671st from 668th Squadron. Completed 65 missions.

The status of various personnel was reported as :

S/Sgt. L. Ashton	From MIA to POW
S/Sgt. J. S. Wing	From MIA to POW
Sgt. A. D. Wylie	From MIA to KIA
Captain R.B. Prentiss	From MIA to KIA
1st Lt. Burseil BN	From MIA to KIA
S/Sgt. D.M. Brown	From MIA to KIA

First Lieutenant Norman V. Shainberg, a POW, was returned to duty in the states under military control, having lost his leg in the hands of German captors, having been injured in his crash landing.

This was the first Easter Holiday that the French people enjoyed since the Germans took over their country, so our group gathered candies the soldiers had accumulated, and doughnuts from the Red Cross and distributed them to 850 French Children. aged four to seven, at the Laon School. There seemed to be no hostility the French people had against our boys because of the destruction of a major part of their city, by our bombers. Some of our boys were invited into the homes of the residents for dinners and entertainment. The Mayor of Laon and other dignitaries joined with our officers and men to make the affair a joyous one, promoting friendships amid their hardships.

Easter services were celebrated during Holy Week, ending up with a Catholic Mass at the famous Rheims Cathedral, attended by group personnel of all religions.

The Distinguished Service Cross, the nation's second highest award, under the Medal of Honor, was awarded to more of our men. First Lieutenant John W. Kehoe who at that time was listed as MIA, earned the award for "extraordinary heroism in action against the enemy while serving as pilot of an A-26 the aircraft on a mission to Munstereifel, Germany 25 December 1944."

Major Leland C. Neilsen received the award for a bomb-strafe mission conducted on 23 January 1945 at Blankenheim, Germany. A third Distinguished Service Cross was been awarded to Lt.Tommie J. Sims, and a fourth such Medal was earned by Captain Paul Atkinson, also on the bomb-strafe mission at Blankenheim on 23 January 1945.

Bronze Star Medals were awarded to Captain William P. Kinney, Group S-4 for "outstanding factor in the success of our operations." The Bronze Star Medal was also awarded to T/Sgt.M.E. Bjertness, a crew chief, plus S/Sgt. W. M. Max of Special Services, and Sgt. Carl Valentine, a crew chief, all for

"Meritorious achievement in direct support of military operations."

Mission #218 - 1 March - Giessen Ordnance Depot. Major Dunn with Lts. Brewer and Basnett, BNs, plus Lts. Buskirk with Lts. Hanna and Muir, BNs, led boxes. Lts. Evans and McCartney, BN flew as deputy. Flights were led by Lts. Mish and Shaft, BN and Lts. Brown and Kerns, BN. B-26 PFF pathfinders had to lead the formation due to cloud cover, The PFF equipment failed to operate, and the fighter rendezvous did not connect, so the formation went for the secondary target, just over the bomb line, the town of Brenn and the Eller bridge. No flak or fighters engaged the formation.

Mission #219 - 2 March - Iserlohn Transport Depot. This depot contained replacement parts for much field equipment plus their required motors, so frag bombs were loaded on our planes, to follow PFF planes again. Captain Evans with Lt. McCartney and F/O Blount as BNs led Box I. Major Price and Lt. Forma, BN flew as deputy to Box I. Captain Anderson with Lts. Babbage and Shaft, BNs, Lts. Brown and Kerns, BN and Captain Pair with Lt. Corum BN led flights. Bombs were dropped through clouds. This was a welcome second "milk-run" for the group.

Mission #220 - 3 March - Giessen Ordnance Depot and Germany Army Quartermaster Hdqs. Lt. Colonel Napier with Lts. Moore and McQuade, BNs and Captain Miller with Lts. Conner and Johnson, BNs led the two boxes. Captain Pair and Lt. Corum BN, Captain Tutt and Lt. Beck, BN,- Lt.Stanley and F/O Blount, BN, plus Lts. Mish and Shaft, BN led flights. Lt. McCready flew a window dropping plane. Bombs were released through cloud cover. Another milk-run?

This day - 3 March - is the first anniversary of the first mission flown from England to the French coast. The experiences of the year have made the group a considerable assist to the war effort and earned a reputation of fine definition. Practically all of the original flying personnel who came overseas with the group have completed their missions and have been replaced by very qualified and ambitious pilots, bombardier-navigators and gunners.

The following personnel will leave the group this month for the states, having put in their required missions:

Major R. F. Price - Captains R. L. Behlmer, - C. C. Mish - E. B. Kreb - First Lieutenants W. F. Tripp, Jr.,- R. Conte,- J. F Smith, - J.C. Sewell, and E. J. Renth, - Staff Sergeants P.C.Euga,- E. L.Shafer,- A. Teran, -D. H. Debower,- R. G. Schrom, and R. F. Tolbert. Technical Sergeant J.F. Goggin. Assigned to the AAF Flexible Gunnery School in the states, are Staff Sergeants K. G. Lagerman ,- M.E. Diaz, and R. W. Cheuveront. Captain F. J. Harrold was to return to the states after completing temporary duty with the ground forces.

Mission #221 - 4 March - Huls Marshalling Yard. Captain Stebbins and Lts. Calloway and McQuade, BNs led the only box making this mission. Major Price with Lt. Shaft BN flew as window droppers. Other flight leaders were Lts. Anderson and Babbage, BN, plus Lts. Brown and Kerns, BN. The mission was supposed to be with PFF but an opening in the clouds permitted the bombardiers to see what they were aiming at. This opening also gave the anticraft gunners something to see and shoot at, with weak inaccurate flak. On the way back to base, the weather thickened up and descent was through clouds. Lt. Hackley of the 669th had his plane go out of control momentarily, and his gunner bailed out without having received instructions to do so. He parachuted in the area of Charleroi. Hackley was able to fight his plane and brought it under control to land safely at base

Mission #222 -5 March - AM - Marburg Marshalling Yard. Major Dunn with Lts. Brewer and Basnett, BNs with Lt. Buskirk and Lts. Hanna and Muir, BNs led the two boxes. Captain Evans and Lt. McCartney BN and Lts. Brown with Kerns, BN plus Lts. Mish and Shaft, BN led flights. Using PFF pathfinder technique, bomb loads of 55 tons, 500 pounders, were dropped. No flak or fighters were encountered.

Mission #223 - 5 March - PM - Bingen Marshalling Yard. Captain Stebbins with Lts. Calloway and McQuade, BNs with Captain Anderson and Lts. Conner and Johnson, BNs led boxes. Captain Tutt and Lt. Beck BN and Lts Lackovich and Muir, BN led flights. PFF planes led the boxes at 12,500 feet. No flak or fighters. The formation landed well after sunset. Photo recon later showed extensive damage was done by the hits. Lt. Bob Basnett, BN of the 671st squadron completed his mission tour with 66 to his credit. He did an outstanding job as flight and box leader, flying with different pilots during his tour. He was one of the original bombardier-navigators to come overseas with the group and the first BN of the 671st to complete the magic 65.

Mission #224 - 6 March - Opladen Marshalling Yard. Lt. Col. Napier with Lts.Moore and McQuade BNs and Captain Miller with Lts. Conner and Johnson, BNs led boxes. Captain Evans and Lt. McCartney, BN,- Lts. Lackovich and Muir BN, -Captain Pair and Lt. Corum BN plus Lts. Buskirk and Hanna BN, led flights. Lt. Mish with Lt.Shaft BN, flew a window dropping plane The usual PFF pathfinder planes led the formation to bomb through the clouds. Recon showed the bombs enveloped the northern end of the yards with considerable damage. The fighter escort did not show up, but the group went on anyway. No flak came up

Mission #225 - 8 March - Wulfrath Motor Transport Depot. A large castle and eight smaller buildings were headquarters for this important target. Captain Stebbins with Lts. McQuade and Calloway, BNs with Lt. Rooney and Lts. Kirk and Koch, BNs led boxes. Lt. Stanley and F/O Blount, BN, - Lt. Anderson and Babbage, BN ,- Lts. Brown and Kerns, BN and Lts. Lackovich and Muir, BN led flights. Bombing was through PFF once more with no results being checked out. No enemy opposition hindered the mission.

Mission #226 - 9 March - AM - Butzbach Marshalling Yard. Major Dunn with Lts. Brewer and Beck, BNs, with Lts. Brown and Kerns - Muir, BNs led boxes. Lts. Mish and Shaft flew flight leads. Lt. Anderson and Lt. Babbage, BN flew deputy to the box leader. Major Price and F/O Blount flew a window plane. Bombing was through clouds with PFF resulting in good results. One of the boxes of our formation missed the signal of the PFF leader and it went on to bomb the communications center at Werterburg with good results. Of the eleven Bomb Groups of the 9th Air Force, six were attacked by enemy fighters today. Three groups actually engaged an estimated 30 ME-109s, along with other German fighters. Three groups felt the brunt of the fighter attacks, with three A-26s shot down. Our gunners claimed damage to some of the Germans. The 416th saw fighters in their bombing area, but they did not attack. The fighter escorts of our groups must have had a great time shooting at the ME 109s. At least they kept those yellow nosed guys away from us.

Mission #227 - 9 March - PM - Wulfen Ammunition Factory. Captain Evans with Lts. McCartney and Babbage, BN team plus Captain Stanley with F/O Blount and Lt. Shaft, BNs headed up the boxes. General Backus, Commander of the 97th Bomb Wing flew as an observer with Captain Evans. Captain Pair and Lt. Corum, BN and Lts. Lackovich and Muir, BN led flights. Lts. Jacobsen and Harvest BN, flew a window ship. With 10/10 cloud cover, PFF B-26s led the formation in to the target. The first box results were not known. The second box bombs were seen through a break in the clouds, and results were rated good, seeing many fires and bursts of flames coming up. Again, FW 190s were seen, but did not attack. Five of our planes received flak damage.

Mission #228 - 10 March - Dillerburg - Neiderscheld Marshalling Yard. Lt. Col. Napier with Lts. McQuade and Moore, BN team.. Captain Miller and Lts. Conner and Enman, BN team headed up the boxes. Other flight leaders were Lts Anderson and Babbage, BN, Captain Pair with Lt. Corum BN, and Lts. Brown and Kerns, BN. Lts. Mish and Shaft flew window planes. The usual cloud cover obscured the target but PFF pathfinders were used. Excellent results were reported. No flak or fighters.

Mission #229 - 11 March - AM - Lippe Airfield. Captain Stebbins with Lts. Calloway and McQuade, BN team on Box I. Captain Stanley with F/O Blount, BN, Captain Evans and Lt. McCartney, BN, Lts. Lackovich and Muir, and Captain Pair with Lt. Corum, BN led flights. Demolition bombs were dropped through clouds with PFF leaders to blanket this field since it housed planes harrassing our troops at the Rhine River beachhead we had established. The import of the target was emphasized by the fact eleven bomb groups of the 9th Bomb Wing were sent to attack and wipe this field out. No flak or fighters.

Mission #230 - 11 March - PM - Wulfen Ammunition Filling Plant which we attacked a few days before. Major Dunn with Lts. Brewer and Beck, BNs and Lts. Brown and Kerns/Muir, as BN team led boxes. Lts. Mish and Shaft took a flight in. Lts. Anderson and Babbage, BN flew window ships. Bombing through clouds with PFF pathfinders was used. After this four hour mission, all planes returned safely, with no flak encountered.

Mission #231 - 12 March AM - Lorch Marshalling Yard. Captain Evans, with Lts. McCartney and Babbage, BNs with Captain Stanley and F/O Blount and Lt. Shaft, BNs took the boxes in. Major Price flew a window ship over the target. Captain Tutt with Lts. Beck and Germana, BNs,- Captain Pair and Lts. Corum and Reed, BNs led flights. PFF aids did the bombing through clouds with no results observed. No flak or fighters.

Mission #232 - 12 March - PM - Posen Marshalling Yard (Mummebech)? Lt. Col. Napier with Lts. Moore and Calloway, BN team in Box I. Box II had Captain Miller and Lts. Conner and Johnson as BNs. Flight leaders were Lts. Andersen and Babbage BN, Captain Pair and Lt.Corum BN and Lts. Lackovich and Muir. PFF bombing was required due to cloud cover. Little, inaccurate flak was seen. German equipment and supplies were being rushed to this marshalling yard in the area of the Ramagen bridgehead the allies held, so it had to be attacked.

During the month of March, Ground Forces personnel were guests of our group, for the purpose of providing information on what missions were all about, how they formulated, and carried out. They became observers on some missions. Not one of the officers or men flying with our crews volunteered to remain with us for this type duty. Much the same feeling of our air crews visiting the front lines, saying the air was better than the ground battle fields. It was an interesting experience for them to relate to their compatriots about what the other side of the war was like.

Mission #233 - 13 March - AM - Rheine Airdrome. This was a German jet plane base, but surprisingly, none of them rose to challenge our group. Captain Stebbins with Lts. Calloway and Powell, BN teams with Major Ferris and Lts. Royalty and Boch BNs were box leaders. Captain Fair and Lt. Corum BN and Lts. Lackovich and BN, led flights. Major Price and Lt. Hand, BN flew window for the group. This was Major Price's 65th mission, the one everybody sweats out.

PFF pathfnders led the group in. As the planes turned off the target, moderate, accurate flak rose and hit six planes. One, piloted by Lt. C. S. Jordan took a bad shot on the under carriage of the plane. When he tried to land, his wheels would not extend, resulting in a crash landing at Station A-70. He did a magnificient job of bringing the ship down, with bent props and skinned underbelly. His gunner, S/Sgt. H. F. Jensen and an observer from the Eleventh Armored Division, S/Sgt. E. E. Bolton, escaped injury. Photo recon showed craters on runways and the general field area attesting to the effectiveness of the 831 bombs dropped by our boys.

Mission #234 - 13 March - PM - Neihem/Huston MarshallingYard. Major Dunn, Lts. Brewer and Corum, BNs and Lts. Brown with Kerns and Muir, BNs headed up the boxes. Captain Sutton with Lt. Reed BN, and Lts. Mish and Shaft, BN led flights. Lts. Anderson and Babbage BN flew deputy on Box I. The PFF plane was unable to keep up with the formation, so they went in to try to bomb visually. Two runs were made due to haze obscuring the aiming point. The boxes wound up dropping on GEE equipment with undetermined results. Moderate, heavy accurate flak hit the planes, with little damage, One gunner shot at an ME 109 which threatened the lead PFF plane. This was Lt. Mish's 65th mission, and he was glad to get it over with.

Mission #235 - 14 March - Neider-Marsburg Railway Bridge. Captain Evans with Lts. McCartney and Shaft, BNs and Lts. Rooney with Kirk and McNutt, BNs were up front on the boxes. Other flights were led by Captain Pair and Lt.Corum, BN, and Captain Tutt with Lt.Germana, BN. This is the first mission in a very long time that did not require PFF leadership. Visual bombing, even though a heavy haze resulted in an excellent pattern destroying the bridge and its approaches. One flight misidentified the target and bombed another bridge instead of the primary, with good results. No flak met the group, all returning to base unharmed.

Mission #236 - 15 March - Pirmasens Road Junction. Ninth Bomb Division sent out eleven groups to wipe out this town which stood in the path of advancing allied armies. Our group scored well, with bombs falling in the center of town, amid smoke and flames. Frag bombs dropped by other groups fell right in between smoke and flames, destroying their objective. In spite of clear weather, no flak came up. This mission was led by Lt. Col. Napier with Lts.Moore and Johnson, BN team on Box I. Captain Miller with Lts. Conner and Enman, BNs led Box II. Lts. Lackovich and Muir, BN,- Lts. Brown and Kerns, BN, Captain Pair and Corum BN, and Captain Sutton and Lt. Reed BN, all led flights.

Mission #237 - 17 March - Alten Kirchen Road Junction. Lts. Rooney with Lts. Kirk and Moore, BNs led Box I. Major Ferris and Lts. Royalty and Koon, BNs on Box II. A solid cloud moved in over the target, PFF was used. No enemy action was experienced.

On March 17 Major General Anderson from Ninth Bomber Command sent this message to the 416th Bomb Group.

> Please inform all crews that examination of approximately 25 Reconnaissance sorties flown on 14 and 15 March reveals that the large number of PFF missions flown by the 9th Bomb Division (M) during February and March were extremely effective. Approximately 90 percent of targets attacked were hit. Damage ranged from moderate to severe. Patterns on the ground reveal that a majority of formations were excellent and that groups did an excellent job of bombing on PFF lead. This is extremely gratifying to me and a source of great credit to all concerned in view of the adverse weather conditions under which most of these missions were flown and difficulties encountered with PFF signals. I realize the adverse effect of bombing blind with no knowledge of how much you are hurting the enemy. I hope the knowledge that on these blind missions you hurt him plenty will be the same shot in the arm that the sight of a bridge you have put in the water is. Anyway, the results are grand and I'm proud of you all.

There are four men from the front lines living with the group now, to learn what mission flying is all about. They feel the experience is spectacular.

Mission #238 - 17 March - Bad Homburg Marshalling Yards. This was a real snafued mission from the start. The formation was late going into the target, due mainly because of bad weather. Ground control notified the PFF planes to hold their bombs. The formation had scattered in the clouds with flight leaders scrounging to seek targets to hit. The first flight used GEE equipment to attack the briefed secondary target, Weilburg. Two other flights of the first box, using GEE equipment attacked Montabeur. Most of the second box attacked Weilburg using GEE equipment. Four planes separated from the rest of the formation, dropping their bombs on German territory. Major Dunn with Lt. Brewer BN and Lt. Claude Brown with Lt. Kerns, BN led Boxes. Captain Pair and Lt.Corum BN,- Captain Sutton with Lt. Reed and Lts. Lackovich and Muir leading flights.

Mission #239 - 18 March - Worms Communication Center. Box leaders were Captain Evans with Lts. McCartney and Freed BNs on Box I. Captain Anderson with Lts. Babbage and Roman, BNs on Box II. Flight leaders were Lts. Buskirk and Hanna, BN, - Lts. Lackovich and Muir BN, - Captain Sutton and Reed, BN. This was a mission of Big Hurts and classified as another Bloody Sunday, one of the worst. PFF was planned for this misssion, but as they neared the target area, clouds cleared,, the lead bombardier dropped visually. Bombs of the first box fell in two patterns in the town, causing extensive damage to buildings, roads and railroad tracks. Box two scored hits in the marshalling yards and a highway overpass. The PFF planes started an unusually long bomb run and the lead bombardier visually sighted the target and dropped. The second box also decided to bomb visually and went to the Initial Point to start their bomb run. Moderate flak met them on the way to the target. The anti aircraft gunners could now see the formation through the cloud break and let loose with everything they had. Four planes were lost near the town of Bingen. Two went down near the target. Twenty three other planes suffered flak damage and as the saying goes, "they must have had their first sergeants manning the guns." They did a good job. The crews that went down presumably did not have a chance to parachute out, although that did not prove to be the fact. The plane piloted by Lt. J. P. Kinney with gunner S/Sgt. J. J. Sittarich received a direct hit in the left engine. It was last seen disintegrating and in flames, going down. Lt. Ross H. Cornell with BN Lt. R. E. Enman, and gunner S/Sgt. A. Carter took a direct hit on the turn off the target. Both engines were smoking and it was going down fast, but apparently under control. After flames broke out in the right engine nacelle, the right wing broke off about 3000 feet above the ground. They were all listed as MIA, but Cornell was returned to Military Command from having been a POW. Enman was lost. Another plane piloted by Lt. W. B. Jokinen and Sgt. E. J. Creeden also received a direct hit and was seen to hit the ground in flames. Their story and that of Lt.Chitty should be related.

This is the first person story of Lt. Chitty:

> On the 18th of March we bombed the town of Worms. I was flying No. 2 position of the second flight, first box. This was a PFF mission but as we crossed the bomb line the weather was CAVU. We reached the IP flying at 11,000 feet and 200 MPH, made a right turn and leveled off for the bomb run. My gunner, Sgt. Raccio called several flak bursts at 6:00 o'clock. At the same time there was a bad explosion and the left engine quit. I advanced full throttle and RPM to my good engine and stayed with the formation. About ten seconds later another burst directly in front of me knocked three holes in my windshield and one in my canopy, spraying me with powdered glass. We opened bomb doors and feathered my left engine with no results. About one minute later Sgt. Raccio called and said there were several pieces of small metal from the top of the bomb bay lying in his compartment. Also he saw several holes in the tail and wings. I released my bombs when the leader dropped his. I knew I couldn't stay in formation during evasive action, so pulled

> away from the formation and crossed the bomb line alone. I noticed my pressure on the left engine showed fuel down. I switched to full booster and the left engine sputtered a few times and caught up although the fuel pressure was still around ten pounds. As the formation reached the RP, I rejoined my flight and set course for the base. Ten minutes later, Sgt Raccio called that smoke was coming into his compartment. I told him to locate the fire and put it out. He then called back and said it was gasoline vapor coming in pretty thick. I called him up to the pilot's compartment. I called in for an emergency landing at our base and went in, cutting off the fuel line. The fire fighters were at the end of the runway, when we got out and ran.

The report of Lt. W. B. Jokinen and Sgt. E. J. Creeden is not detailed, but they were reported to have gone down and crashed, exploding. Lt. Jokinen was on his 17th mission and Sgt. Creeden was on his 10th. The story related in the history of the 671 squadron, put together by Gordon Russell, and assembled by Lt. Jim Kerns requires repeating:

It Happened at the Front

A story which might have originated with “Believe it or Not Ripley” broke here at A-69 when Lt. John B. Cooke and his two gunners, S/Sgt. MacCartney and Sgt. Redding returned from their trip to the front on 28 March. It had to with Lt. Jokinen and Sgt.Creeden and their plane ... and it definitely was “good news.” Here's the way it happened:

> Sgt. MacCartney and Redding were putting in some Jeep Time near the town of Gemunden which the Third Army had just taken. The boys spotted a crashed plane in the distance and took the Jeep cross country to take a look at it. As they got closer they

noticed it was a familiar A-26 Invader, their interest rising. The boys got quite a start when they got close enough to see the black rudder markings, the number and letter for it was their own ship, No. 237-D. The ship had bellied in on the flat surface on top of a hill outside town. The pair made a thorough search of the plane and the area. Both hatches were lying on the ground beside the plane, evidence that Lt. Jokinen and Sgt.Creeden had gotten out of the plane but the plane was not torn up badly. There was no sign of blood in either section of the ship. MacCartney found the flak jackets a short distance from the plane. The nose guns had been removed, probably by the Germans for their use..

The ground troops which had gathered around the plane were very skeptical when the two gunners exclaimed that it was their own plane and one in which they had flown several missions. MacCartney answered their "Oh Yeahs" by turning his back to them saying, "Take a look at the number and letter on the A-26 and the back of my jacket!" And sure enough, there was old No. 237 D on the jacket.

They told Lt. Cooke of their find and he returned with them to the plane. It seemed apparent to Lt. Cooke that the pilot and gunner climbed out of the plane themselves and were taken prisoner by the Jerris who occupied the territory when they went down. The three agreed that Jokinen had made a perfect crash landing, although at the time and until they returned to A-69 they did not know who was flying the ship.

Lt. Jokinen's plane received several flak bursts in the engines over the target - Worms. With the oil system in both engines leaking, he made a vain attempt to get back across the bomb line, but apparently the engines burned out and he was forced to set it down. It was a story of so close and yet so far, for he was just six miles from the Fourth Armored Division.

The squadron is now anxiously awaiting further word about Lt. Jokinen, and it is hoped that he and Sgt. Creeden may be freed in the Allied drive into Germany.

The sequel to that story is that on April 7, Squadron D Operations received a call from Lt.William R. Jokinen that he had escaped from the Germans and was at USTAFF Hdqs in Paris. Jokinen returned to the squadron on April 13th, telling that when he found he could not make it to friendly lines, he sought a crash landing spot and went in. He and Sgt. Creeden jumped out of the plane and threw a grenade into it, but it was a dud. It did not explode. He returned to the plane to retrieve a few things, when the Germans arrived and took them in as prisoners. They separated the pilot from the gunner and started a long march which resulted in foot blisters from the long treks. They marched at night for two weeks. When they got to the destination three other prisoners and Lt. Jokinen made their escape. During their long night marches, they only received black bread and water. Aside of the hikes and poor food, they were not mistreated. After the break-out, the four crept, crawled, hid and ran until they reached the Seventh Army and were then taken back to Paris.

Mission #240 - 18 March - PM - Kreutztel Marshalling Yard. Lt. Col. Napier with Lts. Miller and Hulgrew BNs and Captain Miller with Lts.Conners and Wrubbelle, BN led the two boxes. The 671st squadron furnished four flight leader teams for this mission, including: Captain Tutt and Lt. Orr, BN,- Captain Sutton and Lt. Reed, BN,- Lts. Buskirk and Hanna, BN, - Lts. Brown and Kerns, BN. The lead PFF plane did not drop, calling for the second flight BN team to take over. The Gee equipment of the second team, Lts. Brown-Kerns Gee equipment did not function so they failed to drop. Brown called “Bullseye” for a vector to the target and after flying for about an hour got back to the target and bombed on GEE which started to work again. Weak inaccurate flak met them on the bombline. The second box dropped on PFF with no problem, but results were not determined.

Mission #241 & 242 - 19 March AM - Lage Railroad Bridge. This is called spreading activities around, taking advantage of the weather and the excellence of the crews. In the morning, two boxes were directed to different targets and a third box in the afternoon zeroed in on the Lage Railroad Bridge with Major Ferris and Lts. Royalty and Moore, BNs leading the first box of 24 planes bombed with excellent results. Moderate accurate flak met them on the bomb run for five minutes damaging nine planes. Lts. Brown and Kerns, BN led flights.

Captain Rooney led the second box of 21 planes to Nassau Communication Center with excellent results. No flak or fighters bothered this formation. Lts. Lackovich and Muir. BN led a flight.

Mission #243 - 19 March - PM - Schweim Marshalling Yard. Major Dunn with Lt. Brewer BN. This box were directed to fly behind a 409th Bomb Group Box. The lead plane was hit, injuring the bombardier and the pilot, so they did not drop. Major Dunn's box dropped, but no results were determined.

Mission #244 - 20 March- Geisecke Marshalling Yard. PFF Pathfinder B-26s led our group. The PFF plane developed engine trouble before the bomb run. Major Shaefer and Lts. Hand and Roman, BNs leading box I took three bomb runs over the target, eventually dropping on the secondary target, Westerberg with success. The second box led by Captain Evans and Lts. McCartney and Freed, BNs had difficulty and changed their aiming point to another part of the town, but his bombs scattered in the woods. However, 76 tons of bombs blanketed the town of Westerberg. Weak, inaccurate flak was experienced. Captain Tutt, Lt. Orr, BN and Lts. Buskirk and Hanna, BN, plus Lts.

Lackovich and Muir led flights. Two pilots of the 671st who joined the squadron in May 1944 flew their 65th missions today as window dropping planes.

Rooney's Sad Mission

Mission #245 - 21 March - AM - Goesfield Communication Center. Incendiaries from 37 planes made this community in Holland a firey mess, Captain Miller with Lts. Conner and McCartney, BNs and Lt. Col. Napier with Lts. Miller and Hullgrew BN, led the boxes. Flights were headed up by Captain Tutt and Lt. Orr BN, Lts. Buskirk and Hanna BN, plus Lts. Lackovich and Muir BN. Captain Tutt had an Infantry Observer, Lt. Robertson riding with him. The bombs were dropped amidst smoke and flames, but the results showed the entire town seemed to be burning.. The formation flew over most of Holland into the target, but weak, inaccurate flak did not bother them. All returned safely.

Mission #246 - 21 March - PM - Vreden Communication Center. Major Ferris with Lts. Royalty and McNutt, BNs in Box I and recently promoted to Captain, Rooney with Lt. Kirk, BN leading Box II. The flights in Rooney's box were each assigned a different target to bomb. Flights were led by Lt. Anderson and Lt. Babbage, BN, - Lts. Brown and Kerns, BN,- Captain Tutt and Lt. Orr, BN. Captain Rooney had another Infantry Observer riding with him, Captain Chester C. Slaughter.

The second box was to have each of its flights to bomb different targets and then join up behind Rooney's flight to go back to base. After dropping their bombs, Captain Anderson leading flight B was coming in to rejoin behind Rooney, all flying west, into a setting sun. The gunner in Lt. Downing's ship, who was flying in the #4 slot right behind and below Rooney's ship called Downing, telling him Anderson was leading his flight straight into theirs, and before any correction could take place, Anderson's plane got into Rooney's flight. This is the story as related by Lt. Robert Bower who was flying on the left side of

Rooney, in the No. 3 position of Box B, known as position B-1-3.

Bower, now a Reverend in Maryland, wrote on 19 February, 1999 as follows:

> Today I rechecked my diary. Now I wish my writing had been more, much more detailed. The date is recorded for my 28th mission with a good bomb report encountering flak going in and exiting. Flight leaders did fine evasive action.
>
> A clear day, away from flak, it had every appearance of being a Sunday afternoon family ride home. It was that, except for flying into the sun necessitating a lot of squinting.
>
> While flying number B-1-3 on Rooney, I was flying my usual formation mode, style, or what have you? One gunner, Ike Hummer said of one mission with me, 'My God, you scared the hell out of me.' 'How did I do that?' 'You flew so damn close,I could count the rivets on the lead ship.' I was in a close position to Rooney. I was in tight enough to readily see him.
>
> The flight was proceeding without incident, figuring we would soon be on the ground without having to do an instrument let-down. My unworried state of mind was abruptly, suddenly, instantaneously alerted when from somewhere a strong command type voice hit my ear phones, 'Bower, move out!' I could tell it wasn't Rooney. Who? Where did it originate? Responding to what I sensed was an urgency in the voice as well as the nature of an order, I instantaneously jammed left rudder and right aileron and slid out!
>
> As I did, I looked to my right. Dumfounded, I saw the nose of an A-26. Immediately, it was obvious that something bad was going to happen.

Consequently, pulled back on my power setting while pulling back on the wheel. This retarded my air speed to the point where I could observe and not fly beyond what was an ensuing tragedy.

The invasive ship had flown into my spot and at a speed that surpassed us. The right wing of the invasive ship struck the tip of Rooney's left wing. About that time, Rooney looked over to where I had been. As he did, I saw a smile on his face - seeming to say 'I'm glad it isn't you.' I can see that handsome face today. The invasive aircraft proceeded in an upward angle, something like a gentle stall. As it did, it fell off on the right wing toward Rooney. The invasive aircraft continued to fall toward Rooney's left wing. I watched the left prop of Rooney's ship cut through the aft bomb bay of the invasive ship. Whirling away that prop looked like a giant pair of scissors.

The empenage of the invasive craft flew over my plane. Both ships then fell off to the right. Someone called out, 'All ships continue on in formation!'

While the two aircraft spun to the right, I continued to hold back on power and went to my left. In no time, I saw them. Realizing that each aircraft was doomed, I hit the mike and called out 'Rooney, for God's sake, jump, jump, go, go!'

I floated around and saw Kirk's chute blossom. What a lovely sight! I understood Kirk called Rooney at 5,000 feet to say he was going. 'Go ahead, Good Luck!' Rooney was reported to say to Kirk. When both aircraft hit the ground, they exploded. A ball of fire formed out from underneath each aircraft.Then I left.

Why didn't Rooney jump? I've wondered. He was conscious. He was functioning. Did the canopy get jammed? Could be quite possible if the invasive craft continued to fall toward the nose of Rooney's craft. Did Captain Slaughter panic - possible and yet he too may have been trapped.

My diary has a note - 'I fell sick and weak - so near and yet so far - it was really wonderful to get back on the ground.'

If I differ from other accounts you'll have to overlook my memoried observations of what? A greatful survivor.

Lt. Downing, flying behind and below Rooney in B-1-4 spot reported the two planes, Rooney's and Anderson's props were slicing up each other's aluminum fuselage, with pieces of metal dropping all over him. Downing said he knew enough not to pull out to right or left, which would be the natural thing to do, because he would crash into the number 5 or 6 plane. Going down would have been out and certainly flying up would be right into the two merged aircraft. Downing held his position, watching all the pieces of both planes going down. Fortunately for him, nothing severely damaged his plane. Downing's gunner, Sgt. Sgroi was injured in the mishap from falling debris.

The massive irony of this incident is that Captain Rooney was on his last, 65th mission, having just received his Captain's bars, and a celebration awaited him by his tent mates, cake and all. The second irony, Captain Slaughter, the Infantry observer, lost his life. Rooney's gunner Sgt. Robert J. Kamischke went down with the plane. The gunners in Anderson's plane perished with Anderson, so six fatalities resulted from this act of God. Was that it? Rooney's flight undoubtedly was flying right into the setting sun, which was blinding Anderson.

Mission #247 - 22 March - AM - Berken Communication Center. Major Dunn with Lt. Brewer and F/O Lehneis BNs led Box I. Lts. Brown and Kerns BN, led Box II. The concentration of troops and equipment on the east bankof the Rhine River signaled a major thrust by Germans. This mission was to invalidate those efforts, by bombing fragmentation bombs in the area. The first box and its flights did well, scoring superior results. Two flights of the second box mis-identified the target and bombed the town of Sudlohn and Stedlohn with good results. Lt.Fero's plane received flak hits on the left engine and the right engine started smoking. Sgt. Rojas was the gunner with Fero. Fero salvoed his bombs and flew toward friendly territory. His bomb bay doors would not close after the bombs dropped, so Rojas had to pump the doors shut by hand. As they approached the field at Station A-55, they found the wheels would not lock, so he went in on his belly, in what was classified as a brilliant crash landing with no injuries.

Mission #248 - 21 March - PM - Berken Communication Center. Again. Major Shaefer, Lts. Hand and Reeves, BNs with Captain Stanley and F/O Blount and Lt. Schlefer, BNs led Boxes. Brigadier General Backus Commander of the 9th Bomber Wing, rode with Captain Shaefer as an observer. Flights were led by Lts. Buskirk and Hanna BN, - Captain Tutt with Lt. Orr BN. the target was still smoking from the morning raids making aiming difficult, so GEE equipment was used to drop the loads of incendiaries on the second run. An enemy fighter made a pass at the formation, firing tracers, with no results. No return fire was made from our gunners. Our P-47 escort turned the enemy away. No flak was received on this mission.

The Ninth Bomb Division handed out a release regarding recent bombing missions we ran. The release said:

> Communications inside seventeen German towns north of the Ruhr had been battered out of usefullness and smoke still covered entire town areas late Thursday, after some 1400 separate attacks by Ninth Bombardment Divison Marauders, Invaders and Havocs. These attacks have been aimed at sealing off the entire road and rail system in the northern sector of the Rhine. Since the air offensive opened in mid-morning Wednesday, nearly 2700 tons of

high explosives and incendiaries have been rained on main road junctions, supply depot and other military installations, in the key German towns. Located in a 50 mile arc running mid-way between Munster and the Rhine, each town is a key in the enemy's chain of communications north of the Ruhr. Object of the current program is to cut off all road and rail facilities leading east from the northern sector of the Rhine, thereby sealing off the battle area north the Ruhr Valley.

Mission #249 - 23 March - AM - Dinslaken Factory Area. Captain Miller, Lts. Conner and Johnson, BNs with Lt. Col. Napier with Lt. Moore and F/O Wrubelle, BNs leading boxes. Lts. Lackovich and Muir, BN,- Captain Sutton with Lt. Reed, BN, led flights. Excellent results were reported destroying a large portion of the factory and adjoining roads and buildings. Allied bombing seems to have rendered most German towns and areas reduced to piles of rubble, smoke and haze. Smoke seems to obscure most everything in the area, The Rhine River has yet to be crossed by enemy forces, with all the bombing allies are doing. There was weak but accurate flak in the area, with five planes suffering damage. Lt. Ford's plane took a hit on the first run toward the target. He broke away from the formation and headed toward friendly territory, still carrying his 1,000 pound bombs, flying on single engine. He was escorted by P-47s. At about 4000 feet, his other engine quit. With his bomb bay full of bombs and no power he managed to glide down for a crash landing, which he did with a slight injury to himself on the landing. His gunner, S/Sgt. Freeland W. Tharp had bailed out over German territory and was listed as MIA. He had not been given the order to bail out

Mission #250 - 23 March - PM - Dinslaken Factory Area. Major Ferris, Lts. Royalty and McNutt, BNs led Box I. Lt. Brewster with Lt. Dennis and F/O Conley, BNs were on Box II.

Captain Tutt and Lt. Orr BN leading Box III. Heavy smoke from the morning mission did not deter the bombs dropped in the PM from adding to the conflagrations, our boys dropping incendiaries. Most of the town was also on fire. Three boxes of eight planes each dropped 64 tons of a new type incendiary bomb, which was supposed to be inextinguishable. Weak inaccurate flak came up. Lts. Buskirk and Hanna BN led a flight with success.

Mission #251 - 24 March - AM - Ihling Kamps near Bocholt flak gun emplacements. Eleven groups were assigned different gun emplacements with frag bombs. Major Dunn, Lt. Brewer and F/O Lehneis BNs on Box I. Lts. Brown and Kerns, BN led Box II. Brigadier General Backus of 9th Bomb Wing rode as an observer with Major Dunn. Direct hits were made amid smoke and fire, with no flak coming up. The lead bombardier misidentified the target and bombed on the edge of town, Rhede, one mile east of the assigned target. He hit railroads, roads, and the buildings. On returning to base, we noticed numerous C-47s and gliders making their way to the Rhine River. Later news reports shouted that our troops had crossed the Rhine and that the Third Army led by General Patton had penetrated the area. Our bombing helped considerably. Two of our planes, led by Lt. Jordan and Lt. Mulgrewe BN were assigned to attack another flak position with the 409th Bomb Group. Our boys scored an excellent shot.

Mission #252 - 24 March - PM Colbe Railroad Bridge. Major Shaefer with Lts. Hand and Reeves, BNs leading the only box of 24 planes. Bombing just ahead of our forces, but to keep the enemy from using the bridge. The bombing scored an excellent, one superior one good and one unsatisfactory. One flight landed its load right on the center of the bridge. Railroad tracks and roads were damaged. Lt. Lackovich and Lt. Muir led a flight.

Mission #253 -25 March - AM - Altenkirchen Communication Center. Forty-eight planes were sent to demolish this road junction. Captain Miller with Lts. Conner and

Johnson, BNs were leading Box I. Captain Stebbins and Lt. Calloway BN led Box II. Lts. Buskirk and Hanna BN,- Captain Sutton and Lt. Reed BN, and Lt. Fero with F/O Langsom BN headed up flights. The planes met varying degrees of flak on the bomb line into the target, causing 22 ships damaged. Bombing results were excellent for some flights. A few flights could not be assessed. Lt. Barausky took a direct hit on the right engine. A large part of the nacelle fell off. He feathered the prop but continued on the bomb run. He headed for field Y-57 after dropping his bombs, to make a crash landing. His BN Lt. Sheehan came back from the nose of the ship and sat on the shot gun position for safety during the crash landing. Going in, Barausky feathered his left engine, gliding in. The gunner and the BN jettisoned their hatches, preparatory to a quick get out on landing.The left engine tore loose from its mounting, but all got out of the plane after it sank into the mud off the runway. Gunner Sgt. Ball was slightly injured.

Mission #254 - 25 March PM - Fulda Marshalling Yard. Two boxes of 37 aircraft attacked this very important and heavily trafficked marshalling yard, a key point for the transfer of supplies and equipment to German troops facing General Patton's bridgehead. Major Ferris with Lts. Royalty and McNutt BNs and Lt. Brewster with Lt. Dennis and F/O Conley led the boxes. Violent explosions indicated that the yards contained ammunition or fuel. One hundred and twenty five freight cars were destroyed or damaged, 47 hits were counted on the tracks, eight hits on the railroad overpass, destroying it, plus there were ten hits on railroad workshops. 23 on other buildings and 15 on roads, cutting them. All these hits attest to the bomb scoring of two superiors and four excellents.

Mission #255 - 26 March - Gemunden Marshalling Yard. This target was quite a distance from our base, but because of the rapid advances made by General Patton's troops, it was just a few miles ahead of the bomb line in his sector. The yards were the junction point of four separate rail lines. Again, two superiors and three excellents were the ratings of the bombing teams. The choke points, tracks, cars, and surrounding work shops were destroyed or severely damaged. New Box leading teams headed up this mission, they being Lt. Claude Brown and Lt. Jim Kerns with Lt. Brewer, BNs and Lts. J. A. Buskirk and R.C. Hanna BN.- Lt. Fero and F/O Langsam led a flight.

Mission #256 - 28 March - Ebrach Fuel Depot. Complete cloud cover caused 38 planes to become separated climbing through the overcast. PFF planes led the boxes. Twenty-nine planes bombed on PFF signal, with bombs falling east of the target. Four planes attacked a railroad and an autobahn crossing. Two planes dropped their bombs near Wurzburg. F/O H. G. Gunkel and gunner Sgt. L. J. Grzpna went down, unaccounted for. Their plane was last seen going down through the overcast at the start of the bomb run. They are listed as MIA. Major Shaefer, Lts. Hand and Reeves, BNs with Captain Evans and Lts McCartney and Myrold BNs led boxes. Captain Tutt, Lt. Orr BN, and Lt. Fero and F/O Langsan BN led flights.There were no battle damages to the formation.

Mission #257 - 30 March - Hann Munden Depot. Another PFF pathfinder mission B-26s leading the formation. Our group box leaders were Major Ferris with Lt. Brewster This was an ordnance depot and barracks area. Captain Tutt, Lt. Orr BN and Lts Lackovich and Muir BN, plus Lt. Van Noorden with F/O Brandt BN, led flights. Five ships received battle damage from moderate flak.

Mission #258 - 31 March - AM - Wurzburg Storage Area. Captain Miller with Lt. Conner and F/O Wrubelle, BNs and Lt. Col. Napier and Lt. Moore BN, led the boxes. Lt Fero and F/O Langsan BN, and Lts. Lackovich and Muir led flights. Patchy clouds obscured the target area so PFF pathfinders were used. The leader of the second box made a visual bomb run scoring an excellent hit. Violent explosions and high rising smoke billowing through the clouds were observed. Moderate, accurate flak damaged four planes, but all returned safely with no personal injuries.

Mission #259 - 31 March - PM - Marianburg Storage Area. This mission was determined to be an uneventful attack, with PFF Pathfinders leading the formation in. A few crews reported hits on the target area. Box I reported excellent results. Lt. Brown and Lts Kerns and Brewer, BNs with Lt. Buskirk and Hanna BN, led boxes. Lt. Van Noorden with F/O Brandt BN and Lt.Ames with Lt. Simpson BN led flights.

The 416th flew 42 missions in March, dropping 2565 tons of bombs, a bit more than 40 percent of the total tonnage dropped during the first year of operation, although we had flown only one-fifth as many missions. This increase in tonnage is certainly attributable to the heavier bomb load carried by the A-26s as compared to that amount the A-20s would carry. In the first full year of operation, to March 2, 1945, our Group flew 219 missions, including 7486 individual sorties, dropping 6394 tons of bombs. During March 1945 our group flew 1615 sorties. During the first year of operation, 72 aircraft were lost either over enemy territory or friendly area, due to enemy action, or 0.9 percent of the total number of sorties flown. The 416th were a major influence in assisting ground forces in their advances toward German forces and encampments, destroying bridges and marshalling yards, plus ammo depots. We were called upon often for support of our allied forces. It was a rewarding experience, with most of the flights being conducted by other than the original crews which came over in January 1944. The newer crews were eminently successful.

Ninth Bomb Division Has Record Month

Commended by Lieutenant General Omar F. Bradley for its sustained offensive, the 9th Bomb Division turned out a record month of operations during which its medium and light bombers flew 15,000 sorties and dropped 24,000 tons of bombs.

The March figures set an all time high for Major General Samuel E. Anderson's bomber forces, eclipsing the previous record of 10,538 sorties and 15,226 tons established in June 1944.

Operational 28 days, including 19 straight days from March 8 through March 26, the division's B-26s, A-20s and A-26s ranged over a 250 mile front from Munster Bay south to the Main Scarplanes to disrupt road and rail communications and deny the Germans facilities for moving reinforcements equipment and supplies to meet current Allied offensives.

Two-thirds of the division's record assault was directed against communications centers, marshalling yards, and bridges on routes feeding battle areas with supplies and reinforcements. Sweeping advances by ground forces over the entire western front testify to the bombers' success in blocking German attempts to strengthen defense lines. Successfully completed campaigns to isolate battle areas, including the Ruhr and Remagen bridgehead, resulted in wide-spread destruction to German transportation facilities. Nine major railroad bridges on main lines were destroyed or left unserviceable, four railroad overpasses damaged and at least 33 marshalling yards severely damaged. Bomber attacks cut all lines in 20 rail yards and left only one line open in eight others. A total of 584 rail cuts were made.

Rail facilities destroyed or damaged included 1,769 cars, nine roundhouses, 12 locomotives and 26 workshops.
Sharing top priority with rail targets in the bombers' March offensive were 81 communications centers, equally important to Germans' defense in the west. Attacking the towns with 8,000 tons of incendiaries and high explosives, the medium and light bombers blocked roads with craters and debris, cut rail lines and leveled warehouses, factories and buildings that would offer protection for house-to-house fighting.

Destroyed or damaged in the bombers' assault on communications centers were 7,851 buildings, 79 factories and 99 warehouses. Main and secondary roads running through the town were cut in 887 places, two highway overpasses destroyed and six highway bridges damaged.

A four day offensive against gun positions, roads and rail lines in and around 21 towns in the area north of the Ruhr where the 21st Army Group now is expanding its Rhine River bridgehead highlighted the bombers attacks on communications centers.

While main weight of their attacks were aimed at road and rail facilities, the bombers backed up their assault to immobilize the German Army by striking at seven fuel and ammunition dumps and 10 ordnance and motor vehicle repair depots.

Twenty-three bombers were lost to flak and enemy fighters during the month, against claims of nine enemy fighters destroyed, three probably destroyed and five damaged.

CHAPTER 14

April 1945 Missions

April 1945 Missions

Mission #260 - 3 April - Hemeln Marshalling Yard. This was an attack on which 76 tons of bombs were dropped, using PFF pathfinder leaders. The formation had to climb to 16,000 feet (remember we didn't have oxygen masks, making us wonder why some of the guys didn't feel the affects. Now if I go to an 11,000 foot altitude on ski slopes, I can't catch my breath). A few crews reported that through a small break in the clouds they saw the bombs bursting in the yards and in the town. The formation encountered weak but accurate flak between the I.P. and the target. A few bursts also came up at the rendezvous point where Lt. James R. Phillips' plane was hit. He feathered his engine and returned to base on single engine.

He was able to get the engine operating over our base and landed with both engines although he was able to get very little power from his damaged engine., The formation split up after leaving the target in bad weather. Major Sommers headed back alone and traveled directly across the Ruhr pocket, which our troops created. His Gunner, Staff Sergeant Kalen Heath, fired at a few flak guns as he sped by, but he could make no claims. The box leaders were Major McNulty with Lts. Powell and Reeves as BNs and Captain Evans with Lts. McCartney and Myrrold, BNs. Captain Tutt and Lt. Orr led a flight.

The Group just received a report that reconnaissance revealed that the Colbe Railroad Bridge, 20 miles north of Geissen was completely destroyed by the 416th's attack on the afternoon of 24 March 1945. Four flights hit the bridge with superior to good results.

Mission #261 - 4 April - Crailsheim Barracks. The formation of 39 aircraft dropped a total of 59 tons of incendiary bombs on this target, unfortunately through clouds using PFF pathfinder leaders. Photo reconnaissance found the barracks almost entirely gutted. This barracks were used for marshalling troops and equipment to reinforce German positions in the path of the U.S.

Seventh Army. Captain Miller with Lts. Conner and Moore BNs led the first box. Lt. Blomgren with Lts. Johnson and Morley BNs led Box II. Lts.Lackovich and Moore, BN, Lt.
Van Noorden and F/O Brandt, BN, and Captain Tutt with Lt. Orr BN, led flights.

On April 6, Five Star General Hap Arnold, Supreme Commander of the Army Air Forces presented the Distinguished Service CROSS to Captain Leland C. Nielsen for his heroism on 23 January on a bomb-strafe mission at Blankenheim

Mission #262 - 8 April - AM - Munchen-Bernsdorf Railroad sidings and oil storage tanks. Three boxes of a total of 42 planes created a very successful mission. Four different groups attacked this target in 20 minute intervals. When our crews got there, smoke and fire were the only thing to aim at and six of our crews did that with perfection. Violent explosions and fire balls rose as our bombs hit. A seventh flight of our group misidentified the target and dropped his bombs about five miles southwest of the primary target. Smoke could be seen for about 70 miles away from our primary target, indicating what the photo recon showed, that three storage tanks destroyed, large storage buildings destroyed and craters blocked four roads leading into the facility. Boxes were led by Major Ferris with Lts. Royalty and McNutt, BNs,-Lt. Brewster with Lt. Dennis and F/O Conley BNs, and Captain Tutt with Lt. Orr, BN. Lts. Lackovich and Orr BN,-Lt. Fero and F/O Langsam BN, - Captain Sears and F/O Przywitowski BN, led flights.

Mission #263 - 8 April - Sondershausen Railroad Junction. This road junction was blocking the attacking Third US Army forces in their thrust toward Leipzig, so it had to be taken out. Despite heavy smoke and haze, four flights scored excellent results. A fifth flight lost the formation and later tagged on to what was thought to be our formation. It bombed with the first flight of the formation on the secondary target, Bad Frankenhousen, with unobserved results. It was not until the formation turned off the target that they could see the rail markings of the 396th Bomb Group. Unable to pick up the primary target, one other flight chose the town of Nordhausen as a casual target. It was later learned that Nordhausen had contained a large death camp, where the Germans had perpetrated some of the greatest crimes against the civilized world. Because of poor visibility, bombing altitudes ranging from 4500 to 9500 feet were reported. The box leaders were Lts. Brown and Kerns with F/O Lehneis BNs, with Lts.Buskirk and Lt. Hanna BN.

Lt. Kerns lead bombardier had a problem with his GEE equipment going into the target on the first run. The flight circled around Germany for about an hour until Lt. Kerns got the GEE stuff to start operating, so he went in and sighted the target with excellent results on the town.

Mission #264 - 9 April AM - Anberg-Kummersbruck Ordnance Depot. This was to be another two mission day with the first one calling for three boxes with a total of 44 planes to hit this target with 500 pound incendiary bombs. Under ideal weather conditions, our bombardiers showed what they can do when they are able to see the aiming point, without clouds in their way. The importance of this target is significant when four different groups are assigned to destroy it. They must have had the greatest confidence in the 416th since they pegged us as the anchor men on the team., asking us to go in as the last bombing team. By the time our group got there, smoke and flames obscured the main aiming point, but there were new aiming points available which our boys cherished. They left more fire and destruction behind, and also cut railroad lines. The three boxes were led by Major McNulty with Lts. Powell and Myrrold BNs, Captain Evans and Lt.Cartney BN, and Captain Default with F/O Cardinale BN. Leading flights were Captain Pair and Lt.Corum BN plus Lt. Remiszewski and F/O Lehneis, BN.

Mission #265 - 9 April PM - Saalfield Marshalling Yard. Two boxes took off in the afternoon on another long range attack on this huge yard. Two other groups were assigned to go in before the 416th. When our boys got there, smoke and haze were present. Two superiors and three excellent ratings were scored by our boys, eliminating the possibility of the yards being used again. The bombs blanketed wagons, trucks, and servicing facilities. The engine roundhouse was 1/3 destroyed and six engines probably destroyed. At least 50 hits on the tracks and 28 on the roads were counted. The box leaders were Captain Miller with Lt. Conner and F/O Wrubelle BN, and Lt. Blomgren with Lt. Johnson BN. Leading flights were Lt. Lackovich and Lt. Muir BN, Captain Tutt and Lt. Orr BN, -Captain Sears and F/O Przwyitowski BN and Lt. Remiszewski and F/O Lehneis. Lt. D. L. Price of the 671 squadron returned early from the mission since his gunner's turret was jammed and unusable. Price tried to contact the box leader, telling him he had to leave, but was unable to raise him on the radio. Price wobbled his wings and then hit an air pocket which jolted his bombs out of their shackles. His gunner, Sgt. J. F. Reicher reported the bombs were rolling around on the closed bay door. The arming vane on one bomb started to turn, getting ready to arm the bomb. Price opened the bomb bay doors and three bombs rolled out on to an open field. The one bomb with the turning arming vane was still left in the plane. Sgt. Reisher crawled in to the open bomb bay and kicked out the arming bomb, undoubtedly saving himself his pilot and the plane from total destruction.

Mission #266 - 10 April - AM - Eger Railroad Viaduct. A first for A-26 Invader planes, a target in Czechosolovakia, now called Sudeten Germany. This was a 1344 foot long viaduct which the Germans were using to escape northern Germany and trying to get to the Redoubt in the south. This was an extremely long trip for our group, well over 800 miles. We only had one box with 25 planes on this mission, but Major Ferris called it the perfect mission, citing ideal weather, excellent navigation, and superior bombing. Our bombardiers sliced the viaduct in half with bombs hitting smack in the center, also knocking down buildings and cratering holes in roads. Aside from our important crews, other dignitaries included General Backus of the 97 Bomb Wing,

Colonel Britt, the Division Flak Officer and Colonel Stramney, the reclassification officer from ETOUSA. Major Ferris led this mission with Lts. Kirk and McNutt as BNs. Leading flights were Captain Pair and Lt.Corum BN, and Lt. Fero and Langsam BN. This was the first mission for Lt. Kirk the BN who was fortunate enough to escape from the two plane crash which killed Captain Rooney and his gunner Sgt. Kamische. The bombing was rated superior.

Mission #267 - 10 April - PM - Stassfurt/Deopolds-Shall Oil Storage Depot. Before the first mission got back from Sudeten, the second mission was taking off with 22 more planes to destroy this storage and loading facility including a mine entrance, a pipeline and underground tanks. We joined up the the 409th Bomb Group. Three out of four of our flights scored excellent results, leaving fires and explosions. Three buildings were left-aflame with sheets of fires visible at 6 to 7000 feet in the air.. Our crews saw three airfields in the area, but no planes rose to attack our formation. Maybe they were out of gas. Lt. Brown with Lts. Kerns and Orr were the BN team.

Mission #268 - 11 April - AM - Bernburg Marshalling Yard. This was a maximum effort mission with 44 planes taking off. Bombs blanketed the southern choke point of the yards, catching wagons, and buildings, plus blowing up railroad tracks and storage sheds.The results were explained to have been devastating. Major McNulty with Lts. Powell and Myrrold BNs, Captain Evans with Lt. McCartney BN and Lt. Lackovich with Lt.Muir, led boxes. Other flight leaders were Captain Tutt and Lt. Orr BN, plus Lts.Warren, Forbes, Gruning, and Morris as flight leaders.

Mission #269 - 11 April - PM - Zwickau Marshalling Yards. This was another deep penetration into Germany with 37 planes. The yards were full of freight cars, estimated to be up to 100 destroyed and damaged. There were 40 to 50 direct hits on the railroad tracks and three buildings. Captain Miller with Lts. Conner and Vollmayer, BNs plus Lt. Blomgren with Lt. Johnson,

BN led boxes. Lt. Lackovich and Muir BN, Captain Pair and Corum BN,- Lt.Withington and Lt. Ashley, BN plus Lt. Popeney and Lt. Fry - Lt. Simpson and F/O Smetanka BN led flights. Bombing was rated as excellent.

Mission #270 - 12 April. - AM - Kempton Ordnance Depot. This target was located near the Swiss border, an area never before attacked by our Group, but we sent 42 planes out, all of which returned with their bombs because they ran into rain and bad weather. The formation flew into the rain for one hour before the recall. The target was to be attacked visually because of it being close to a POW Camp. The cloud cover was up to 5500 feet, making visual contact out of the question. To drop any lower, the planes would have been scraping the top of very high mountains. One bomb in Major Ferris' plane came loose and dropped on the bomb bay door. Major Ferris dropped it on the bombing range before landing at our base. Through some breaks in the clouds crews reported seeing German Airfields, deserted, but in apparent excellent condition. Major Ferris with Lts. Kirk and McNutt BNs, and Lts. Brewster and Dennis BN, Captain Pair and Corum BN, led the boxes. Captain Tutt and Lt. Orr BN led flights. Captain Moore had Colonel J. L. Stromme with him as an observer.

Mission #271 -12 April - PM - Hof Railroad Bridge. The weather did not improve later in the day, but 27 planes took off anyway, going a little further than the target assigned in the-morning. Weather forced the formation down to 5200 feet to make the attack (watch out for the high mountains!) There were four direct hits on the railroad tracks, eight on the roads, and 20 buildings destroyed or damaged, in addition to the bridge being destructed. The planes returned and landed in the middle of a driving rainstorm. Only one plane , Lt. Downing, was diverted to another field. No flak met the formation. Lt. Brown with Lt. Kerns and Hanna BNs led the formation. Lt. Hall and F/O Goss led a flight. Ninth Bomb Division Commander General Samuel E. Anderson sent congratulations to the 416th for the excellent bombing at the Hof Bridge. Our four flights scored one superior and three excellent.

Mission #272 - 15 April - Ulm Marshalling Yard. The battle lines are moving so fast and so far, very few nearby targets were available for us to attack. About noon, our planes took off to this target near Stuttgart. The object of this mission was to prevent troops from reaching the "Redoubt" area, the Germans had established for their men. An almost solid cloud cover necessitated the use of PFF equipment. Results were unobserved. Photo recon the next day showed 12 hits just south of the main sorting sidings, causing minor damage to tracks and rolling stock. Through traffic was still possible, however. Weak, inaccurate flak was experienced coming out over the bomb line near Freiburg. The formation was led by Captain Evans, but he had to abort so Captain Stanley with F/O Blount and Lt. Myrrold, BNs took the lead. Flights were led by Lt. Errotabere with Lt. Wilber BN. -Lt. Heinke and Lt. Rosenquist, BN led the second box.

Mission #273 -16 April - AM - Zerbst Marshalling Yard. .Of the 38 planes on this mission, 31 dropped 500 pound incendiary bombs, seven miles in front of the advancing U. S. Second Armored Division and the 83rd Infantry Division. One flight was unable to bomb and he hoped to make a second run at the target. His TOT would have caused a collision course with another flight scheduled for that moment, so they did not drop. Although smoke from a previous attack hung over the target, excellent results were scored on the marshalling yards and in the town itself. In the Yards, 100 to 150 wagons were destroyed, eight sheds, three warehouses and 25 to 30 other buildings were set afire. Smoke made it impossible to estimate the damage done to the town, although flames were seen shooting up through the smoke. Major Shaefer with Lts. Hand and Conner, BNs, and Major Sommers with Lts. Kupits and Vollmayer, BNs led the boxes. Lt. Warren and Forbes, BN , Captain Pair and Lt. Corum BN and Lt. Lackovich and Lt. Muir led flights

Mission #274 - 16 April - PM - Wittenberg Marshalling Yard. The flight to the target was uneventful except bad weather moved in making the aiming point invisible to all flights except one. This flight took a different bomb run from the scheduled Initial Point and got to drop his bombs with what was determined to be an excellent shot. Moderate intense, accurate flak came up at the target area and on the turn off, with two planes receiving battle damage. Captain Evans with Lt. McCartney BN led Box I with Lt. Brewster and Lt. Dennis and F/O Conley BNs on Box II. Captain Tutt and Lt. Orr BN led a flight.

Mission #275 - 17 April - AM - Magdeburg Town. The Ninth Army was advancing across the Elbe River and this target was in the path they had detailed. There were eleven other bomb groups bombing this heavily defended town. Our ground forces were-withdrawn about 1500 yards from the town, which was destined to be totally destroyed according to the high command. This was done, with all those groups going after it. This town was the heaviest organized resistance our ground forces had run into, signifying its importance to both fighting forces. The 416th provided three boxes to do their part, resulting in superior and excellent patterns of bomb drops. Major Dunn with BNs Brewer and Kerns led Box I. Lt. Buskirk with Lt. Hanna and F/O Przywitowski led the second box with Lt. Parker and Lt. Shaft,BN on Box II. Flights were headed up by Lt. Hall with F/O Coss BN and Lt. Errotabere and Lt. Wilbur BN. No flak was met.

Mission #276 - 17 April - PM - Tubingen Ordnance Depot. This was a supply center for the Germans in the Bavarian Alps in southwestern Germany 18 miles south of Stuttgart. Five flights scored good to excellent pattern with many drops on ordnance buildings warehouses and tracks. It was determined that large amount of supplies were stored here. Visual reports came in as excellent hits. Bomb release malfunctions caused flights to make four separate runs at the target, but they were unable to get the machines to cooperate, so no bombs were dropped. The first box was led by Captain Evans with BNs Lts. McCartney and

Myrrold. Box two leader was Captain Stanley with F/O Blount. Lts. Lackovich and Muir, BN,-Lt. Popeney and Lt. Fry BN, and Lts. Heinke and Rosenquist BN led flights. This was the first mission for 670th BNs, Lt. Pavey and Lt.Peppers. Lt. Lackovich flew his last mission this afternoon after flying as flight leader with Lt. Muir and also flew as deputy leader. He is on his way back to the states.

Mission #277 - 19 April - Ulm Marshalling Yard. This is the afternoon mission , the first mission in the morning took off and just about reached enemy territory when it was recalled, so no credit was given to the boys. This marshalling yard is the second largest between Munich and Nuremburg. We've been there before and wreaked havoc on it on previous missions. All 38 planes got to drop their bombs, destroying 150 to 160 boxcars, 40 bursts on the tracks between them, 22 buildings demolished and several roads cut. One enemy fighter made a pass at the formation with gunner Sergeant DiOrio firing two short bursts at him, with no claims made on either side. DiOrio was the only gunner to have sighted the invader, who moved away when he got to within 800 yards of the formation. Of the six flights attacking, four scored superior and two rated excellent. With no hindering clouds, our bombardiers show their mettle. The two box leaders were Captain Miller with Lts.Conner and Vollmayer BNs, and Major Sommers with Lts. Kupits and F/O Cardinale, BNs. Flight leaders included Lt. Warren and Lt. Forbes BN, Captain Sutton and Lt. Reed BN, and Lt. Van Noorden and F/O Brandt BN.

Mission #278 - 20 April - AM - Deggendorf Ordnance Depot. This target on the DanubeRiver not too far from Munich was hit with 1000 pound bombs, again with devastating results. Flames and smoke rose to 9000 feet, attesting to the accuracy of the hits. Again, superior and Excellent results were scored. The depot was severely damaged with 30 to 35 hits on smaller buildings and ten hits on the roads. One plane had a problem getting his bombs to release, but his flight leader took him over Viechtach, where they shook the bombs out, doing considerable damage there. No flak or fighters came close to the formation.

The two boxes of a total of 44 planes were led by Major Ferris with Lts. Kirk and McNutt, BNs, Lt. Brewster with Lt. Dennis and F/O Conley, BNs. Captain Pair and Lt. Corum BN,- Captain Tutt and Lt. Orr BN, and Lt. Fero and Lt. Sampson led flights.

Mission #279 - 20 April - PM - Annaburg Fuel Depot. Demolition bombs started many fires on this target (When aren't any bombs demolition?) scoring very successful results. About 500 hits were counted on the fuel storage area, and roads leading in /out of the target were severly damaged. Superior and excellents were scored by the flights. Three boxes made this mission with Box I led by Major Dunn with Lts. Brewer and Hanna BNs Lts. Brown with Lt. Kerns BN, and Lt.Prucha with Lt. Reeves, as BN. Another brand new pilot BN team Lt. Barausky and Lt. Sheehan led a flight, with success.

Mission #280 - 21 April - Attang-Pucheim Marshalling Yard. We were the first 9th Air Force group to bomb in Austrian territory for the second time in a month. This target was on the main route to the National Redoubt (retreat?) area in western Austria. This was a 970 mile trip for our formation, pretty long for A-26s. Inclement weather forced the formation down to about 8200 feet and the bombing was again scored superior and excellents. Getting down to near 8000 feet was just about scraping the tops of the Austrian Alps, but no one bumped into one. From 300 to 350 railroad cars, along with a roundhouse and 25 buildings were demolished. All tracks were severed and roads cratered. Four flights used impulse bombing No flak bothered the group. Weather caused returning flights down low and as the formation approached an airfield near Erding, our crews reported they saw Germans scurrying for cover, probably expecting to be bombed. When no bombs dropped, they ran to their anti-aircraft guns and started firing at the last flight, with no damage. As many as 50 planes were reported parked at this airfield, including ME109s,

JU 88s, JU 52s and ME 163s, none of which challenged our group, A large convoy was sighted and reported to fighter-ground control for them to go in and blow them off the roads. Weather at our base was closing in, so the 40 planes were diverted to A-64 for the night. Two were diverted to A-67. The leaders of the boxes were Captain Evans with Lts. McCartney and Myrrold BNs, Captain Stanley with F/O Blount BN and Lt. D. O. Turner with Lts. McGivern and Morley, BNs. Flight leaders included Lt. Popeney with Lts. Fry and Pepper BNs, -Lt. Hall with F/O Goss and Lt. Pavey, and Lt. Van Noorden and F/O Brandt.

Mission #281 - 24 April - Landau Airdrome. A new blind bombing technique was introduced here today to replace or improve on the PFF equipment used by B-26s in the past. Grinches got into the equipment and after two bomb runs, the formation returned with their bombs. The 9/10th cloud cover called for something other than visual bombing. Since the Sharon didn't function, the usual PFF was tried and that didn't work either. Our own GEE equipment was inoperative, so it too was abandoned Major Shaefer with Lts. Hand and Conner, BN led Box I with Lt. Blomgren and Lt. Johnson on Box II. Flight leaders included Lt. Errotabere and Lt. Wilbur, BN, Captain Pair and Corum BN, Captain Sutton and Lt. Reed, BN and Lts. Fero and Sampson.

Mission #282 - 25 April - Freilassing Ordnance Depot. One flight of six planes attacked two flak positions near the target in elements of three, about two minutes before the main attack. They dropped 132 x 100 pound fragmentation bombs with excellent results. The formation encountered no flak. This was the last ditch stand with ordnance supplies for the National Redoubt area. Our bombs deterred that action with six flights hitting the depot and starting large fires, severely damaging roads and railroad tracks. This target was about 20 miles from Hitler's mountain retreat at Berchtesgarden. The two boxes were led by Major Ferris with Lts. Kirk and McNutt BNs, and Lt. Hall with Lt. Goss and F/O Conley, BN. The two elements attacking the flak positions were Lt. Van Noorden and F/O Brandt, BN and Captain Default with F/O Cardinale BN. Captain Tutt and Lt. Orr led the other flight.

Mission #283 - 26 April - Plattling Airfield, 40 miles southeast of Regensburg. This field hangared planes which were harrassing our ground troops. Fragmentation bombs peppered the landing runways and also the gun positions, silencing them while our formation flew over. Results of bombing showed two superiors and four excellents. Lts. Brown with Kerns and Brewer BNs led Box I with Lts. Buskirk and Hanna and F/O Smetanka BNs on Box II. Flight leaders were Lts. Heinke and Rosenquist BN and Lts. Warren and Forbes, BN.

Mission #284 - 1 May - Stod, Czechoslovakia Airdrome. Bad weather prevented bombing. When the formation crossed the bomb line they were forced to abandon the attack after flying just two minutes. No flak or enemy fighters were seen. Box leaders were Captain Evans with Lts McCartney and Myrrold, BNs and Captain Stanley with F/O Blount BN. Captain Pair and Lt. Corum BN led a flight.

Mission #285 - 3 May - Stodt Ammunition Dump. Czechoslovakia. The Shoran system was again attempted on this mission, evidently with success, at least the bombs were dropped. Results were scored between good and excellent. Major Shaefer led Box I with Captain Hand and Lt. Dant BNs plus Captain Blomgren with Lt. Johnson, BN. Flight leaders were Captain Pair and Lt. Corum BN and Captain Sutton and Lt. Reed BN

The Last Mission for the Glorious 416th Bombardment Group

Historical Data, April 1945

Easter Day, April 1945 with its religious service and significance, ushered in one of the strangest months in the history of World War II. No longer did we think that the bombs we dropped were as a pebble on a beach, lost among the others. Instead, as the month slipped by each ton of bombs dropped seemed to show a definite reaction and bring about a new change in the bomb line. The Germans were on the run and we now knew that it was only a matter of time before an unconditional surrender would be made.

The question in the minds of most of us, now, seemed not to be, when will V-E Day come, but what will the terms of surrender be, so that we will not have to fight again in another decade or two? The Yalta conference, held some months ago, had decided on some of the terms to be demanded. The San Francisco conference to begin in April 25, attended by delegates from the Allied Nations, was to decide on the terms of final settlement. Our champion at these conferences was our President Franklin D. Roosevelt. His astuteness, understanding of the problems, and diplomacy had won him the confidence of the whole world. Then a wall fell on us. The news reached us on the morning of the 13th that President Roosevelt had died at his summer home at Hot Springs, Georgia, on the 12th. The average American soldier knew that with his passing, had gone one of our greatest assurance of a just and lasting peace. A period of 30 days of mourning was proclaimed by the new President, Harry S. Truman. A memorial service was held on the 670th Bomb Squadron's athletic field on the 15th. Chaplains Penticoff and Doyle conducted the service, attended by all available personnel from all units on the base.

The events of the following few days were watched closely to see what changes in policy would be made by the new President. Mr. Truman issued a statement that he would continue to carry out the policies of the late President and would make no immediate changes in the cabinet.

April might easily be called Inspection Month. On the 3rd and 4th, the Office of the Inspector General of the 9th Bombardment Division made a complete administrative inspection of the Group and Station. The Group and Station received a Superior rating. This was the second consecutive Superior rating given to the Group in an administrative inspection by that office.

On the 9th, Colonel Stramney, a reclassification specialist from ETOUSA, arrived to spend a few days on the base. He flew on a couple of missions so that he might understand the conditions under which our combat crewmen worked and lived and thereby make any needed recommendations for improvements.

A Bombardment Division Personnel survey, audit , and inspection team arrived on the 28th to make a 10 day inspection of personnel records, checking them for accuracy and agreement. The team of an officer and three enlisted men was under the supervision of Captain James M. Lynch, Jr.

Throughout the month, there were changes in personnel and assignment, Major William P.Thomas, Intelligence Officer for the Group since its activation in February, 1943, was transferred to the headquarters of the European Civil Affairs Division on 6 April. He was succeeded by Captain H.B. Sheridan, who had been I.O. of the 670th Bomb Sq. since the Group's inception. Captain H.W. Anderson and Lt. L.H. Perkins were appointed Top Secret control officer and assistant control officer. Lt. Col. Napier returned to the U. S. after completing his tour of duty. Major Shaefer became commanding officer of the 669th Squadron. Captain R. V. Wheeler was appointed Assistant Group Operations officer on the 22nd. Strength of the Group on the last day of April was:

668th Squadron	48 Officers	275 Enlisted Men
669th "	56 Officers	272 Enlisted Men
670th "	61 Officers	269 Enlisted Men
671st "	54 Officers	269 Enlisted Men
Hq. 416th	33 Officers	56 Enlisted Men
Totals	252 Officers	1141 Enlisted Men

Among those who had completed their tours of duty and had returned to the Zone of the Interior were Lt. Col. J. G. Napier,- First Lieutenants F.W.Henderson,-A.E. Herman, - W.A.Merchant, F.H. Miller,-A.F. Maltby, -E. R. Hayter - R.J. Basnett - R J. McQuade,-J. K.Colquitt,-H. J. Montrose,- J. J.Lackovich,-D. L. Withington III, -Staff Sergeants E.P. Brzesinski,-R. J. Brown,-R. W. Carstene,-H. E. Fessler,-C. Fetko, Jr.,-C. F. Floyd,-H. J. Nowoskieiski,-H. J.Roberts,-J. W. Robinson,-R. P.Sharp Jr.,-S. Kochan Jr.,-J.A.Hummer,-D. E. Burns,.- M. Bookach,-F.P. Basford,-H. R. Davis,-T.Connery Jr.,- A. H.Vinson Jr.,- L.McElhattan,-C. F. Huss,-M. Hall, - A.A.Cianciose, and H. G. Wiggins.

On the 6th, an old familiar face returned to pay a short visit. It was Brigadier General Harold L. Mace, who had been Commanding Officer of the Group when it arrived overseas. His familiar "Hi Boys!" greeted everyone at Colonel Aylesworth's staff meeting. General Mace now commands the 98 Combat Wing. During the month, a Soldier's Medal was awarded to S/Sgt. C. V. Hinker for having promptly and courageously defus-ing a 1000 pound bomb when it had fallen on the bomb bay doors, forcing them partly open. Wind blowing on the arming vane, had started to arm, the bomb. His courage saved himself, his pilot and the plane from sure destruction. Staff Sergeant Harold G. Wiggins, a gunner in the 670th squadron devised a gadget which would enable a gunner to release any bombs hung up on its shackles. The main escape hatch for gunners was down through the open bomb bay doors. A switch in the gunner's compartment opened the bomb bay doors and salvoed the bombs. A hung up bomb, however, might block the passage of the escaping gunner. The design was passed on to higher quarters for possible inclusion on other planes.

CHAPTER 15

Numerical Mission Listings

Missions of the 416th Bombardment Group (L)

Mission No.	Target	Date
		March 1944
1.	Poix Airdrome	3
2.	Bernay St Martin Airdrome	4
3.	Conches Airdrome	6
4.	Conches Airdrome	7
5.	Vacqueriette Noball	18
6.	Wisque Noball	19
7.	Foret Nationale de Tourneben	20
8.	Montdidier Airfield	23
9.	Vacqueriette Noball*	26

*Noball is a V-1 Self Propelled Buzz-Bomb Launching Site

Mission No.	Target	Date
		April 1944
10.	Bois de Huit Noball	10
11.	LeHavre Gun Emplacement	10
12.	Lingham Noball	10
13.	Beauvour Noball	11
14.	Bonniers Noball	11
15.	Vacqueriette Noball	12
16.	Noball (not identified)	12
17.	Yvrench Bois Carre Noball	13
18.	Petite Bois Tillencourt Boball	13
19.	Charleroi-St.Martin Marshalling Yard	18
20.	Bois de Huit Noball	19
21.	Gorenflos Noball	20
22.	Yvrench Carre Noball	20
23.	Yvrench Bois Carre Noball	21
24.	Behen Noball	22
25.	Linghem Noball	22
26.	Bonnieres Noball	23

Mission No.	Target	Date
		April 1944
27.	Bois D'Enfer Noball	25
28.	St.Pierre du Mont Coastal Gun	25
29.	Louvain Railroad	26
30.	Monseau Su Sombre Marshalling Yard	27
31.	Arraa Marshalling Yard	27
32.	Bonnieres Noball	30
33.	Busigny Marshalling Yard	30
		May 1944
34.	Charlois Montignies Marshalling Yard	1
35.	Blanc Misseron Marshalling Yard	1
36.	Blanc Misseron Marshalling Yard	2
37.	Blanc Misseron Marshalling Yard	7
38.	Behen Noball	8
39.	Aerschot Marshalling Yard	8
40.	Ailly L'Haut Cloches Noball	8
41.	Aerschot Marshalling Yard	9
42.	Bois d'enfer Noball	9
43.	Corneille eu Vexin Airdrome	11
44.	Aerschot Marshalling Yard	11
45.	Monchy Breton Airdrome	12
46.	Beauvoir Noball	12
47.	Beauvois Tille Airdrome	13
48.	Creil Airdrome	15
49.	Beauville Fille Coastal Guns	19
50.	Beauville Tolle Airdrome	20
51.	Cormeilles-eu-Vexin Airdrome	20
52.	Cormeilles-eu-Vixen Airdrome	22
53.	Beaumont leoger Airfield	24
54.	Abbeyville-Drucat Airfield	24
55.	Monchy-Breton Airdrome	25
56.	Beauville Tille Airdrome	26
57.	Ameins Marshalling Yard	27
58.	Amiens Marshalling Yard	27
59.	Bruges/St. MichelRadar Station	28

Mission No.	Target	Date
		May 1944
60.	Vacqueriette Noball	28
61.	Behan Noball	28
62.	Achiet Airdrome	29
63.	Denain Prouvy Airdrome	30
		June 1944
64.	Gorenflos Noball	2
65.	Chartres Airdrome	3
66.	St. Pierre du Mont Coastal Gun	4
67.	Argentan Cross Roads	6
68.	Serquex Marshalling Yard	6
69.	Lessay Bridge	7
70.	Balleroy Road Junction	7
71.	Vitre Railroad Bridge	8
72.	Falaise Railroad Junction	11
73.	Epernon Railroad Junction	12
74.	St. Sauveur LeVicomte Railway Junction	13
75.	Aunay-Sur-Odon Railway Junction	14
76	St. Hillaire de Harcourt Railroad Jujnction	14
77.	Lessay Bridge	15
78.	Domfront Fuel Dump	15
79.	Foret De Conches Fuel Depot	18
80.	Ligescourt Noball	20
81.	LeGrand Rossegnol Noball	20
82.	Middel Straete Noball	21
83.	Cherbourgh Hewavy Gun Emplacement	22
84.	Middel Straete Noball	24
85.	Bagnoles D'Andaine Fuel Depot	24
86.	Foret D'Andaine Fuel Depot	25
87.	St. Hillaire-Vitre Railroad Junction	29
88.	Thury-Harcourt Railroad Junction	30
		July 1944
89.	LaMorintiere Defended Area	4
90.	Merlemont Headquarters Building	5
91.	Epernon Railroad Junction	6

Mission No.	Target	Date
		July 1944
92.	Verneuil LaLoupe Railroad	6
93.	St. Pierre Sur Dives Bridge	7
94.	Caen Strong Point	8
95.	Combourg and Avranches Railroads	8
96.	Bourth Railway Bridge	11
97.	Foret D'Andaine Fuel Depot	12
98.	Bourth Railway Bridge	14
99.	St. Hillaire De Harcourt Railroad	16
100.	Giberville Strong Point	18
101.	Gles-Sur-Risle Railroad Junction	18
102.	Bruz Fuel Depot	19
103.	Bourth Bridge	22
104.	Evreaux Railroad Embankment	23
105.	St. Giles Strong Point	25
106.	Marigny Strong Point	26
107.	LaGouesniere Fuel Depot	28
108.	Caumont Area	30
109.	Liseaux Marshalling Yard	31
110.	Mantes-Gassicourt Railroad Bridge	31
		August 1944
111	CaudebeckAirdrome	2
112.	Beauvais Marshalling Yard	4
113.	Marigny-Compeigne Marshalling Yard	5
114.	Laigle Railroad Bridge	5
115.	Oissel Bridge	6
116.	Oissel Bridge	6
117.	Frevent Railroad Junction	8
118.	Bois De Pierre Chateau Radar	8
119.	Bois De Pierre Chateau Radar	9
120.	Chauny Railroad Bridge	9
121.	Foret De Romare Ammunition Depot	10
122.	Le Lande de Louge Ammunition Depot	10
123.	Foret de Romare Ammunition Depot	11
124.	St. Malo Gun Defenses	11

Mission No.	Target	Date
		August 1944
125.	La Ferte Mace Ecouche Highway	12
126.	Pont D'Eveque Railroad Junction	13
127.	Foret De Chantilly Fuel Depot	15
128.	Montfort Sur Risle Bridge	17
129.	Brest/Kerviniou Coastal Defense Gun	25
130.	Champeigne-Clairox Fuel Depot	26
131.	Roeun Troop Concentration	26
132.	Roeun Troop Concentration	27
133.	Doulen Fuel Depot	28
		September 1944
134.	Brest Stronghold	1
135.	Brest Stronghold	3
136.	Brest Stronghold	3
137.	Brest Stronghold	5
138.	Brest Stronghold	6
139.	Brest Stronghold	6
140.	Foret de Haye Strong Point	
141.	St. Julian de Haye Communication Center	11
142.	St. Wendel Marshalling Yard	12
143.	Foret de Haye Strong Point	12
144.	Brest	14
145.	Bergen op Zoom	16
146.	Foret de Parroy Fuel Depot	27
147.	Foret de Parroy Fuel Depot	28
148.	Bitburg Marshalling Yard	29
149.	Julich Marshalling Yard	29
		Octcber 1944
150.	Urbach Area	2
151.	Duren Marshalling Yard	3
152.	Duren Marshalling Yard	6
153.	Trier Supply Dump	7
154.	Linnich Town	8
155.	Langerwehe Town	12
156.	Langerwehe Town	13

Mission No.	Target	Date
		October 1944
157.	Mayen Railroad Bridge	14
158.	Trier Railroad Bridge	17
		November 1944
159	Haguenau Supply Depot	17
160.	Breisach Railroad Bridge	18
161.	Merzig Troop Concentration	19
162.	Landau Airdrome	19
163.	Mariamweiler Town	29
		December 1944
164.	Saarlautern Highway	2
165.	Kall Town	5
166.	Erkelenz Town	6
167.	Sinzig Railroad Bridge	8
168.	Saarwellengen Supply Depot	9
169.	Dilsburg Town	9
170.	Schleiden Town	12
171.	Germund Town	13
172.	Heimbach Town	15
173.	Saarburg Bridge	23
174.	Waxweiler Marshalling Yard	23
175.	Zulpich Railroad	24
176.	Munstereifeil Communication Center	25
177.	Hillersheim Railroad Junction	25
178.	Eller Bridge	27
179.	Keuchinger Bridge	29
		January 1945
180.	Mont Le Ban Troop Command Post	1
181.	Simmern Bridge	2
182.	Simmern Bridge	5
183.	Simmern Bridge	11
184.	Steinbruck Bridge	13
185.	Schleiden Railroad Junction	14
186.	Simmern Bridge	15
187.	Sinzig Bridge	16

Mission No.	Target	Date
		January 1945
188.	Euskirchen Bridge	16
189.	Simmern Bridge	21
190.	Dasburg Area Convoy	22
191.	Arzfeld Dasburg Area	23
192.	Blankenheim Troop Concentration	23
193.	Schleiden Railroad Junction	24
194.	Kall Railroad Junction	25
195.	Nonnweiller Railroad Bridge	29
		February 1945
196.	Schleiden Railroad Junction	1
197.	Euskirshen Railroad Bridge	2
198.	Berg- Gladbach Supply Depot	3
199.	Berg- Gladbach Supply Depot	6
200.	Nutterden-Cranneberg, Holland	8
201.	Kempen Command Headquarters	9
202.	Munstereifel Troop Concentration	10
203.	Iserlohn Motor Transport Station	13
204.	Mechernich Motor Repair Depot	14
205.	Rheinbach Airdrome	14
206.	Unna Ordnance Depot	16
207.	Weisbaden Ordnance Depot	19
208.	Geldern Bridge	21
209.	Lage Bridge	21
210.	Mittenburg-Horchst-Munster Bridge	22
211.	Simmern Bridge	23
212.	Golzheim Railroad Junction	23
213.	Vierson Communication Center	24
214.	Kerpen Railroad Junction	25
215.	Munstereifel Town (Norvenich)	25
216.	Sindorf Communication Center	26
217.	Unna Ordnance Depot	28
		March 1945
218.	Giessen Ordnance Depot	1
219.	Iserlohn Communication Center	2

Mission No.	Target	Date March 1945
220.	Giessen Ordnance Depot	3
221.	Huls Marshalling Yard	4
222.	Marburg Marshalling Yard	5
223.	Bingen Marshalling Yard	5
224.	Opladen Marshalling Yard	6
225.	Wulrath Marshalling Yard	8
226.	Butzbach Marshalling Yard	9
227.	Wulfen Airdrome	9
228.	Dillerberg/Neiderscheld Marshalling Yard	10
229.	Lippe Town	11
230.	Wulfen Airdrome	11
231.	Lorch Marshalling Yard	12
232.	Au Mummelbach Marshalling Yard	12
233.	Rhein Jet Airdrome	13
234.	Husten Marshalling Yard	14
235.	Neider-Marsberg Bridge	14
236.	Pirmasens Town	15
237.	Alten Kirchen Railroad Junction	17
238.	Bad Homberg Marshalling Yard	17
239.	Worms Communication Center	18
240.	Kreuztel Marshalling Yard	18
241.	Lage Bridge	19
242.	Nassau Railroad Junction	19
243.	Schwelm Marshalling Yard	19
244.	Geisecke-Westerburg Town	20
245.	Goesfeld Town	21
246.	Vreden Railroad Junction	21
247.	Berken Communication Center	22
248.	Berken Communication Center	22
249.	Dinslaken Factory Area	23
250.	Dinslaken Factory Area	23
251.	Ihlingkamps Gun Position	24
252.	Colbe Railroad Bridge	24
253.	Alten Kirchen Railroad Junction	25

Mission No.	Target	Date
		March 1945
254.	Fulds Marshalling Yard	25
255.	Gemunden Marshalling Yard	25
256.	Erbrach Oil Storage Yards	28
257.	Hann Munden Depot	30
258.	Wurzburg Ordnance Depot	31
259.	Marianburg Storage Area	31
		April 1945
260.	Hemeln Marshalling Yard	3
261.	Crailsheim Barracks	4
262.	MunchenBernsdorf Railroad	8
263.	Sondershausen Railroad Junction	8
264.	Amberg-Kummersbruck Ordnance Depot	9
265.	Saalfeld Marshalling Yard	9
266.	Egar Railroad Viaduct	10
267.	Stassfurt/Leopoldshall Fuel Oil Depot	10
268.	Bernberg Marshalling Yard	11
269.	Zwicken Marshalling Yard	11
270.	Kempton Ordnance Depot	12
271.	Hof Railroad Bridge	12
272.	Ulm Marshalling Yard	15
273.	Zerbst Marshalling Yard	16
274.	Wittenberg Marshalling Yard	16
275.	Magdeburg Town	17
276.	Tubingen Ordnance Depot	17
277.	Ulm Marshalling Yard	19
278.	Deggendorf Ordnance Depot	20
279.	Annaburg Fuel Depot	20
280.	Attang-Pucheim Marshalling Yard	21
281.	Landau Airdrome	24
282.	Freilassing Ordnance Depot	25
283.	Plattling Airdrome	25
		May 1945
284.	Stodt Airdrome, Czechoslovakia	1
285.	Stodt Airdrome, Czechoslovakia	3

CHAPTER 16

Loading Lists - Various Missions

Loading List **Mission #3** **6 March 1944**
Box 1 **Conches Airdrome**

#207
Lt. P.F.E.McManus
S/S J.L.Rogers, Jr.
S/S G.I.Fleischman

#224
Lt. A.A.Raines
S/S J.O.Nielsen
S/S G.J.Bender

#219
Lt. M.S. Street
S/S C.A.Prindle
S/S A.J.Huber

#202
Lt. E.E.Demun
Sgt.Rosenstein
S/S W.G.Ferguson

#194
Lt. R.F.Shaefer
S/S E.R.Judd
S/S/J.A.Fejes

#223
Lt.L.G.Peede
S/S C.L.Hibbs
S/S L.M.Daugherty

Flight I
#380
Lt. Col. T.R.Ford
Lt. W.L.Smith
S/S J.D.Bresnak
S/S G.F.Cope

#387
Major J.G.Napier
Lt. W.A.Lytle
S/S S.F.Alden
S/S R.F.Bellinger

Flight II
#377
Major M.W.Campbell
Lt. J. Kupits
S/S.E.T.Epps
S/S J.J.Shields

#181
Lt. R.J.Morton
S/S C.Q.Norton
S/S E.M.City

Flight III
#385
Major R.F.Price
Lt. A.R.Hand
Sgt. V.E.Malver
T.S L.E.Robbins

#379
Capt.H.F.Conant
S/S J.R.Herttus
S/S J.E.McCreary

#200
Lt. A.W.Gullion
S/S C.L.Webb
S/S G.L.Coffey

#227
Lt. P. Dontas
PFC R.W.Nicks
S/S W.E.Fields

#203
Lt. W.A.Peck
S/S.A.E.Bergeron
S/S H.E.Kelton

#226
Lt. W.C.Siggs
H.L.Neilsen
S/S N.Radlich

#195
Lt. M.E.Kleopfel
Sgt.D.H.Simpson
Sgt. R.Bankston

#182
Lt.B.H.Bradford
S/S R.W.McDonald
S/S A.A.Hill

Spare: Col.H.L.Mace S/S B.C.Seig & S/S J.R.Orr Lt.L.J.Siracusa Sgt.S.P.Newell &H.Perkins - Capt. Battersby S/S L.R.Shaw & S/S C.M.Gray

Loading List

Mission #5
Vacqueriette NoBall

18 March 1944

#707
Lt.R.D.Poindexter
Sgt. V.E.Molver
T/S L.E.Robbins

#194
Lt.R.V.Miracle
S/S B.C.Seig
S/S J.C.Burkhalkter

#243
Lt. R.K.Cruze
S/S F.L.Adair
S/S C.F.Love

#195
Lt. P.G.Atkinson
S/S P.F.Glynn
Sgt. J.O.Swafford

#220
Lt. B.H.Bradford
S/S E.R.Judd
S/S J.A.Fehes

Box I
Flight I
#914
Major W.W.Farmer
Lt. M.A.Pape
Capt. A.McClellan #899
S/S O.D.Lanave

#444
Major R.F.Price
Lt. A.R.Hand
S/S R.W.MacDonald

Flight II
#215
Capt. W. Battersby
Lt. W.M.Lytle
Sgt. D.H.Simpson
S/S R.Bankston

#182
Lt. L.J.Siracusa
S/S J.F.Hume
S/S F.E.Brown

Flight III
#225
Capt. R.S.Prentiss
S/S C.L.Hibbs
S/S L.M.Daugherty

#219
Lt. A.E.Osborne
S/S E.E.Kelly
S/S W.H.Coe

Lt. L.E.Hill
S/S C.H.Yost
S/S R.W.Burch

#360
Lt. S.B.Ritchie
S/S A.W.Newkirk
S/S A.A.Anderson

#378
Lt. J.F.Meagher
S/S E.A.Damico
S/S E.F.Dickenson

#745
Lt. M.Kleopfel
Sgt. A.Antanaitis
S/S H.A.Hedrick

#218
Lt. R.G.Meredith
S/S L.R.Shaw
S/S C.M.Gray

#203
Major K.T.Honey
S/S .R.E.Lee
Sgt. F.G.Falk

Loading List **Mission #20** **19 April 1944**
Bois de Huit BoBal

#181
Lt. W.H.Land
S/S S.F.Alden
S/S R.L.Ballinger

#215
Lt. R.G.Meredith
S/S V.E.Molver
S/S C.M.Gray

#390
Lt. M.S. Street
S/S C.A.Prindle
S/S G.F.Cope

#189
Lt. A.W.Gullion
S/S C.L.Webb
S/S G.L.Coffey

#227
Lt. A.W.Nordstrom
S/S J.D.Gossett
S/S R.L.Miller

Box II
Flight I
#450
Major M.W.Campbell
Lt. W.H.Palin
S/S A.E.Bergeron
S/S H.E.Kelton

Major H.A.Radetsky
Lt. W.L.Smith
S/S W.J.Donahue
S/S M.R.Bryan

Flight II
#444
Capt. R.A.Clark
Lt. C.W.Jones
S/S J.B.Thompson
S/S H.L.Hatch

#717
Lt. R.J.Morton
S/S C.Q.Norton
Sgt. F.M.City

Flight III
#200
Capt. C.R.Jackson
S/S E.L.Griffin
S/S C.W.Maziasz

SPARE
#225
Lt. R.D.Perkins
S/S V.H.Sherry
S/S R.H.Linneman

#376
Lt. E.J.Renth
S/S R.J.Colosimo
S/SJ.S.Wing

#194
Lt. S.B.Ritchie
S/S A.W.Newkirk
S/S E.A.Anderson

#673
Lt. P.Dontas
S/S A.L.Nielson
S/S W.E.Fields

#211
Lt. E.E.Demun
S/S M.Rosenstein
S/S H.O.Carney

#750
Lt. W.B.Ostrander
S.S. J.E.Wilson
S/S I.Binney

Loading List **Mission #21** **20 April 1944**
Gorenflos NoBall

#689
Lt. J.C. Crispino
S/S T.I.Walsh
S/S R.E.Conopask

#696
Lt. N.G.Brown
S/S W.J.Donahue
Sgt. M.Brayn

#379
Lt. R.D.Lesher
S/S A.J.Antanaitis
S/S H.R.Hedrick

#195
Lt. E.B.Kreh
S/S A.W.Newkirk
S/S E.A.Anderson

#224
Lt. H.A.Monroe
S/S W.L.Kidd
S/S R.Eustler

#216
Lt. R.G.Meredith
S/S C.M.Gray
S/S V.E.Molver

Box I
Flight I
#439
Major W.J.Meng
Lt. V.H.Powell
S/S R.F.Stobert
S/S P.F.Glynn

#455
Capt. C.R.Jackson
Lt. R.Conte
Pvt. J.C.McKee
S/S A.J.Bonamo

Flight II
#444
Lt. A.E.Osborne
Lt. A.H.Maltby
S/S E.E.Kelly
S/S W.H.Coe

#223
Lt. R.F.Shaefer
S/S E.R.Judd
S/S J.A.Fejes

Flight III
#200
Lt. R.S.Rudisill
S/S F.D.Allred
Sgt. D.W.Stephens

#194
Lt. L.J.Siracusa
S/S F.E.Brown
S/S J.C.Burkhalter

Spare
#750
Lt. J.P.Hillerman
S/S J.E.Wilson, S/S I. Binney

#978
Lt. R.J.Rooney
S/S H.M.McCleary
S/S S.F.DiNapoli

#227
Lt. A.W.Nordstrom
S/S W.J.Gossett
S/S R.L.Miller

#684
Lt. J.F.Meagher
S/S E.A.Damico
S/S E.S.Dickenson

#963
Lt. L.E.Hill
S/S C.H.Yost
S/S R.W.Burch

#217
Lt. W.L.Greene
S/S J.A.Ochaba
S/S W.F.Colbert

#893
Lt. R.D.Poindexter
T/S L.E.Robbins
S/S D.M.Simpson

Loading List **Mission #49** **19 May 1944**

Beauville Fille Coastal Guns

Box I

Flight I

#125
Major R.F.Price
Lt. A.H.Hand
S/S E.A.Anderson
Sgt. K.E.Hornbeck

#907
Lt. R. Poindexter
T/S L.G.Robbins
S/S D.H.Simpson

#444
Capt. H.F.Conant
Lt. R.F.McBrien
S/S J.E.McCreery
S/S H.J.Sylva

#195
Lt. G.F.Bartmus
S/S J.R.Orr
S/S F.L.Flacks

#379
Lt. R.K.Cruze
S/S B.C.Sieg
S/S J.C.Burkhalter

#0194
Lt.H. E. Hill
S/S C.H.Yost
S/S R.W.Burch

Flight II

#225
Lt. E.T.Platter
S/S K.L.Johnson
S/S J.L.Czech

#214
Lt. R.H.Smith
S/S A.A.Stockham
Sgt. R.J.Mahoney

#219
Lt. J.D.Adams
S/S P.L.Clearman
Sgt. A.J.Zeikus

#711
Lt. H.P.Cole
S/S F.R.Chvatel
S/S B.G.Fandre

#211
Lt. F.W.Henderson
Sgt. R.M.Griswold
Sgt. P.E.Coulombe

#714
Lt. R.A.Wipperman
S/S H.S.Ahrens
Sgt. L.C.Mazza

Flight III

#363
Lt.F.W.DeMand
S/S C.W.Middleton
Sgt. R.J.Troyer

#937
Lt. A.R.Durante
S/S H.T.Best
S/S I.R.DeGiusti

#155
Lt. H.D.Andrews
S/S G.M.Cook
S/S E.R.Werley

#393
Lt. R.S.Greenley
S/S H.C.Worden
S/S J.J.Rzepka

#493
Lt. R.W.York
S/S H.A.Marion
S/S V.P.Adams

#221
Lt. W.A.Merchant
S/S C.J.Harp
S/S K.P.Brown

SPARE
#216
Lt. R.G.Meredith
S/S V.E.Molver
S/S C.H.Gray

Loading List **Mission #53** **24 May 1944**
Beaumont le Roger Airfield

#953
Lt. L.G.Peede
S/S A.A.Hill
S/S C.L.Hibbs

#176
Lt. C.C.Mish
Sgt. C.J.Clark
Sgt. R.F.Shustz

#0226
Lt. R.G.Meredith
S/S H.J.Sylva
Sgt. H.W. Smith

#907
Lt. G.Ebenstein
S/S H.Perkins
Sgt. S.P.Newell

#983
Lt. L.V.Shainberg
S/S A.E.Bergeron
S/S G.F.Cope

#743
Lt. J.H.Smith
Sgt. C.Vafiadis
Sgt. R.C. Hoffman

Box II
Flight I
#442
Capt. H.F.Conant
Lt. R.T.McBrien
Sgt. J.S.McCreery
Sgt. C.W.Scott

#195
Lt. J.F.Meagher
S/S E.A.Damico
Sgt. D. Hantske

Flight II
#0203
Lt. L.J.Siracusa
S/S F.L.Brown
S/S J.N.Hume

#0210
Lt. R.F.Shaefer
S/S J.A.Fejes
S/S E.R.Judd

Flight III
#673
Lt. R.J.Morton
S/S R.W.Nicks
S/S N. Radlich

#840
Lt. P.F.E.MacManus
S/S J.L.Rogers
S/S G.I.Fleischman #717

SPARE
Lt. R.L.Behlmer
T/S.W.J.Kelly
S/S W.G.Ferguson

#455
Capt. G.M.McNulty
Lt. F.R.Burseil
S/S H.E.White
S/S R.F.Addleman

#194
Lt. R.D.Lesher
S.S H.R.Hedrick
S/S A.A.Antanaitis

#684
Lt. E.B.Kreh
Sgt. E.Shelton
S/S D.R.Schenck

#0194
Lt. R.D.Poindexter
T/S L.G.Robbins
S/S D.H.Simpson

#376
Lt. E.E.DeMun
S/S M.Rosenstein
S/S H.O.Carney

Lt. A.J.Vleghels
Sgt. C.E.Rice
S/S R.W.Young

Loading List	**Mission #52** **Carmille-En-Vexin Airfield** **Box II**	**22 May 1944**
#227 Lt. A.W.Nordstrom Sgt. J.L.Johnson S.SF.G.Falk	**Flight I** #455 Capt. C.R.Jackson Lt. A.H.Maltby S/S H.M.McCleary S/S S.E.DiNapoli Capt.	#914 R.R.Prentiss Lt. W.M.Lytle S/S J.E.McCreery S/S H.J.Sylva
#689 Lt. P.G.Atkinson S/S J.O.Swafford Sgt. L.Martinez	#224 Lt. H.A.Monroe S/S W.L.Kidd S/S S.Risko	#978 Lt. F.D.Sommers S/S I.Binney Sgt. L.C.Burger
#907 Lt.E.B.Kreh Sgt. E.Shelton S/S D.R.Schenck	**Flight II** #684 Lt. R.F.Shaefer S/S J.A.Fejes S/S E.R.Judd	#195 Lt. R.G.Meredith S/S J.R.Orr S/S F.L.Flacks
#0194 Lt. R.D.Lesher S/S H.R.Hedrick S/S A.J.Antanaitis	#176 Lt. L.J.Siracusa S/S F.E.Brown S/S F.N.Hume	#0203 Lt. L.G.Peede Sgt. D.Hantske S/S C.L.Hibbs
#840 Lt T.Boukamp *** S/S R.J.Colosimo S/S G.F.Cope	**Flight III** #442 Capt. M.J.Huff *** Lt. J.Kupits S/S J.B.Thompson S/S H.F.Hatch	#376 Lt. P.F.E.MacManus *** S/S J.L.Rogers S/S G.I.Fleischman
#717 Lt. P.Dontas S/S A.L.Nielsen S/S W.E.Fields	#743 Lt. W.C.Siggs *** S/S N.Radlich S/S R.W.Nicks	#900 Lt. N.V.Shainberg S/S C.A.Prindle S.S E.T.Epps
***NoSortie Flight All Returned	SPARE #0210 Lt. H.E,Hewes S/S J.F.Kasper S/S H.E.Boyer	

Loading List

Mission #56
Beauville Tille Airdrome

26 May 1944

#176
Capt. R.E.Prentiss
S/S J.E.McCreery
S/S H.J.Sylva

#203
Lt. C.C.Mish
S/S C.J.Clark
Sgt. R.F.Chustz

#893
Lt. R.D.Poindexter
S/S D.H.Simpson
T/S L.G.Robbins

#226
Lt.R.G.Meredith
S/S A.J. Antaniatis
S/S H.R.Hedrick

Box III
Flight I
#452
Lt. A.E.Osborne
Lt. W.Forma
S/S E.E.Kelly
S/S W.H.Coe

#745
Lt. J.F.Meagher
S/S E.A.Damico
Sgt. D.Hantske

Flight II
#210
Lt. R.F.Shaefer
S/S J.A.Fejes
S/S E.R.Judd

#0194
Lt. W.E.Downing
S/S E.Dickensen
Sgt. K.E.Hornbeck

Flight III
#687
Lt. G.Ebenstein
S/S H.Perkins
Sgt. S.P.Newell

#393
Lt. W.A.Merchant
S/S C.J.Harp
S.S K.R.Brown

SPARE
Lt. J.D.Adams
S/S P.L.Clearman
Sgt. A.J.Zeikus

#450
Major H.A.Radetsky
S/S A.A.Hill
S/S G.E.Pfenning

#684
Lt. S.B.Ritchie
S/S E.A.Anderson
S/S A.W.Newkirk

#0194
Lt. L.G.Peede
S/S C.L.Hibbs
Sgt. P.J.Fild

#195
Lt. R.VMiracle
S/S B.C.Seig
S/S J.C.Burkhalter

Loading List **Mission #63** **30 May 1944**
Abbeyville Drucat Airfield

Box I
Flight I

#914
Major D.L.Willetts
Lt. P.G.Royalty
T/S F.H.Larronde
S/S H.A.Lempka

#711
Lt. J.D.Adams
S/S P.L.Clearman
S/S A.J.Zeikus

#439
Lt. H.L.Sommers
Lt. R.J.McQuade
S/S C.D.Lanave
S/S D.F.Mallory

#957
Lt. E.T.Platter
S/S K.L.Johnson
S/S Czech

#231
Lt.W.A.Merchant
S/S C.J.Harp
S/S K.P.Brown

#951
Lt. R.W.York
S/S R.J.Wilds
Sgt. L.A.Ashton

Flight II

#701
Lt. R.F.Shaefer
S/S E.R.Judd
S/S J.A.Fejes

#560
Lt. R.K.Cruze
S/S F.L.Adair
S/S C.F.Love

#963
Lt. L.E.Hill
S/S C.H.Yost
S/S R.W.Burch

#226
Lt. R.G.Meredith
S/S A.A.Hill
S/S B.C.Sieg

#0194
Lt. C.C.Mish
S/S C.J.Clark
Sgt. R.F.Chustz

#684
Lt. E.B.Kreh
Sgt. E.Shelton
S/S D.R.Schenck

Flight III

#900
Lt. P.F.E.Macmanus
S/S J.L.Rogers
S/S G.I.Fleischman

#961
Lt. M.S.Street
S/S C.A.Prindle
S/S E.T.Epps

#189
Lt. N.V.Shainberg
Sgt. J.W.Sabadosh
Sgt. C.W.Floyd

#743
Lt. W.A.Peck
S/S A.E.Bergeron
S/S H.E.Kelton

#673
Lt. P.Dontas
S/S W.E.Fields
S/S A.L.Nielsen

#202
Lt. J.F.Smith
S/S C.Vafiacis
Sgt. H.C.Hoffman

SPARE

#393
Lt. R.H.Smith
S/S A.A.Stockham
Sgt. R.J.Mahoney

Loading List | **Mission #64** | **2 June 1944**

Gorenflos NoBall

Box I

Flight I

#135
Major M.W.Campbell
Lt. W.H.Palin
J.B Thompson
S/S H.L.Hatch

#181 S/S
Lt. W.H.Land
S/S S.F.Alden
S/S R.L.Ballinger

#439
Capt. D.A.Hulse
Lt. R. Conte
S/S F.D.Allred
Capt.A.McClellan

#202
Lt. P.F.E.MacManus
S/S J.L.Rogers
S/S G.I.Fleischman

#148
Lt. H.B.Clark
Sgt. J.W.Sabadosh
Sgt. G.F.Floyd

#189
Lt. E.R.Hayter
Sgt. F.E.Melchoir
S/S R.C.Halloway

Flight II

#684
Lt. R.F.Shaefer
S/S J.A.Fejes
S/S E.R.Judd

#894
Lt. S.B.Ritchie
S/S A.W.Newkirk
S/S E.A.Anderson

#226
Lt. R.G.Meredith
S/S A.A.Hill
S/S R.W.MacDonald

#701
Lt. J.F.Meagher
S/S D.Hantske
S/S E.A.Damico

#0194
LT. R.V.Svenson
S/S P.F.Fild
S/S G.E.Pfenning

#195
Lt. W.E.Downing
S/S E.S.Dickenson
Sgt. K.E.Hornbeck

Flight III

#0176
Lt. G.F.Bartmus
S/S J.R.Orr
Pvt. J.R.Herttua

#360
Lt. R.K.Cruze
S/S F.L.Adair
S/S C.F.Love

#745
Lt. R.V.Miracle
S/S B.C.Sieg
S/S J.C.Burkhalter

#362
Lt. L.E.Hill
S/S R.W.Burch
S/S C.H.Yost

#0210
Lt. A.P.Nikas
Sgt. H.W.Smith
Sgt. G.W.Scott

#963
Lt. E.B.Kreh
Sgt. E.Shelton
S/S D.R.Schenck

SPARE
#840
Lt. T.Boukamp
S/S R.J.Colosimo
S/S D.F.Mallory

Loading List **Mission #65** **3 June 1944**
Chartres Airdrome

Box II
Flight I

#125
Captain H.F.Conant
Lt. R.T.McBrien
S/S J.R.Orr
Pvt. J.R.Herttua

#745
Lt. R.D.Lesher
S/S H.R.Hedrick
S/S A.J.Antanaitis

#455
Major J.G.Napier
Lt. W.L.Smith
S/S A.E.Bergeron
S/S H.E.Kelton

#362
Lt. J.F.Meagher
S/S E.A.Damico
Sgt. D.Hantske

#195
Lt. R.R.Svenson
Sgt. P.G,Fild
Sgt. G.H.Pfenning

#684
Lt. E.B.Kreh
Sgt. E.Shelton
S/S D.R.Schenck

Flight II

#227
Lt. R.S.Rudisill (Not Airborne)
S/S A.J.Bonamo
S/S R.K.Riley

#689
Lt. P.G.Atkinson
Sgt. J.O.Swafford
S/S P.F.Glynn

#217
Lt. D.F.Shea
S/S R.E.Lee
S/S F.G.Falk

#207
Lt. F.J.Harrold
S/S E.L.Griffin
S/S C.W.Maziasz

#750
Capt. Z.R.Moore
S/S J.A.Ochaba
S/S D.D.Burns

#680
Lt. J.P.Hillerman
Sgt. E.F.Paules
Sgt. L.Martinez

Flight III

#147
Lt. R.J.Morton
S/S A.L.Nielsen
S/S W.E.Fields

#717
Lt. W.F.Tripp
Sgt. J.W.Sabadosh
S/S D.F.Mallory

#743
Lt. W.C.Siggs
S/S R.J.Colosimo
S/S N.Radlich

#943
Lt. E.J.Renth
S/S O.D.LaNave
S/S F.M.Citty

#900
Lt. C.Church
S/S P.E.Maciulewicz
S/S H.E.Shatzer

#189
Lt. E.R.Hayter
Sgt. F.E.Melchcir
S/S R.C.Halloway

SPARE
#226
Lt. R.G.Meredith
S/S A.A.Hill
S/S R.W.MacDonald

D-Day 6 June 1944 Group Mission #67
First Mission — AM
Loading List—-Argentan, France

Box I

Flight I

#914
Major D.L. Willetts
Lt. P. G. Royalty
T/S R. W. MacDonald
S/S H. A. Lempka

#214
Lt. R. V. Wheeler
S/S J.S.Brower
S/S E. Corrin

#937
Lt. A. R. Durante
S/S H.T. Best
S/S I. R. DeGiusti

#363
Lt. R. W. York
S/S H. J. Wild

#645
Lt. Col. W. W. Farmer
Lt. M. A. Pape
S/S R. W. MacDonald
S/S A. A. Hill

#714
Lt. F.W. Henderson
Sgt. R. M. Griswold

Flight II

#1711
Lt. L.A. Marso
Lt. R. J. Basnett
S/S H. E. Wellin

#393
Lt. R. E. Greenley
S/S H. C. Worden
S/S J. J. Rzepka

#493
Lt. R. C. Morehouse
S/S L. A. Zygiel
Sgt. A. J. Burgess

#951
Lt. E. A. Herman
Sgt. J. O. Young
Sgt. A. D. Garrett

#221
Lt. W. A. Merchant
S/S C. J. Harp
S/S K. P. Brown

#220
Lt. J. H. Miller
Sgt. R. G. Schrom
Sgt. J. Galender

Flight III

#164
Lt. H. P. Cole
S/S B. G. Chvatal
S/S F. R. Fandre

#840
Lt. T. Boukamp
Sgt. C. Vafiadas
Sgt. R. C. Hoffman

#711
Lt. T. J. Murray
Sgt. R. J. Jones
Sgt. D. H. Debower

#929
Lt. A. J. Vleghels
Sgt. R. W. Rice
Sgt. C. E. Young

#219
Lt. M. Zubon
T/S J. R. L. Turner
S/S W. Crussell

#189
Lt. J. S. Conner
Sgt. H. C. Rogers
Sgt. J. E. VanDuyne

Spare #943 - Lt. E. J. Renth with gunners S/Sgts. O. D. LaNave and F. M. Citty

D-Day 6 June 1944, Group Mission #67, Argentan, France

Box II
Flight I

#444
Major R. F. Price
Lt. A. R. Hand
S/S E. R. Judd
S/S A. J. Fejes

#894
Lt. R. D. Pointdexter
T/S L. E. Robbins
S/S D. H. Simposon

#450
Lt. H. L. Sommers
Lt. R. J. McQuade
S/S A. E. Bergeron

#226
Lt. J.F. Meagher
Sgt. D. Hantske
S/S E. A. Damico

#195
Lt. R. R. Svenson
Sgt. P. G. Fild
S/S G. H. Pfenning

#684
Lt. E. B. Kreh
Sgt. E. Shelton
S/S D. R. Schenck

Flight II

#439
Capt. D. A. Hulse
Lt. R. Conte
S/S F. D. Allred
S/S D. J. Stephens

#207
Lt. L. R. McBride
Cpl. J. McKee
Sgt. L. Burger

#211
Lt. A. W. Nordstrom
S/S J. D. Gossett
S/S R. L. Miller

#978
Lt. R. J. Rooney
S/S H. M. Mc Cleary
S/S S. B. DiNapoli

#157
Lt. D. F. Shea
S/S R. E. Lee
S/S F. G. Falk

#907
Lt. P. G. Atkinson
S/S J. O. Stafford
S/S P. F. Glynn
(Returned-Early-No Sortie)

Flight III

#0194
Lt. G. Ebenstein
Sgt. S. P. Newell
S/S H. Perkins

#154
Lt. E. Hill
S/S R. W. Burch
S/S C. H. Yost

#202
Lt. R. K. Cruse
S/S H. E. Shatzer
S/S P. P. Maciulewicz

SPARE
#925
Lt. E. T. Platter
S/S K. L. Johnson

D-Day 6 June 1944, Group Mission #67, Argentan, France

Box III

Flight I

#640
Lt. E. A. Osborne
Lt. Forma
S/S E. E. Kelley
S/S W. H. Coe

#745
Lt. R. D. Lesher
S/S H. D. Hedrick
S/S A. J. Antanaitis

#442
Capt. M. J. Huff
Lt. J. Kupits
S/S J.B. Thompson
S/S H. F. Hatch

#176
Lt. R. V. Miracle
S/S B.C. Sieg
S/S J.C.Burklhalter

#210
Lt. W. E. Downing
S/S E.S.Dickenson
Sgt. K.E.Hombeck

#194
Lt. B..Ritchie
S/S E. A. Anderson
S/S C.J.Clark

Flight II

#147
Lt. R.L.Morton
Sgt. J.W.Sabados
Sgt. C.F.Floyd

#390
Lt. P. Dontas
S/S A.L.Nielson
S/S W.E. Fields

#148
Lt. E.E. Demun
S/S M.Rosenstein
S/S H.O. Carney

#961
Lt. M. S. Street
S/S C.A. Prindle
S/S E.T. Epps

#900
Lt. E.R. Hayter
Sgt. F.E. Melchoir
S/S R. G. Holloway

#743
Lt. W. F. Tripp
Sgt. J.O. Scott
S/S D.F. Mallory

Flight III

#455
Capt. C.R. Jackson
Lt. A. H. Maltby
S/S H. E. Shite
S/S R. F. Addleman

#380
Lt. E.J. Johnson
S/S W.J.Donahue
S/S M.R. Brayu

#750
Lt. C.L. McGlohn
S/S J.W. Moran
S/S P.B. Driskill

#224
Lt. H. a. Monroe
S/S W. L. Kidd
S/S S. Riako

#680
Lt. H. P. Hillerman
Sft. E. F. Paules
Sgt. L. Martinez

#892
Lt. R. O. Gruetzemacher
Sgt. S. R. Zahlikiewics
Sgt. J.L. Johnson

SPARE

#165
Lt. N.G. Brown
Sgt. D.D. Burns
Sgt. W.J. Daniel

Loading List **Mission #68** **6 June 1944** **D-Day PM**
Serquez Marshalling Yard

Box I

Flight I

#439
Major W.J.Meng
Lt. V.H.Powell
S/S F.P.Glynn
S/S R.F.Stobert

#224
Lt.Col.T.R.Ford
S/S R.J.Colosimo
Sgt. N. Radlich

#914
Capt. G.M.McNulty
Lt. F.H.Burseil
S/S H.E.White
S.S R.F.Addleman

#750
Lt. W.B.Ostrander
S/S J.E.Wilson
S/S I.Binney

#892
Lt. R.O.Gruetzmacher
Sgt. S.R.Zaklikiewicz
Sgt. J.L.Johnson

$207
Lt. F.J.Harrold
S/S E.L.Griffin
Sgt. C.W.Maziasz

Flight II

#380
Lt. R.S.Rudisill
S/S R.R.Riley
S/S A.J.Bonamo

#689
Lt. P.G.Atkinson
S/S J.O.Swafford
S/S P.F.Glynn

#680
Lt. C.L.McGlohn
S/S J.W.Moran
Lt. G.E.Lindsey

Flight III

#1717
Lt. R.F.Shaefer
Lt. J.E.Burg
S/S J.A.Fejes
S/S F.R.Judd

#226
Lt. R.G.Meredith
S/S A.A.Hill
S/S R.W.MacDonald

#0154
Lt. C.C.Mish
S/S C.J.Clark
Sgt. R.P.Chustz

SPARE
#745
Lt. R.D.Lesher
S/S H.R.Hedrick
S/S A.J.Antanaitis

(See addendum on pages 359-360 for additional loading lists for this mission)

Loading List	**Mission #71** **Vitre Railroad Bridge**	**8 June 1944**
#227 Lt. P.G.Atkinson S/S J.O.Swafford S/S P.F.Glynn #157 Lt. D.F.Shea S/S R.E.Lee S/S F.G.Falk	**Box I** **Flight I** #455 Major W.J.Meng Lt. V.H.Powell S/S R.F.Stobert S/S F.P.Glynn #207 Lt. F.J.Harrold S/S E.L.Griffin Sgt. C.W.Maziasz	#467 Capt. D.A.Hulse Lt. R. Conte S/S F.D.Allred S/S D.W.Stephens #224 Lt. N.G.Brown S/S J.E.Wilson S/S I.Binney
#9194 Lr. R.G.Meredith S/S A.A.Hill S/S R.W.MacDonald	**Flight II** #907 Lt. G. Ebenstein Sgt. C.P.Newell Sgt. H.Perkins #217 Lt. T.J.Leonard S/S O.D.Evans S/S T.A.Palmer	#195 Lt. W.E.Downing S/S K.E.Hornbeck S/S.B.Kemper
#210 Lt. L.G.Peede S/S L.M.Daugherty S/S/ C.W.Hibbs	**Flight III** #176 Lt. G.F.Bartmus S/S J.R.Orr S/S H.W.Smith #0194 Lt. L.E.Hill S/S C.H.Yost Sgt. R.W.Birch	#894 Lt. R.D.Lesher S/S H.R.Hedrick S/S A.J.Antanaitis

Loading List

#951
Major J.G.Napier
S/S W.H.Coe
S/S E.E.Kelly

#221
Lt. J.H.Miller
Sgt. R.B.Schrom
Sgt. J.Galender

#684
Lt. E.B.Kreh
Sgt. E.Shelton
S/S D.R.Schenck

#0194
Lt. R.G.Meredith
S/S A.A.Hill
S/S R.W.MacDonald

#227
Lt. L.E.Hill
S/S R.W.Burch
S/S C.H.Yost

#217
Lt. R.K.Cruze
S/S F.L.Adair
S/S C.F.Love

Mission #69
Lessay Bridge
Box II
Flight I

#1711
Lt. L.A.Marzolf
Lt. R.J.Basnett
S/S H.E.Wellin
S/S L.G.Kutzer

#393
Lt. R.E.Greenley
S/S C.J.Harp
S/S K.P.Brown

Flight II

#0210
Capt. H.F.Conant
S/S J.A.Fejes
S/S E.R.Judd

#987
Lt. G.Ebenstein
S/S H.Perkins
Sgt. S.P.Newell

Flight III

Lt. J.F.Meagher
Sgt. D.Hantske
S/S E.A.Damico

#894
Lt. R.D.Poindexter
T/S L.G.Robbins
S/S D.H.Simpson

SPARE
#493
Lt. R.H.Smith
S/S A.A.Stockham
Sgt. R.J.Mahoney

7 June 1944

#135
Capt. H.J.Huff
Lt. J.Kupits
Sgt. J.W.Sabadosh
Sgt. C.E.Young

#937
Lt. A. R..Durante
S/S H.T.Best
S/S I.R.DeGiusti

#0176
Lt. W.E.Downing
Sgt. E.S.Dickenson
S/S K.E.Hornbeck

#9194
Lt. S.B.Ritchie
S/S E.A.Anderson
S/S J.R.Orr

#207
Lt. R.V.Miracle
S/S J.C.Burkhalter
S/S B.C.Sieg

#195
Lt. R.R.Svenson
Sgt. P.G.Fild
S/S G.E.Pfenning

Loading List **Mission #72** **11 June 1944**
Falaise Railroad Junction

Box III
Flight I

#452
Capt. D.A.Hulse
Lt. R. Conte
S/S F.D.Allred
S/S D.E.Stephens

#227
Lt. A.W.Nordstrom
S/S J.D.Gossett
S/S R.L.Miller

#467
Lt. R.S.Rudisill
Lt. R.H.Joost
S/S R.K.Riley
S/S A.J.Bonamo

#750
Lt. W.B.Ostrander
S/S J.E.Wilson
S/S I.Binney

#207
Lt. P.G.Atkinson
S/S J.O.Swafford
S/S P.F.Glynn

#380
Lt. D.T.Sommers
Sgt.S.R. Zaklikiewicz
Sgt. J.L.Johnson

Flight II

#1750
Lt. R.F.Shaefer
Lt. J.C.Burg
S/S A.J.Fejes
S/S E.R.Judd

#0226
Lt. R.G.Meredith
S/S B.C.Sieg
S/S R.W.MacDonald

#9194
Lt. S.B.Ritchie
S/S E.A.Anderson
Sgt. H.W.Smith

Flight III

#907
Lt. G. Ebenstein
Sgt. S.P.Newell
S/S H.Perkins

#0194
Lt. C.C.Mish
S/S C.J.Clark
Sgt. R.F.Chustz

#195
Lt. R.R.Svenson
Sgt. P.G.Fild
S/S G.E.Pfenning

SPARE
#978
Lt. R.J.Rooney
S/S H.M.McCleary
S/S S.P. DiNapoli

Loading List

Mission #74 13 June 1944
St. Sauveur Le Vicomte
Railway Junction

Box I
Flight I

#439
Major W.J.Meng
Lt. V. H. Powell
S/S R.F.Stobert
S/S F.P.Glynn

#380
Lt. E.L.Johnson
S/S W.J.Donahue
S/S M.R.Brayn

#1711
Lt. L.A.Marzolf
Lt. R.J.Basnett
S/S H.E.Wellin
S/S L.G.Kutzer

#750
Lt. W.B.Ostrander
S/S J.E.Wilson
S/S I.Binney

#689
Lt. P.G.Atkinson
S/S J.O.Swafford
S/S P.F.Glynn

#211
Lt. N.G.Brown
Sgt. L.Martinez
Sgt. E.F.Paules

Flight II

#764
Capt. R.B.Prentiss
S/S J.E.McCreery
S/S H.J.Sylva

#9194
Lt. S.B.Ritchie
S/S E.A.Anderson
Sgt. H.W.Smith

#226
Lt. R.G.Meredith
S/S L.B.Kemper
S/S R.W.MacDonald

Flight III

#0194
Lt. J.F.Meagher
S/S E.A.Damico
Sgt. D.Hantske

#973
Lt. E.B.Kreh
Sgt. E.Shelton
S/S D.R.Schenck

#176
Lt. R.D.Lesher
S/S H.R.Hedrick
S/S A.J.Antanaitis

SPARE

#224
Lt. A.W.Nordstrom
S/S J.D.Gossett
S/S R.L.Miller

Loading List **Mission #77** **15 June 1944**

Lessay Bridge
Box I
Flight I

#444
Major R.F.Price
Lt. A.R.Hand
T/S L.G.Robbins
S/S D.H.Simpson

#935
Lt. J.F.Meagher
Sgt. D.Hantske
S/S E.A.Damico

Flight II
#450
Lt. R.J.Morton
Lt. J.Madenfort
S/S R.J.Colosimo
S/S F.M.Citty

#390
Lt. W.A.Peck
S/S A.E.Bergeron
S/S H.E.Kelton

Flight III
#135
Capt. M.J.Huff
Lt. J.Kupits
Sgt. C.Vafiadis
Sgt. R.C.Hoffman

#900
Lt. R.L.Behlmer
T/S W.J.Kelly
S/S W.G.Ferguson

#0194
Lt. L.G.Peede
S/S L.M.Daugherty
S/S C.L.Hibbs

#176
Lt. G.F.Bartmus
S/S J.R.Orr
S/S G.F.Pfenning

#469
Major H.A.Radetsky
Lt. M.A.Pape
S/S H.O.Carney
S/S M.Rosenstein

#717
Lt. H.B.Clark
Sgt. Sgt. J.W.Sabadosh
Sgt. F.G.Floyd

#961
Lt. M.S.Street
S/S C.A.Prindle
S/S E.T.Epps

#202
Lt. E.R.Hayter
S/S F.M.Melchoir
S/S R.C.Holloway

#1719
Capt. H.F.Conant
Lt. R.T.McBrien
S/S C.J.Clark
Lt. R.F.Lindsay

#226
Lt. R.G.Meredith
S/S A.A.Hill
S/S R.W.MacDonald

#189
Lt. J.S.Conner
Sgt. H.C.Rodgers
Sgt. J.E.Van Duyne

#743
Lt. W.C.Siggs
S/S O.D.Lanave
S/S N.Radlish

#147
Lt. W.F.Tripp
Sgt. J.O.Scott
S/S D.R.Mallory

#929
Lt. A.J.Vleghels
Sgt. R.W.Rice
Sgt. C.E.Young

SPARE: #9711 Lt. W.A.Merchant w/ S/S C.J.Harp & S/S K.P.Brown

Loading List **Mission #80** **19 June 1944**
Ligescourt NoBall

Box II
Flight I
#1711
Lt. L.A.Marzolf
Lt. R.J.Basnett
S/S H.E.Wellin
S/S L.G.Kutzer

#220
Lt. R.D.Perkins
S/S V.N.Sherry
S/S.H.Linneman

#714
Lt. H.D.Andrews
S/S G.M.Cook
S/S E.R.Werley

#221
Lt. A.E.Herman

Sgt. A.D.Garrett
Sgt.J.O.Young

#900
Lt. R.L.Behlmer
S/S O.D.Lanave
S/S W.G.Ferguson

#929
Lt. J.F.Smith
Sgt. V. Vafiadis
Sgt. R.C.Hoffman

#907
Lt. W.E.Downing
S/S E.S.Dickenson
Sgt. K.E.Hornbeck

#226
Lt. R.G.Meredith
S/S A.A.Hill
S/S R.W.MacDonald

#165
Lt. M.Zubon
T/S J.R.L.Tanner
S/S W.C.Russell

#951
LT.R.C.Morehouse
(Returned Early)
Sgt.L.A.Zygiel
Sgt. A.J.Burgess

Flight II
Lt. R.J.Morton
Lt. J.Madenfort
S/S C.L.Webb
S/S F.M.Citty

#147
Lt. W.A.Peck
S/S A.E.Bergeron
S.S G.I.Fleischman

#390
Lt. A.J.Vleghels
Sgt. R.W.Rice
Sgt. C.E.Young

#840
Lt. H.B.Clark
Sgt. J.W.Sabodosh
Sgt. C.F.Floyd

Flight III
#719
Lt. R.F.Shaefer
Lt. J. Burg
S/S J.A.Fejes
S/S E.R.Judd
#894
Lt. R.D.Poindexter
T/S L.G.Robbins
S/S D.H.Simpson

#764
Lt. L.E.Hill
S/S R.W.Burch
S/S C.H.Yost

#210
Lt. R.V.Miracle
S/S J.C.Burkhalter
S/S B.C.Sieg

SPARE: R.D.Lesher W/ S/S H.R.Hedrick & A.J.Antanaitis

WINDOW: #450 Lt.H.L.Sommers - Lt.R.J.McQuade-S/S C.A.Prindle & S/S E.T.Epps
#961 Lt. W.F.Tripp-w/ Sgt. J.O.Scott & S/S D.F.Mallory
#189 Lt. J.S.Connor - w/ Sgt. H.C.Rodgers & Sgt.J.E.VanDuyn

Loading List **Mission #81** **20 June 1944**
LeGrand Rossegnol NoBall

Box I
Flight I

#444
Major R. F. Price
Lt. A.R. Hand
S/S J.A.Fejes
S/S E.R.Judd

#9194
Lt. S.B.Ritchie
S/S E.A.Anderson
S.S. H.W.Smith

#745
Lt. R.D.Poindexter
S/S D.H.Simpson
T/S L.G.Robbins

#0176
Lt. G.F.Bartmus
S/S J.R.Orr
S/S S.P.Newell

#935
Lt. W.E.Downing
S/S E.S.Dickenson
S/S K.E.Hornbeck

#0266
Lt. R.G.Meredith
S/S A.A.Hill
S/S R.W.MacDonald

Flight II

#135
Capt. M.J.Huff
Lt. J.Kupits
S/S A.E.Bergeron
S/S D.R.Mallory

#743
Lt. W.C.Siggs
S/S R.W.Nicks
S/S N.Radlich

#390
Lt. N.V.Shainberg
S/S H.C.Rodgers
Sgt. J.E.Van Duyne

#189
Lt. P.F.E.MacManus
S/S J.L.Rogers
S/S G.I.Fleischman

#147
Lt. W.F.Tripp
Sgt. C.Vafiadis
Sgt. R.C.Hoffman

#840
Lt. T. Boukamp
S/S R.J.Colosimo
S/S A.L.Nielsen

Flight III

#469
Lt. R.J.Morton
Lt. J. Madenfort
S.S C.L.Webb
S/S F.M.Chitty

#961
Lt. M.S.Street
S/S C.A.Prindle
S/S E.T.Epps

#181
Lt. W.H.Land
S/S S.F.Alden
S/S R.L.Ballinger

#900
Lt. R.L.Behlmer
S/S O.D.Lanave
S/S R.C.Hoffman

#717
Lt. H.B.Clark
Sgt. J.W.Sabadosh
Sgt. C.F.Floyd

#943
Lt. J.F.Smith
Sgt. R.W.Rice
Sgt. C.E.Young

SPARE
#211
Lt. J.C.Sewell
Cpl. J.McKee
S/S R.Eutsler

Loading List **Mission #82** **21 June 1944**
Middel Straete NoBall

Box I
Flight I

#439
Major W.J.Meng
Lt. V.H.Powell
S/S R.F.Stobert
S/S F.P.Glynn

#227
Lt. A.W.Nordstrom
S/S J.D.Gosset
S/S R.L.Miller

#712
Lt.Col.T.R.Aylesworth
Lt. W.M.Lytle
S/S J.N.Sabadosh
S/S C.F.Floyd

#455
Lt. Col. W.W.Farmer
Major W.P.Thomas
S/S J.E.Wilson
S/S I.Binney

Flight II

#907
Lt. G.Ebenstein
S/S H. Perkins
Sgt. S.P.Newell

#745
Lt. R.D.Lesher
S/S A.J.Antanaitis
S/S H.R.Hedrick

#0210
Lt. R.V.Miracle
S/S B.C.Sieg
S/S J.C.Burkhalter

#894
Lt. R.D.Poindexter
S/S D.H.Simpson
T/S L.G.Robbins

#764
Lt. L.E.Hill
S/S R.W.Burch
S/S C.H.Yost

#0226
Lt. R.G.Meredith
S/S A.A.Hill
S/S R.W.MacDonald

Flight III

#224
Lt. H.A.Monroe
S/S W.L.Kidd
S/S S.Risko

#689
Lt. P.G.Atkinson
S/S J.O.Swafford
S/S P.F.Glynn

#680
Lt. J.P.Hillerman
Sgt. L.Martinez
Sgt. E.F.Paules

#147
Lt. W.J.Greene
S/S J.A.Ochaba
S/S W.F.Colbert

#978
Lt. R.J.Rooney
S/S H.M.McCleary
S/S S.F.DiNapoli

#387
Lt. C.L.McGlohn
S/S J.W.Moran
S/S P.B.Driskill

SPARE
#892
Lt. L.R.McBride
S/S S.J.McKee
S/S R.Eustler

Loading List **Mission #83** **22 June 1944**
Cherbourg Heavy Gun Emplacement

#224
Lt. Col. T.R.Ford
S/S R.F.Stobert
S/S F.P.Glynn

#227
Lt. A.W.Nordstrom
S/S R.L.Miller
Sgt. H.G.Wiggins

#210
Lt. R.V.Miracle
S/S B.C.Sieg
S/S J.C.Burkhalter

#0194
Lt. W.E.Downing
S/S E.S.Dickenson
S/S K.E.Hornbeck

#975
Lt. R.W.Cruze
S/S C.F.Love
S/S F.L.Adair

#195
Lt. R.R.Svenson
S/S P.G.Fild
S/S G.H.Pfenning

Box I
Flight I
#455
Capt. C.R.Jackson
Lt. A.H.Maltby
Sgt. D.E.Burns
S/S W.J.Daniels

#209
Lt. F.J.Harrold
S/S E.L.Griffin
Sgt. M.E.Dias

Flight II
#907
Lt. G.Ebenstein
S/S H.Perkins
Sgt. S.P.Newell

#176
Lt. G.F.Bartmus
S/S J.R.Orr
S/S R.J.Chustz

Flight III
#935
Capt. R.B.Prentiss
S/S J.E.McCreery
S/S J.Sylva

#9194
Lt. S.B.Ritchie
S/S E.A.Anderson
S/S H.W.Smith

SPARE
#157
Lt. D.F.Shea
S/S R.E.Lee
S/S F.G.Falk

#452
Capt. D.A.Hulse
Lt. R. Conte
S/S F.D.Allred
S/S D.W.Stephens

#689
Lt.D.T.Sommers
Sgt. S.R.Zaklikiewicz
Sgt. J.L.Johnson

#894
Lt. R.D.Poindexter
T/S L.G.Robbins
S/S D.H.Simpson

#745
Lt. L.G.Peede
S/S C.L.Hibbs
S/S E.A.Damico

#226
Lt. R.G.Meredith
S/S A.A.Hill
S/S R.W.MacDonald

#764
Lt. L.E.Hill
S/S C.H.Yost
S/S R.W.Burch

Loading List | **Mission #90** | **Merlemont Headquarters Building** | **5 July 1944**

Box II

Flight I

#450
Lt. H.L.Sommers
Lt. R.J.McQuade
S/S M.Rosenstein
S/S H.O.Carney

#929
Lt. L.W.Pentilla
Sgt. J.D.Dugan
Sgt.L.E.Curtis

#1717
Captain G.M.McNulty
Lt. F.H.Burseil
S/S A.E.Mayhew
Sgt. S.G.Novak

#840
Lt. T.Boukamp
S/S R.J.Colosimo
S/S J.S.Wing

Flight II

#689
Lt. P.G.Atkinson
S/S J.O.Swafford
S/S P.F.Glynn

#224
Lt. D.B.Grunig
Sgt. M.Dias
Sgt. H.J.Nowosielski

#380
Lt. D.T.Sommers
Sgt. J.L.Johnson
Sgt. S.R.Zaklikiewicz

#892
Lt. J.P.Hillerman
Sgt. E.F.Paules
Sgt. B.R.Wilson

Flight III

#973
Lt. R.J.Rooney
S/S H.M.McCleary
Sgt. L.C.Leahigh

#750
Lt. R.B.Singletary
Sgt. A.A.Cianciosi
Sgt. H.C.Wiggens

#209
Lt. R.B.Hall
Sgt. L.C.Burger
Sgt. D.S.Blackford

#387
Lt. L.H.McBride
S/S J.McKee
S/S R.Kutsler

Flight IV

#210
Lt. R.V.Miracle
S/S L.M.Daugherty
S/S C.L.Hibbs

#935
Lt. J.P.Kenny
Sgt. J.K.Spadon
Sgt.F.Noteriani

#764
Lt. T.Clausen
Sgt. C.Fetko
Sgt. D.M.Brown

#379
Lt. W.E.Downing
S/S E.S.Dickenson
S/S K.E.Hornbeck

SPARE: Lt. R.G.Meredith w/ S/S R.W.MacDonald & Sgt. S.P.Newell

Loading List **Mission #91** **6 July 1944**
Epernon Railroad Junction

#493
Lt. R.C.Morehouse
S/S L.A.Zygiel
S/S A.J.Butgess

#214
Lt. D.L.Withington
Sgt. C.F.Huss
Sgt. D.L.McElhattan

#200
Lt. D.F.Shea
S/S R.E.Lee
S/S F.G.Falk

#387
Lt. L.R.McBride
S/S R.Eutsler
Sgt. E.L.Shaw

#745
Lt. R.D.Lesher
Sgt. R.E.Wright
Sgt. S.G.Novak

#210
Lt. R.V.Miracle
Sgt. S.H.Giesy
Sgt. F.E.Cherry

Box I
Flight I
#645
Lt. L.A.Marzolf
Lt. R.J.Basnett
S/S H.E.Wellin

#393
Lt. R.E.Greenley
S/S H.C.Worden
S/S.J.Rzepka

Flight II
#457
Lt. R.S.Rudisill
Lt. R.K.Joost
S/S R.K.Riley
S/S A.J.Bonamo

#211
Lt. W.J.Greene
S/S J.A.Ochaba
S/S W.F.Colbert

Flight III
#640
Lt. A.E.Osborne
Lt. W.Forma
S/S E.E.Kelly
S/S W.H.Coe

#379
Lt. W.E.Downing
S/S E.S.Dickenson
S/S K.E.Hornbeck

SPARE
#209
Lt. A.W.Nordstrom
S/S J.D.Gossett
S/S R.L.Miller

#925
Lt. R.W.York
S/S J.L.Czech
S/S J.L.Johnson

#219
Lt. H.D.Andrews, Jr.
S/S G.M.Cook
S/S E.R.Werley

#224
Lt. H.A.Monroe
S/S W.L.Kidd
S/S S.Risko

#892
Lt. T.J.Leonard
S/S O.D.Evans
S/S T.I.Palmer

#975
Lt. L.E.Hill
S/S R.W.MacDonald
S/S E.Shelton

#362
Lt. L.G.Peede
S/S L.M.Daugherty
S/S C.L.Hibbs

Loading List | **Mission #91-2** | **6 July 1944**

Epernon Railroad Junction

Box II

Flight I

#914
Major D.L.Willetts
Lt. P.G.Royalty
T/S F.H.Larronde
S/S H.A.Lempka

#951
Lt. R.H.Smith
S/S R.J.Mahoney
S/S A.A.Stockham

#221
Lt. M.Zubon
S/S W.C.Russell
T/S J.R.L.Turner

#363
Lt. R.V.Wheeler
S/S J.S.Brower
S/S H.J.Wilds

#967
Lt. W.H.Ames
Sgt. H.S.Fessler
Sgt. R.J.Brown

#9711
Lt. C.L.Estes
S/S.C.R.Orvold
Sgt. A.E.Dimartino

Flight II

#135
Capt. M.J.Huff
Lt. J.Kupits
Sgt. R.A.Clark
Sgt. F.P.Basford

#961**
Lt. J.E.Blomgren
Sgt. M.Bookach
Sgt. L.R.Fleming

#189
Lt. J.S.Connor
S/S J.E.VanDuyne
S/S H.C.Rodgers

#840
Lt. T.Boukamp
S/S R.J.Colosimo
S/S J.S.Wing

#147
Lt. D.W.Elliott
Sgt. J.Mani
Sgt. J.J.McQuire

#376
Lt. W.L.Penttila
Sgt. J.D.Dugan
Sgt. L.B.Curtis

Flight III

#712
Lt. E.E.DeMun
Lt. W.L.Smith
S/S M.Rosenstein
S/S H.O.Carney

#176
Lt. E.J.Renth
S/S O.D.Lanave
S/S R.L.Ballinger

#929
Lt. W.F.Tripp
S/S J.C.Scott
S/S D.F.Mallory

#907
Lt. N.V.Shainberg
S/S J.L.Rogers
S/S G.I.Fleischman

#717
Lt. E.R.Hayter
S/S F.E.Melchoir
S/S R.G.Holloway

#673
Lt. L.E.Poundstone
Sgt. A.J.Burland
Sgt. K.Heath

SPARE
#907
Lt. G.Ebenstein
Sgt. S.P.Newell
Sgt. C.Fetko

**Failed to Become Airborne (Magneto Problem)

Loading List **Mission #93** **7 July 1944**
St. Pierre Sur Dives Bridge

Box II
Flight I
#467
Lt. R.S.Rudisill
Lt. R.H.Joost
S/S R.K.Riley
S/S A.J.Bonamo

#209
Lt. R.B.Hall
Sgt. B.S.Blackford
Sgt. L.C.Burger

#135
Capt. M.J.Huff
Lt. J.Kupits
Sgt. R.A.Clark
Sgt. F.P.Basford

#387
Lt. E.L.Johnson
S/S W.J.Donahue
S/S A.A.Cinanosi

#689
Lt. R.O.Gruetzsmacher
S/S J.D.Gossett
Sgt. R.L.Cochran

#224
Lt. D.G.Grunig
Sgt. M.K.Dias
Sgt. H.J.Nowosielski

Flight II
#907
Lt. G.Ebenstein
S/S D.H.Simpson
T/S L.E.Robbins

#819
Lt. E.B.Kreh
S/S E.Shelton
S/S D.R.Schenck

#943
Lt. T.Clausen
Sgt. C.Fetko
Sgt. D.M.Brown

#390
Lt. R.K.Cruze
S/S F.L./Adair
S/S C.F.Love

#764
Lt. F.W.Harris
S/S D.Hantske
Sgt. S.P.Newell

#176
Lt. A.J.Welsh
Sgt. S.G.Novak
Sgt. R.E.Wright

Flight III
#210
Lt. R.V.Miracle
S/S R.W.Burch
S/S C.H.Yost

#226
Lt. R.G.Meredith
S/S P.G.Fild
S/S G.H.Pfenning

#745
Lt.C.C.Mish
S/S C.J.Clark
S/S R.F.Chustz

#379
Lt. W.E.Downing
S/S E.S.Dickenson
S/S K.E.Hornbeck

#221
Lt. A.E.Herman
S/S D.H. DeBower
S/S R.J.Jones

#935
Lt. J.K.Colquitt
Sgt. S.H.Giesy
Sgt. F.E.Cherry

Flight IV
#450
Lt. H.L.Sommers
Lt. R.J.McQuade
Sgt. F.E.Melchoir
Sgt. R.G.Holloway

#9711
Lt. R.D.Perkins
S/S V.N.Sherry
S/S R.H.Linneman

#743
Lt. R.L.Behlmer
T/S W.J.Kelly
S/S W.G.Ferguson

Loading List **Mission #94** **8 July 1944**

Caen Strong Point

#819
Lt. C.C.Mish
S/S C.J.Clark
S/S R.F.Chustz

#975
Lt. F.W.Harris
S/S D.Hantske
S/S C.F.Love

#714
Lt. F.W.Henderson
S/S R.M.Griswold
S/S P.E.Coulombe

#951
Lt. W.H.Ames
Sgt. H.S.Fessler
Sgt. H.J.Brown

#219
Lt. R.C.Morehouse
S/S A.J.Burgess
S/S L.A.Zygiel

#956
Lt. D.L.Withington
S/S C.F.Huss
Sgt. L.D.McElhatten

Box II
Flight I
#444
Major R.F.Price
Lt. A.R.Hand
T/S L.G.Robbins
S/S D.H.Simpson

#764
Lt. L.E.Hill
S/S C.H.Yost
S/S R.W.Burch

Flight II
#1724
Lt. H.P.Cole
Lt. R.J.Basnett
S/S F.R.Chvatel
S/S B.G.Fandre

#493
Lt. R.H.Smith
S/S R.J.Mahoney
S/S J.O.Young

Flight III
#1711
Lt. L.A.Marzolf
Lt. J.T.Beck
S/S H.E.Wellin
S/S L.G.Kutzer

#937
Lt. A.R.Durante
S/S H.T.Best
S/S S.R.DeGiussti

SPARE
#390
Lt. N.V.Shainberg
S/S F.E.Melchoir
S/S R.C.Holloway

#226
Lt. R.G.Meredith
S/S R.W.MacDonald
Sgt. S.G.Novak

#195
Lt. R.R.Svenson
S/S P.G.Fild
S/S G.H.Pfenning

#165
Lt. H.F.Pair
S/S W.C.Russell
T/S J.R.L.Tanner

#363
Lt. C.L.Estes
S/S A.E.DiMartino
S/S R.V.Orvold

#220
Lt. J.H.Miller
S/S R.G.Schrom
S/S J.Galender

#221
Lt. T.J.Murray
S/S R.J.Jones
S/S D.H.DeBower

Loading List **Mission #96** **11 July 1944**
Bourth Railway Bridge

Box II
Flight I

#640
Lt. A.E.Osborne
Lt. W. Forma
S/S H.T.Sylva
S/S J.E.McCreery

#764
Lt. L.E.Hill
S/S C.H.Yost
S/S R.W.Burch

#1717
Lt. J.F.Meagher
Lt. J.J.Burg
S/S D.H..Simpson

Flight II

#362
Lt. L.G.Peede
S/S L.Daugherty
S/S H.L.Hibbs

#9195
Lt. C.J.Anderson
Sgt. P.G.Euga
Sgt. E.L.Shaefer

#819
Lt. V.T.Clausen
Sgt. C.Fetko
Sgt. T.D.M.Brown

#745
Lt. R.G.Meredith
S/S R.W.MacDonald
Sgt. R.E.Wright

Flight III

#176
Lt. G.F.Bartmus
S/S F.L.Flacks
Sgt. J.K.Spadoni

#907
Lt. C.C.Mish
S/S C.J.Clark
S/S R.F.Chaustz

#210
Lt. R.V.Miracle
S/S B.C.Sieg
S/S J.C.Burkhalter

#975
Lt. R.K.Cruze
S/S C.F.Love
S/S F.L.Adair

Flight IV

#390
Lt. N.V.Shainberg
Sgt. M.Bookach
Sgt. L.R.Fleming

#900
Lt. H.B.Clark
S/S J.W.Sabadosh
S/S C.F.Floyd

#840
Lt. J.F.Smith
S/S C.Vafiadis
S/S R.C.Hoffman

#929
Lt. J.S.Connor
S/S H.C.Rodgers
S/S J.E.VanDuyne

SPARE: #943 - Lt.D.W.Elliott -Sgt.J.J.McQuire & Sgt. J.Mani

Loading List **Mission #98** **14 July 1944**
Bourth Railway Bridge

Box II
Flight I

#640
Lt. A.E.Osborne
Lt. W.Forma
Sgt. J.W.Robinson
Sgt. W.P.Newell

#226
Lt. R.G.Meredith
Sgt. P.G.Euga
S/S R.W.MacDonald

#058
Capt. C.R.Jackson
Lt. A.H.Maltby
Sgt. W.J.Daniel
Sgt. D.E.Burns

Flight II

#907
Capt. R.B.Prentiss
S/S J.E.McCreery
S/S H.J.Sylva

#935
Lt. J.K.Colquitt
Sgt. S.H.Giesy
Sgt. F.E.Cherry

#764
Lt. J.P.Kenny
Sgt. J.K.Spadoni
Sgt. F.Noteriani

#362
Lt. R.D.Lesher
S/S H.R.Hedrick
S/S A.J.Antanaitis

Flight III

#819
Lt. G.F.Bartmus
S/S D.Hantske
S/S F.L.Flacks

#195
Lt. R.R.Svenson
S/S P.C.Fild
S/S G.E.Pfenning

#176
Lt. C.C.Mish
S/S C.J.Clark
S/S R.F.Chustz

#975
Lt. A.J.Welsh
Sgt. R.E.Wright
Sgt. S.G.Novak

Flight IV

#211
Lt. W.J.Greene
S/S J.A.Ochaba
S/S W.F.Colbert

#200
Lt. N.G.Brown
S/S H.E.White
S/S R.F.Addleman

#207
Lt. F.J.Harrold
S/S E.L.Griffin
S/S C.W.Haziasz

#689
Lt. .G.Atkinson
S/S J.O.Swafford
S/S P.F.Glynn

SPARE

#209
Lt. J.C.Sewell
S/S B.R.Wilson
S/S C.L.Shaw

Loading List **Mission #105** **25 July 1944**

St. Giles Strong Point

Box II

Flight I

#452
Capt. R.B.Rudisill
Lt. R.H.Joost
S/S R.K.Riley
S/S A.J.Bonamo

#211
Lt. W.J.Greene
S/S J.A.Ochaba
S/S W.F.Colbert

Flight II

#907
Lt. G.Ebenstein
Sgt. C.F.Parchman
Sgt. W.F.Fuehrer

#362
Lt. R.G.Meredith
S/Sgt.C.F.Love
Lt. F.J.Mazanec

Flight III

#745
Lt. R.D.Lesher
S/S H.R.Hedrick
S/S A.J.Antanaitis

#379
Lt. W.E.Downing
S/S E.S.Dickenson
S/S K.E.Hornbeck

SPARE

#943
Lt. E.J.Renth
S/S O.D.Lanave
Pvt. J.Moskowitz

#224
Lt. T.J.Leonard
S/S O.D.Evans
S/S T.A.Palmer

#227
Lt. P.P.Parausky
Sgt. B.R.Wilson
Sgt. M.Hall

#173
Lt. C.C.Mish
Capt. R.G.Bailey
S/S R.F.Chustz

#210
Lt. P.E.Parker
Sgt. A.F.Galloway
Sgt. S.Kochan

#294
Lt. J.P.Kenny
Sgt. J.K.Spadoni
Sgt. F.Notariani

#919
Lt. J.H.Montrose
Sgt.R.S.Gandy
Sgt. J.W.Felkel

#1711
Lt. F.W.DeMand
Lt. R.J.Hanlon
S/S R.J.Troyer
S/S C.W.Middleton

#209
Lt. D.T.Sommers
Sgt. S.R.Zaklikiewicz
Sgt. J.L.Johnson

#160
Lt. J.L.Colquitt
S/S E.Shelton
Sgt. E.B.Schafer

#480
Lt. L.E.Cannon
Sgt. J.W.Robinson
Sgt. F.P.Brzezinski

#764
Lt. L.E.Hill
S/S R.W.Burch
S.H.Yost

#193
Lt. F.W.Harris
S/S D.Hanstke
S/Sgt.E.A.Damico

Loading List

Mission #108
Caumont Town

30 July 1944

#764
Lt. R.G.Meredith
S/S R.W.MacDonald
S/S A.A.Hill

#176
Lt. A.J.Welsh
Sgt. R.E.Wright
Sgt. S.G.Novak

#925
Lt. C.L.Estes
S/S C.R.Orvold
S/S A.E.DiMartino

#951
Lt. J.H.Miller
S/S J.Galender
S.S.R.G.Schrom

#165
Lt. M.Zubon
T/S J.R.L.Tanner
S/S W.C.Russell

#956
Lt. J.J.Lackovich
Sgt. T.Connery
Sgt. R.M.Barry

Box II
Flight I
#640
Lt. A.E.Osborne
Lt. W. Forma
S/S E.E.Kelly
S/S K.G.Lagerman

#907
Lt. G.Ebenstein
Sgt. J.H.Roberts
S/S D.E.Raines

Flight II
#493
Lt. R.E.Greenley
S/S H.C.Worden
S/S J.J.Rzepka

#220
Lt. R.D.Perkins
S/S V.N.Sherry
S/S R.H.Linneman

Flight III
#214
Lt. R.V.Wheeler
S/S J.S.Brewer
S/S J.L.Czech

#937
Lt. A.R.Durante
S/S H.T.Best
S/S I.R.DeGiusti

SPARE S/S R.J.Jones
Lt. J.R.Sparling
Sgt. L.L.Leahigh
Sgt. C.L.Shaw

#135
Capt. M.J.Huff
Lt. J.Kupits
Sgt. R.A.Clark
Sgt. F.P.Basford

#894
Lt. C.J.Anderson
Sgt. T.G.Euga
Sgt. E.L.Schafer

#219
Lt. H.D.Andrews
S/S G.M.Cook
S/S E.R.Werley

#363
Lt. R.C.Morehouse
S/S A.J.Burgess
S/S L.A.Zygiel

#719
Lt. W.H.Ames
Sgt. H.S.Fessler
Sgt. R.J.Brown

#221
Lt. T.J.Murray
S/S D.H.DeBower

Loading List **Mission #109** **31 July 1944**

Liseaux Marshalling Yard

Box I

Flight I

#712
Major R.A.Clark
Lt. C.W.Jones
Sgt. K.Heath
Sgt. H.A.Burland

#181
Lt. J.S.Connor
S/S J.E.Van Duyne
S/S H.C.Rodgers

#937
Lt. H.B.Clark
S/S J.W.Sabadosh
S/S D.F.Floyd

#147
Lt. T.Boukamp
S/S R.J.Colosimo
S/S J.S.Wing

#943
Lt. E.J.Renth
S/S O.D.Lanave
S/S G.I.Fleischman

#900
Lt. E.P.Hall
Sgt.R.P.Sharp
Sgt. R.W.Carstens

Flight II

#1717
Lt. J.F.Meagher
Lt. J.J.Burg
T/S L.G.Robbins
S/S D.H.Simpson

#150
Lt. T.Clausen
Sgt. C.Fetko
Sgt. D.M.Brown

#907
Lt. W.E.Downing
S/S E.S.Dickenson
S/S K.E.Hornbeck

#362
Lt. L.G.Peede
Sgt. F.Noteriani
S/S C.L.Hibbs

#195
Lt. L.E.Cannon
Sgt. J.W.Robinson
Sgt. F.P.Brzezinski

#480
Lt. J.K.Colquitt
S/S J.E.McCreery
S/S D.E.Raines

Flight III

#724
Lt. F.W.DeMand
Lt. R.J.Hanlon
S/S R.J.Troyer
S/S C.W.Middleton

#221
Lt. A.E.Herman
S/S A.D.Garrett
S/S J.O.Young

#951
Lt. F.W.Henderson
S/S R.M.Griswold
S/S P.E.Coulombe

#220
Lt. R.D.Perkins
S/S V.N.Sherry
S/S R.H.Linneman

#493
Lt. J.H.Murray
S/S D.H.Debower
S/S R.J.Jones

#925
Lt. D.L.Withington
Sgt. C.F.Huss
Sgt. L.D.McElhattan

SPARE
#719
Lt. H.F.Pair
T/S J.R.L.Tanner
S/S V.P.Adams

Loading List **Mission #110** **31 July 1944**

Mantes-Gassicourt Railroad Bridge

#214
Lt. W.H.Ames
Sgt. H.S.Fessler
Sgt. R.J.Brown

#9711
Lt. J.H.Miller
S/S R.G.Schrom
S.S J.Galender

#176
Lt. W.E.Downing
S/S E.S.Dickenson
S/S K.E.Hornbeck

#150
Lt. F.W.Harris
S/S E.A.Damico
Sgt. A.F.Galloway

#819
Lt. E.B.Kreh
S/S E.Shelton
S/S D.R.Schenck

#894
Lt. J.P.Kenny
Sgt. J.K.Spadoni
Sgt. F.Noteriani

Box II

Flight I

#724
Lt. H.P.Cole
Lt. R.J.Basnett
S/S F.R.Chvatal
S/S B.G.Fandre

#719
Lt. H.F.Fair
S/S J.S.Brower
S/S V.P.Adams

Flight II

#1719
Lt. J.F.Meagher
Lt. J.J.Burg
T/S L.G.Robbins
S/S D.H.Simpson

#907
Lt. R.V.Miracle
S/S B.C.Sieg
S/S J.C.Burkhalter

Flight III

#640
Lt. A.E.Osborne
Lt. W.Forma
S/S K.G.Lagerman
S/S E.E.Kelly

#745 **
Lt. R.D.Lesher
S/S A.J.Antanaitis
S/S H.R.Hedrick

SPARE
#380
Lt. R.B.Singletary
Sgt. H.C.Wiggins
Sgt. A.A.Ciaciosi

#219
Lt. H.D.Andrews
S/S G.M.Cook
S/S E.R.Werley

#956
Lt. J.J.Lackovich
Sgt. R.Connery, Jr.
Sgt. R.M.Barry

#362
Lt. L.G.Peede
Sgt. R.S.Gandy
S/S C.L.Hibbs

#195
Lt. R.R.Svenson
S/S P.G.Fild
S/S G.H.Pfenning

#480
Lt. R.G.Meredith
S/S R.W.MacDonald
S/S A.A.Hill

#764
Lt. C.J.Anderson
Sgt. T.G.Euga
Sgt. E.L.Schafer

** Crash Landed in England - Did not make mission.

Loading List **Mission #116** **6 August 1944**
Oissel Bridge

Box I
Flight I
#640
Lt. A.E. Osborne
Lt. W. Forma
S/Sgt. E.E. Kelly
S/S K.G. Lagerman

#894
Lt. C.J. Anderson
Sgt. T.J. Euga
Sgt. E.L. Schafer

#935
Lt. P.E. Parker
Sgt. A.F. Galloway
Sgt. S. Kochan

#819
Capt. R.B. Prentiss
S/S H.J. Silva
S/S J.L. McCreary

#770
Lt. A.J. Walsh
Sgt. R.E. Wright
Sgt. S.G. Novak

#150
Lt. J.R. Monroe
Sgt. R.S. Gandy
Sgt. J.W. Felkel

Flight II
#452
Capt. D.A. Hulse
Lt. R. Conte
S/S F.D. Allred
S/S F.P. Glynn

#224
Lt. A.W. Nordstrom
Sgt. J.A. Hummer
S/S D.A. Sampson

#387
Lt. N.G. Brown
S/S H.E. White
S/S R.F. Addleman

#211
Lt. R.J. Greene
S/S J.A. Ochaba
S/S W.F. Colbert

#978
Lt. T.W. McManus
Sgt. G.E. Hart
Sgt. J.A. Lapointe

#750
Lt. R.T. Byrne
Sgt. W.D. Cummings
Sgt. L. Paules

#874
Col. J. Backus (Wing C.O.)

Flight III
#467
Capt. C.R. Jackson
Lt. A.H. Maltby
Sgt. D.E. Burns
Sgt. W.J. Daniel

#200
Lt. D.T. Summers
Sgt. S.R. Zaklikiewicz
Sgt. J.L. Johnson

#380
Lt. T.R. Leonard
S/S O.D. Evans
T/S T.J. Goggin

#209
Lt. C.L. McGlohn
S/S J.W. Moran
S/S P.B. Driskill

#227
Lt. P.P. Barausky
Sgt. M. Hall
Sgt. B.R. Wilson

#674
Lt. J.R. Sparling
Sgt. C.L. Shaw
Sgt. L.L. Leahigh

#490 (Spare) Lt. T.D. McCready with Sgts. W.F. Fuehrer & C. Fetko

Loading List **Mission #116** **6 August 1944**
Oissel Bridge

Box II

Flight I
#712
Major J.G. Napier
Lt. J. Madenfort
Pvt. R.W. Perkins
S/S R.R. Lowe

#390
Lt. T. Boukamp
S/S O.D. Lanave
S/S J.S. Wing

Flight II
#711
Lt. A. Marzolf
Lt. J.T. Beck
S/S C.J. Czeck
S/S J.L. Johnson

#719
Lt. H.F. Pair
S.S. H.A. Marion
S/S V.P. Adams

Flight III
#135
Capt. M.J. Huff
Lt. J. Kupits
Sgt. R.A. Clark
Sgt. F.P. Basford

#900
Lt. R.L. Behlmer
T/S W.J. Kelly
S/S W.G. Ferguson

#717
Lt. Col. W.W. Farmer
Sgt. J.E. Hay
Sgt. J.A. Buskirk

#743
Lt. J.F. Allen
Sgt. L.R. Getgen
Sgt. C.W. Veazy

#493
Lt. J.H. Miller
S/S R.G. Schrom
S/S J. Gallender

#956
Lt. J. Lackovich
Sgt. T. Connery
Sgt. R. Barry

#961
Lt. M.S. Street
S/S C.A. Prindle
S/S E.T. Epps

#202
Lt. D.W. Elliott
Sgt. J.J. McGuire
Sgt. J. Manx

#147
Lt. J.F. Smith
S/S C. Vafiadis
S/S C. Hoffman

#943
Lt. J.E. Blomgren
Sgt. M. Bockach
Sgt. L.R. Fleming

#714
Lt. M. Zubon
T/Sgt. J.R.L. Tanner
S/S W.C. Russell

#925
Lt. A.R. Durante
S/S H.T. Best
S/S R.I. DiGuisti

#181
Lt. W.H. Land
S/S S.F. Alden
S/S R.L. Ballenger

#929
Lt. E.R. Hayter
S/S F.E. Melchoir
S/S R.C. Holloway

#219 Spare Lt. W.H. Ames with Sgt. H.S. Fessler & S/S R.J. Brown

Chapter 17
Individual Anecdotes

Don Sorrells

Don Sorrels Joined the 669th Squadron of the Group in September 1944.

I liked flying the A-20 - it felt and acted more like a fighter. the plane was easy to fly in formation, easier than the B25 or A-26. Going down the bomb run, straight and level was a scary feeling, but I was so intent on keeping formation and watching for the bomb drop, that I didn't have time to think about anything else.

I didn't have any emergency landings from damage, although I did have a tire blow out on landing due to flak hits. I ran off the side of the runway damaging the prop and engine. I still have that piece of flak that our crew chief Sgt. Gehrels, saved for me.

On one of our missions, we experienced a lot of flak hits on my plane.I could hear the stuff hitting the ship so after the bomb run, I called my gunner to see if he was all right and he did not answer. I called several times without success and so I thought he was dead or badly wounded. When we landed, he crawled out of the ship in good condition. I asked him why he had not answered the intercom. He said that when we were on the bomb run, he leaned back from the periscope sight and a piece of flak came between him and the sight. Said he was so scared, he couldn't talk for a while.

I first flew the A-20 in Charlotte, NC after going to B-25 school in Mather Field in Sacramento, California and then another B-25 school in Columbia, SC. There I had an opportunity to go to A-20s in Charlotte.

I ferried an A-20 K from Hunter Field, GA to Scotland and then went to combat training in Belfast, Ireland.

I was billeted with Dolph Whitten, Ed Bond, Charlie Stewart, Sheffy McBroom, Thaddeus P. Hall, and pilots Jack Blomgren and Ross Cornell. The first night I was sitting on my cot writing a letter when the air raid siren went off. No one paid any attention so not wanting to appear frightened, I didn't either. About the time we heard this V1 bomb approaching, it got louder and louder, and louder, when I decided to seek shelter. I could not move, I was paralyzed! The thing went over the top of our hut and hit the ground a hundred yards past our hut, exploding with a big boom and doing some damage to the hut and other buildings. That was my introduction to the 416th.

I don't remember much about all the guys we were with, but I do remember a couple of them I can't forget.

On December 24, 1944, we had a mission to Hillsheim and I watched a good friend get shot down. He was Bob Svenson from the 668th. We had gone all through cadet training together. He was flying an A-20, the only one on that mission, so I knew who it was when I saw him go down.

Christmas Day 1944, my friend and fellow Seattleite was shot down and killed on a mission to Munsteifel. He was Johnnie Kehoe, we had made a lot of bicycle trips around France on our days off.

Another unforgettable mission was on January 2, 1945. It was very cold, foggy and we were waiting to take off. Emil Martin was right in front of me and Van Meter was in front of him. Van Meter took off and crashed with a loud explosion. A fog bank settled over the runway and the windshield frosted over. Emil Martin turned back and I decided to make an instrument take off. About halfway down the runway I checked the airspeed indicator and it said zero so I firewalled the throttles, prayed a lot and eased back on the control - the airplane flew up out of the-fog and I joined up with the flight leader.

The mission was Simmern bridge. I don't think it was a success, because we had to go back on Jan. 11th.

Sorrels remembers his trip to the "front" in the spring of 1945.

He was given a jeep in Spring 1945 with a trailer to haul his equipment. He took his two gunners to Sittard, Holland to join the 35th Infantry Division, a part of General Patton's Third

Army. He was assigned to a Company that was living in a pill box. They asked what type plane he flew. When he told them the A-26, that turned them off because they were bombed by that type plane. They didn't believe his story that his group could never do a dumb thing like that, but their misbelief was mollified when they shared the extra bottle of gin he carried with him.

The Tech Sergeant assigned to keep Sorrels and his gunners out of trouble took them across a field, which the T/Sgt told them to step in his footprints because it was a mine field. The import of that instruction was fortified when they heard a whomp up ahead. A misstep took the life of a soldier. Sorrels said it was not a pretty sight, but his first view of a war causalty. They eventually made it okay.

Carl Weinert

Carl Weinert joined the 416th Group when they were flying A-26s, so he did not fly the A-20s although he did say he was told by A-20 pilots that the plane flew like a fighter.

I joined the 669th squadron and was elated with the crew chiefs from that squadron. I lost an engine on an A-26 training flight. That night, after lights out, the crew chief came over to tell me what had happened. I flew most of my 43 missions with crew chief Fred Stemler. If you remember, before taxing out, the crew chiefs would salute then pull the chocks. On one mission he waived off the salute climbed up to the cockpit and hit me on the flak helmet three times,. After returning from the mission I asked 'why?' His answer,' I have never lost an airplane when I did that.' To hell with the pilot? On the Worms mission, he said, 'What did you do to my airplane?' when he saw the flak damage. I loved the love of the airplane-later.

Take off on my first mission was wierd because it was my first flight with a bomb load and it made the airplane much less responsive to maneuvers, I soon got used to that. I came back from that mission soaking wet for the first and only time.

During the bomb run, I just focused on flying a tight formation. It was always a big relief to see the bomb bay doors open and the bombs fall. I then jettisoned them and had the gunner confirm that the bombs were released.

On one mission, a bomb hung up. I had the gunner remove the fuze and the bomb started rolling around on the bomb bay door during rough air descent. I requested special permission to land and had to remind myself while taxiing back not the open the bomb bay doors after cutting one engine.

We went in on Pathfinder on the Worms mission. When the clouds disappeared, at the Rhine River, the commander of my group, Ross Cornell, I found out later, said, 'we're going in visually'. I choked on the three sticks of gum which I chewed on every mission. Now, gum gags me after the flavor is gone. Going in visually meant flying around the target, in very heavy flak, back to the IP. Sweat time!

After we dropped our bombs on one mission, going through heavy clouds, I kept losing visual contact from my #2 position so decided to leave the formation. I banked right and dropped my nose then went on instruments. The artificial horizon had tumbled and the airspeed was frozen and I was losing altitude fast. I had to put both feet on the instrument panel to pull it out of the dive. As I pulled out of the dive, I saw some green grass, probably blacked out, and ended back in the clouds. The bomb bay doors flew open, my gunner lost his helmet, calling my name. I closed the doors and had him join me. I gave a short call for my heading and ETA.

At about 5,000 feet the sky filled with 20 and 40mm tracers. I thought that I was in friendly territory so shot the colors of the day with my Very pistol. A mistake. Some time later, I was joined by two P-38s who flew with me for a short time then said goodby. They scrapped the airplane because there were skin wrinkles just aft of the bomb bay doors and the airplane couldn't be trimmed.

As you recall, we felt that when your number is up - that's it, so don't sweat it. On my 35th mission, I got stuck in the mud on take-off, while taxiing out. By the time the tractor pulled me out, the flight were well on the way. I saw one flight with 5 aircraft so I joined it in the #5 position, just under my usual #2 spot, my normal position. The #2 plane received a direct hit. It wasn't my time, but was it coming up soon?

As you remember, we didn't discuss missions then. One reason that I enjoy the reunions is that I have had lots of questions answered.

Claude Brown

Claude Brown had interesting history before joining the 416th Bomb Group. He had gotten his wings the early part of 1943 and flew B-25 and B-26 medium bombers in the states, and became an instructor. Then the A-26 came along and only 18 B-26 pilots were selected to test fly and evaluate the A-26s. Claude almost didn't make that group of selected fliers, but his heavy experience in twin engine mediums, opened the door for him to participate in that training period.

Following exciting moments on a torturous trip over the North Atlantic, through Greenland, taking A-26s over seas, Brown wound up with the 386th Bomb Group, 553rd Squadron, in England. They flew a few milk runs with the A-26s in what may be called "test" combat missions for those new, swift, bombers. But then their luck ran out,they were assigned a run at Bergen op Zoom in Holland. Brown said the Germans knew the exact fly route planes heading for op Zoom would follow, so they set their heavy anti-aircraft guns on barges on the estuary just ahead of the target. The formation got shot up real badly, with Brown's plane having received over 100 flak hits. His right engine failed on the bomb ran, but he made the drop and returned to Englnd on one engine.

The planes were judged to be ready for combat after the ten or twelve missions the386th flew. Eighteen shiny aluminum skinned A-26s were flown to the 416th's base at Villa Roche, France to hold transition flights for pilots there to fly the new units. The members of the 416th excitedly remember seeing that formation of shiny planes fly over their base and peel off for landing. The 416th had a 30 day transition period between 17 October and 17 November, when no combat missions occured.

Villa Roche, (A-55) was 'borrowed' after the Germans retreated, much as the Germans had borrowed it from the French. The Germans had left little in their retreat. There was only one building left standing in our area. This building was claimed by the A-26 pilots as their quarters and as the 671st squadron operations. This went well for only a few days, as the only option was a tent.

We rigged a 55 gallon oil drum to burn our used plane oil as heater fuel. One morning someone started the fire as usual but he failed to regulate the flow of fuel to the firebox. During breakfast, shouts told us the building was on fire. She was burning gently, when someone hit the drum with a bucket of water. Away it blew, spreading the fire everywhere. We lost everything from our rooms, but were able to salvage records from the front office.When the fire burned out we found that the Germans had booby-trapped the foundation with land mines, but for some reason the mines did not explode although they were very much alive. We had been sleeping over these things for some time.

The transition training pilots became regular members of the 416th group, with four assigned to each of the four squadrons. The transition training went well with the 416th pilots getting to love flying the A-26s, but the A-20s were still easier to fly, so they said.

J. K. Colquit

Pilot Colquitt flew 65 missions with the 416th Bomb Group in the 668th Squadron.

I love to fly an airplane more than anything else that I have ever done. I could go on for months about the great feelings that you have when you are flying an airplane.

About the war, I think that most of us felt that it was a job we were dealt and we had to deal with it as best we could. We did what we were told to do and did it the best that we could. I think that most of us were more afraid of not doing our assigned job well than of anything else.

I first flew the A-20 in Florence, SC. It was a great airplane and was lots of fun to fly. It was great in formation because of the narrow fuselage and you could turn without having to slow down and drop down so you could see the plane you were flying formation with. I flew 65 missions and had no major problems with my tour. I had lots of holes in my airplane and do not know why everything went so well for me. Someone had their hand on my shoulder and I do not know why. I am still looking for the answer.

There is no doubt in my mind that the best part of the thing that went on over there was the people that I met and lived with. Most of them are just a name that I remember and I cannot tie anything to them. There are a few stories I remember and that is about all.

Richard V. Wheeler

Dick Wheeler, a West Point graduate and a pilot for the 671st Bomb Squadron of the 416th, had completed his normal tour of about 65 missions, and was assigned to be a liason between Air Force pilots and the Commanders of Ground Forces just about before the Battle of the Bulge. Dick, with pilots from heavy aircraft groups, medium and fighter groups were advisors to ground forces on which targets either one of the type bomber or fighter groups would be best suited to handle when the time came to call on the Air Force for aerial assistance. While passing the time of day with a fighter pilot representative, Dick relates how this story evolved.

Wheeler was leading a six plane flight of A-20 and A-26 light bombers. His flight, #2 in the formation, moved out of position because the lead flight got into trouble. Wheeler took his flight out. German fighters were swirling around overhead, looking for targets of opportunity, like straggler lone planes or flights separated from their group formation. The Germans evidently spotted Wheeler's six planes, and they swooped down for an attack.

Wheeler said,

> A German ME-109 came zipping across my line of flight, and crossed my nose by no more than 50 yards. Right behind the 109 came a P-38, guns blazing toward the 109. Immediately behind the P-38 came another 109, guns blazing at the P-38, AND A FOURTH PLANE, another P-38 was shooting at the second 109. So, we had a 109 - a P-38 - a 109 - a P-38 all lined up. As our flight got close to the last P-38, a flak burst hit one of the two engines of the last P-38, which flipped over on its side and dove down to what I thought was his grave. Fortunately, my flight got back into the formation, and no other German fighters attacked. I said a prayer for the P-38 pilot for trying to save my flight.

While at the gathering of pilots, they all seemed to exchange stories about their experiences, and when a P-38 pilot said that he flew that type of plane, Wheeler told his story about how a P-38 saved his flight. he said he was real sorry to see that plane go down and he felt sorry for the pilot who went down that day. The P-38 pilot then broke in and elaborated on the story, surprising Wheeler by telling him that he was the P-38 that got flipped over and was going down. He said he got his plane under control on the way down, and on one engine got close to the ground. At reduced speed, he managed to fly to a friendly airfield, landed, and got out without a scratch.

Talk about surprise endings!

Debby Smith

Debby Smith is the daughter of the wife of a former pilot of the 416th Bomb Group, Andy Vleghels of the 669th Squadron. Andy lost his life on a mission to Bergen op Zoom in Belgium on September 16, 1944. Debby became interested in her mother's first husband and contacted members of the group. She attended two reunions of the group, gathering as much information as available on Andy's exploits, and learning about the workings of the group. Debby investigated all aspects of Andy's demise, and is writing a book which will include background on how and why Andy died, naming the people in Belgium who took care of the deceased, who brought the body in from the ocean between England and Belgium where Andy's plane went down, and where he was buried. In May, 1999, Debby wrote this.

"As Memorial Day approaches (in 1999), my thoughts turn to my mother and her first husband, Andy, a pilot who fought and died in World War II. Andy left behind a mother, a father, a thirteen-year-old sister, and my mother, a twenty-five year old wife and mother to be. It was a devastating loss for one so young and in love, a life-changing experience that colored everything to follow.

"Memorial Day was an important day for my mother; it was important for her to remember. But as the flag-waving of the war years has faded, Memorial Day has evolved into a national holiday where families gather for a little 'R and R.' The origin of its observance often seems to go unrecognized. It was different for my mother. I imagine that she could think of little else than the day she was notified that her beloved husband of nine months was missing in action.

"So, each Memorial Day for the past thirteen years, my mom and I would make our way to the serene ground of the Grosse Pointe (Michigan) War memorial to commemmorate the hundreds of thousands of soldiers who never returned home to their loved ones. It was a responsibility I gladly assumed after the death of my father. I was there to support my mother and to honor Andy. Few words were ever exchanged upon these occasions. I was simply there for her. We stood at attention, pledged our allegiance to the flag, listened to the speeches, joined in prayerful thanksgiving, and shed some tears as the bugler played the mournful melody of taps. The mood was somber and respectful.

"This past July, my mother died suddenly. On her bedside was an opened letter from Andy dated July 12, 1944 - so strong a tie was her first love.

"The week of my mother's funeral, my family and I went to see 'Saving Private Ryan,' Steven Spielberg's extraordinary, uncompromising film. With his honest and vivid depiction of World War II, Spielberg honors the men who defended our freedom. Anything less would have been an injustice. He spares us no detail, juxtaposing a matrix of pristine crosses and Stars of David at Normandy with the brutal, bloody battlefield at the beachhead below. Spielberg's images jolt our emotions. We are shocked to be vicarious witnesses to the undiluted terror of war, yet riveted by a harsh dose of reality as it existed on June 6, 1944, Omaha Beach.

"The enormity of it all is hard to comprehend, mere boys and young men by the millions, enlisted or drafted, mobilized to face the nightmare of war. All the while, families did their best to carry on, keeping vigil as their loved ones fought in foreign lands, constantly praying for their safe return. Some were called upon further to rebuild their lives, and struggle with their overwhelming feelings of loss. Collectively, their fortitude, bravery and sacrifice rid the world of a genocidal maniac whose death grip on occupied Europe threatened our freedom. World War II stole the lives, the hopes, and dreams of so many, forever changing the families left in the wake of combat. The cost was immeasurable. I sincerely hope that it is matched only by our gratitude and by our resolve to protect our liberty.

"For me, this memorial Day will be bittersweet. I'll still raise the flag and head down to the War Memorial, this time without my mother by my side. Our annual ritual had grown into a special tradition that we shared, and I will miss her. But now she has been reunited with Andy and my father. This brings me some consolation and peace. So, this year as the drone of taps fills the air, once again I will remember Andy and his fellow countrymen who fought the good fight. I will remember all the families that buried their sons, brothers, husbands and fathers. And I will remember my mother. It is a very important day for me."

Wayne E. Downing

One Spring day in 1944, an A-20 of the 668th Squadron of the 416th Bomb Group was sent from England along with 17 other Havocs to bomb targets in France. Its name was "L" for LIMA. The German antiaircraft guns were waiting to shoot it down. These guns were called 88s because their projectile was an 88mm shell. The shell has two fuses to explode it: a nose fuse to explode it if it hits its target. A tailfuse that was set to explode at a certain number of seconds after it left its gun barrel, if it did not hit anything in the sky. When it was exploded by the tail fuse, the shell's fragments would poke holes in anything within a seventy-five foot radius of the explosion. Many of these shells came up to meet "L" for LIMA's formation that day over France.

On previous missions over France there were occasions where an 88 shell made a direct hit on an A-20 Havoc. The result was to blow the airplane in half or to blow up the gas tanks and cause it to burn up in the sky. In either case, it was unusual for the airplane's crew of top gunner, bottom gunner, pilot, and in the glass-nosed version the navigator-bombadier, to survive. There are photos of this A-20 directly after it was hit, flat spinning down, without its tail attached to the fuselage.

On this day an 88 shell hit "L" for Lima directly under the top turret gunner's position. There was a very thick metal sheet of armor plating under this position. The shell bent this sheet around the top turret gunner's legs, bruising them. This deflected the shell out of the right side of the A-20 where it tore a large hole in the aircraft fuselage. The nose fuse did not explode the shell. The tail fuse did explode the shell after it got above the aircraft.

Why? The pilot carried a four-leaf clover with him in his flying suit pocket. It had been given to him by his fiance to carry as a good luck charm. Did it work?

The Havoc went on to bomb its target and return to its base in Wethersfield, England with a couple of cold wind-blown gunners.

Top Turret Ginner	— Ken Hornbeck
Bottom Gunner	— Ed Dickinson
Pilot	— Wayne Dowling

"L" for LIMA was now referred to as "L" for LUCKY.

John Buskirk

One of the A-26 transition training pilots joining the 671st Squadron was 1st Lt. John A. Buskirk. He flew A-20 planes during training in the states and first flew that type plane with the 416th Bomb Group while the group were at Melun, France, (Villa Roche), Field A-55. During his training in the states, he had hoped to be assigned to fly the B-26, Marauder.

His assessment of flying the A-20, "It was easy!" He also said he felt great, flying down the bomb run, adding, "hoping the flak didn't get us." This what he recalled.

> On the first mission the group flew after the 'Battle of the Bulge' December 23, 1944, I lost oil from the left engine. Prop ran away on the bomb run to bomb the bridge at Saarburg.
>
> The prop wouldn't feather because we found later, the prop governor broke on the wrong side of the feathering valve.
>
> We ran out of altitude approximately 2 - 3 miles from A-59 and closer to the wing Headquarters.

They were in a chateau belonging to Prince Ranier. It was used as a hunting lodge and one part of the chateau was left for the owner's use.

We landed in a field where a French farmer was plowing with two oxen. The sister of Prince Ranier came out to the airplane along with several of her male companions.

We were told that the FFI (French Underground) had captured two German parachutists that were hiding in a haystack that morning,

We returned to A-55 in time for Christmas and before our buddies had divided our personal possessions.

Buskirk said he hadn't experienced emergency landings due to flak or enemy fighters. Pretty Lucky!

APPENDIX

Transfer List
Laurel to Camp Shanks 27 December, 1943

1458-R Group Headquarters

	OFFICERS
COL.	MACE, HAROLD L.
LT.COL.	AYLESWORTH, THEODORE R.
MAJOR	CONEN, WARREN J.
MAJOR	TOWNSEND, JAMES W.
CAPT.	CLARK, ROBERT A.
CAPT.	LAUFER, MORRIS H.
CAPT.	NAPIER, JOHN G.
CAPT	PENTICOFF, PRENTISS C.
CAPT.	RADETSKY, HAROLD A.
CAPT.	RONEY, KENNETH T.
CAPT.	ZESINGER, CLAYTON W.
1ST. LT.	KINNEY, WILLIAM L.
1ST LT.	McDONALD, WILLIAM A.
1ST LT.	MAYER, WILLIAM H.
1ST.LT.	NUSSBAUM, HAROLD J.
1ST.LT.	SCHENKEIN, GEORGE
1ST.LT.	SWEENEY, BERNARD P.
2ND.LT.	BONURA, JOHN M.
2ND.LT.	CACHAT, FRANCIS J.
2ND.LT.	CASTLE, WALTER D.
2ND.LT	GUREASKO, MARTIN H.
2ND LT.	PAPE, MAX A.
2ND.LT	SUTTNER, HARRY G.
CWO	MOFFETT, WILLIAM H.
MR	RUGLAND, SIGVARD L.

ENLISTED MEN

Air Corps

M Sgt Alexander Houston	M Sgt Bernard John T	M Sgt Holmgren Joseph
M Sgt Young Clarence	T Sgt Blair Mathew G	T Sgt Corwin Stephen A
S Sgt Froehlich Kenneth A	T Sgt Stone Norman L	T Sgt Wilson David M

TRANSFER LIST
LAUREL TO CAMP SHANKS

S Sgt Calderon John M	S Sgt Connor Bernard J	S Sgt Eck Donald B
S Sgt Ezelle James S	S Sgt Hull Loren R	S Sgt Laning Paul W
S Sgt Mihalek Charles J	S Sgt Russo Edward J	
Sgt Boolos Leo Jr	Sgt Conrad Douglas K	Sgt Cormier O'Neil A
Sgt Dollar William F	Sgt Goodman Harold	Sgt Huey Dansley A
Sgt Loomis Norman R	Sgt MacNeil Hector J	Sgt Max Edwin M
Sgt Reski Henry E	Sgt Stolp Paul B	Sgt Wyman David L
Cpl Bird Sylvan L	Cpl Byrne John M	Cpl Clapp Wallace I
Cpl Gallahue Edward W	Cpl Gottlieb Irvin J	Cpl Hoffman Harrison H
Cpl Hughes William A	Cpl Leach Robert M	Cpl Leatherwood Harry R
Cpl Laguens Paul H	Cpl Martin Robert C	Cpl Noble John M
Cpl Talerico Frank A	Cpl Tiffany Paul B	Cpl Yost James S
Cpl Jeffcott Emory W		
Pfc Conlon Anthony R	Pvt Cates Robie W	Pvt Murph Bruce G
Pvt Fairhurst Frederick	Pvt Mustaka John A	Pvt Rehmann Edmond M
Pvt Watkins O Pakley M Jr		

Ordnance

T Sgt Hoover Donald C	Sgt Rea David J

Medical

T Sgt Jablonsky Jack R	Cpl Brier Ora C	Cpl Hinkle James J
Cpl Poplawski JohnW	Pvt Wagner Charles F	Pvt Pacheco Frank J

416th Bombardment Group (L)
668th Bomb Squadron

Acker, Kenneth L.
Acree, Ellis C.
Adair, Fred L.
Adkisson, Owen R.
Alexander, C. B.
Alexander, Harrison
Allen, Charles A.
Allison John C.
Alsleben, Lester
Alves, Laurence
Amend, Frank, C. Jr.
Amick, Robert L.
Amodeo, Joseph P.
Anatanatis, A. J.
Anderson,Charles E.
Anderson, Charles E.
Anderson, Charles J.
Anderson, Edwin A.
Anderson, Harold V.
Anderson, Roy
Andree, Harry T., Jr.
Annin, William W.
Arens, Frank L.
Arnes, Harold
Atchinson, Robert
Atkins, Claude N.
Bacon, Booker, B.
Bailey, Robert G.
Bailey, Thomas C.
Bales, Zane G.
Ball, Charles L.
Bankston, Roy Jr
Baran, Eugene
Bartmus, Galen F.
Baseo, John W.
Bass, William M.
Baxter, Bruce
Beatty, Griffin R.
Beck, John T.
Benton, Jessie
Bentzler, Daniel
Bergfelder, Paul H.
Bernard, John T.
Best, Alton F.
Bills, Richard K.
Bilotti, Gaetano
Bilunas, Frank A.
Bird, Joseph
Bird, Sylvester L.
Bjertness, Melvin
Bladykas, Walter T.
Blair, Matthew G.
Blakley, Evan E., Jr
Blanchard, Charles
Blevins, David L.
Blevins, John W.
Blount, Judson H.
Bocchieri, Emanuele
Bode, Raymond J.
Bollinger, Robert
Boolos, Leo
Born, Paul S.
Bostonian, D. A.
Bottlinger, M. A.
Bower, William M.
Bowling, Paul E.
Boykin, William M.
Brabham, James A.
Bradford, B. H.
Breece, Horace
Brigode, George A.
Brossett, Denny B.
Brown, Allen J.
Brown, Daniel M.
Brown, Floyd E.
Brown, Forrest C.
Brown, Jack H.
Brunetti, Dominick
Brzezinski, Ed P.
Buchanan, James Jr.,
Buchanan, Rhonda "
Buen, C
Buinski, Stanley. J.
Burch, Robert W.
Burg, Jack J.
Burkhalter, Joe C.
Busony, John Jr.,
Caivano, Walter J.
Calabrese, Conrad
Calderon, John M.
Call, George F.
Callahan, William Jr..,
Cannon, L.
Carver, James A.
Casbar, Anthony
Cates, Robie W.
Cathcart, Charles C.
Cavanaugh, Albert F.
Cavossi,Gino J.
Cebourne,Arthur
Cee, William M.
Chapin, Joe Jack
Chalmers, John J.
Charles, Fred M.
Cherry, F. E.
Chessmore,Roy
Christiaoa, Joseph A.
Chustz, Roy F.
Ciemiakoski, Henry J.
Cinguegrapa, Frank L.
Ciryak, Joseph C.
Clapp, Wallace T.
Clark, Claude J.
Clark, Michael
Clark, William E.
Clary, Amos H.
Clausen, Tom
Clearman, Percy L.
Cochran, Ernest N.
Coe, William H.

416th Bombardment Group (L)
668th Bomb Squadron

Cole, Christopher R.
Collier, Charles, B.
Conrod,Douglas K.
Cottle, Charles H.
Cross, Richard M.
Currie, John H., Jr.
Decaro, Nicholas A.
Deloriea, Leroy M.
Denetone, Clyde
Deutcher,Charlie J.
Dike, Charles F.
Doule, Gordon
Drum, Ezra B.
Dunlop, John E., Jr.
East, Bailey
Eck, Donald E.
Edenburn, James C.
Evans, Hugh M.
Evarts, Alan V.
Eyler, Joseph K.
Faulkner, James C.
Fejes, John A. Jr,
Fetko, Charles Jr.
Fild, Philip E.
Flacks, Francis L.
Ford,William
Freed, Don
Fuehrer, Wilkie F.
Gandy, Robert S.
Gentry, F.
Geyer, John
Gomez, A.
Gottberg, Alfred J.
Grodowitz, Phillip
Gunkel, Harry G.
Hale, Wilber L.
Hampton, Edward
Hantske, Douglas
Harris, Frank
Harvest, R. W.
Colden, Dean F.
Combs, Carmin
Cooper, Dean W.
Craig, John S.
Cruze, Raymond K.
Curtis, Charles S., Jr.
Dejes, John A., Jr.
DeMars, Willaim H.
Desimone, John
Dickenson, Edward S.
Doherty, Wilbur R.
Downing, Wayne
Duffield, William E.
Durrach, David S.
Eastwood, John E.
Eckard, David
Ernstrom, Reed L.
Evans, Reece
Ewing, Byron
Fagan, C. D.
Feasel, Roy
Felkel, James W.
Few, Maurice
Findley, Lloyd R.
Flaig, Kenneth S.
Forma, Warren
Freese, Arthur L. Jr.
Furtado, Edward R.
Gasper, John
Geraghty, Fred C. Jr.
Giesy, Samual H.
Gonlon, Anthony R.
Gray, Clarence M.
Grzona, LeRoy J.
Gunter, Joseph G.
Halligan, David M.
Hanks, Don W.
Harmon, Fredrick B.
Hart, Dyel
Havoc, Douglas(Mascot)
Colquitt, J. K.
Conant, Hiram F.
Cooper, John V.
Crane, Wilbur F.
Curran, John E.
Damico, Elpidio A.
Delano, Robert E.
Demartiono,Charles
DeStefano, Richard
Dickinson, Richard S.
Dooley, James R.
Drake, Emmet W.
Dullnig, Roland E.
Eastman, Dave
Ebenstein, Gustave
Eckard, L. W.
Euga, Philborn
Evans, Richard E.
Ewing, William W.
Fairhurst, Fredrick
Feese, Wayne, F.
Ferguston, Leland C.
Fidler, Wesley H.
Fisher, Jack
Fleming, John P.
Fortner, Kim
Fryman, William T.
Galloway, Arthur
Geffinger, Lowell E.
Gerger,
Goldman, Gene R.
Gooch, H. I.
Gregory, Harold E.
Guillow, Harry H
Hagerman, Orville
Hametch, Edward A.
Hand, Arvin R.
Harrington, John P.
Hartman, Philip E.
Hawk, Donald W.

416th Bombardment Group (L)
668th Bomb Squadron

Hayes, Ellis E.
Hedrick, Harold R.
Henderson, Artie T.
Herttua, John R.
Hicks, Cornelius M.
Hill, John
Hinkle, James J.
Holy, Johnnie A.
Horvath, John
Huey,Dansel J,
Hume, James A.
Jackson, Chet
Jablonsky, Jack R.
Jordan, Donald R.
Kaminski, Casmir
Kelly, Ernest E.
Kleopfel, Michael F.
Knudsen, George J.
Kotre, Frank J.
Kuhlahan, Richard W.
Lagerman, K. G.
Lanier, J.
LaPuma, Anthony J.
Leach, Robert
Leguens, Paul H.
Leonard, B. W. Jr.
Lewis, James P.
Lloyd, Felix B.
Love, Carl. F.
Luckasen, Wilford L.
Marcus, Stanley
Martin, Ray L.
Max, Edwin L.
McBrien, Richard T.
McCready, Thomas O
McDonald, Harold V.
McGary, Frank J. Jr.
McNulty, Gerald M.
Medlock, James H.
Meredith, Robert G.
Hazel, Lawrence L.
Heiland, Hugh
Hendricks, Myrrel C.
Hess, Ervin
Higgins, William J.
Hill, Luther
Hoeflein, William
Hood, Albert R.
Hough, Raymond
Hughes, William A.
Hutton, Forrest R.
Jacobsen, Otto F.
Jimenez, Jesus
Judd, Earl R.
Kearney, Martin P.
Ketchin, Veto R.
Klumpp, Rudy
Kochan, Stanley Jr.
Krebs, Bernard L.
Kuhlman, Virgil A.
Lambert, Robert L.
Laning, Paul W.
Larsin, Harry W.
Leatherwood, Harry R.
Leinert, Richard J.
Lesher, Robert D.
Lindser, Fred
Long, Robert H.
Lowe, R. R.
MacDonald, Robert W.
Markowitz, Arnold
Martinez, Lucio
Mayhew, A. E.
McCarthy,Cornelius J.
McCreery, Joe E.
McDonald Robert W.
McGehes, Elisha B.
Meaden, Stanley J.
Meek, Howard E.
Merrit, Olen N. Jr.
Heald, R
Heitell, Stanley L.
Henry, Frank
Hibbs, Charles L.
Hill, Atha A.
Hindman, Roy G.
Hoist, Eldon R.
Hornbeck, Kenneth E.
Hudson, Homer L.
Hull, Loren
Hytale, Scotty
Jeffcoat, Emory W.
Jolly, Hester L.
Kable, Roderick J.
Kellner, Wilmont F.
Kinney, James
Knight, Robert M.
Kohout, George
Kreh, Eldon B.
Lackner, Ralph J.
Lancelotti, Anthony
LaPoint, Jack
Laseter, William H.
Legg, Arthur
Lemonds,Winford E.
Lewis, George R.Jr.
Little, James S.
Lorenz, Richard T.
Luchon, Vincent W.
Mansley, Walter E. Jr.
Marsh, Robert R.
Mason, John D.
Mazanec, Frank
McCartney,Thomas
McDaniel,Thomas
McFeeton, Paul
McHugh, Walter S.
Meagher, Joseph F.
Melver, Verne S.
Metcalf, Russell L.

416th Bombardment Group (L)
668th Bomb Squadron

Metzler, Lawerance V.
Mirabella, P. A.
Misisco, Louis J.
Montrose, James H.
Mowry, John H.
Murch, Bruce G.
Mussarra, Anthony J.
Naifer, F.
Neupert, Elmer H.
Newman, F.
Nikas, Anton P.
Noel, Raymond
Norris, Earl J.
Nowell, S. P.
Olsen, John R.
Owens, Harry L.
Papa, Michael E.
Parkhurst, George
Partaledis, Ernest M.
Pedi, Frank N.
Peterson, Oscar S.
Phenning, George H.
Pointdexter, R. Danny
Potter, Harold A.
Price, Robert W.
Przona, LeRoy
Pyszozynske, Ed
Raines, Vernon E.
Reed, Will C.
Reski, Henry E.
Ritchie, Scott B. Jr
Romell,
Robertson, Frank J.
Rott, Jacob
Russo, Edward J.
Saxton, Robert S.
Schier, Lester A.
Schlisserman, Aaron
Screws, Bill
Sereno, Frank L.

Miller, Wallace W.
Miracle, Richard V.
Moegel, Alfred L.
Morrissey, Albert G.
Muliver, Verne E.
Murphy, Frank P.
Mustard, Robert D.
Nathanson, Allen S.
Newell, S. P.
Nichols, Howard W.
Nobel, John M.
Nolfa, James C.
Noteriani, Frank
Ohlrogge, Paul Jr.
Orr, John R.
Pacheco, Frank J.
Parker, Joseph L.
Parris, Deaver F.
Pauker, J. R.
Peede, Loring G.
Peterson, Seym,our
Phillips, James P.
Poplawski, Harry V.
Prentiss, Richard B.
Profita, Paul
Pugh, Grover C.
Rainhart, Coolidge
Ramaika, Lawrence
Rehman, Edmond M.
Rezek, Harold P.
Rivard, Charles J.
Roberts, J. H.
Robinson, J. W.
Russell, Roger A.
Salimbene, Ross
Schafer, Ernest L.
Schilling, Gilbert H.
Schwartzkopf, Joseph
Sears, Robert J.
Shaefer, Ernest L.

Miller, William A.
Mish, Charles C.
Mohr, C. M.
Moss, Thomas R.
Muraski, Walter H.
Murtaugh, Joseph G.
Myrold, Herman E.
Neller, Richard W.
Newkirk, Arlington
Nichy, Albert W.
Noegel, Alfred L.
Nordhioff, William E.
Novak, S. C.
Olsen, Andrew R.
Osborne, Arthur Jr.
Pagan, Cornelius D.
Parker, Paul E.
Parsons, Bertis V.
Pederson, Russell V
Pentzler, Daniel H.
Pettinicchi,Americo
Pisarski, Joseph E.
Popp, John P.
Price, Robert F.
Pricha, Lumir J.
Puskas, Nicholas.
Raines, D. E.
Ray, Robert K.
Reitz, James A.
Rich, William W.
Robbins, Leo E.
Roberts, William H.
Ross, Floyd T.
Russhon,
Salkowitz, Eddie
Schenck, Daniel R.
Schlefer, M. P.
Scott, George W.
Seely, Milo E.
Shaefer, Richard

416th Bombardment Group (L)
668th Bomb Squadron

Shaffer, Tom
Shaft, Robert E.
Shaw, Leroy R.
Sherhan, Joe
Shields, Bernard L.
Seig, Bennet C.
Simmons, John
Simpson, Doyle, H.
Sims, Tommie J.
Siracuse, Lucian J.
Sittarich, Jack
Skeens, Clarence L.
Smead, Charles S.
Smith, Clarence V.
Smith, Edward
Smith, Francis C.
Smith, Harold W.
Snider, Samuel
Spadoni, James K.
Spence, James I.
Squires, Harold L
Stauber, Hyman
Stanford, Lester R.
Stanford,Wilbur A. Jr.
Stanley, C. S.
Stern, Claude E.
Stevens, Harold L.
Stevens, John A.
Stewart, Alvin B.
Stewart, Walter C.
Strong, Richard C.
Sullivan, William J.
Sutter, John
Svenson, Robert R.
Sylva, Howard J.
Syobo, abriel J.
Tank, Frank R.
Taylor, Louis E.
Temple, William P.
Thompson, Monte
Thompson, Oris O.
Tiffany, Paul E.
Torres, Ianacio
Towles, Clarence
Urbanicio, Frank R.
Valentine, Carl
Van Galder, Donald W.
Van Over, Thomas
Vars, Clifford J.
Vaughan, Raymond C.
Veazey, Charles W.
Wagner, Charles C.
Warden, Paul C.
Watkins,Oakley M.Jr
Waugh, Earl H.
Weinbrenner, E. B.
Wells, Allan T.
Welsh, A. J.
Wheeler, George J.
White, John W.
Williams, Corda B.
Williamson, Julius C
Wilson, Glenn C.
Windisch, Raymond P.
Winkler, Harold G.
Winship, Richard C.
Wishart, Thomas
Woodward, Jess A.
Wright, Raymond E.
Wright, W. Jake
Wylie, Alvin C.
Wysocki, Chester C.
Yost, Clarence R. Jr.
Youlice, Dennis Jr.
Zeimet, LeRoy R.

416th Bombardment Group (L)
669th Squadron

Abriola, Daniel F.	Ada, Bitl. E.	Adams, Joseph D.
Adkins, Nealy	Albertson, Charles H.	Alden, Sterling F.
Allen, Julian F.	Allred, F. D.	Anderson, Albin C.
Anderson, Clayton	Anderson, Robert V.	Anderson, Roy E.
Andrews, John T.	Andros, John T.	Anlauf, Norman Z.
Anthony, Edward N.	Arendt, Emil A.	Ayo, Edward
Bach, Herman C.	Backe, Lare T.	Bailey, Kenneth W.
Baker, Clarence E.	Baker, Warren C.	Ballagamba, Silvo Jr
Ballinger, Robert L.	Banasky, Geza S.	Banfill, Walter H.
Barnard Leroy G.	Basford, Franklin P.	Batreay, William M.
Beamish, Wallace C.	Behlmer, Robert L.	Bellagamba, Silvo J.
Bender, Glenn J.	Berger, R.	Bergeron,Amos E.
Bergsma, Edward C.	Bergum, Ivan	Bernhardt, Paul L.
Bethard, Myron C.	Bethel, Paul	Bigelow, Gordon C.
Biggs William E.	Bilfield, Bernard B.	Binge, Hilton T.
Black,Robert M.	Blanchard, Charles U.	Blanchard, Jim
Block, Paul J.	Blomgren, John E.	Blum, Bernard
Bollinger,Robert	Bond, Edward V.	Bookach, Michael
Borgeson, Allen E.	Bouecher, Joseph L.	Boukamp Tonnis
Boulton, Richard L.	Bounds, Jesse S.	Bourland, James C.
Boyer, Vernon U.	Bradford, Blair H.	Brady, Edward J.
Brandt, Henry E.	Brennan, William	Bresnak, Joseph D.
Brier Ora C.	Brindle, Charles T.	Brinkman, E
Britt, Jesse W.	Brown, Charles E.	Brown, G. E.
Burland, Arnold J.	Burns, Roy L.	Burton, Robert E.
Buskirk, Joseph A.	Butcher, Wade H.	Butler, Geroge S.
Cardinale, Otto A.	Callaway, Adolphus	Campbell, Jack L.
Campbell, Murdock W.	Caprol John C.	Cardinale, Otto A.
Carney, Herman C.	Carpenter, Micuston	Carter, Ashton
Carter, James A.	Carter, John H.	Carstens, R. W.
Chapman, John E.	Cheney George E.	Cheney, N. W.
Chestnut, James N.	Charles, Charles	Cicarelli, Henry A.
Citty, Foster M.	Clark, Harry E.	Clark, Hiram B.
Clark, Robert A.	Clearman, P. L.	Clements, Joseph
Cohola, J.	Colbert, R.	Colden, Dean F.
Coleman, Charles W.	Colosimo, Russell J.	Conner, Jack K.
Conner, Joe S.	Conte, Ralph F.	Cook, J.
Cornell, Ross Jr.	Couglan, Raymond W.	Craig, Edwin H.
Curtis, David G.	Curtis, Layford B.	Dahlbeck, Russel M

416th Bombardment Group (L)
669th Squadron

Dalton, Albert h.	Daugherty, Lewis M.	Deatherage, J. B.
DeMarco, Albert	DeMoss, Harold A.	DeMun, Earl E.
Dent, N. B.	Depner, Alfred W.	DeSTefano, Richard
Donnelly, Walter W.	Dontas, Peter	Dove, Bernard
Draft, Leo B.	Drake, Charles N.	Driskill, P. B.
Dubi, Robert G.	DuBose, Willad W.	Duda, Joseph J.
Dudding, Karl F.	Dufault, William F.	Dugan, John D.
Dunn, Cleo C.	Dunn, Fletcher G.	Dupell, Edmund J.
Durkin,Clifford J.	Dyke, William	Eads, William C.
Eiseaman, Earl C.	Elliott, Donald E.	Ellis, Lloyd D.
Ellis, Richard W.	Entrikon, William F.	Epps, Evert T.
Ericson, William	Esseltine, ARthur J.	Fair, Vincent
Farene, Joseph E.	Farley, Jon J.	Farmer, Walter W.
Farrer, Leslie	Fee, R. E.	Ferguston,WilliamG
Field, Robert G.	Fields, William E.	Fild, Phillip G.
Findley, Frank L.	Flag, Kenneth, S.	Fleischman, Glenn I
Fleming, Leonard G.	Floyd, Claredon W.	Forshell, Robert L.
Fortune, Robert J.	Foster, Clayton R.	Foute, Harold D.
Frambers, Raymond D.	Francis, Richard D.	Frangudakis,PeterW
Fransden, Cleo W.	Frantrz, Roy C.	Fuller, Howard J.
Fury, Joseph G.	Gage, Jack S.	Gantt, Hershel N.
Garrity, James E.	Gaskins, William M.	Gebart, John W
Gehreds, Hugo A.	Getgen, Leo R.	Gettle, Roy E.
Giguere, Gerald G.	Gilbert, Allen B.	Gilbert, Cletus
Gillespie, Ross H.	Gillis, Edward	Glandarf, KennethE.
Glover, Gifford T.	Globin, Clayton W.	Gossett, Jasper
Gottlieb, Irvin J.	Goughlin, Raymond W.	Graham Clyde E.
Grahamewers, R. F.	Green, Willie	Greico, Ben J.
Griffin, Daniel L.	Grimes, Jesse F.	Grisham W. Pierce
Gullion, Allen E.	Gur, Edwin L.	Hackley, Robley H.
Hagan, Wayne A.	Haggand, Glenn E.	Hall, E..P.
Hall, Thaddeus	Halladay, Richard S.	Halloway,RichardG.
Hamilton, Frank H.	Hammel, Thomas C.	Hancock, Larry
Hanes, Harry H.	Hanson, Robert R.	Haptonstall, Richard
Hardesty, G.	Hargis, William W	Hartel, William
Hashem, Alec	Haskell, Robert W.	Hatch, Harold F.
Haver, Harry E.	Hawk, Olin T.	Hay, Jamie E
Hayter, Earl L.	Heath, Kalen	Heenan, David K
Heim, Theodore L.	Heimman, Thomas L.	Henyone, RobertW.
Hewes, H. E.	Hill, Luther E.	Hinck, WEsley E.

416th Bombardment Group (L)
669th Squadron

Hinker, Cletus V.
Hissen, Donald W.
Hobbs, George C.
Hoeflin, William A.
Hoeft, Harley
Hoffman, Ralph C.
Hoffman, Ronald C.
Hollaway, R. G.
Holton, Osborne H.
Hoover, Melvin H.
Hopfner,
Hoppe, Frank M.
Hornbeck, Kenneth E.
Housley, Claude H.
Howard, James T.
Huber, Alexander J.
Huff, Meredith J.
Hulse, Dave
Huss,Charles F.
Islas, Francisco S.
Jacmel, Albert E.
Jagielski, Louis J.
Jensen, Kenneth F.
Joe, Edwin J.
Johnson,Arthur G.
Johnson, George G.
Johnson, Harlan C.
Johnson, M. K.
Johnson, Robert K.
Jones, Claude W.
Jordan, Clyde S.
Jose, Richard C.
Joyner, Horace L.
Judge, Richard
Katz, Bernard
Keat, Harold F.
Keebaugh, Herman R.
Keefe, James J.
Kehoe, K. W.
Kelly, William J.
Kelton, Harvey E.
Kempernolte,
Key, Ted A.
Kiker, C. M.
Kirik, Stanley J.
Kiser, James E.
Klingman, W. H.
Knotts, Clarence R.
Knowlton, Warren P.
Knutsen, Jennings C.
Konnely, John K.
Konn, Harold A.
Kroboth, Harlan
Kruger, Charles J.
Kuhlman, Richard W.
Kupits, Joseph
Lamb, Wosley T.
Lamonds, Theodore, R.
LaNave, Orlando D.
Land, Willard H.
Lane, Vincent L.
Lane, William E.
Larsen, Claude L.
Lawrence, Max
Lazore, Buford A.
Lea, Edwin W.
Lee, Gerald F.
Legere, Joseph E.
Lewis, Ralph
Lindsley, Charles D.
Lloyd, Lawrence D.
Locke, Campbell
Loeb, William H.
Los, Mitzio T.
Lucas,
Luria, Sydney
Lyde, Joseph W.
Lynch, Howard V.
Maciulewicz, Peter P.
MacManus, Patrick
Madenfort, J.
Malara, Valo A.
Mallory,Donald F.
Mallory, J. F.
Mani, Jack
Mann, Charles A.
Marden, Herbert E.
Marks, Jackson, L.
Martin, Audry F.
Martin, Emile C.
Martin, George A.
Martin, John T.
Martino, Michael S.
Marton, Robert
Marturo, Carmiac A.
Maykulaky, Joseph F.
McBroom, Sheffy
McCabe, Lawrence E.
McCarren, Edwin L.
McClusky, John W.
McDonald, Arthur A.
McDonald John J.
McDonald, Thomas A.
McElhatten, L. D.
McGaughy, William S
McGivern, Peter J.
McGuire, John J.
McLain, Howard B.
McLeroy, Orico Jr.
McManus, T.W.
McNeil, Hector J.
McQuade, Robert J.
McVoy, Fred H.
Melchoir, Frank F.
Meliniotis, Nick
Melte, Thomas E.
Merkin, Soleman

416th Bombardment Group (L)
669th Squadron

Merritt, Olen N.
Messina, William H.
Metzler, Cyrus E.
Meyer Frank J. Jr.
Michel, Donald C.
Michels,
Mihler,
Miller, Doyle R.
Miller, Edward L.
Mitchell, Wilshire F.
Mohler, Stewart E.
Moore, Donald L.
Moore, Elmer
Moore, Hiram E.
Morcik, Louis J.
Morely, Bernard J.
Morris, Chester A. III
Morris, Earl E.
Morton, Robert J.
Moskowitz, Louis
Mowaczewski,Eugene
Muldoon, Joseph D.
Mulgrew, R. P.
Mullins, Elmer W.
Murphy, Garland D.
Musgrove, Wayne
Myers, Dorsey M. Jr.
Nahill, Joseph A.
Napier, John G.
Nardone, Marlin W.
Nearing, Lloyd T.
Neilson, Arthur L.
Neilson, Jack O.
Nelms, Fred L.
Neskowitz, J.
Nichols, J. R.
Nicks, Roger W.
Norton, Chalres Q.
Nossman, Trafton K.
Nowaczewski, Eugene
O'Hare, Arthur G.
O'Malley, Bentol
O'Neil, Merrill C.
Opatowsky, David L.
Orvis, William F.
Osborne,
Otis, Nick
Ozmore, Keith
Palin, William A.
Parker, Leroy
Paulettea,Richard C.
Payne, C. E.
Payne, George E.
Pearlman, Bernard
Peck, William A.
Pemberton, James M.
Pentilla, W. L.
Perkins, Clyde R.
Perkins, Homer W.
Pikel, Joseph M.
Platkin, Murray
Ponticoff, Rev.
Potts, Albert W.
Poundstone, Leo
Priest, James E.
Prindle, Charles A.
Proctor, Willie J.
Radlick, Nathan
Raine, Joseph T.
Raines, Arthur A.
Randall, Earl H.
Ray, Bethel E.
Reed, Conner M.
Reeves, Frank
Reid, Kenneth A.
Reiter, Glenn E.
Renth,Edward J.
Reyes, M.R.
Rhodes, Earl F.
Rice, Roger W.
Rich, Francis M. Jr.
Richards, T.
Richards, David A.
Ridenour,Brookem
Riffey, Gordon L.
Robert, Lewis
Robertson, Reece B.
Rodgers, H. C.
Rodgers, John L.
Roehen, Clarence C.
Rogers, John L.
Rooney, Thomas
Rosenstein, Morton
Rubar, Donald H.
Sabadosh, John W.
Santandrea, Michael
Schafer, Dick
Schenkein, George
Schlemmer, Russell
Schmigel, Anthony G.
Scott, James O.
Scully, R.
Seese, Nahone E.
Seibert, Lester C.
Shainberg, Norman V.
Shapard, John M.
Sharp,
Shatzer, Herbert E
Shaw, Calvin L.
Shields, Joseph J.
Siggs, Wilford C.
Simms, Arthur E.
Slifko, Raymond M.
Smahel, Daniel
Smith, Benjamin A.
Smioth, Daniel E.
Smith, J. D.

416th Bombardment Group (L)
669th Squadron

Smith, Jack F. Jr.
Smith, John N.
Smyth, Richard L.
Sommers, Harold L.
Sorkin, Hymie
Sorrels, Don
Sparling, J. R.
Spencer, George, E.
Spiro, D.
Springer, William R.
Squires, Basil J.
Stebbins, Burton D.
Stead, C.H.
Stein, Irvin
Stein, Llewellyn C.
Stemler, Frederick L.
Stephens, Hartzewll
Stephens, James E.
Stephens, Robert M.
Stewart, Charles H.
Stewart, Donald D.
Stewart, Marion, S.
Stone, Norman L.
Street, Marion E.
Strictland, Thurmon
Stroup, Neal
Sturgeon, George W.
Sturgeon, Donald O.
Sumner, Walter R.
Swap, Floyd W.
Tewksberry, Floyd W.
Thompson, James B.
Thompson, Richard R
Thorngreen, Loenard
Tolin,William M. Jr.
Transhina, C.E.
Triber, Harry L.
Tripp, William F.
Truesdale, Roy
Turner, Dan O.
Valiadis, Constantine
Vallot, Clifford T.
VanderHoeven, Lloyd P.
Van Duyne, J.E.
Van Meter, G. O.
Vanrope, Roy W.
Veazey, C. W.
Venazo, George
Viloman, Harry C.
Vincze, John
Vleghels, Andre J.
Vorce, Kenneth B.
Warters, James H.
Webb, Charles L.
Weinert, Carl
Weisman, H. John
Wells, Drexel. R.
West, N. D.
Western, Glenn G.
White, Roy L.
Whitten, Dolphus Jr.
Wilds, H. J.
Willard, Jack A.
Wills, Paul W.
Wilson, David M.
Wilson, Ralph
Wing, Jeong
Winkler, Melvin P.
Witulski, Clarence A.
Withington, David L.
Woods, Dwight E.
Woodward, Ernest Jr
Wright, George
Wright, Jake
Wyche,
Wyman, David L.
Wysocki, Joseph C.
Yardbrough, John R.
Yarnell, Thomas M.
Yee, Robert E.
Young, Calvin C.
Young, Clay E.
Zander, Victor D.
Ziekus, A. J.

416th Bombardment Group (L)
670th Squadron

Abbott, James S. III
Abbott, Joseph G.
Acker, Kenneth L.
Ackerson, Dale C.
Addleman, Raymond F.
Ahlstrom, Karl Y.
Akula, Alexander G.
Alexander, Houston
Allen, Byron K.
Ammerpohl, Frederick
Ammott, Victor R.
Anderson, Harold J.
Anderson, Walter G.
Arnett, Willard E.
Atchinson, Robert E
Atkinson, Paul G. Jr.
Backorski, Mile
Baginski, Anthony
Bailey George T.
Balair, M. G.
Balch, William M.
Baldwin, George E.
Ballangee, Charles R.
Barsusky, Peter. P.
Basile, Albert C.
Beachler, Wesley, Jr.
Beck, William
Bekrowski, Cassmer
Belcas, James O.
Bennet, Edward F.
Berry, Mark E.
Berry, Zorns D.
Bird, Joe
Binney, Irving
Bischoff, Walter
Bishop Edward G.
Black, George M.
Blackford Alton D.
Blackford, Dayton S
Blair, Gordon
Bodiford, James W.
Body, Clifford D.
Boerner, Stewart B.
Bohles, Charles R.
Bond, Edmond V.
Bonderman, Neil A.
Bonamo, Albert J.
Bos, Richard Jr.
Bouchane, Warren
Bower, Robert S.
Bradford,Charles K
Brasher, Louios M.
Brayn, M. R.
Brennan, James B.
Brenner, Walter
Brewer,William E.
Brewster, Francis
Brown, James W.
Brown, Joseph K.
Brown, Kenneth F.
Brown, Lawrence .
Brown, Neil G.
Brown, Warren E.
Brownlee, Milton A.
Bullin, Wesley M.
Bullock, Franklin W.
Buono
Buras,
Burch, Horace H.
Burger, LaVerne C.
Burgess, James E.
Burns, Donald E.
Burns, Donald E.
Burseil, Francis C.
Bush, Lewis C.
Butler, Henry W.
Butschek, Walter H.
Byrne, R. T.
Byrnes, David H.
Cain, Laurel M.
Caldwell, Charles H.
Calhoun, Howard H.
Cameli,Vincent
Candler, Harry
Carney, James F.
Carney, Thomas D.
Carvell, John P.
Casteen, William T.
Caughan,
Cendellire,Frank D
Cerney, Frank J.
Cernich
Champion, Clyde L.
Champlin, Carl S.
Chapin, Ernest N.
Chaplin, Milburn
Chitty, Westey D.
Cianciosa, ADam A.
Clark, Noel E.
Clark, Wendell O.
Cleave, Benjamin T.
Cochran, Ralph L.
Colamonico, Michael
Colbert, William F.
Combs, Harry F.
Conant, Hiram F.
Conley, Frank J.
Conner, Jack E.
Conopask,Floyden
Cook, L.
Cockingham, Paul D.
Cooper, Grimsley L.
Corey, Francis E.
Costa, Jonas M.
Craig, John T.
Crispino, Joseph C.
Cromwell,Richard C

416th Bombardment Group (L)
670th Squadron

Cummings, William E.	Cummings, Bernard V.	Curdy, Paul F.
Curtis, John C.	Daniel, William J.	Daniels, Joseph T.
Daverio, Carlo	Deane, Everett	Decker, Fred R.
Dennis, Lewis W.	Dias, Melvin E.	Dick, Roscoe
Diehl, Elmore O.	Dietzel, Frederick H.	DiFerdinando,Tony
DiNapoli, S. F.	Doane, Everett S.	Donahue, William J.
Donato, Joseph E.	Dondero, Harold C.	Donovan, Charles D.
Dontas, Joseph W.	Downing, Ernest V.	Duemig, Joseph
Dunn, Albert H.	Dunn, Lloyd	Dunnington,JuneW
Duquette, Robert L.	Durham, Morris W.	Durham, William J.
Duthu, Robert J.	Dutsler,	Dyre, Bartly, J.
Eaves, Robert J.	Eddy,K. A.	Ehrlich, Bernard W.
Eickoff, Clifford	Eizel, Joseph W.	Elliott, F. W.
Ellis, Kenneth, L.	Elston, Bernard E.	Ennis, William J.
Enslow, Charles E.	Euster, Ralph Jr.	Evans, O. D.
Everts, Royal S.	Falk, Francis, G.	Ferrell, Phillip
Ferris, Collins H.	Fidac, Lloyd L.	Finnell, Donald L.
Fisher, Richard T.	Flamagan, Kenneth W.	Flint, William J.
Flynn, James M.	Ford, Russell	Foresman, John R.
Forsythe, James M	Fougereusse, William	Frankenberg,Harold
Frath, Roy A.	French, Clifford E.	Friedlob, Eugene M.
Furman	Gallbreath, Gordon D.	Garlington, R. S.
Garrison, Vernon W.	Garvin, Harold H.	Gatti, Raymond J.
Gaughan, Johnny	Geffinger, Lowell E.	Giancola, Romer F.
Gill, Charles E.	Glandorf, Kenneth E.	Glynn, Francis P.
Glynn, Patrick. F.	Goggin, Joseph P.	Goff, Charles
Golmez, Quirino	Gollen, Archie L.	Gomez, Anthony A.
Goodman, Harold	Gorski, Joh n P.	Goss, Thurman L.
Gossett, Joseph D.	Gossner, John E.	Gray, Bennie F.
Gray, George J.	Green, Joe	Greene, William J.
Griffin, William L.	Gruetzemacher, Robert	Gruning, David B.
Gulley, Kenneth B.	Gunn, Few A.	Hadden, Edson P
Hagerstrom, Raymond	Haire, Henry J.	Hall, Rosell B.
Hammon, Samuel	Hardwick, Walter F.	Harm, Robert L.
Harmon, Carson, D.	Harrold, Frank J.	Harris, Mack C.
Harrison, Clay B.	Hart, G. E.	Hart, Wesley F.
Hawkins, Orin R. Jr.	Heafy, Edward F.	Heiland, Hugh
Hebert,Donald A.	Heinke, Dick. W. R.	Heisel, Clarence L
Hendrix, James	Henry, Asa V.	Henson, Albert G.

416th Bombardment Group (L)
670th Squadron

Herradan, Lester E.	Herrman, ester P.	Hiatt, Kenneth B.
Hibbard, Carlton J.	Hillerman, John P.	Hixon, Stuart M.
Houge, Clifford E.	Holloway, William R.,	Homler, Robert K.
Hoover, Donald C.	Hordatroon,	Horning, Ernest L.
Houser,Roland J.	Howard, Adrian M.	Howard, Elwin F.
Howard, Joseph E.	Hubbard, Carlton J.	Hudnutt, Lyle
Hulete, Eugene S.	Hulse,David	Hulsey
Hummer, James A.	Hunter, Edward P.	Hunter, Jack M.
Jackson, C.Ronald	Jackson, Edward C.	Jacob, Wilbur P.
Jacobs, Ernest P.	Jednak, John	Johanna, Lawrence
Johnson, Ernest L.	Johnson, Henry	Johnson, John H.
Johnson, J. L.	Jones, Harry E.	Jones, Herman C.
Jones, Leland, L	Jones, Sylvester W.	Joost, Robert H.
Kamenistky,	Kaminschko, Robert J.	Kaplan, Michael J.
Keables, Haller F.	Kehres, Bob J.	Kerbauaz,Richard J
Kerr,	Kidd, William L.	Killerbrew, Roy L.
Kinball, Alfred H.	King, Jack W.	Kinney, Del. J.
Kirk, Robert L.	Kline, Elmo W.	Knott, Judson A.
Koch, Otto K.	Kohl, Myron H.	Koons, Chalmer T.
Krantz, John G.	Kubjalko, A.	Lally, John G.
Lamm, Roscoe, R.	Landano, Frank J.	Langley, Thomas R.
LaPointe, J. A.	Larimore, John D.	LaVallee, John A.
Leahigh, Lawrence L.	Lee, Robert E.	Leeds, Henry H.
Lehman, Martin T.	Leishman, Samuel	Leonard, Thomas J.
Leva, Joe C.	Levengood, Donald	Levin, Henry
Ley, Joseph R.	Licker, Morton	Lindsey, J. L.
Love, Nathan D.	Luke, Francis X.	Luria, Sydney A.
Lykins, Charles R.	Lynch, Charles	Lynch, Phillip R.
MacGillivery, Finlay	MacMicking, James T.	Mailman
Mallery, Alfred	Maltby, Alfred H.	Maltby, Harold
Mamulski, Fred L.	Mangwith,	Mapes, James A.
Markle,.	Marks, George W.	Marsh, Clark A.
Martinez, Lucio	Mazianec, Chester W.	McBride, Leonard R.
McCellan, Eugene W.	McCleary, Herbert M.	McCrary, George A.
McCurry, Donald L.	McDonald, William	McElroy, George V.
McFadden, Roy R.	McFaul, Vincent J.	McFier, Norman W.
McGlohn, Charles	McKee, James C.	McPeak,Lester H.
Meng, William J.	Merritt, Theron S.	Meyers, Rudolph
Meyers, Wallace D.	Mihalek, Charles J.	Miller, Robert L.

416th Bombardment Group (L)
670th Squadron

Miller,	Miller, Veto	Miranda, Angelo F.
Mobley, James T.	Monroe, Hugh A.	Moore, Alex E.
Moore, Guy T.	Moore, Zean R.	Moos, Louis M.
Moran, John W.	Moranske, Gusie J. Jr.	Morris, John T. S.
Moydell, Lester, E.	Mulzet, Otto F.	Murphy, Richard L.
Murro, Daniel J.	Nagorski, Frank	Nanni, Edmond R.
Napoli, Sebastian D.	Neal, Dory E., Jr.	Nelson, Ray W.
Neupauer, William D.	Nickolson, Thomas W.	Nicolay, Edward R.
Nitz, Eugene A.	Nolan, Daniel J.	Nordstrom,Arthur W
Nowack, Clarence C.	Nowosielski, H.J.	O'Brien, Jack V.
Ochaba, Joseph A.	O'Neil, William F.	Orvold, Chester R.
Osterrischer, John C.	Ostrander, Gus W.	Otoso, Felix
Ott, Richard C.	Ottaviano, Joseph O.	Overmeyer,Donald E
Page, Lester, J.	Paladino, Domenic V.	Palmer, Thomas A.
Parker, Newman G.	Patric, Clayton	Paules, Eugene F.
Pavilauts, Joseph F.	Payne, Clifford R.	Payne, Lawrence
Payton, Monroe O.	Pellegrino, Frank	Perujo, Raphael J.
Philips, Dick	Phillips, Oseola D.	Pichler, Rudolph
Plant, Richard	Polackwich, Adolphus	Polk, James W.
Pollins, Cal. R.	Popeney,Harry V.	Porter, Allen V.
Powell, John V.	Powell, S..R.	Powell, Vernon H.
Prenger, Raymond J.	Prestek, Ernest J.	Prester, Francis S.
Procter, Charles H.	Puskas, Nicholas G.	Purch, Horace R.
Quigley, Neal M	Raccio,Vincent B.	Rada, James
Ramer, Melvin L	Rancour, Norbert F.	Rape, Zimmer L.
Rauche, William E.	Rasport, Richard R.	Ray, Clarence C.
Recchia, Frank	Richard, Donald B.	Reichert, Donald J.
Reid, William R.	Reynolds, Virgil	Rhoney, Clarence B.
Rice, Tom	Richard, Wesley C.	Richards, Charles C.
Richards, Donald B.	Ricketson, Joseph J.	Riempp, William F.
Riggs, Paul H.	Riley, John	Riley, Robert K.
Riley, Thomas F.	Rio, D. J.	Risko, Steve
Risser, Jameson	Riston, Bernard R.	Robbins, Clement E.
Robertson, Glendon W.	Robinson, Lynwood M.	Rogers, Lilburn Jr.
Rooney, Robert J.	Rozeki, Ben G.	Rudisill, Frank
Rudisill, Robert S.	Rulette, Eugene	Rush, Lawrence F.
Ryan, Francis P.	Ryan, Joseph T.	Safranek, George J.
Saklidiewics,Stanley R.	Saltonstall, Richard L.	Sampson, Dale A.
Sannino Andrew D.	Saunders, Edwin B.	Schlanzer,Raymond T

416th Bombardment Group (L)
670th Squadron

Schmidt, Harry
Schwartz, Leo H.
Sefranek, George J.
Seibert, Russell G.
Sewell, Jackson C.
Sgroi, Anthony P
Shanks, Don
Shanks,Ollie V.
Shapiro, Harold H.
Shaw, Calvin L.
Shea, Danial F.
Sheehan, William E.Jr
Sheley, Stanley
Sherer, Hollis G.
Sheridan, Maurice B
Shempren, Eugene H.
Shite, H. E.
Sicola, Adolph E.
Siebert
Siedlicki, John M.
Sienkiewicz,Joseph
Silva, Arnold L.
Simkins, John
Simmons
Singley, Earl M.
Singletary, Robert B.
Siracuse, Joseph F.
Sleeper, Donald E.
Smith, George H.
Smith, Leo. R.
Smith, Van P.
Smolincek, Walter M.
Smyser, Robert L.
Snapp, William W.
Snyder, James W.
Snyder, Robert N.
Snyder, Robert J.
Sommers, Douglas T.
Spatafore,Anthony N
Spilleet, Sidney
Stafford,
Stankowski, John F.
Starr, Giles J.
Steel, Dan E.
Stemm, Harry A.
Stephens, Donald W.
Stephens, Robert M.
Stewart, James S. Jr.
Stewart, Paul L.
Stobert, Ralph F.
Stoy, Robert L.
StPierre, Laurier L.
Strictland, Thurman
Strikol, Leonard T.
Swafford, Joseph O.
Sweeny, Bernard P.
Switzer, Harold W.
Szakovits, William
Talerico, Frank A.
Thompson, Charles Jr.
Thompson, Clark J.
Tilton, Donald F.
Tollett, Joseph E.
Torcivia, Charles S.
Tracey, Lloyd E.
Trechock, John
Trudeau, James A.
Turman, Alton R.
Turner, Elizabeth O.
Turpin, Samuel J.
Tyson, Robert C.
Valley, Francis E.
VanWert, George R.
Vellinga, John R.
Verbish, George J.
Vesley, George M.
Vesley, Henry A.
Vienneau, Arthur J.
Vitrano, Andrew A.
Volpe, Alexander V.
Wagner, Paul C.
Wallace, John F.
Walsh, Thomas I.
Walten, Dean A.
Walters, Chester A.
Wark, LaMoine
Warren, Jay
Wasner, James H.
Wenter, William
Wentling,Richard L.
Whitacre, Carl W.
White, Howard E.
Whitemire, Harold F.
Wiggins, Harold G
Wilbur, Murray F.
Wilkerson, Earl A.
Wilkinson, Ernest S.
Willever, Wilmer J.
Wilson, George W.
Wilson, John E.
Winans, Glendon C.
Wojton, Henry P.
Wood, Evel T.
Wooste, William F.
Wright, Hillary T.
Wright, Raymond E.
Wurzburg, William R.
Young, Clarence R.
Zaklikiewicz, S. R.
Zelly, Lawrence E.
Zetterberg, Victor Y.
Zukauskas, Veto G.
Zurbrick, Robert M.
Ztwicki, Norman

416th Bombardment Group (L)
671st Squadron

Acrey, Robert L.
Adams, Victor P.
Aherns, Henry S
Ahouse, Bernard F.
Amadora, Vincent
Ames, William
Anderson, Harold W.
Anderson, Olaf E.
Andrews, Harold D.Jr
Angel, John T.
Appleman, Myer
Arnold, Edward P.
Arrington, Harry, T.
Ahston, Lewis A.
Babinec, Edward M.
Baddick, Jacob J.
Balogh, Steve B. Jr
Barausky, Peter P.
Barber, Floyd E.
Barry, Rollins M.
Bartnowski, Matthew
Basnett, Robert J.
Baxter, Elmer W.
Bays, Lonnie O.
Beck, J. T.
Behny, Robert E.
Beibleheimer,Bardell
Bena, Sale M.
Bergum, John B.
Berman, Henry W.
Berner, Howard J.
Besett, Howard L.
Best, Harry T.
Biaesch, Henry W.
Blacklock, Robert E.
Blodgett, Ollie L.
Blount, Henry G.
Booth, Wesley R.
Bovan, Harold R.
Bower, J. S.
Brady, Patrick P.
Brenner, Walter E.
Brewer, Albert L.
Brewer, William E.
Briggs, Robert H.
Brooks, Paul F.
Brower, Jack G.
Brown, Clarence E.
Brown, Claude J.
Brown, Kenneth P.
Brown, Robert J.
Brown, William E.
Bryan, Robert A.
Buckley, Walter C.
Buhrmaster, Harold
Burgess, Arthur G.
Burkhart, Phillip J.
Burke, Frank E.
Burke, James F.
Burke, Walter J.
Burns, Donald E.
Burton, Robert W.
Buskirk, John A.
Calhoun, Howard E.
Call, George F.
Campbell, Sam T.
Campos, Jose S.
Capp, Harry H.
Carlile, Charles D.
Carroll, John T.
Cashell, John F.
Cennery, T.
Chest, D.
Cheuvront, Robert W.
Childress, Roy C.
Chitty, Wesley D.
Chunn, William O.
Chvatal, Franklin R.
Ciber, John
Ciner, Oscar H.
Clark, Ivan C.
Clarkston, John L.
Clearman, Percy L.
Clearush, Benjamin T.
Click, Herbert L.
Cocke, John B.
Cole, Hillary P.
Collins, Joseph M.
Condinho, Jesse
Conley,
Connery Theodore Jr.
Connor, Bernard J.
Cook, Charles J.
Cook, George M.
Cooke, Willis N.
Cope, Andrew J.
Cope, Grady F.
Copeland, Dennis M.
Corbitt, Charles H.
Corrin, Earl
Corum, John P.
Cossner, John E.
Costa, Julius M.
Cota, John B.
Coulombe,Phillippe E
Cousin, Norman
Cowgill George W.
Cramsie, William P.
Crassio.
Crates, Edward M.
Creamans, Carl E
Cress, Robert F.
Crnavic, Stephen
Crumpston, Duance
Culwell, Marvin J.
Cutting, Arthur C.
Curl, Edgar C.
Czech, Joseph L.
Davis, Harry R.
Davis, Lyle E.

416th Bombardment Group (L)
671st Squadron

Davis, Warren G.
DeBower, Delbert W.
Deckard, Clarke
DeMond, Francis P.
DiGiusto, Italo R.
Dennis,
DiMartino, Arthur E.
DiOrio, Felix
Doan, Mildredge C.
Dowe, Stanley
Doyle, P.
Duff, Benjamin B.
Dulicia, Anthony
Dunbar, Joe
Dunbhase,Henry W.
Dunn, Lloyd F.
Durante, Anthony R.
Durham, Morris W.
Duthu, Robert J.
Dzendzel, Michael
Eaton, Arthur B.
Edholm, Robert
Edstrom, Lawrence
Ehrmann, Leonard W.
Elliott, Edward R.
Elliott, James F.
Elmore, Everett K.
Elmore, Theodore V.
Emery, William C.
Errotabere, Martin
Estes, Coleman L.
Eurich, George L.
Fabic, Frank
Fair, Horace F.
Fandre, Benjamin
Farmer, Luther J.
Farrow, Hosea H.
Favey,
Fazio, Lee
Feistl. J.
Feldman, David
Feldman,David M.
Fero, Donald A.
Fessler, Herman S.
Fidler, Paul E.
Figgins, Harry E.
Fitzsimmons, Robert
Flummerfelt, John
Foltz, John F.
Forbes, T. M.
Ford, Arthur M.
Forsythe, James M.
Foscaldo, Joseph
Foster, Hollis A.
France, James L.
Frank, Harry B.
Franzel, Herman
Friedrick, Franklin
Fry,
Funkhowser, Carl
Galender, Julius
Gann, Oscar A.
Gardiner, Thomas W.
Garrett, Alvin D.
Gary, John
Geddes, William
Gedinak, Albert
George, Melvin
Germany, Joseph
Gerould
Gillet, Elmer W.
Gilliam, Delbert C.
Goetzker, Wallace R.
Goldberg, Louis
Gordon, Jim
Gose,
Gossner, John E.
Gottlieb, Sherwood
Graeber, Ted E.
Grant, Lee A.
Graub, Robert E.
Graves, Philip D.
Greaney, Robert
Greeley, Richard E.
Green, Willard
Grimes, Charles C.
Griswold, Richard M.
Grooms, Thomas M.
Gross, Victor
Gurkin, Charles W.
Gurnea, Ernest H.
Hall, Millard
Hall, Rosell B.
Halleran, Barthelomew
Halliman, William C.
Hamman, Samuel
Hammill, James B.
Hammond, Shirley K.
Hanlon, Robert J.
Hanna, Louis B.
Hanna, Robert C.
Hardwin, Melvin F.
Harland, Dan
Harp, Clifford J.
Harper, Craig M.
Harper, Robert E.
Harrington, Charles
Harrington, William
Haubrick, Joseph A.
Hausch, Eugene
Haverland, Louis
Helphenstine, Raymond E.
Hayes,
Helt, Robert
Helton, Charles
Hemphill, John E.
Henerson, Floyd W.

416th Bombardment Group (L)
671st Squadron

Henderson, Scott L.
Henderson, Woodrow W.
Henshaw, Charles R.
Henshaw, J. Stewart
Herman, Arthur W.
Heuman, Joseph P.
Hill, Herbert F.
Hinson, Arthur L.
Hlivko, Alex E.
Hodge, Thomas H.
Hotzschieter, Fred
Houman, Joseph P.
Hudnutt, Lyle
Hudson, L.
Hummer, James A.
Humphrey, Richard L.
Hunter, John S.
Huss, Charles F.
Huston, L.
Indiviglia, Fildelfio
Ingalls, Donald M.
Irwin, Jewell F.
Jacobs, Ernest P.
Jedinak, Albert
Johnson, Curtis
Johnson, J. J.
Johnson, J. L.
Johnson, Keith L.
Johnson, Robert J.
Jokinen, W.B.
Jones, Raymond J.
Kahn, Earl
Kalitich, Steve
Kamischle, Robert J.
Kaplan, Michael E.
Kaste, Walter P.
Katchin, Veto H.
Keating, John A.
Kefran, John C.
Keh, Earl
Kenball, Alfred W.
Kent, Harold F.
Kenshaw, Charles, R.
Kerns, James E.
Kerr,
Kessler, William T.
Kiebell, Alvin M.
Killian, Paul B.
Kimball, Alfred W.
King, Carl G.
King, Maurice O.
Kitchen, Herman W.
Klamberry, Willard
Klipp, Raymond
Kofron, John C.
Kommer, Robert J.
Konsig, Paul
Kozlowski, Vincent A
Kuebler, Paul J.
Kutzer, Louis G.
Lackovich, J. J.
LaFonde, Felix
Laman, Elmore J.
LaMarca, Joseph
Lamphiec, Cyril
Lander, John J.
Laroache, Leo T.
Larrence, T.
Larronde, Felix H.
Lawrence, Francis D.
Leker, Harold H.
Lempka, Henry A.
Leneave, Edwin C.
Leonard, Robert E. Jr.
Levin, David
Lew, John M.
Linder, John J.
Linn, Leslim
Linneman, Robert H.
Lombardy, Peter
Loruse, Domenic W.
Lozowski, Edward J
MacFaul,
MacCartney, William A.
Macrina, Victor G.
Madison, Clifford
Mahoney, Robert J.
Makowski, Barney J.
Mallery, Richard C.
Mapes, James A.
Marashian, George
Marion, Herbert A.
Martinez, Lucio
Maruffi, John J.
Marzolf, LaVerne A.
Matlock, Ernest
Maupin, Wendell W.
Maurice, Valerio
May, Joseph A.
Mazza, Louis C.
McAfee, John W.
McAvoy, Edward F. Jr.
McClung, Merle E
McCullah, C. Gray
McElhattan, Les D.
McGovern, Charles H
McNutt,
McPherson, Joseph
Meadows, Harry L.
Merchant William A.
Merwin, Harold E.
Messinger, Robert W.
Meyer, Armand A.
Meyer, Clarence M.
Middleton, Clyde W
Miguez, Jack H.
Milhorn, G. L.
Millard, Hall
Miller, Alvin H.
Miller, Horace K.

416th Bombardment Group (L)
671st Squadron

Miller, James G.	Miller, James H.	Miller, Leon
Miller, Phil	Miller, Wilbert	Minnicks, William D.
Morehouse, Ray C.	Mooney, S.	Moore, Zean R.
Morris, John T. S.	Morton, Robert W.	Mowell, R. F.
Moyer, Clarence M.	Muir, Richard C.	Mundell, William J.
Mundy, James H.	Murphy, Paul E.	Murray, Thomas J.
Nadeau, Albert J.	Nanney, Lawrence E.	Napri, Orlanda P.
Nelson, Donald E.	Nelson, Louis G.	Newpert, Elmer H.
Newsome, Carl A.	Nicosia, Dominic	Nielsen, Leland C.
Novak, William J.	O'Brien, Thomas J.	Ochoa, Laure C.
Ohannesian, Paul	Olmer, Richard J.	Olmstead, Elton R.
Oravec, William D.	Orr, Lloyd A.	Orvold, Chester R.
Osterman, B. V.	Ostrander, L.	Owens, Douglas
Pair, Horace, F.	Palmer, Wallace B.	Parker, Burdette D.
Paules, Eugene F.	Pavey,	Peppers, Robert B.
Peppiatt, F. M.	Perkins, Holly, Jr.	Perkins, Leroy
Perkins, Ronald D.	Perrol, Clifford L.	Peters, Warren R.
Pettis, Russell T.	Pittinger, Fred	Pitts, Laverne D.
Platter,Evert T.	Pledger, Leon D.	Pocharicke, Edward C.
Pochatko, Edward G.	Pofl, Henry J.	Pogue, Roswell F.
Pointer, Edgar	Pomps, Steven A.	Porter, Edward
Porter, Martin D.	Povery,	Powell, H. Basil
Powell, Stanley I.	Powell, Morris E.	Prey, Alvin W.
Price, Donald L.	Przywitowski, Stanley J.	Raithel, Arthur W.
Randles, Dr. Leland	Rawling, Richard A.	Ray, Darrell T.
Reavis, Gilbert	Redding Russell D.	Reed, John V.
Reily, John	Remisszewski, Alfred	Rittenhouser, William
Roenquist, Arvid E.	Rojas, Andrew A.	Roohrdanz, Raymond R
Rose, Donald E.	Ross, Junior	Rosser, Evan J.
Rowbothan, Egar R.	Roy, Roger M.	Royalty, Peter G.
Rubon, M.	Runyan, Charles C.	Ruskiewich, John J.
Russell, Gordon D,	Russell, William C.	Rust, Egos W
Rzepka, Joseph J.	Sampson, Thomas W.	Sanderson, Arthur J.
Scalia, Samuel J.	Scharas, George N.	Schmidt, Kenneth, W.
Schoen, Alfred E.	Schouten, Joseph T.	Schrom, Robert G.
Schuchardt, Ed W.	Schumacher, Fred C.	Schumacker, Robert C.
Schutzberg, Murray	Schwartzapol, Donald	Sears, Audry C.
Semtanka, P. L.	Senkiewicz, J.	Seighman, Harold G.
Sewell, Jackson	Shaffer, George H	Sheehan, Robert E.
Shehan, Robert D.	Shelhammer, James W	Sherry, Vincent N.

416th Bombardment Group (L)
671st Squadron

Sherwood, Ted	Simon, David O,	Simpson, Russell L.
Sinclair, H. Gordon	Skelton,ThurmanW.	Skidmore, James A.
Slovenkai, Frank	Smith, Arthur H.	Smith, Francis L.
Smith, Jack L.	Smith, Jesse L.	Smith, Lewis
Smith, Robert H.	Smith, Seaman	Smolleck, Mickey R.
Smyth, John A.	Snodgrass, Richard	Sorenson, Harold W.
Sparks, Alan A.	Spires, Homer R.	Spires, John W.
Stanley, Meredith E	Staving, William A.	St. Clair, James W.
Steffy, Robert I.	Stephens, Hartzell O.	Stephenson, Glenn G.
Stinchen, John P.	Stockman, Arnold A.	Stockwell, J.C.
Stockwell, Robert E	Stolp, Paul	Stoner, Daniel J.
Strobel, Richard T.	Stroup, C. C.	Stypenski, Valentine S.
Summers, Julius B.	Sumpter, Irvin L.	Sunderland, Herbert E.
Sutton, L. J.	Swabb, Robert S.	Swank, Ollie E.
Swantek, Irvin J.	Tanner, Jean K.	Tatum, Ben K.
Tate, Luther R.	Teciusti, I. R.	Terris, Raymond A.
Tharp,	Thee, Roy F.	Theusen, Paul J.
Thiele, A. H.	Thomas, Elmer E.	Thomasco, Paul R.
Thompson,GeorgeJr	Thompson, Milo J.	Thrasher, Hugh
Tidwell, John H.	Townsend, Gerald L	Troyer, Reuben J.
Tschudin, John W.	Tudor, Sidney A.	Tutt, Richard P.
Valerio, Maurice	Van Noorden, Hartwig M.	Vaughan, Odis H.
Vellinga, John R.	Verville, Roger	Waddell, Russell, W.
Walker, Garrad R.	Wallman, Milton	Walter, James
Warden, Paul C.	Warren, Jay R.	Wash, Alec R.
Waugh, Earl H.	Waugh, James E.	Weatherford, Max F.
Weathers,	Weaver, John W.	Wellin, Horace E.
Wells, Jimmie J.	Werlry, Ernest R.	West, Lawrence A.
Wheeler, Richard V	Wilds, Harley J.	Willetts, David L.
Williams, John B.	Williams, Richard M.	Williamson, Robert R.
Willis, John R.	Willson, Clarke	Wilson, Beverly R.
Winn, A. J.	Wipperman, Ronald A.	Worden, Howard C.
Wright, John R.	Wyatt, William F.	Yons, James E.
York, Robert W.	Young, James O.	Zaretsky, Paul
Zeanah, George L.	Zeikus, Allen J.	Ziebell, Alvin M.
Zubon, Michael	Zygiel, Leonard R.	

Casualty List of 416th Bombardment Group members

Legend:

MIA Missing in Action	POW Prisoner of War	KIA Killed inAction
KIT Killed in Training	KILD Killed in Line of Duty	RET Returned toDuty
SWA Severely Wounded in Action	EUS Evacuated to U.S.A.	
G Gunner	P Pilot	BN Navigator	CC Crew Chief

Abriola, D. R.	669 G	MIA-RET	2-2-45
Ahrens, H. S.	671 G	MIA D-Day	6-6-44
Allen, B. K.	670 CC	KIT Parachute Failed to Open	6-30-44
Anderson	668 P	MIA KIA	3-21-45
Anderson, E. A.	668 G	KIT	6-30-44
Ashton, L. A.	671 G	POW-RET	9-29-44
Atkinson, P. G.	670 P	SWA - EUS	1-23-45
Babbage	668 BN	MIA KIA	3-21-45
Bankston, R	668 G	MIA-POW-RET	5-20-44
Barnard, L. G.	669 G	KIA	4-24-44
Battersby, W.	668 P	KIT Test Flight on Base	5-9-44
Baxter, B.	668 P	MIA	6-29-44
Bender, G. J.	669 G	MIA	4-10-44
Berks, E. F.	671 G	MIA-RET	2-16-45
Boukamp, J.	669 P	MIA-KIA	9-29-44
Boyer, V. U.	669 G	MIA-RET	
Bradford, B. H.	669 P	MIA	5-20-44
Brown, D. M.	668 G	KIA	12-25-44
Brown, F. E.	668 G	MIA-POW-RET	5-27-44
Burns, A. C.	671 BN	MIA	9-29-44
Burns, D. E.	670 G	MIA	5-29-44
Burgess, A. J.	671 G	MIA	
Burg, J. J.	668 BN	KIA	12- -44
Burke, W. J.	671 P	KIT	
Burseil, F. H.	670 BN	KIA	12-25-44
Buskirk, J. A.	669 G	MIA-RET	8-6-44
Campbell, M. W.	669 P	MIA-RET	6-6-44
Carter, A.	669 G	MIA	3-18-45
Carstens, R. W.	669 G	MIA	
Cavanaugh, A. F.	668 G	MIA-RET	10-7-44
Chalmers, J. J.	668 P	MIA-RET	2-14-45
Cheney, M. W.	669 G	MIA	
Cherry, F. E.	668 G	KIA	7-18-44
Church, C.	669 P	MIA-POW-RET	
Clark, H. B.	669 P	KIA	1-2-45

Casualty List of 416th Bombardment Group members

Cochran, R. L.	670 G	KIA	7-19-44
Coe, W. H.	668 G	KIA	6-4-44
Coffee, G. L.	669 G	MIA-POW-RET	5-27-44
Columbe, P. E.	G		
Coleman, C. W.	669	KIT Parachute Rigger	5-9-44
Collier, J. L.	668/670 G	MIA-RET	1-23-45
Colosimo, R. J.	669 G	MIA-POW-RET	9-29-44
Conocpak, F. E.	670 G	KIA	5-19-44
Cook, J.	669 P	KIA	2-21-45
Cope, G. P.	671 G	MIA-POW-RET	5-27-44
Cornell, R. H.	669 P	MIA-POW-RET	3-18-45
Cramsie, W.	671 P	KIA	4-10-44
Crandle, W.	671 P	MIA	
Creeden, E. J.	671 G	MIA-POW-RET	3-18-45
Cruze, R. K.	668 P	KIA (Ditched in Channel)	7-18-44
Curdy, P. F.	670 P	KIT	6-25-44
Colquit, J. L.	668 P	MIA-POW-RET	
Curtis, L. B.	669 G	MIA-POW-RET	8-8-44
Daniel, W. J.	670 G	KIA	9-29-44
DeMond, F. W.	671 P	MIA	
DeStefano, R.	668 G	KIA	2-2-45
Dontas, P.	669 P	MIA-KIA	8-8-44
Drugan, C. L.		MIA	
Dugan, J. B.	669 G	MIA-POW-RET	8-8-44
Dunnington, J. W.	670 G	KIT	7- -43
Eckard, D.	668 G	KIT	10-29-43
Eckard, L. A.	668 BN	MIA	2-14-45
Enman, R, E.	669 BN	KIA	3-18-45
Ernstrom, R. L.	668 G	MIA-KIA	6-29-44
Farley, J. J.	669 P	MIA	2-25-45
Farmer, W. W.	669 P	KIA	8-6-44
Field, P. C.	668 G	MIA-KIA	12-25-44
Feistl, J.	671 G	MIA	4-23-44
Fields, W. E.	669 G	MIA-POW-RET	8-8-44
Ford, R.	670 P	MIA	3-23-45
Fortner, K.	668 G	MIA-POW-RET	2-14-45
Floyd, C. F.	669 P	KIA	
Galloway, A.	668 G	MIA-KIA	12-25-44
Gandy, R. S.	668 G	KIA	8-6-44
Garrett, A. D.	671 G	MIA-RET	
Gillespie, R. H.	669 G	MIA-RET	12-25-44

Casualty List of 416th Bombardment Group members

Gollen, A.	670 G	KIT	7- -43
Gossett, J. D.	670 G	MIA-RET	9-29-44
Graham, C. E.	669 G	KIT	
Grahamewers, R. F.	669 G	MIA	
Gray, C. M.	668 G	MIA-POW-RET	5-20-44
Griswold, R. M.	G	MIA	
Grzpna, L. J.	668 G	MIA	3-28-45
Gullion, A. W.	669 P	MIA-POW-RET	5-27-44
Gunkel, H. G.	668 P	KIA	3-28-45
Hall, E. P.	669 P	MIA	
Haney, N. B.	670 P	KIT	8-22-44
Haptonstall, R.	669 CC	KILD-Hard Stand Accident-9-24-44	
Hardesty, E. R.	669 G	MIA-KIA	2-25-45
Harns, J. M..	668 G	MIA-POW-RET	10-7-44
Hatch, H. F.	669 G	MIA-POW-RET	
Haver, H. E.	669 G	MIA-POW-RET	
Harmon, C. D.	670 G	MIA	8-6-44
Hart, G. E.	670 G	MIA	8-6-44
Hay, J. E.	669 G	MIA-RET	8-6-44
Heitell, S. L.	668 G	KIA	
Henderson, L. W.	P	MIA	
Henshaw, C. R.	671 G	KIA	4-10-44
Hewes, H. E.	669 P	MIA-POW-RET	5-27-44
Holtzschieter, F.	671 P	KIT	
Hullette, E. S.	670 P	KIT	4-15-44
Hytale, S.	668 G	KIA	8-6-44
Hume, J. S.	668 G	MIA	5-27-44
Jedinak, A.	671 BN	MIA-POW-RET	5-12-44
Joe, E. Wing	669 G	MIA-POW-RET	9-29-44
Johnson, J. L.	670 G	KIA	6-6-44
Johnson, R. J.	671 G	MIA	
Jokinen, W. B.	671 P	MIA-RET	3-18-45
Jones, Herman C.	670 BN	KIT	10-20-44
Kamischke, R. J.	671 G	KIA	3-21-45
Keeper, J. L.	G	MIA-POW-RET	
Kehoe, K. W.	669 P	MIA	9-29-44
Kelley, W. G.	668 BN	KIT	11-11-44
Kempernolte,	669 P	KIT	
Kenshaw, C. R.	671 G	MIA	
Kiker, C. M.	669 G	KIA	1-14-45
Kinney, J.	668 P	KIA	3-18-45

Casualty List of 416th Bombardment Group members

Kleopfel, M. F.	668 P	MIA-KIA	5-20-44
Kylie	668 G	MIA	
LaPoint, J. M.	668/670 G	MIA-KIA	8-6-44
Larson, H. W.	668 G	MIA-POW-RET	5-27-44
Leishman, S. P.	670 P	KIA	10-15-44
Maciulewicz, P. P.	669 G	MIA-POW-RET	
Mazza, L.	671 G	MIA-POW-RET	6-6-44
McDonald, A. A.	669 P	KIA	4-24-44
McIver, V. E.	668 G	MIA-POW-RET	5-20-44
McManus, T. A., Jr.		MIA-KIA	6-6-44
McManus, T. W.	670 P	MIA	8-6-44
McVoy, F. H.	669/671 KIT		
Meagher, J. F.	668 P	SWA-EUS	
Middleton, C. W.	671 G	MIA-POW-RET	9-29-44
Miquez, J. H.	671 G	MIA-POW-RET	
Miles, R. C.	668 P	KIT	11-11-44
Miller, R. L.	670 G	MIA	9-29-44
Minnicks, W. D.	671 P	KIT	2-14-44
Miracle, R. V.	668 P	MIA-KIA	1-22-45
Mish, C. C.	668 P	MIA-RET	6-6-44
Morehouse, R. G.	671 P	MIA	9-29-44
Morrissey,	668 G	KIT	11-11-44
Morton, R. W.	671 P	KIT	
Murphy, T. A.	670 P	KIA	1-1-45
Neilson, J. O.	669 G	MIA	
Newkirk, A. W.	668 G	MIA-RET	6-3-44
Nielson, A. L.	669 G	MIA-KIA	8-8-44
Nikas, A. P.	668 P	MIA-POW-RET	6-3-44
Nordstrom, A. W.	670 P	KIA	9-29-44
Novak, S. C.	668 G	MIA-RET	8-6-44
O'Connell, L. W.	670 G	MIA-RET	1-1-45
Pentilla, W. L.	669 P	KIA	
Phenning, G. H.	668 G	MIA-RET	
Palin, W. H.	669 BN	MIA-RET	6-6-44
Portn, K.	G	MIA	2-24-45
Potter, H. A.	668 G	MIA-POW-RET(Escaped)	6-29-44
Prentiss, R. B.	668 P	MIA-KIA	12-25-44
Raines, A. A.	669 P	MIA	
Ray, J. E.		MIA-RET	
Rice, R. W.	669 G	MIA-KIA	9-16-44
Riley, T. F.	670 CC	KIT	6-25-43

Casualty List of 416th Bombardment Group members

Ritchie, S. B.	668 P	KIA	6-30-44
Robertson, R. B.	669 P	MIA-POW-RET	12-25-44
Rooney, R. J.	670 P	KIA	3-21-45
Rust, E. W.	671 G	MIA-POW-RET	5-12-44
Ryan, E. W.	671 G	MIA-POW-RET	
Sabadosh, J. W.	669 G	KIA	1-2-45
Saidla, J. B.	668 P	MIA-POW-RET	10-7-44
Schouten, J. T.	671 P	MIA-KIA	4-23-44
Schainberg, N. V.	669 P	MIA-RET	8-8-44
Scott, G. W.	668 G	MIA-POW-RET	6-3-44
Scully,	669 P	KIT	
Sharp,	669G	MIA	
Shatzer, H. E.	669 G	MIA-POW-RET	
Shaw, C. I.		SWA-EUS	
Shaw, L. R.	668 G	MIA-POW-RET	5-20-44
Shempren, E. H.	670 G	KIT	10-15-44
Shields, J. J.	669 G	KIA	
Simmons, J.	668 G	MIA	12-25-44
Siracusa, J. F.	670 P	KIT	10-15-44
Siracusa, L. J.	668 P	MIA-POW-RET	5-27-44
Sittarich, J. J.	668 G	MIA-RET	3-18-45
Slaughter, Capt.	29th Inf. Div	KIA (Observer for Ground Forces)	3-21-45
Smith, H. W.	668 G	KIT	6-30-44
Smith, J. D.	669 P	KIA	8-30-44
Sommers, D. T.	670 P	MIA	8-6-44
Spadoni, J. K.	668 G	SWA-EUS	
Stead, C. H.	669 P	KIA	2-8-45
Stewart, J.	671 G	MIA-KIA	4-10-44
Stockwell, R. E.	671 P	MIA-KIA	5-12-44
Svenson, R. R.	668 P	MIA-KIA	12-25-44
Tharp, F. M.	671 G	MIA-KIA	3-23-45
Thompson, J. B.	669 G	MIA-POW-RET	
Transhina, C. A.	669 G	KIA	2-8-45
Troyer, R. J.	671 G	MIA	9-29-44
Valentine, O.	668 CC	SWA-EUS	
Van Meter, G. O.	669 P	KIA	1-14-45
Vars, C. J.	670 G	MIA-KIA	
Vienneau, A. J.	670 G	KIT	10-15-43
Vleghels, A.	669 P	MIA-KIA	9-16-44
Walsh, T. J.	670 G	KIA	3-4-44
Welch, A. J.	668 P	MIA-POW-RET	8-6-44

Casualty List of 416th Bombardment Group members

Wentling,	670 G	KIT	6-25-43
White, J. W.	668 P	KIT	10-18-43
Wilds, H. J.	669 G	MIA-POW-RET	9-29-44
Williamson, J. C. 668 G		MIA-POW-RET	5-27-44
Williamson, R. R.	671 G	MIA	9-2-44
Wilson, W. D.	671 P	MIA	2-16-45
Wipperman, R. A.	671 P	MIA-POW-RET	6-6-44
Wright, R. E.	668 G	MIA-POW-RET	8-6-44
Wylie, A. C.	668 G	MIA-KIA	12-25-44
York, R. W.	671 P	MIA	10-20-44
Young, C. E.	669 G	MIA	9-16-44
Zakliliewicz	670 G	KIA	6-6-44
Zelly, L. E.	670 G	KIT	6-26-43
Zygiel, L. R.	671 G	MIA	9-29-44

N.B. Many of the MIA's mentioned have returned to Military Duty, released from POW camps, but their return has not been recorded in the files and records available in official repositories.

Another problem, the official records from the squadrons and group are stored in government repositories on micro-fiche, or 16 mm reels, which have deteriorated and much of the information is undiscernible. Deciphering much of the information is difficult, and was done with the best techniques available.

The above listing of casualties represent the best information available for recording. Our apologies to families of our group, or to any one whose record is not listed, if omission took place, or incorrect data is recorded.

The following members were Returned to Military Command from POW camps.

S/Sgt/ D.R. Abriola
S/Sgt. R. Bankston, Jr.
S/Sgt. E.G. Berkes
S/Sgt. F.E. Brown
Major M.W. Campbell
S/Sgt. A.J. Cavanaugh
1st Lt. J.J. Chalmers
2nd Lt. Charles Church
S/Sgt. G.L. Coffey
S/Sgt. J.L. Collier
S/Sgt. R.J. Colosimo
S/Sgt. G.F. Cope
Captain R.H. Cornell
Sgt. E.J. Creeden
S/Sgt. L.B. Curtis
S/Sgt. W.E. Fields
S/Sgt. J.D. Gossett
S/Sgt. C.M. Gray
S/Sgt. J.M. Harris
S/Sgt. H.F. Hatch
S/Sgt. J.N. Hume
2nd Lt. A. Jedinak
Sgt. H.W. Larson
S/Sgt. P.P. Maciulewicz
S/Sgt. C.W. Middleton
2nd Lt. A.P. Nikas
Sgt. S.G. Novack
S/Sgt. L.W. O'Connell
2nd Lt. J.B. Saidla
S/Sgt. G.W. Scott
S/Sgt. L.R. Shaw
1st Lt. L.J. Siracusa
S/Sgt. J.J. Sittarich
Sgt. J.K. Spadoni
1st Lt. R.B. Robertson
S/Sgt. E.W. Rust
S/Sgt. J.B. Thompson
S/Sgt. H.J. Wilds
Sgt. J.C. Williamson
2nd Lt. R.A. Wipperman
S/Sgt. R.E. Wright
S/Sgt.C. Valentine

War Record of 416th Bombardment Group (L)
(Data furnished by Larry Hancock)

Organized at Oklahoma City, Oklahoma,
15 February 1943
Arrived Lake Charles, Louisiana, 4 June 1943
Arrived Laurel, Missisippi, 1 November 1943
Arrived Camp Shanks, New York, 3 January 1944
Left for Overseas on 17 January 1944
Arrived Glasgow, Scotland, 31 February 1944
Arrived Wethersfield, England, Station 170, 2 February 1944
Flew First Combat Mission 3 March 1944
Flew 158 Missions with A-20 Havoc, Aircraft
Arrived Melun, France Station A-55, 15 September 1944
Converted to A-26 Aircraft, 1 November 1944
Flew First Mission with A-26 Invader Aircraft,
17 November 1944
Arrived Laon France, Station A-69, 11 February 1945
Flew 127 Missions with A-26 Aircraft
War ended 5 May 1945
Arrived Cormielles, France 20 May 1945
Arrived Camp Chicago, France 28 July 1945
Left Camp Chicago 15 September 1945
Arrived Marseilles, France 17 September 1945
Left for states, 1 October 1945
Arrived in states 10 October 1945
Disbanded, October 1945

^^

Dispatched	10,865 Aircraft
Sorties	10,009 Aircraft
Combat Hours	33,479
Tonnage Dropped	11,119 Tons
Lost in Action	40 Aircraft
Battle Damage	40 Aircraft

PERSONNEL

Missing in Action	85
Killed	30
Prisoners of War	19

Dropped in Month of March 1945, 58% of total tonnage of entire A-20 Missions

BATTLE STARS AND CITATIONS

Air Offensive Europe	WD GO 85	1945
Normandy	WD GO 102	1945
Northern France	WD GO 103	1945
Rhineland	WD GO 118	1945
Ardennes	WD GO 114	1945
Central Europe	WD GO 116	1945
Distinguished Unit Citation	WD GO 84	Aug 6 to 9

French Croix de Guerre with Silver Star: Organization Award By Corps Order of French Air Force 4 July 1945 for Action from 18 October 1943 to 8 May 1945.

Mace's Aces

We're some of Mace's Aces,
We're now in his good graces,
He talks to us and says, "Hi Boys" each day.
And when we go a-flying
He starts right on a-crying
He sweats with us and worries all the way.
It's not the flak he's sweating,
It's a silver star he's getting
And that's what makes him look so old and grey.
Flying hours, he's got many
He's got seven in the twenty
No wonder he can tell us what to do
And when our flying's stinkin'
Our orders come from Schenkin.
He really knows his flying through and through.
All our trainees are synthetic
It really is pathetic
When Radetsky snaps the whip for me and you.
Old Farmer has a folly
He cackles like a polly
At briefings you are sure to hear him say.
"All briefings will be formal
All join ups will be normal
On take off, flaps will be put down half-way."
And when our wheels we pull up
He tells us that we foul up
Another pass is gone the normal way.
And when he's on a mission
Baldy's never in position
Especially when we cross Pas de Calais.
He's twisting and a-curving
He's always out observing
His shiny head is always miles away.
So keep your cowl flaps open
Keep a-praying and a-hopin
That flak will get the Jerries any day.

Anonymous

War Ends, May 1945

Following the end of hostilities on 8 May 1945, ground personnel who had been serving the flying crews so admirably. were given an opportunity to fly over the devastated war zones by our plane crews. Each day different members were given the sighseeing tour, with all becoming enthralled at the results of our bombing missions.

In the meantime, preparations were under way to transfer the group to the Pacific Theater with moves to Camp Chicago, near Laon, France, and subsequently to Marseilles France. In October 1945, the group was disbanded at Camp Miles Standish, Massachusetts .

The number of awards presented to group members included Distinguished Service Crosses, Silver Stars, Bronze Stars, Distinguished Flying Crosses, French Government Croix De Guerre, Air Medals and Purple Hearts and in only one instance, the Legion of Merit was awarded to then Corporal Lester H. McPeak of the 670th Squadron. He was an Armament Mechanic and had improvised many adjustments and improvements for parts of the A-20 and A-26 planes. The improvements were so important that the Army Air Force incorporated many of them in their training manuals for their service crews.

The Group was awarded the Distinguished Unit Citation for its excellent record of bombing important targets from 6 August through 9 August 1944 closing up the last remaining escape route for German Forces caught in the Falaise Gap region.

Group Commanders were Lt.Colonel Richard D. Dick February 1943 to October 1943, Colonel Harold L.Mace from October 1943 to August 1944 and Colonel Theodore R .Aylesworth from August 1944 to October 1945.

In closing this history, it is important to say that if the efforts of the late Dolph Whitten and his constant companion and Chief Assistant, wife, Marie were not mentioned in gratitude for everything they did in keeping the group together with their annual newsletter and bi-annual reunions, this group would have undoubtedly floundered out of existence. So, we take our hats off to the Whittens, in Dolph's heavenly abode, and Marie in Arkadelphia; a Million Kudos to you.

Loading List **Mission #68** **6 June 1944** **D-Day PM**
Serquez Marshalling Yard

Box II
Flight I

#468
Major M.J.Campbell
Lt. W.A.Palin
S/S J.B.Thompson
S/S H.L.Hatch

#717
Lt. N.V.Shainberg
Sgt .R.W.Rice
Sgt .C.E.Young

#645
Captain L.F.Dunn
Lt. H.T.Arrington
S/S H.A.Marion
S/S H.O.Carney

#390
Lt .E.E.DeMun
S/S M.Rosenstein
S/S H.O.Carney

#743
Lt. H.E.Clark
Sgt .J.W.Sabasosh
Sgt .C.F.Floyd

#900
Lt .R.L.Behlmer
T/Sgt. W.E.Kelly
S/S W.G.Ferguson

Flight II

#147
Lt. R.J.Morton
S/S J.L.Rogers
S/S G.I.Fleischman

#929
Lt. P.Dontas
S/S A.L.Nielson
S/S W.E.Fields

#181
Lt. W.H.Hand
S/S F.Alden
S/S R.L.Ballinger

Flight III

#202
Lt W.A.Peck
S/S A.E.Bergeron
S/S H.E.Kelton

#148
Lt. C.Church
S/S H.E.Shatzer
S/S P.P.Maciulewicz

#943
Lt. J.F.Smith
Sgt. C.Valiadis
Sgt. R.C.Hoffman

Spare
#0210
Lt. G.F.Bartmus
S/S J.R.Orr
Sgt. D.Hantske

Loading List **Mission #68** **6 June 1944** **D-Day PM**
Serquez Marshalling Yard

Box III
Flight I

#442
Major R.A.Clark
Lt. C.W.Jones
Sgt. J.O.Scott
S/S D.F.Mallory

#189
Lt. J.S.Conner
Sgt. H.C.Rodgers
Sgt. J.E.Van Duyne

#553
Captain R.B.Prentiss
Lt. W.M.Lytle
S/S J.E.McCreary

#217
Lt. T.J.Leonard
S/S O.D.Evans
S/S T.A.Palmer

#0211
Lt. D.T.Sommers
S/S W.J.Donahue
S/S M.R.Brayn

#157
Lt. J.C.Sewell
Sgt. E.F.Paules
Sgt. L.Martinez

Flight II

#951
Lt. F.W.DeMand
Sgt. R.J.Troyer
S/S C.W.Middleton

#220
Lt. R.D.Perkins
S/S V.N.Sherry
S/S R.H.Linneman

#363
Lt. J.D.Adams
S/S P.L.Clearman
S/S A.J.Zeikus

Flight III

#714
Lt. S.M.Hixon
S/S H.C.Worden
S/S J.J.Rzepka

#164
Lt. R.A.Wipperman
S/S H.S.Ahrens
Sgt. L.C.Mazza

#219
Lt. H.D.Andrews
S/S G.M.Cook

Spare
#963
Lt. L.G.Peede
S/S L.M.Daugherty
S/S C.L.Hibbs